Kiss Your Baby Sooner

Kiss Your Baby Sooner

The Guide to Maximizing Fertility & IVF Success

Tasha Blasi

©2026 All Rights Reserved. No portion of this book may be reproduced, stored in a retrieval system, or transmitted in any form or by any means—electronic, mechanical, photocopy, recording, scanning, or other—except for brief quotations in critical reviews or articles without the prior permission of the author.

Published by Game Changer Publishing

Trademark Notice: All trademarks and registered trademarks appearing in this publication are the property of their respective owners. Their inclusion is for identification and reference purposes only and does not imply any affiliation with or endorsement by the trademark holders.

Paperback ISBN: 979-8-90158-108-7

Hardcover ISBN: 979-8-90158-109-4

Digital ISBN: 979-8-90158-110-0

Disclaimer: The information provided in this book is for educational and informational purposes only and is not intended as medical advice, diagnosis, or treatment. What you're about to read is meant for educational purposes, not medical advice. **Always check with your healthcare provider** before adding or changing any supplements, medications, or treatments to make sure they're safe and the right fit for you. The author and publisher are not responsible for any adverse effects resulting from the use of the information contained herein.

www.GameChangerPublishing.com

Praise for Kiss Your Baby Sooner

"When Tasha and I share patients, I know they'll feel calm, supported, and empowered by her thoughtful guidance, compassion, and strategic coaching through IVF."

–Dr. Maria Costantini, MD, PhD, FACOG, East Coast Medical Director, RMA of NJ

"I was set for IVF for my first child but ended up pregnant naturally with Tasha's advice! This book could save your time, sanity, marriage, and tens of thousands of dollars in unnecessary treatments."

–Hanna, Proud Mama of 3, USA

"Save yourself time, money, and heartache, and listen to the wisdom of Tasha Blasi. As someone who went through this process herself, she developed the savvy and practical know-how to successfully guide you as she has so many others. You, and your future baby, are in good hands with Tasha."

–Andrea Beaman, HHC, Nationally renowned, award-winning Holistic Health Coach, Natural Foods Chef, and Herbalist

"Tasha's 'Science Protocols' helped me beat secondary infertility at 42 years old, and her 'Spirit Protocol' carried me through my son's difficult NICU stay. I'm forever grateful for her advice."

–Heather, Proud Mama of 2, UK

"Tasha's expertise and guidance went far beyond fertility, nurturing my emotional, mental, and physical well-being at every step. Thanks to her unwavering support, I didn't just make it through IVF—I entered twin motherhood grounded, whole, and ready."

–Tiffany, Proud New Mama of 2, USA

"My sister gets more people pregnant than NBA players."

–Rosa Blasi, Award-winning Actress, Licensed Marriage and Family Therapist (LMFT) and Author of Jock Itch

Unlock Even More Fertility and IVF Success Strategies

The journey to fertility and IVF success is always evolving, just like the knowledge and tools available to help you along the way.

The following QR code gives you access to valuable additional resources such as checklists, exercises, documents, sourcing, and even updated information that you won't find in the book itself.

Whether you're looking for a list of questions to ask your doctor, a worksheet for powerful exercises, supplemental videos to the written content, or the latest insights to make your IVF journey more successful, it's all right here.

To begin, simply scan the code to visit the website:

This book is dedicated to all the warrior mamas who refuse to settle for anything less than what they feel is possible. Your instincts are your superpower. Never doubt them.

And to my husband, Brian, and our two extraordinary children, Hudson and Mila: you are living proof that divine timing and plans are wiser than anything I could have designed myself.

Kiss Your Baby Sooner

The Guide to Maximizing Fertility & IVF Success

Tasha Blasi

Contents

Part Two
The Book on IVF

Before We Get in Bed Together

On December 15, 2013, I took a pregnancy test, knowing that I probably wasn't pregnant.

I had started spotting a couple of days prior, which for me was the usual sign the embryo didn't implant.

The test was simply confirmation that I could go to my friend's fortieth birthday party and drink as my consolation prize for seeing that minus sign yet again.

I wasn't angry or sad.

I was numb.

This was my tenth round of IVF.

I expected the negative result because that was all I had seen for the last three years. In five years total, I had only seen one positive pregnancy test. I had no more energy or emotion to give to this journey of trying to become pregnant.

Every doctor told me that I had "perfect" fertility, yet not one of them could get me pregnant, and no one had an answer as to why.

Let's back up a little...

When Brian and I got married, we started trying for a baby almost immediately. After a year of trying naturally with no success, I went to my OB/GYN looking for answers.

They ran the standard infertility tests, and that's when we learned something I never saw coming. I could get pregnant through sex... just not with my husband. Brian had a low sperm count.

So IVF was the prescription for us.

At first, this news was devastating to me. I couldn't stop crying about it. I only knew one other person who was going through IVF, and it seemed horrible. Sticking yourself with needles... the expense... the heartbreak... the disgusting-smelling Chinese teas she drank? Ugh!

Brian was devastated, too... he could have been a lot less careful in college.

Once we got through the devastation phase, I suddenly realized that IVF sounded great. I was a control fanatic (which sounds way better than "control freak," right?). I was thirty-three, and I could meticulously plan each pregnancy, deliver two kids every two years, and have three or four total before forty. The perfect plan!

I felt a bit (okay, a lot) cocky going into my first round of IVF because of my pristine fertility and the only issue being a minor male factor.

So IVF treatment began, and in round one, fifteen eggs were retrieved. I thought, *OMG! What will I do with fifteen embryos?*

However, the final result was very different: I only had *three* day-3 embryos —meaning embryos that have reached the third day of development post-fertilization—and the recommendation was to put them back in on a fresh transfer ASAP.

I wasn't upset or heartbroken (yet). I was stunned and confused. And I didn't have time to sit down with the doctor and ask what I was thinking, which was, *Wait, um, what just happened?!! I have three embryos out of FIFTEEN eggs? How is that possible?* Instead, I just followed directions.

They completed a fresh transfer of the two best embryos. They had attempted to grow the third and remaining embryo to the blastocyst stage, a developmental stage for embryos on days 5, 6, or 7, but it didn't develop further.

Two weeks later, we got a positive pregnancy test. A week after that, we saw on an ultrasound that one embryo had implanted. But by the next appointment, when we were supposed to hear the heartbeat, there was none.

That was my first official heartbreak.

When I finally got a chance to talk to the doctor to find out what had gone wrong, all I got from him was a bored stare and an "I don't know." I waited for the rest of his explanation, but there wasn't one.

In an instant, I felt helpless, hopeless, and hurt. I remember thinking, *Who is this person, and what happened to the attentive man who talked us into working with him?*

The obvious next question I asked him was, "Okay, so what would you do differently next time to help improve these results?"

He replied, "Not much, because what I did worked."

Again, I waited for the rest of the explanation, but he said nothing else.

It suddenly dawned on me that our definitions of "success" were very different. To me, "success" meant getting pregnant, having multiple future embryos on ice, and *never* having to spend another $20,000 on an egg retrieval.

But to him, "success" was simply making any number of embryos and achieving implantation, even if just for a couple of weeks.

I was not okay.

Then I asked, "What do we do?"

He shrugged. "Well, you could try again if you want."

And that, my friend, is when I entered what I call the "FU" phase in my IVF journey, because all I could think after that last statement of his was *Faaaaaaahhhhhhk Yoooooou.*

I know it's not appropriate to mentally tell people "FU," but neither was a five-year infertility and IVF journey for "no reason." So, I think it was a fair exchange.

"FU" became the main vibe for the rest of my journey, especially once a few rude realities set in:

1. I had to start the whole process over: the shots, the coordination of doctor appointments before work, trying to make my 8:30 a.m. meetings... to maybe get a baby. (And did I mention it was $20,000?!)
2. What was my doctor's incentive to make this work? If IVF failed, nothing negative happened on the doctor's end. No review. No consequences. Just another paycheck. Was I financing his success while absorbing the loss?
3. Creating my family was not in my control.

If that wasn't enough of a gut punch, what I learned next was worse. Insurance covered my second round of IVF, which felt like a miracle. But they only paid the clinic $11,000.

The same clinic.

The same procedure.

So that $20,000 price tag I paid for the first round? It wasn't the cost of IVF.

It was the cost of being a self-pay patient.

Oof. That hurt.

You now see why "FU" became the anthem for my IVF journey, right?

So in the second round, when the doctor chose to do basically the same protocol, there was one major change: my attitude. I. Was. *Pissed.*

I hated the receptionist. I hated the happy nurses who took my blood. I hated my pompous doctor, with his bored demeanor and house in the Hamptons (which I knew he had because Hamptons photos are easily recognizable when you live on the East Coast—the photo actually smelled of money).

I hated everyone involved and gave them a mental "FU" whenever I saw them.

And no, I am not proud of this behavior.

The second egg retrieval followed a similar protocol and, of course, came with similar results: three day-3 embryos again. Again, two were transferred, and the third embryo did not grow enough to be frozen for future use.

I did not know what to expect this time. Everything felt the same except for one thing: I accidentally messed up the timing of my trigger shot.

But even with that mistake of mine, one of the two day-3 embryos stuck for the long haul, and my son, Hudson, was born on September 29, 2009.

Was it the strategy of changing the timing of the trigger shot that did it this time, or did I just get lucky? No one knew, and I didn't care enough to focus on it then. I had my healthy baby boy.

A year after Hudson was born, I was ready for baby number two. It was time for a third round of IVF. I felt confident, believing we had cracked the code to conception. So I went back to the same clinic, and of course, they did the same thing that worked the last time.

If I had been naïve in thinking I would only need one egg retrieval and transfer for my first child, I was even more naïve to think the same would be true for the second.

Over the next three years, I did seven egg retrievals and eight transfers with four different doctors. Every single one of them said they could get me pregnant, but not one of them figured out why I was not making more embryos or why they were not implanting. With each round, I became less patient.

By the seventh egg retrieval, my internal agitation became external. My personality started to shift, and not in a good way. I was no longer the upbeat, energetic, positive person I had always been. Instead, I felt triggered by anyone who claimed to have answers. Everyone seemed confident. No one was right.

I went from anger to shame, which is the lowest emotion energetically. It drains you of your ability to easily love or feel joy. More on that later. I let the toxic emotion take over and allowed myself to change.

I did not even recognize myself anymore.

It was *bad.*

I remember one doctor doing an ultrasound and, after counting the follicles, telling me I had "perfect" follicles and that he was certain I would get pregnant that round.

Anyone else might have loved hearing that. Not me. So while he was still doing the exam—and yes, I was naked from the waist down, and he was still sitting between my legs—I shot forward, got in his face, and said, "Perfect? It has been 'perfect' every single time, and I am still not pregnant. So I would not comment on things you clearly know *nothing* about."

Then I lay back down.

Yikes.

And if you were not infertile and tried to give me advice, you were really taking your chances. I cannot tell you how many times someone said, "I know what you need to do. You just need to get drunk and relax," or "My friend couldn't get pregnant, but then she started filling out adoption papers, and poof, she got pregnant!" These are things someone with infertility *never* wants to hear.

Since I could no longer politely smile, nod, and wait for people to finish these kinds of comments, like I would have before my three-year journey for baby number two, I developed a response that was very effective at making them as uncomfortable as I was.

I would say, "You are so right." Then I would pause and let them nod proudly, feeling wise. That is when I would add, "But the thing is, Brian has a low sperm count."

Their nodding would stop instantly. I'd continue, "So, if I relaxed, got drunk, and had sex with *your* husband, then yes, I could get pregnant!"

There would be a long pause while they processed whether I had actually said what I said. Then I'd break the tension with a fake laugh, and they'd fake laugh right back.

And if what they said wasn't insanely ignorant enough, I also knew they were wondering if I was actually considering having sex with *their* husband. (Gross!!! And, um, have you seen *my* husband?!)

Some might say it was shocking, and some might even say I sounded like an a-hole, but someone without fertility issues telling an infertile woman that her infertility is her fault and easily solvable if she were "just less stressed" (or less sober) is something only an a-hole would do. So technically, we were even.

The sad truth was that I was drowning in shame. And shame looks for company. So without even realizing it, I started handing it out to everyone around me, but mostly to myself.

I shamed myself for not appreciating my life with one child, especially when everyone around me told me I should. I desperately wanted to be okay with just one so I could finally end the infertility and IVF roller coaster, but having one child did not feel right to me at all. What I wanted was planted firmly in my heart. That is the only way to describe it.

Looking back, I can see it was okay to feel that way. The problem was never the desire. It was the toxic shame wrapped around it. And I will show you how to remove that.

But before we get there, if you are experiencing something similar, just know this. It is the biggest lesson in the fertility journey, and I will come back to it again and again throughout this book: **If it doesn't feel right, it's not.**

The people urging you to stop wanting a baby, or another one, are probably doing it because they *love you* and cannot stand watching you hurt anymore.

And while that comes from a good place, they are not the ones living in your body or carrying this desire in their heart. You are. It is okay to honor what you want and do what it takes to make it happen.

Back to the story...

I went to a fourth clinic for my ninth egg retrieval and tenth transfer. In the initial consultation, the doctor started with, "So, how can I help you?"

I immediately realized that taking the time to gather five years of medical records from three previous clinics and then waiting three months for the appointment had all been for show. (FU!)

So I gave him the elevator pitch of my IVF journey, after which he said, "You might hold the record for doing the most egg retrievals."

Now that I know this doctor, I think this was his attempt at humor. But I didn't yet know him then, and in that moment, it made me feel... you got it... ashamed for still wanting baby number two.

By the end of the meeting, he told me he would give me a try or two, but if it didn't work, my next option would have to be an egg donor. He also suggested doing genetic testing on my embryos because, clearly, I had egg-quality issues, and he wanted to prove it.

We did a similar protocol as the previous doctors and got similar results: two embryos grew to blastocysts, and they were both normal, which disproved his theory that it was my now old eggs that were the issue. We did a frozen transfer with both of them.

So, let's go back to the beginning. Remember when I took that pregnancy test to get the official "okay" that I wasn't pregnant, so I could give myself permission to drink too much at the party?

Well, I ended up not drinking at all that night. In fact, I didn't even go to the party... because the second line on the test finally showed up.

I couldn't believe it was real. This was my first positive since Hudson. My three-year journey of trying for baby number two, through ten transfers, hundreds of shots, and dozens of embryos, was finally over.

This is the photo of Hudson holding that pregnancy test right after I took it.

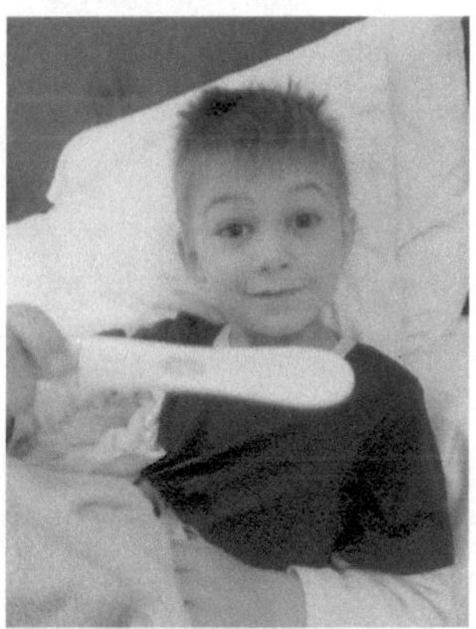

Hudson holding the pregnancy test for Mila, December 15, 2013

Everyone in my life wanted to know how I was finally able to get and stay pregnant after all those IVF rounds.

But this is not one of those neat stories where you figure it out in real time and then proudly share the formula that worked.

So let's start with why I now believe it took me five years to create my family, even though I was young and constantly told by doctors that I was "fertile."

After dedicating my life to understanding fertility and IVF success and studying thousands of protocols and professionals over the last ten years, I can finally see the full picture:

1. Despite what I was told, my body was not fertile. I was living in chronic survival mode. No amount of medications or procedures could override that. My body was depleted, stressed, and conserving energy, yet I kept pushing forward with treatments instead of listening to the signs that something deeper needed attention.
2. My journey was driven by anger, fear, and shame, which drained my energy and kept my body in survival mode. Looking back, I can see how much harder that likely made it for me to get and stay pregnant.
3. I did not have the right medical approach, and more importantly, the execution was off. I have since tracked down my medical records and can clearly see which adjustments could have optimized my results. With the knowledge I have today, I can confidently say that I unnecessarily went through ten rounds of IVF to have two children.

Together, these three pieces shape the pregnancy protocols I now teach. When they're all addressed together, your body, specifically your reproductive organs, can function more easily as designed.

While I am now grateful for my difficult, depleting, and honestly depressing infertility and IVF journey, since it qualified and motivated me to pioneer this work, there is no reason that anyone else should have to go through what I did.

I had to live it, obsessively study it, and turn it into repeatable strategies. You don't. You get to learn from it, apply it, and move forward with clarity and confidence.

With what I now know, I truly believe infertility, miscarriage, and unnecessary IVF could decline around the world! And that shift begins with women like you who choose to be informed, take ownership of their family's future, and demand better answers.

MY THREE PROTOCOLS FOR PREGNANCY

Through years of research and studying thousands of protocols prescribed for my clients around the world, I've found that the core reasons someone struggles to get or stay pregnant usually come down to three things: their body is stuck in survival mode, their mindset is so fear-driven that their hormones are completely out of sync, and they're either doing the wrong medical treatments or the right treatments are being used, but the execution is off.

So, when I'm consulting with someone trying to get pregnant, whether they're starting naturally or doing IVF, I focus on three protocols, often all at once. Here's a quick overview before we go deeper into each one in this book.

1. SURVIVING TO THRIVING PROTOCOL

This protocol is your *foundation* because no medication or procedure can ever force a pregnancy. If your body is stuck in survival mode (the opposite of conception mode), getting or staying pregnant becomes a struggle. The *Surviving to Thriving Protocol* gives your body the energy, stability, and safety signals it needs so your brain knows it is finally okay to conceive. When that happens, your body can more easily get pregnant and take care of you at the same time.

2. SPIRIT PROTOCOL

Long fertility journeys can wear you down until your brain is stuck in fear mode instead of trust mode. Shame, guilt, grief, and old stories can keep you on high alert, and over time, your brain starts linking pregnancy with stress. That makes your hormones respond in ways that work against you. The *Spirit Protocol* helps you shift into emotions such as willingness, acceptance, and peace, so your body stops feeling under attack. This work is about *alignment* with your true self, the version of you that thinks with clarity, confidence, and reason instead of fear. In simple terms, it "tames the mean girl" in your head who has been running the show for way too long, so your mind and body can finally work together again.

3. *SCIENCE PROTOCOL*

Once your body and mind are working together, it is time to bring in the science. This is where you uncover your fertility mystery and make sure every part of your reproductive system is doing what it is meant to do. The *Science Protocol* is where we get into testing, procedures, and my specialty: creating perfect protocols and knowing the exact execution needed for you to successfully get and stay pregnant. You will learn which tests to consider based on your symptoms and how to recognize whether medical interventions are being done correctly so conception becomes as easy as possible. This is not where you start your goal of easily getting and staying pregnant; it is the *optimizer* once the first two protocols are in place.

VISUALIZATION OF THE PROTOCOLS

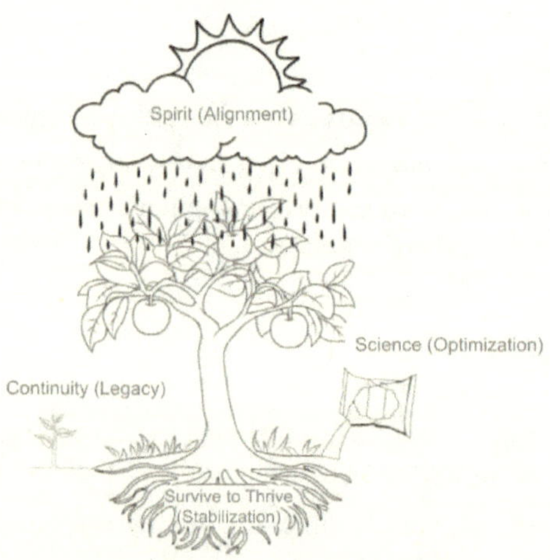

If you want a simple picture of how these protocols work, think of a fruit tree. The Surviving to Thriving Protocol is the soil. If the soil is dry, weak, or missing the nutrients it needs, the tree struggles no matter what you do. The Spirit Protocol is the sun and the rain. When the tree is in alignment with the weather, it grows with ease because it is getting exactly what nature intended. Lastly, the Science Protocol is the fertilizer. It works beautifully, but only after the soil, sun, and rain are incorporated.

Think about what happens when fruit grows without the right soil, sun, and rain. No amount of fertilizer could fix that fruit. But once the foundation is strong and the tree is getting what it needs, fertilizer can help it produce even more fruit with far less effort. That is how I picture your baby blooms growing, too.

There is one more piece that I will not be going into more deeply in this book, but it naturally happens when you follow the other three protocols. I call this the *Continuity Protocol.* This is about the health, wellness, happiness, and future fertility of your children. It is the way your choices today shape their epigenetics tomorrow. The lessons you learn in this book could break generational patterns of illness. The seeds that grow from your baby blooms will start their life out stronger because of the work you did long before they arrived.

HOW I FIGURED THIS OUT

I'm not a functional medicine expert or a naturopath. I'm not a psychologist or therapist. And I'm not an IVF doctor. I believe that's actually to my advantage.

I'm a science nerd who studied and taught biology and chemistry, and I love, love, love formulas. They feel safe to me.

So since 2016, I've studied all types of infertility and IVF professionals, mostly doctors, watching how their recommendations actually play out in real life and paying close attention to factors that support or hinder someone getting and staying pregnant.

How I discovered the formulas for IVF protocols and execution will be shared in more detail later in the section called "The Story Behind IVF Uncovered."

For now, know this: everything you are about to read comes from what I have *seen* work in the real world. It may not appear in medical school curricula or published studies, and it may not match what is supposed to work "in theory," but it reflects what I have helped my clients create in building the families they dreamed of, no matter which doctor or clinic they were working with or the country they were working in.

That said, if you only take advice from people with letters after their names, or you only trust advice backed by large research studies, this is not the book for you.

But if your goal is results, you're in the right place.

TWO BOOKS, ONE GOAL: YOUR PATH TO PREGNANCY

The fertility world is overflowing with information: books, coaches, professionals, doctors, and programs. But most of it leans too far in one direction. You'll either find resources that skip the medical side completely and focus only on nutrition, mindset, and lifestyle, or ones that cover mostly the medical options, even though medicine alone can't get you pregnant.

That's why I broke this book down into two separate parts: one on fertility and one on IVF. It's also my official excuse to the editors for why the book ended up so long. The real reason? I talk too much.

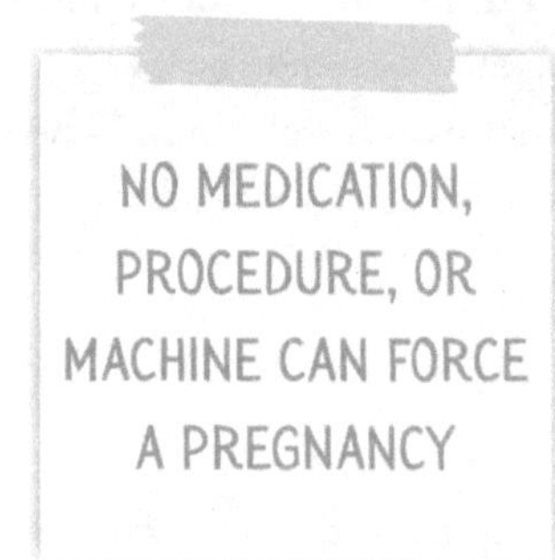

Whether you're trying naturally or using treatments, you need to understand what's inside "Part 1: The Book on Fertility." You'll hear me say this throughout: **no medicine, machine, or procedure can force a pregnancy.** The goal is to uncover what could be contributing to infertility so you can become as naturally fertile as possible, even if natural conception is not an option. These strategies can support you not only in getting pregnant, but also in having a healthier, more supported pregnancy and postpartum experience.

Next is "Part 2: The Book on IVF." It walks you through how to approach IVF strategically to protect your investment. If you are considering IVF and don't know how to optimize it from the start, you risk depleting your time, energy, egg reserve, money, and emotional bandwidth on treatment plans that were never designed to help you create your family.

When you understand how to optimize both your fertility and your IVF treatments, you can have more strategic conversations with your doctor, create a plan that fits your unique biology from the very beginning, and ultimately set yourself up to kiss your baby sooner.

HOW TO WORK THIS BOOK LIKE IT OWES YOU A BABY

The best way to use this book is exactly how I believe you should approach your fertility journey: become as fertile as possible first, and then add medications and treatments. When you do it in this order, you may need fewer medications and treatments, or possibly none at all.

Start with the Surviving to Thriving Protocol. These steps rebuild the foundation for fertility by restoring energy and pulling your body out of survival mode.

Next, layer in the Spirit Protocol. Together, these two create more usable energy for conception by calming the nervous system and aligning your body for growth rather than protection.

(This is where you might want to tell me off...) If possible, spend two to three months focusing on these two protocols before moving into the Science Protocol.

I know what you're thinking: *Three months? Are you kidding me?!* I get it. When you've been trying for months or years and only get one shot each cycle, three months can feel like forever. I thought the same thing when someone told me to wait, so I didn't.

But here's what I know now. Skipping this step is how so many people end up with unnecessary treatments, medications, and years of heartbreak that could have been avoided.

I've worked with many clients preparing for IVF or recovering from multiple failed rounds who discovered that after doing the Surviving to Thriving and Spirit protocols, they didn't even need IVF. What they really needed was *a bit more* hormonal balance and energy so their bodies could more easily get and stay pregnant.

You can't force a pregnancy, no matter how expensive the treatment. Your body needs to feel safe to have a baby. The Surviving to Thriving and Spirit protocols help create that sense of safety and readiness. Giving your body and mind the tools they need to function well is the best foundation for getting and staying pregnant, with or without IVF.

However, if that timing doesn't feel right for you, and you decide to start with the Science Protocol or "Part 2: The Book on IVF," that's okay! Promise me two things:

1. Make sure your choices come from feeling ready and confident, not from pressure or panic coming from others.
2. Commit to the Survive to Thrive and Spirit protocols at the same time, because that's what could help your body respond better to

treatment and create the healthiest possible environment for pregnancy.

HOW YOU'LL GROW

Fertility is a byproduct of overall health. What you learn in this book goes far beyond getting pregnant. These protocols help you uncover root causes, restore energy, and build a body that is resilient, adaptable, and capable of growth, now and for years to come.

This work also changes how you experience your life. As your body moves out of survival mode, clarity replaces urgency, and confidence returns. Your brain regains the ability to reason, plan, and choose rather than react.

You'll learn how to advocate for yourself and your family in any medical setting, ask smarter questions, and participate in your care as an informed partner instead of a passive patient.

And maybe most importantly, these protocols give you the chance to change the story your family has been living. You can interrupt emotional and physical patterns that quietly keep families stuck or unwell and rewrite what success looks like for the generations that come after you.

Okay, Mama, are you ready? Let's get...

Wait!

One more thing before we move forward. I want you to know that **your child is so lucky to have you as their mom.**

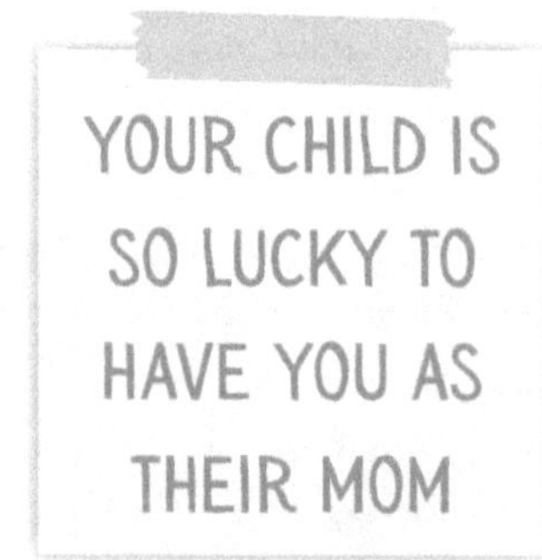

Look at how much time, energy, and love you're pouring into them before they're even here. That is incredible. You are doing something so beautiful and selfless, and that little soul is blessed to have you.

I truly believe that when your baby arrives, the world will be a better place because of them.

Okay, now we're really ready. Let's get growing!

Part One
The Book on Fertility

1. There is No Such Thing as "Unexplained Infertility"

**Quick Note: Moving forward, all doctors doing IVF treatments will be referred to as "IVF Doctors."*

Let's tackle one of the biggest myths in the fertility world: unexplained infertility. Unless someone was born with a compromised reproductive system, there is always a reason the system is struggling. "Unexplained" means the real cause hasn't been uncovered yet.

Many women are told, "We ran the standard tests, and everything looks fine. You're probably not getting pregnant because of your age or poor egg or sperm quality."

But egg and sperm quality, similar to thyroid irregularities, acne, thin uterine lining, migraines, constipation, eczema, mood swings, heavy or missing periods, PCOS, endometriosis, and more, is not the *problem*. They are *clues*.

UNCOVERING YOUR FERTILITY MYSTERY SHOULD NOT START WITH WHAT IS WRONG, BUT WHY IT'S HAPPENING

And **uncovering your fertility mystery should not start with *what* is wrong, but *why* it's happening.** Fertility is not a collection of disconnected symptoms. It is a whole-body process.

When we do not ask why, we keep treating symptoms: the "whats," while the real issue: the "why," stays hidden and quietly works against every effort you make.

I see this with menstrual cycle issues all the time. Women are told their infertility is unexplained because heavy, painful, or missing periods are "managed" with birth control. But your cycle is one of the loudest signals of your overall health. Understanding why your cycle is off can dramatically improve fertility, energy, mood, long-term health, and quality of life. It can also help you avoid unnecessary medications and expensive procedures.

While my specialty includes the precise dosing and execution of medications used to achieve and maintain pregnancy, medication should not be the starting point for fertility treatment.

IF YOU ARE TRYING TO DO SOMETHING AS NATURAL AS GETTING PREGNANT, MEDICATION SHOULD BE A LAST RESORT, NOT THE FIRST

Remember, no medication, procedure, or machine can force a pregnancy. They can support your body, but they cannot override it. So, **if you are trying to do something as natural as getting pregnant, medication should be a last resort, not the first.**

This book shows you what your body needs to support pregnancy, starting with the things you can begin doing today to improve your fertility. From there, we identify what is actually getting in the way, whether structural, hormonal, or metabolic, and what to do about it. This is about finding and fixing what's blocking your body from getting and staying pregnant.

My Story of Surviving to Thriving

After having my children, I transitioned from traditional OB/GYN care to an integrative medicine doctor. I initially saw her just to support her new practice. I figured I was fine, but maybe she could help me with a faster metabolism and help me grow long, gorgeous hair—the really important things when it comes to health, right?

Sure, I had occasional migraines, constipation, and stomachaches that hit like a truck (but only a few times a year), a thyroid issue, stress (who doesn't?), thinner hair, and a sluggish metabolism. In other words, I was like everyone else I knew.

What she uncovered floored me. My "normal" wasn't normal at all. She found the reasons behind all those symptoms: hormonal imbalances I didn't even know I had, like barely detectable testosterone and unusually high estrogen, plus significant mineral deficiencies. Also, my cortisol levels were double the national averages.

Looking back now, I believe the reason I needed eight additional transfers to have a second child, despite everything I was doing,was that my body had been living in severe, chronic survival mode. It felt normal to me at the time, but it wasn't.

FIXING THE FOUNDATION IS WHERE THE BABY-MAKING MUST BEGIN

Modern medicine can do incredible things, but it still has limits. A cardiologist can restart a stopped heart. A thoracic surgeon can give you a machine that breathes for you. A plastic surgeon can resurrect breasts that look like they've given up on life. But no doctor, medication, or machine can force an embryo to be created, implanted, and stay for forty weeks. The body has to feel safe enough to allow it. **Fixing the foundation is where baby-making must begin.**

Once I addressed survival mode, my body began responding differently. The nagging issues I had lived with for years faded, and for the first time, my menstrual cycle felt like almost nothing. No cramps. No clots. No dramatic hormonal swings. I hadn't even realized how difficult my cycle had been until I experienced what an easy one actually felt like.

I hear this same experience from my clients all the time. They didn't know how much they were suffering until they started feeling better, because when you've lived in survival mode long enough, it becomes your baseline.

When the body and nervous system are no longer stuck in survival, you get to experience what "normal" is really supposed to feel like. The kind of normal that supports fertility instead of working against it. The kind that doesn't require endless appointments, extreme diets, or desperation-driven rituals.

And if you're curious about how far I went when I was deep in it, you can listen to Episode 51 of my podcast about the craziest thing I ever did to get pregnant. It involved a watermelon, molasses, a yellow cloth, and the ocean.

(And no, I still can't believe I did it either!)

SURVIVAL VS. CONCEPTION MODE: THE FERTILITY FORMULA

There is one organ that can make getting or staying pregnant feel nearly impossible, and it is not your uterus, your ovaries, or your partner's testicles. It is the boss of all of them. Actually, it is the boss of every organ system in your body: your brain.

Your brain has one primary mission: keeping you alive today. Not sixty years from now or even one year from now. Just today.

When your brain is exposed to ongoing stressors, whether physical, emotional, or environmental, it flips the body into a stress response. Energy gets prioritized for survival and redirected away from something as energy-demanding as conception. The organs that keep you alive, like your heart, lungs, and muscles, get first dibs. Over time, this is when the reproductive system can take a hit, showing up as irregular cycles, PCOS, endometriosis, poor sperm quality, and more.

This is what I call survival mode, and it is the opposite of conception mode.

Despite what people without infertility often tell you, struggling to get or stay pregnant is not about having a busy or stressful life. Almost everyone is busy and stressed, but not everyone struggles with fertility.

At its core, infertility is about not having enough of the one thing required for conception: energy.

Chronic survival mode is driven by severe energy drains, both emotional and physical. Emotional drains can include trauma, anxiety, or people-pleasing. Physical drains can include inflammation, mold exposure, blood sugar swings, hormonal chaos, and the sheer amount of energy your unique body needs to keep you functioning.

AT ITS CORE, INFERTILITY IS ABOUT NOT HAVING ENOUGH OF THE ONE THING REQUIRED FOR CONCEPTION: ENERGY

Think of energy like currency. If your body is constantly overdrawn, it is not going to approve a big baby budget. But when you start replenishing your reserves and cutting unnecessary withdrawals, your body begins to trust that it has what it needs to thrive, not just survive.

One of the biggest contributors to energy loss is toxins. In the upcoming section on daily detoxing, we will get into the dirty details. For now, know this: toxins are not something most doctors are trained to look for, which makes them hard to identify in traditional medicine. And toxins are not only physical. Emotional toxins are real, too, and together they increase the workload on your body, drain energy, disrupt hormones, affect your mood, and contribute to infertility.

Here are simple formulas to explain how toxins and energy impact fertility:

SURVIVAL MODE

↑ Toxins (Physical + Emotional) = ↑ Energy Requirements = ↓ Energy Reserves = ↓ Fertility

CONCEPTION MODE

↓ Toxins (Physical + Emotional) = ↓ Energy Requirements = ↑ Energy Reserves = ↑ Fertility

The survival mode formula is: **no energy for Mama = no creating a baby.** Although it may seem like your body is punishing you, Survival mode is ultimately an act of love because it's your body's way of trying to protect you.

Conception mode creates the *Fertility Formula*, which happens when you lower the toxic load you are carrying, both physical and emotional. With less cleanup work to do, your body has more available energy, and your brain is far more willing to give the green light for pregnancy.

So, knowing what you know now, is your brain supporting pregnancy or protecting you from it?

Are you in survival mode or conception mode?

Next, we'll look at the ways your sperm and eggs quietly reveal the answer.

HOW SPERM AND EGGS SIGNAL SURVIVAL MODE

Before we talk about sperm or egg signals for survival, we need to zoom out and understand how so many of us ended up stuck in survival mode in the first place.

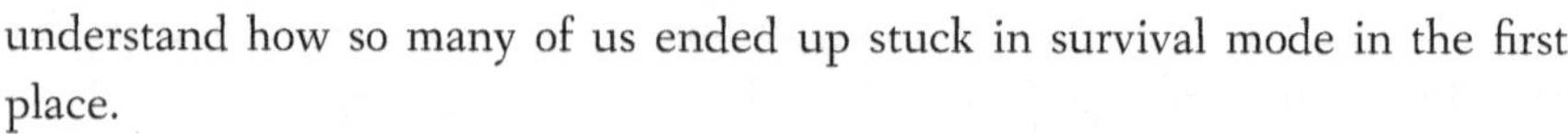

Our modern world, with all its incredible conveniences and innovations, has also created new challenges for our hormones. It's not that your body or your partner's isn't doing its job. Both are doing exactly what they were designed to do: protect you first.

Are you surrounded by artificial light at night? Your body is saying to you, *Got it, you're staying up late again. I can handle it.* But that means you miss the time when hormones and cells regenerate, both of which support egg and sperm health.

Are you eating too little or eating things that don't fuel your body? Your body says, *That's okay! I'll make this work with what we have,* which usually means slowing down your metabolism and putting your reproductive organs on the back burner so your body doesn't have to feed two when it barely has enough for one.

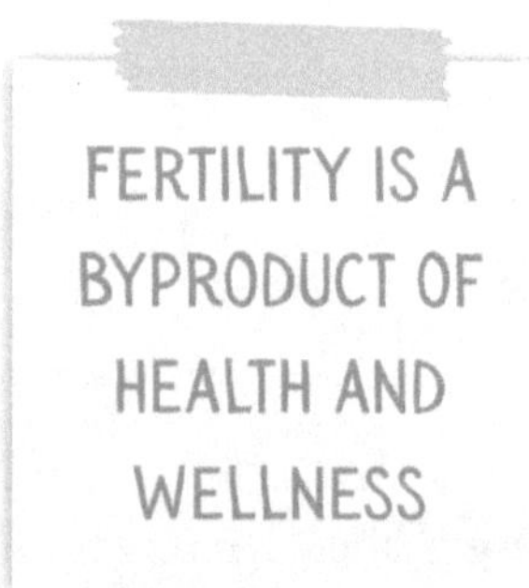

Do you breathe shallowly, live in constant motion, or rarely feel truly rested? Your body says, *Okay, we're still in danger today, just like we were yesterday, last year, and the decade before.*

Every modern habit that disrupts our bodies' natural rhythm carries a cost. Fertility is often the first thing to take a hit because reproducing is the last thing your body wants when it barely has enough resources to take care of the most important person in the world: you.

Remember, **fertility is a byproduct of health and wellness.** Many practitioners have observed that both egg and sperm health respond to the environment they are in. When you nourish, rest, support detoxification, and regulate your body's stress response, the reproductive system may receive the signal to function more smoothly again. Whether it is egg health, sperm health, or both, fertility is not fixed; it is flexible.

And since survival mode shows up first, where cells are least protected, we start with sperm.

His Sperm, Your Pregnancy

I spent nine weeks in the hospital with complete placenta previa before Hudson was born. At 19 weeks, I was told I'd need a C-section. At 22 weeks, after several heavy bleeds, they said if it happened again after 26 weeks, I'd be on hospital bed-rest. So naturally, I did what any desperate woman might do. I tried to "manifest" it away.

I even watched The Secret to will the bleeding to stop.

Well, the very next day, I had another bleed. It felt like God was saying, How'd that work out for ya?

So there I was, admitted at 26 weeks. I begged my way out a week later, only to end up right back after another bleed. This time, they told me I was there for good, until Hudson's scheduled birth on September 29, 2009.

I'm sharing this because, back then, no one connected the dots between Brian's "low sperm count for no reason" and the complications I had, not just getting pregnant but also during my pregnancy. When I started IVF in 2008, I was told what many women still hear today: that a low sperm count or high DNA fragmentation (the breaking up of sperm DNA) isn't something to worry about.

But now we know so much more. Sperm not only plays a major role in embryo creation, but it also affects the health and success of the pregnancy itself.

Thankfully, more functional medicine experts are finally speaking up and saying what should have been obvious all along: there is always a reason for infertility, male or female. And if there is a sperm issue, that is not just a lab number to work around. It is a signal. Something upstream needs attention.

So if your partner has an abnormal semen analysis or high DNA fragmentation, remember that this is information about his overall health and the genetic material being used to create your family. Encourage him to focus on the steps that could help improve or even reverse those findings while continuing to work with your care team. You'll learn many of these in the Survive to Thrive Protocol.

I'll go deeper into sperm health in the Science Protocol section, but for now, know this: Male sperm are incredibly adaptable. With the right changes, meaningful improvement is often possible in as little as three months. And yes, it may require some annoying adjustments, but for something as important as creating your child, it is a small and temporary inconvenience for a lifelong payoff.

It's always better to assume an abnormal semen analysis or high DNA fragmentation could be playing a role, especially if testing hasn't been done yet, than to assume it's normal and miss the opportunity to improve it. Sperm quality is often one of the easiest factors to optimize. Focusing on it can only help.

Oh, and if you ever need hospital bedrest tips for the busy, impatient professional, I'm your girl. I had a system. Some of my best hacks were definitely against the rules. I hung a "Napping" sign on my door so Brian could sneak my dog in for visits. I hosted a few small parties in my room. And every weekend, Brian would take me on wheelchair rides straight out the hospital doors and into Central Park, where we'd spend hours reading and playing cards together.

Those little things kept me sane.

Every night, I crossed off another day on my calendar, as if I were counting down a pregnancy prison sentence, and said, "Today was a great day." And I meant it. Every day Hudson didn't arrive early felt like the best day of my life.

I look back on that bedrest period with a lot of love now, but it's also a not-so-gentle reminder of how much is influenced long before pregnancy even begins. It's why I'm so passionate about making sure he's doing the few key things that could improve sperm quality and potentially prevent a lot of chaos during the pregnancy journey.

SPERM: STARTING THE FERTILITY FORMULA

I mostly hear about egg-quality issues being the assumed reason for infertility or failed IVF, with no data supporting it. What is even more interesting is that, if data does support a sperm issue, doctors usually say it isn't the reason for failed IVF—it's the egg quality. That doesn't make sense to me, and I don't agree. Sperm isn't a supporting actor in the fertility story. It's a co-lead.

And poor sperm quality doesn't only make it harder to get pregnant; it can directly impact the health of the embryo, the success of the pregnancy, and even how that pregnancy ends, like an unplanned C-section due to placental issues (see my story in the callout box above).

Sperm are also highly vulnerable to damage, but they respond quickly to change. Their health often reflects a man's overall health and wellness in real time. For all of these reasons, I like to start the fertility investigation by looking for signs that the male partner is in survival mode.

WHY SPERM ARE SO VULNERABLE TO DAMAGE

Sperm is built for one job: speed. They are stripped down to the bare minimum to reach the egg fast, but that also means they have almost no protection. They:

- Have almost no cytoplasm, so there's nothing to shield them from damage.
- Are packed with polyunsaturated fats, which makes them break down easily and leaves them vulnerable to damage from toxins and a poor diet.
- Can't repair their own DNA, so any damage they pick up gets delivered straight into the embryo with no edits and no do-overs.
- Are constantly exposed to toxins from the environment, diet, and lifestyle, which means their quality depends heavily on how your partner eats, sleeps, moves, and manages stress every day.

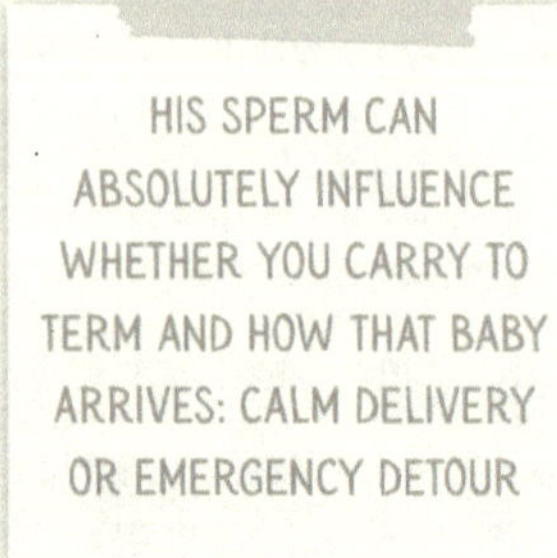

Sperm are like flimsy umbrellas in a windstorm (and I mean that in the most loving way possible). They are easily damaged, and once that happens, those issues are carried straight into the embryo. That can lead to poor fertilization, slow embryo development, failed implantation, miscarriage, or complications like poor placental development. **His sperm can absolutely influence whether you carry to term and how that baby arrives: calm delivery or emergency detour.**

SIGNS HE'S IN SURVIVAL MODE

Male fertility is on the decline. Sperm counts worldwide have dropped by more than 50 percent in the last 50 years, and the decline has sped up since 2000. Much of this is due to modern lifestyles and environmental factors that keep the body in a constant state of low-grade stress.

When a man's body is focused on survival, it shifts energy away from reproduction. The body's message becomes clear: stay alive now, create later.

The signs that he is in survival mode are similar to yours.

Inflammation Clues

- Joint pain or muscle stiffness

- Chronic sinus issues or allergies
- Skin problems like acne, eczema, or psoriasis
- Poor recovery after workouts or injuries
- Bloating or visible inflammation around the midsection

These are all signs of inflammation and oxidative stress, which directly impact sperm quality and hormone balance (especially testosterone).

Gut Distress

- Constipation, bloating, or IBS-like symptoms
- Reflux or chronic indigestion
- Frequent sugar cravings or energy crashes

A disrupted gut microbiome affects detoxification and hormone regulation, two key systems that protect sperm DNA from damage.

Mental and Emotional Signs

- Quick to anger or irritability
- Chronic stress or burnout
- Low motivation or drive
- Brain fog, trouble focusing, or poor memory
- Anxiety or depression

These are classic indicators that his body and brain are operating in fight-or-flight mode instead of rest-and-repair mode.

Other Physical Signs

- Low libido or erectile issues
- Weight gain (especially belly fat)
- Fatigue or waking up tired
- Poor sleep quality
- Hair thinning
- Low testosterone or other hormonal imbalances

These symptoms show that his body is reallocating energy away from reproduction toward survival. All of these can interfere with hormone balance and sperm production.

EGGS: COMPLETING THE FERTILITY FORMULA

Your eggs tell the story of how your body has been living, not just over the last month but over the last several years. They reflect your environment, your daily pace, your nutrition, your sleep, and how safe your body feels to create a baby. When your body is in survival mode, egg health takes a back seat because survival always wins over reproduction.

If your cycles feel unpredictable, your hormones are out of sync, or you've been told your egg quality is "poor" with data to support it, your body is not failing; it's adapting. And once your system feels safe and supported again, your eggs can thrive.

YOUR EGGS TELL THE STORY OF HOW YOUR BODY HAS BEEN LIVING, NOT JUST OVER THE LAST MONTH BUT OVER THE LAST SEVERAL YEARS

Yes, that's right, I just said that your egg quality and hormones that support it, like AMH and FSH, can improve.

What's that you say? You were told that improving your AMH and FSH is impossible, that you're doomed to a life of "bad eggs," and your only hope for a baby is an egg donor? My clients have heard that same story dozens of times, too. But I'm here to tell you: I've seen it happen, again and again. The right Survival Protocol (the set of guidelines designed to help you thrive in challenging situations) could be the very thing to make your eggs *egg-cited* again!

(I know that was rough. But buckle up, there's more where that came from!)

SIGNS YOU'RE IN SURVIVAL MODE

How do you know if your body is stuck in survival mode? Here are some clues that your body might be protecting you instead of preparing for pregnancy.

Menstrual Cycle Red Flags

- Cycles that are too short (26 days or less) or too long (30+ days)

- Heavy, clotty, or painful periods
- Major PMS, back pain, cramps
- Missing periods or ovulation

Inflammation Clues

- Endometriosis, adenomyosis, or PCOS
- Skin issues like acne, eczema, or psoriasis
- Joint pain, arthritis, or chronic allergies

Gut Distress

- Constipation
- IBS or bloating
- Other ongoing digestive issues

Mental and Emotional Signs

- Quickness to anger or irritability
- Chronic stress or overwhelm
- Depression, anxiety, or feeling emotionally flat
- Focus issues or brain fog

Other Physical Symptoms

- Low egg reserve at a younger age
- Naturally thin uterine lining
- Hormonal imbalances (low or high testosterone, estrogen, or progesterone)
- Sensitivity to synthetic estrogen (from birth control pills or patches)
- Sleep issues (trouble falling or staying asleep)
- Low energy or waking up tired

Some of these symptoms might be common, but that doesn't make them normal. I often remind my clients, "If it doesn't feel right, it's not." Your body shouldn't be inflamed, uncomfortable, or in pain, even during your menstrual cycle. These are signals from your body that something is out of balance, and that's where we start to rebuild the foundation of your natural fertility.

CHAPTER 1 SUMMARY

- **No Such Thing as Unexplained Infertility:** If you were not born with a compromised reproductive system, there is always a reason fertility feels hard right now. "Unexplained" usually means the right questions have not yet been asked.
- **Symptoms Are Clues, Not Failures:** Egg quality, sperm quality, hormone issues, painful cycles, or irregular ovulation are not the problem. They are signals pointing to a deeper imbalance that deserves attention.
- **Medicine Supports the Body, Not the Outcome:** Even the best medications and technologies support the process but cannot force implantation or pregnancy.
- **Survival Mode Blocks Baby-Making:** Your brain's main job is to keep you alive, not to get you pregnant. When it senses stress, danger, or low energy, reproduction is the first system to be put on pause.
- **Energy Determines Fertility:** When toxins and stress overwhelm the body's energy supply, the body stays in survival mode. When energy supply wins, the body shifts into creation mode.
- **Toxins Drain the Baby Budget:** Physical and emotional toxins create an extra workload for the body, draining energy, disrupting hormones, affecting mood, and contributing to infertility.
- **Sperm Matters From Day One:** Sperm is not a side character. It influences embryo health, implantation, and pregnancy outcomes, and it is often one of the easiest places to make meaningful improvements.
- **Eggs Reflect Your Environment:** Egg health mirrors how safe, nourished, and supported your body has felt over time. When survival mode lifts, hormones and egg quality can improve.
- **Fertility Is Flexible:** When you nourish, rest, support detox pathways, and calm the nervous system, the reproductive system may finally get the green light to do what it was designed to do.

Before heading to the next section...

If you'd like the link to the podcast on the craziest thing I ever did to get pregnant (but only if you promise not to judge me) and want to check out the extra resources that go hand in hand with this book, just scan the QR code.

2. Survive to Thrive Protocol: The Foundation for Fertility

This section shows you how to shift your body out of survival mode and into conception mode by steadily tipping the energy balance in your favor. These are the same strategies that have helped my clients improve labs (yes, even AMH), strengthen embryos, and get pregnant sooner.

The steps are simple and, more importantly, doable. Small, consistent changes add up fast. When your body finally has the energy it has been asking for, conception mode wins.

One important heads-up: simple does not always mean easy. Your brain loves what feels familiar, so a little pushback at first is expected. My brain acts like a toddler having a tantrum whenever I try to build new, healthier habits. To make this transition easier, start slow. Choose one or two practices at a time. Let them settle in. Then stack them together so it doesn't feel like you are constantly adding to your to-do list.

And when your brain argues against change, remind it that you are safe, supported, and choosing something new on purpose. Change is how this baby works.

Though I am going to keep the Survive to Thrive protocol as practical as possible, I will also share the science behind each recommendation so you understand how it supports your health and, ultimately, your fertility.

If you would like to hear this explained from a traditionally trained physician's perspective, I highly recommend the book *Good Energy* by Dr. Casey

Means. She is a Stanford-trained physician who later moved into integrative medicine. She explains how modern medicine is excellent at acute care, but chronic conditions like infertility often require identifying and addressing root causes at the cellular level so the body can function the way it was designed to.

Fair warning, the first chapter is a little science-heavy. Stay with it. After that, it becomes a fascinating and very readable breakdown of how energy production in the body affects everything from hormone balance to egg quality and why true healing or disease reversal often requires more than medications and procedures alone.

THE GUT-FERTILITY CONNECTION

On the podcast, I asked Andrea Beaman, internationally renowned holistic health coach and best-selling author, who also happens to be one of the most gifted healers I have ever worked with, "If you wanted to create worldwide health, what is the very first thing you would have everyone do?"

Her answer? Eat real food. That's it.

You could change nothing else except make meals with whole foods such as any meat, fish, vegetables, fruit, and other foods in their natural form, using healthy oils like avocado, olive, and coconut oil, and I believe your health, wellness, and fertility would flourish.

Now, I am not going to pretend this is easy. I love plenty of processed foods right up until my body reminds me otherwise, usually with a nice combo of bloating, constipation, or a random wave of anxiety.

But if we are talking about one simple shift, especially in the United States, where many processed foods and even certain breads can create more inflammatory responses than in other countries, this is it.

Your gut is a major control center for how your body produces hormones, manages energy, and decides whether it feels safe enough to support conception. Give your gut the whole foods that fuel it, and your brain is far more willing to give your reproductive system the green light. Feed it ultra-processed, inflammatory foods instead, and your body shifts into survival mode, pushing pregnancy to the backseat.

If the gut struggles, the ripple effects show up quickly. A diet low in whole, nutrient-dense foods and poor absorption both lead to deficiencies, making it harder to build hormones, repair cells, and support reproduction. Gut-driven inflammation raises cortisol, which disrupts estrogen, progesterone, and testosterone. Impaired detox pathways allow old hormones and toxins to build up, increasing your body's workload and draining energy that should be supporting fertility.

SIGNS YOUR GUT IS IN SOS MODE

Your gut doesn't have a mouth, but it knows how to get your attention. When things are off, it doesn't whisper; it screams.

Common signs include:

- **Digestive Distress:** Bloating, gas, constipation, or sudden food sensitivities
- **Skin Signals:** Acne, eczema, or psoriasis (Yep, that inflammation showing up on your face is often gut-related.)
- **Brain Fog and Mood Swings:** Your gut makes neurotransmitters like serotonin, so when it's off, your mood and focus take a hit.
- **Energy Drain:** That "I'm so tired no matter how much I sleep" feeling
- **Immune Struggles:** Frequent colds or infections (70% of your immune system lives in your gut.)

A HEALTHY GUT COULD HELP STABILIZE YOUR HORMONES, IMPROVE EGG QUALITY, AND SUPPORT YOUR BODY IN SUSTAINING A HEALTHY PREGNANCY

When your gut is thriving, inflammation quiets down, detox works more efficiently, and energy becomes available again, helping your body shift into conception mode. **A healthy gut could help stabilize your hormones, improve egg quality, and support your body in sustaining a healthy pregnancy.**

After years of working with and learning from brilliant nutritionists and holistic health practitioners, including Andrea Beaman, I am going to share a few key steps to help you reset your gut, calm sensitivities, and clear the energy drains that may be quietly stalling your progress.

BEFORE YOU START EATING "PERFECTLY"... LET'S TALK

Before we dive into nutrition for fertility, I need you to promise me one thing: that you'll approach this with the goal of becoming healthier, happier, and more balanced, not more "perfect."

I say that because many women who start working with me are already stuck in overly restrictive nutrition plans that become one more way they feel trapped. I call it "infertility jail." They are no longer living their actual lives because of everything they think they have to do to get pregnant. Nutrition almost always becomes the main obsession, with acupuncture and supplements close behind, because these are things you can control in a process that often feels completely out of control.

And I get it, because I did the same thing. After another failed embryo transfer, I would snap at Brian for all the things I thought he could be doing better, and then I would turn around and shame myself even harder for not doing everything perfectly. I convinced myself that if I had tried harder or been more disciplined, I would have gotten pregnant.

It was not helpful. And it was not true.

Nothing needs to be perfect for you to get and stay pregnant. Eating for fertility is not about doing everything right. It is about making a few strategic changes that tip the Fertility Formula just enough in your favor, where energy outweighs toxins.

Striving for perfection may be one of the most energy-draining practices there is. Perfection is an impossible standard, and chasing it pulls energy away from your body instead of supporting it. When you aim for perfection, you are constantly setting yourself up to feel like you have failed, rather than recognizing the progress you are making.

So yes, I'm going to give you tools to eat in a way that supports hormone balance, replenishes nutrient stores, and helps your body feel safe enough to conceive. But if food starts to feel like the enemy, or your meals bring up anxiety or shame, that is a sign to pause. It may be time to reach out to a professional who can help you with a customized plan.

STEP-BY-STEP GUT RESET FOR FERTILITY

Your gut plays a powerful role in hormone balance and fertility, and shifting it does not have to mean flipping your entire life upside down overnight. Yes, eating only whole foods is the gold standard. But most women do better with smaller, strategic shifts that build momentum instead of triggering overwhelm.

That is why I like to approach gut repair in stages. Instead of overhauling everything overnight, we simplify and layer.

Each stage removes common stressors and strengthens your foundation before adding the next step. Most women only need the first three stages to see meaningful change.

Focus on one stage for two to three weeks, or until it starts to feel normal, before moving forward. This is not about restriction. It is about giving your body consistent signals of safety so it can shift out of survival mode and back into conception mode.

Step 1: Sabotager Swaps

The first step is to make slight upgrades to what you eat and use for cooking, rather than a major overhaul, so you avoid unknowingly adding toxins to your body. I know these swaps can sometimes be more expensive, and it may not be realistic to change everything at once. That is okay; do what you can, when you can.

Here are a few simple upgrades you can make, along with how each one could support your fertility:

- **Fruits and Vegetables:** Check out EWG.org for the Clean 15 and Dirty Dozen so you know which produce is worth buying organic and where you can save with conventional. Fewer pesticides means less hormonal cleanup work for your body, which matters when you are trying to conceive.
- **Meats and Dairy:** Choose meats and dairy without added hormones, antibiotics, or steroids whenever possible. These additives contribute to your body's hormone workload, which can quietly interfere with fertility over time.
- **Kitchen Essentials:** Swap plastic utensils, water bottles, and storage containers for glass or stainless steel. Plastics often contain chemicals like BPA and phthalates that confuse hormone signaling and increase toxic load.
- **Food Storage and Heating:** Avoid heating or freezing food in plastic. Temperature changes can cause chemicals to leach into

your food and increase exposure to hormone-disrupting compounds. Stick with glass or stainless steel for storing, reheating, and freezing.

- **Personal Care Products:** Start with laundry detergent. Your skin is in constant contact with your clothes and bedding, so this swap matters more than you think. I love Molly's Suds. Then move on to shower products. Heat and steam increase absorption through the skin, which makes this an easy place to reduce daily chemical exposure. You can find safer options on EWG.org.
- **Dressings and Sauces:** Keep it simple. Olive oil, salt, and lemon go a long way. When buying store-bought, look for brands like Primal Kitchen that avoid inflammatory seed oils and unnecessary additives.
- **Oils to Use:** Avocado, coconut, extra virgin olive, flaxseed, walnut, sesame, ghee, and macadamia oil. These support steadier blood sugar levels and lower inflammation, both of which are important for fertility. *Quick note:* Be mindful of smoke points. Heating oils beyond their limit creates oxidative stress, which puts extra work on your body.
- **Oils to Avoid:** Canola, soybean, corn, refined sunflower, and hydrogenated oils. These are highly processed and often contribute to inflammation, something we are actively trying to lower when fertility feels difficult.

You do not need to overhaul everything. Start with what feels doable and build from there.

Step 2: Add in Superfoods

The second step is to start *adding* foods that support your health, without taking anything else away yet. Think of these as "superfoods" or nutrient-dense options that fuel the bodily systems most connected to fertility. These can help balance hormones, reduce inflammation, and create a healthier, more receptive body for pregnancy.

Here's a comprehensive list of superfoods for gut and hormone health, including examples, benefits, usage tips, and research-backed reasons they belong on your plate.

- **Fermented Foods:** Sauerkraut, kimchi, kefir, yogurt (if tolerated), miso, and tempeh contain probiotics that support a healthy gut microbiome. A balanced gut helps you absorb nutrients, produce hormones, and reduce inflammation. Add sauerkraut on top of salads or "bowls" with a protein and vegetable.
- **Bone Broth:** Made from beef, chicken, or fish, bone broth is packed with collagen, glycine, and amino acids that help heal and strengthen the gut lining. A strong gut lining supports immune health and hormone regulation. Use bone broth in soups, or cook your grains in it.
- **Leafy Greens:** Spinach, kale, arugula, and Swiss chard are rich in folate, magnesium, and fiber. These nutrients support detox, balance blood sugar, and lower inflammation. Folate is especially important for reproductive health. You can add them to smoothies, salads, eggs, stir-fries, or sauté with olive oil, salt, and garlic.
- **Healthy Fats:** Avocados, extra-virgin olive oil, and coconut oil support hormone production, stabilize blood sugar, and reduce inflammation. Use olive oil as a dressing, cook with avocado oil (or ghee), and bake with avocado or coconut oil. And add avocados on top of (almost) anything!
- **Fiber-Rich Foods:** Sweet potatoes, carrots, and beets feed good gut bacteria, improve regularity, and help clear out excess estrogen. Roast them, shred them into salads, or toss into stir-fries.
- **Seeds:** Pumpkin, chia, and flaxseeds are packed with omega-3s, zinc, and lignans to support hormone balance, reduce inflammation, and boost egg quality. Sprinkle them on salads, blend into smoothies, or bake with them.
- **Berries:** Blueberries, raspberries, and blackberries are high in antioxidants and vitamin C, which help combat oxidative stress and support egg and sperm quality. Their fiber also supports gut health. Eat them as a snack, toss into smoothies, or add to yogurt.
- **Fatty Fish:** Salmon, sardines, and mackerel provide omega-3s like DHA and EPA, which reduce inflammation, support egg and sperm quality, and help regulate hormones. Aim for two to three servings per week. Bake or air fry salmon with olive oil and sea salt, add smoked salmon to eggs or salads, mix canned wild salmon into

avocado for an easy lunch, or choose high-quality fish oil if you truly cannot tolerate fish.

- **Garlic and Onions:** Red onions, shallots, and garlic are rich in prebiotics that feed beneficial gut bacteria and support detoxification. Use as a base in soups, stir-fries, or roasted veggie dishes.
- **Cruciferous Vegetables:** Broccoli, cauliflower, and Brussels sprouts contain compounds that help eliminate excess estrogen and support gut microbiota diversity. Roast them, steam and toss with lemon, or shred into salads.
- **Eggs (Pasture-Raised):** Loaded with choline, B vitamins, and protein, eggs support fetal brain development, hormone production, and gut repair. If your body tolerates eggs, they're one of the most nutrient-dense fertility foods.
- **EGG-ceptions:** Eggs can be a fertility superfood, unless your body sees them as the enemy. If you're sensitive to eggs, they may trigger inflammation that disrupts hormones and implantation. Common red flags include bloating, skin issues, brain fog, joint pain, or digestive discomfort after eating them.
    - To find out if you're sensitive to eggs, eliminate them for 2–4 weeks, then reintroduce them and see how your body reacts.
    - If you suspect a sensitivity, removing eggs and supporting gut repair could free up the energy your body needs for conception.
- **Herbal Teas:** Ginger, peppermint, and fennel teas help digestion, lower inflammation, and support hormonal balance. Ginger also supports blood sugar regulation. Sip herbal teas throughout the day or add fresh ginger to meals.
- **Organ Meats:** Liver from beef or chicken is packed with vitamins A, D, and B12, plus iron and zinc, key for hormone production, gut repair, and egg quality.

Confession: I don't eat organ meat myself, and in full transparency, I have never done any of these. But if you want the benefits without the taste, the following are a few workarounds:

- Mix a small amount into ground meat for burgers, meatballs, or tacos.
- Slow-cook it into stews with garlic and spices.
- Take it in capsule form as a supplement.
- Freeze small pieces and swallow like a pill with orange juice to mask the taste and boost absorption.

Step 3: Eat Only WHOLE Ingredient Foods

As you will see in the next callout box, even when I thought I was living a pretty healthy lifestyle, a month of eating only whole foods forced me to change way more habits than I expected.

Now, I'm not pretending this is easy. I love my chocolate and peanut butter protein bars, and I absolutely fall into the trap of grabbing packaged foods that taste amazing, right up until my body reminds me otherwise.

But as I mentioned earlier, if we are talking about one simple shift that could create a massive impact, this is it.

One-ingredient, whole foods are not exactly sexy until you realize they could help you skip the pricey fertility appointments, clear out half the supplements cluttering your counter, finally get to kiss your baby sooner, look younger, feel amazing, sleep better, and have clear, smooth skin that actually glows. Then they get real sexy, real fast.

Here's how whole foods can make you a whole lot healthier... and a whole lot more fertile.

- **They feed your fertility... literally!** Whole foods are packed with the nutrients your body needs to grow healthy eggs and sperm, balance hormones, and repair cells. Leafy greens like spinach provide folate (something you likely get in a prenatal vitamin) that supports early neural development. Eggs? Full of choline that helps build fetal brain and liver cells. Real food equals real building blocks for your baby.
- **They calm the chaos.** Processed foods tend to drive up inflammation, and chronic inflammation messes with ovulation, implantation, and hormone communication. Whole foods, like wild-caught salmon (rich in omega-3s) and turmeric (with its

compound curcumin), help reduce inflammatory markers and keep the reproductive system running more smoothly.

- **They keep your gut in the game.** Your gut isn't only about digestion; it helps detox estrogen, regulate immunity, and absorb the nutrients your hormones rely on. Whole foods high in fiber, like asparagus and garlic, feed your beneficial gut bacteria. Fermented foods like yogurt and sauerkraut provide probiotics that help keep your gut flora balanced, which is essential for hormone and immune balance.
- **They stabilize your blood sugar (and your hormones).** Blood sugar spikes and crashes are one of the fastest ways to throw your hormones off track, especially insulin, which directly affects ovulation. Whole foods with healthy fats and slow-digesting carbs (like sweet potatoes, lentils, and avocados) help prevent that rollercoaster and keep your cycle more stable.
- **They lower your toxic load.** Many processed foods contain additives, preservatives, and synthetic chemicals that stress your liver and can disrupt hormones. Whole foods, especially organic or pasture-raised options, reduce that toxic burden. Cruciferous vegetables like broccoli and Brussels sprouts help your liver break down excess estrogen more effectively.
- **They help your body absorb what it needs.** Nutrients don't do much if your body can't absorb them. Whole foods bring natural fiber and digestive enzymes that support gut function and nutrient uptake. Beets support bile flow from the liver, while fiber-rich fruits and vegetables help keep things moving and repair the gut lining, so more of what you eat actually gets used.
- **They make it easier to spot troublemakers.** When your meals are made of simple, whole ingredients, it's way easier to figure out what's bothering you. Processed foods often hide gluten, dairy, soy, or seed oils in ways that make it hard to track what's triggering inflammation or digestive issues. Eating real food simplifies that feedback loop.
- **They're easier to stick with.** This is the part no one talks about: whole foods make healthy eating simpler, not harder. A big batch of roasted vegetables, some cooked rice or quinoa, and grilled protein can last you for days. And the more consistent you are with

whole foods, the more you're rewarded with steadier cycles, better energy, and finally having the reserves to create life.

Ways to Win When Moving to a Wholefood-Only Plan:

- **Batch-Prep Your Meals:** Set aside time to prep by food group. Think proteins, roasted vegetables, chopped raw veggies, fresh or frozen fruit, trail mix, hard-boiled eggs, and baked sweet or regular potatoes. In our house, this works far better than batching full recipes. When you prep the basics, you can mix and match all week without getting bored.

  Keep Simple Sauces on Hand: Find or batch sauces made with real ingredients to add flavor and variety. A tasty sauce can turn the same bowl into a completely different meal.

  Use Fresh Herbs: Want to feel fancy? Keep a few fresh herbs on hand. Rosemary is one of my go-tos. Toss them on whatever protein or vegetables you are eating, and suddenly it feels like a brand new meal.

  No, this is not a gourmet cooking class. It's how you keep things simple, efficient, and actually doable. The key is having real food ready and options within reach.

- **Get a Support System:** Don't do it alone. Grab a friend, a family member, or a partner to join you. Make it fun by setting a challenge, planning a reward, or turning it into a reason for a trip when you and your partner reach the 30-day mark.
- **Expect Detox Symptoms:** That first week might feel a little rough. Mild headaches, low energy, or brain fog can show up as your body clears out the junk. I used to describe it as a hangover without the party. This is completely normal... It means the detox is working!
- And if you're cutting out caffeine (optional, by the way, since coffee beans *are* technically a whole food), do it slowly. Cut back by about 25 percent a day and swap in an organic decaf (made with the Swiss water method) or a coffee alternative.

- **Patience Before Progress:** You might feel nothing after that initial detox. And yes, you may wonder if this whole food thing is actually a whole big waste of time and energy. Promise me you will keep going. As long as you're sticking with it and not sneaking in processed foods on the side, the results will come. When I am doing whole foods only, I usually notice a real difference in my health around the three-week mark... which can feel like a lifetime when you are doing something outside your comfort zone.
- **Feel Amazing After 30+ Days:** This stage is when you'll really start noticing changes and might even feel motivated to keep going. If you're already feeling better but still working through lingering health issues, stay the course. Two to three months on whole foods gives your body the deep reset it's been waiting for. This level of nourishment supports cellular regeneration, which can lead to organ repair and revitalized organ systems (including your reproductive system!) and could be the turning point for your fertility.

Step 4: Plans For Autoimmune Issues

This step is the last in a four-step gut reset process. It is *not*, and let me repeat, *not* necessary for everyone. But it can be a helpful short-term option if your goal is to better understand your personal food sensitivities without spending money on expensive testing that is not always accurate.

If you are dealing with more significant issues like autoimmune conditions, you could talk with a qualified practitioner about options like the Autoimmune Paleo Diet (AIP) or doing a round of Whole30. AIP is *very* restrictive. I have done AIP once and Whole30 many times. It is not easy, but for the right person, AIP can help identify inflammatory foods and reset a gut that feels stuck.

I typically only suggest even *considering* AIP when someone is dealing with multiple, ongoing symptoms like major gut issues, migraines, lack of ovulation, heavy and painful menstrual cycles, or chronic allergies. That said, I have only recommended it to two clients.

What I do recommend often is Whole30 or simply eating whole foods, depending on someone's biology and the specific fertility challenges we are working through. Whole30 is essentially a whole food approach with a few extra restrictions on foods that, while technically whole, can still trigger inflammation or sensitivities in some people.

At the end of the day, this step is optional, not essential. If you are already making progress with whole foods, you likely do not need anything more intense. But if symptoms persist and you want clarity on how food may be affecting your health, a short-term reset like Whole30 or AIP can be a useful tool.

Remember, the goal is to feel more energized and supported, not to feel like you have landed deeper in infertility jail.

My Whole Truth

Many years ago, a friend suggested that a group of us try the Whole30 program in September. Imagine eating only single-ingredient foods for an entire month, with even more restrictions layered on top, such as no grains. The goal of the program is to reset your gut and experience the health benefits that come with it. But let's be honest, my friends and I were doing it purely for vanity. We wanted to see how good our bodies would look after thirty days of "clean" eating.

What it quickly became was a crash course revealing the extent to which our brains cling to comfort, how many processed foods we unknowingly consume, and the profound response our bodies exhibit when we give them real food.

Here's how it went for me:

Day 1: I was excited! I prepped a ton of meals, and we all shared photos of what we were eating.

Day 3: I had a headache so bad it felt like I was hungover without the fun part. Later, I learned that this was my body detoxing. Yuck and ouch. But it only lasted a day.

Day 7: It felt like the longest week of my life (because I can be a bit dramatic). I was waiting for someone to cheat, but no one did. My friends are the competitive type who never tap out. I am not like that; I will absolutely tap out if you give me an out.

Day 14: I was bratty. I avoided fun because I couldn't eat or drink what I wanted. But the positives started creeping in, whether I wanted to acknowledge them or not.

First, I realized how many processed foods I was actually eating, even though I thought I was "healthy." Second, my sleep improved dramatically, and I had the data from my tracker to prove it. And third, I was pooping regularly. (I know, TMI, but I had always been a bit constipated.) (I even pooped on a plane. Pooping while traveling? Completely unheard of.)

(Okay, I'll stop. But seriously, it felt like a miracle.)

Day 21: Less bratty, more bored. Really, really bored with my food choices, which I could have changed, but instead I complained. The results, though, were undeniable. I hadn't changed my workouts, yet I was noticeably more toned. That was the inflammation going down. My skin was smooth and glowing. I hadn't realized how dull it had been until I saw the shift. When inflammation drops, your skin shows it. Since what goes in comes out, eating clean gave me that healthy glow. Who knew?

Day 30: My first thought was, That wasn't so bad. I couldn't deny the results. My body looked and felt incredible, and my gut was definitely reset. How do I know? Because as soon as I finished, I went a little wild with the foods I'd missed. My face blew up, red, hot, and swollen, and I felt awful. Turns out, you're supposed to reintroduce foods slowly. No one told me that part.

Eating only whole foods, especially the kind Whole30 recommends, is hard in our modern world, but it's also one of the simplest ways to detox your body, boost energy, and get back on the right side of the "formula for fertility." Whole foods are what your body recognizes and knows how to use. They send your system a clear message: We have what we need to create a baby.

When you stick with it, even for a few weeks, your symptoms can start to fade. I've had a client in her mid-forties with PCOS go from decades of irregular cycles (where the pill was the only solution offered) to consistent 28-day cycles. All from changing her diet. And yes, she got pregnant with her own eggs.

It is also a powerful reminder that you are in control, not the part of your brain screaming for comfort. When you recognize that those urges to stop are simply your brain trying to keep you safe, even when the change is good for you, it becomes easier to tell it to calm down… in a loving way. That is how you allow a little discomfort to lead to real progress, instead of staying comfortable and stuck.

So here's your challenge. Whether your partner's sperm is part of the equation or not, make an eating plan together. One month. Only whole foods. Try the Whole30 program if you want a clear plan (look online for the rules and meal ideas; I'll also link my favorite recipes in the resources section).

I still do Whole30 two to three times a year, usually before a beach vacation because, yes, I am still a little vain. I never look forward to it, but I am always glad I did. I would love to say it is because the discomfort reminds me I can do hard things or because it resets bad habits that keep me sick. But if I am honest, it's because I feel and look like a million bucks when I do it.

BEFORE YOU CONSIDER A NUTRITION PLAN

There's a big difference between nourishing your body and micromanaging it, and that difference really matters, especially if you've ever struggled with your relationship with food in the past. So before diving into any fertility-focused nutrition strategy, here are a few things I want you to keep in mind.

- **Is There Anxiety?** If reading about cutting out certain foods makes you anxious or brings up old patterns of guilt or control, pause. That's your body waving a red flag, and you should not move forward with it. You need nourishment, not more rules. Plenty of women get pregnant without ever following a specific food plan, even with health issues in the mix. And putting restrictions on yourself could be exactly what puts your body into survival mode, and that's what we want to avoid.

EATING FOR FERTILITY SHOULD FEEL SUPPORTIVE, NOT STRESSFUL. THE GOAL ISN'T TO CONTROL YOUR BODY, IT'S TO CREATE SAFETY, BALANCE, AND TRUST WITHIN IT

- **Eat Enough and Plan Ahead.** Having a loose plan for meals each week helps you avoid that panic at 6 p.m. of "What do I eat?" Skipping meals or eating too little sends your body a signal that it is unsafe, and when it feels unsafe, it starts conserving energy rather than creating it. That is the opposite of what we want when you are trying to get pregnant. Make sure you have plenty of food available and a variety of options you actually enjoy. And promise me this one thing: do not restrict calories. Your body needs fuel to feel safe enough to create life.
- **Reintroduce Foods Slowly.** If you've removed a food group for more than a few weeks, how you bring it back matters. Start small and try a little once or twice a day, then increase over the next few days. Only add one food group at a time so you can tell what feels good and what doesn't. Go slowly, adding one new food every 3 to 4 days, and watch for signs such as bloating, fatigue, skin reactions, or digestive issues. If anything feels off, pause and give your body a few days before trying something new.

Eating for fertility should feel supportive, not stressful. The goal isn't to control your body; it's to create safety, balance, and trust within it.

GUT SUPPORT WITH SUPPLEMENTS

If you have already worked on improving your diet and lifestyle but still need extra support for digestion and gut balance, certain supplements could help. I will cover supplements in more detail later, but for gut-specific support, these are the ones I have seen be most helpful.

- Probiotics could help replenish beneficial bacteria.
- Slippery elm powder could help soothe and support the gut lining.
- Oregon grape root extract could help rebalance harmful bacteria or yeast.

TIPS FOR VEGETARIANS

If you are trying to conceive while following a vegetarian or vegan diet, let me say this first: it is absolutely possible to support fertility within your dietary choices.

That said, after years of working with fertility specialists, nutrition experts, and real clients in the trenches, I have seen a consistent pattern. Vegetarian and vegan diets often make fertility more challenging because some of the most critical nutrients for reproduction are harder to get in adequate amounts.

Nutrients like vitamin B12, iron, DHA, and L-carnitine play a big role in egg quality, hormone production, and energy availability. These nutrients are most easily absorbed from animal sources, which is why some bodies struggle to stay out of survival mode on plant-based diets alone.

If your diet choice is flexible, adding in some animal-based foods is something to consider, even temporarily, while trying to conceive. Think of it as giving your body extra support during a very energy-demanding season.

And if staying vegetarian or vegan is non-negotiable, that is completely okay. It simply means we need to be more intentional. With thoughtful planning and the right supplements, you can absolutely support a fertile environment without compromising your values.

Here are some tips inspired by Lily Nichols and Lisa Hendrickson-Jack's book *Real Food for Fertility.*

Dietary Tips:

- Track your protein intake and aim for adequate daily amounts. A good amount is typically 0.75 grams of protein per pound of body weight.
- Include two eggs per day if possible.
- Eat full-fat dairy from pasture-raised animals (yogurt, cheese, kefir).
- Add seaweed regularly to boost iodine levels.
- Soak grains, beans, and legumes in water for at least seven hours or sprout them before cooking to enhance nutrient absorption.
- Avoid seed oils; replace them with healthier fats like those mentioned in earlier sections.
- Consider eating oysters a few times a week (if "ostroveganism," which refers to the practice of eating animals that do not feel pain, is acceptable to you).

Supplements to Add:

- High-Quality Prenatal Vitamins: Ensure that they include B12, iron, and zinc.
- Algae-Based DHA: A plant-based source of omega-3 fatty acids.
- Acetyl L-Carnitine (500 mg): If you have the MTHFR mutation, this building block, found only in meat, may need to be added to your diet due to its critical role in pregnancy.

Iron-Rich Plant Foods and Absorption Tips:

Pair iron-rich foods with vitamin C to enhance absorption:

- Chickpeas and black beans with broccoli, cauliflower, or citrus fruits.
- Lentils with a squeeze of lemon or tomato sauce.
- Hemp seeds on a spinach salad.
- Potatoes with the skin, paired with bell peppers.
- Tomato paste or sun-dried tomatoes in a vitamin C-rich dish.

- Super-dark chocolate (because fertility-friendly doesn't have to mean boring).

You can support fertility on a vegetarian diet. It just requires thoughtful planning so your body feels nourished, safe, and well-fueled enough to create life.

Before heading to the next section...

If you'd like links to the recipes I used while eating whole foods only, resources I rely on to check for toxins in foods and produce, supplement discounts, and more, just scan the QR code.

GET MORE FERTILE WHILE YOU SLEEP

I always knew sleep mattered, but I had no idea how powerfully it affects fertility until I started digging into the research. When it comes to what actually improves fertility, the research on sleep is some of the most *eye-opening*.

One of the best resources I found was *Sleep Smarter* by Shawn Stevenson. That is where I learned what our bodies are actually doing when we get restorative sleep.

Think of restorative sleep as nature's built-in way to tip the Fertility Formula in your favor. It lowers toxic stress, rebuilds energy reserves, and restores your body at the cellular level, including your eggs and sperm.

Restorative sleep is also your body's free pharmacy. **When you get quality sleep, your body naturally produces hormones that would otherwise cost thousands of dollars to replace.**

WHEN YOU GET QUALITY SLEEP, YOUR BODY NATURALLY PRODUCES HORMONES THAT WOULD OTHERWISE COST THOUSANDS OF DOLLARS TO REPLACE

One of the biggest players is human growth hormone, or HGH. This so-called "fountain of youth" hormone is released in its highest amounts during your first deep sleep cycle, peaking in what Shawn Stevenson calls the "magic hour," between

10 p.m. and 1 a.m. This is when your body enters its deepest, most restorative sleep and releases HGH in the greatest quantities.

If you are staying up late, scrolling on your phone, or pushing past your natural bedtime, you are missing out on this powerful hormone, which supports things like:

- cellular repair
- muscle recovery
- healing from daily stressors
- preparing your body for optimal performance, including conception

And HGH is not the only hormone doing important work while you sleep. When your sleep timing is aligned, here is what is happening behind the scenes:

- **Melatonin** begins rising about two hours before bedtime to help you fall into deep sleep. It is also a powerful antioxidant that protects your eggs from oxidative stress.
- **Cortisol,** your stress hormone, naturally lowers overnight and reaches its lowest point in the early morning hours. Around 6 to 7 a.m., it begins to rise again, helping you wake up feeling refreshed, assuming you slept enough.

When you stay up too late or wake frequently throughout the night, your body misses the full benefit of these hormonal cycles. It is like your body is running an exclusive flash sale on fertility-supporting hormones, and you only get access if you are asleep during the right window.

I also learned that sleep does not start at bedtime. **The quality of your sleep at night depends heavily on what you do during the day.**

THE QUALITY OF YOUR SLEEP AT NIGHT DEPENDS HEAVILY ON WHAT YOU DO DURING THE DAY

How you wake up, eat, move, manage stress, and wind down—all of these send signals to your circadian rhythm, your internal clock that regulates hormones, mood, detoxification, and energy production. When that rhythm is supported, your body can finally shift out of survival mode and into repair and creation mode.

HOW TO TELL IF YOUR SLEEP IS RESTORATIVE

Want to know if your sleep is actually supporting your fertility? These questions help you get a quick, honest snapshot of whether your sleep is restorative enough to build energy and support your hormones or if your circadian rhythm may be out of sync.

Ask yourself:

- *Do I fall asleep easily, and am I asleep by around 10 p.m.?*
- *Do I stay asleep through the night?*
- *Do I wake up feeling rested, not groggy or depleted?*
- *Can I function well in the morning without caffeine?*
- *Do I still have steady energy around 3 p.m.?*
- *Do I naturally wake up before or by 7 a.m. without an alarm?*

If you answered no to most of these questions, your sleep is likely not yet fully restorative. That is okay because this section will walk you through simple practices to improve it. If you answered yes to most of the questions, your sleep is likely supporting your fertility. And if you want objective confirmation, consider getting a sleep tracking device.

PRESCRIPTION FOR RESTORATIVE SLEEP

Most people struggle with sleep because of their daily habits. It all starts with your morning routine: what time you wake up and how you begin your day. What you eat, how you move, and how you unwind at night also play a big role in how deeply you sleep.

Each of these choices affects your ability to get restorative sleep, which is essential for your health, energy, and fertility. To help you reset your rhythm, here are simple shifts that make a big difference.

(Asterisks (*) indicate items covered more extensively in later sections.

Eating for Sleeping*

What you eat all day shows up at night. Blood sugar swings, processed foods, and inflammation do not magically clock out at bedtime. If your body has been chasing spikes and crashes or working overtime to clean up chemicals, it is much harder to drop into deep, restorative sleep. Whole foods keep your blood sugar steadier, lower inflammation, and give your nervous system the signal that it is safe to rest. When your body feels nourished and stable, sleep comes more easily.

Focus on magnesium-rich foods like spinach, almonds, pumpkin seeds, and dark chocolate earlier in the day, and avoid heavy or sugary meals right before bed. Balanced blood sugar is key to staying asleep.

If you tend to wake between 2 a.m. and 4 a.m., try a small bedtime snack with protein, fat, and carbs. Good options include:

- Apple slices with nut butter
- A small handful of trail mix with nuts and dried fruit
- Greek yogurt with honey and a sprinkle of nuts

Drinking for Sleeping

I hate to say it, because I enjoy both, but caffeine and alcohol are sleep killers for some people.

Caffeine blocks adenosine, the chemical that helps you feel sleepy, and it can interfere with deep sleep even if you drink it earlier in the day. It also spikes cortisol, which can throw off your energy and hormones. If you love coffee but suspect it's getting in the way of restorative sleep, try switching to organic decaf espresso, ideally decaffeinated using the Swiss water process, as I've previously mentioned. Just taper slowly to avoid headaches.

Alcohol might make you feel sleepy at first, but it disrupts deep sleep, spikes cortisol, and messes with blood sugar, which is why it can wake you in the middle of the night. And beyond sleep, your body treats alcohol as a top-priority detox job, which I explain more fully in the *Survive to Thrive* Detox section later in the book.

Toxic Load and Sleep*

Sleep does not just restore energy. It also requires energy to detoxify, repair tissues, regulate blood sugar, and balance hormones. When your toxic load is high, your body spends more time managing cleanup and less time dropping into deep, restorative sleep. Lowering that load frees up energy for repair, hormone balance, and fertility.

Morning and Afternoon Sunlight

For all of us, getting natural sunlight without sunglasses within thirty minutes of waking helps reset our sleep-wake cycle, also known as the circadian rhythm, and supports a healthy balance of melatonin and cortisol.

If you struggle with insomnia, what I am about to suggest may help, but it is not easy: get up at sunrise for seven to ten days in a row to help reset your circadian rhythm. It may feel uncomfortable and inconvenient, but chronic insomnia often feels worse and can have long-term effects on both your overall health and your fertility.

Getting sunlight throughout the day matters too. Aim for at least an hour of natural light exposure daily, spread out if needed.

At nighttime, do the opposite. Avoid bright light after sunset whenever possible. Wearing blue light-blocking glasses is an easy way to support this shift and help your body wind down for sleep.

Move!*

Daily movement, especially in the morning, helps regulate your circadian rhythm, and sweating during exercise or in a sauna supports detox pathways.

Don't Move!*

Resting during the day can actually help you sleep better at night. Five minutes with your feet up (and your phone down) once or twice a day can make a real difference.

Habit stack by adding a few slow belly breaths during these pauses, especially before meals. This activates your parasympathetic nervous system, also known as "rest and digest" mode. When you do this before eating, it could improve digestion by increasing blood flow to your digestive system and lowering the overall workload on your body.

These small pauses throughout the day signal to your nervous system that it is safe, supported, and not in a constant state of urgency. That sense of safety carries into the evening, making it easier for your body to relax, repair, and settle into deep, restorative sleep.

Stick to the Sleep Schedule

Aim to be asleep by 10 p.m. to take full advantage of your hormonal repair cycle. Waking by 7 a.m. helps you sync with your body's natural cortisol peak for an energetic start to the day.

Create a Transition Routine

The hour before bed should be your wind-down time. Avoid screens, dim the lights, and do something calming like stretching, journaling, connecting with your partner, or reading.

Optimize Your Bedroom

Keep your room cool (around 65°F or 18°C), dark, and free from electronics.

Turn your phone on airplane mode at the very least, or turn off your Wi-Fi at night if you can. Many of my clients report better sleep after making this simple change. Airplane mode reduces emissions from your phone, while turning off Wi-Fi reduces emissions from your home network. Both can lower overall nighttime EMF (electromagnetic field) exposure and support deeper, more restorative sleep.

Supplements*

If you've already upgraded your restorative sleep routine but still struggle with falling or staying asleep, certain supplements can help. Melatonin (a natural hormone your body produces), magnesium glycinate, glycine, L-theanine, and apigenin could each help promote better rest.

These small but powerful habits could save you years of frustration, thousands of dollars, and endless energy trying to piece together why your body isn't functioning the way it should. Instead of chasing symptoms and scrambling for quick fixes, you're building a foundation that supports longevity, vitality, and a body that is thriving instead of barely surviving for the rest of your life.

Before heading to the next section...

If you'd like a checklist you can personalize for morning and evening routines to support restorative sleep, plus links to some of the products I use for better sleep, just scan the QR code.

JUUUST BREEEEEEATHE

(Please sing this like Faith Hill when you read it.)

We're eating real foods, the kind that makes symptoms disappear and reminds you what "normal" is supposed to feel like. We've got sleep dialed in. Now it's time to bring in one of the most overlooked but powerful tools for fertility: breathing.

I know, it sounds too simple, right? You're currently breathing right now, so clearly you've got it covered and can move on to the next section, right? Probably not. If you're anything like the rest of us, your breathing is usually shallow, and those quick, incomplete breaths could keep you stuck in chronic survival mode that quietly drains your health and, over time, your fertility too.

Here is how deep, intentional breathing could help improve your fertility:

- **Activates the Parasympathetic Nervous System:** This is your "rest and digest" zone, the opposite of "fight or flight." Deep breathing calms your stress response, lowers cortisol levels, and signals to your body that it's safe. And a body that feels safe is one that's more likely to make a baby.
- **Delivers Oxygen to Your Cells:** Every cell in your body needs oxygen to function well, including the ones that grow eggs, build uterine lining, and support sperm. Deep breathing keeps those cells fed and firing.
- **Helps Balance Hormones:** Stress hormones like cortisol love to mess with your reproductive hormones. Deep breathing helps

lower cortisol so hormones like estrogen, progesterone, and LH can actually do their jobs.

- **Improves Blood Flow:** You want nutrient-rich blood reaching your uterus, ovaries, and all the other MVPs of reproduction. Deep breathing supports circulation and helps those areas get what they need.
- **Reduces Inflammation:** Chronic stress triggers inflammation, which leads to hormonal chaos. Deep breathing helps calm that whole cycle down and creates a more fertile internal environment.

By giving your body the oxygen your cells crave, you help retrain your nervous system so it's not always on high alert. You shift out of survival mode and remind your body that it is safe now. It's okay to grow life.

Breathing deeply gives your body permission to rest, repair, and create.

So let's breathe like your future depends on it, because in many ways, it does!

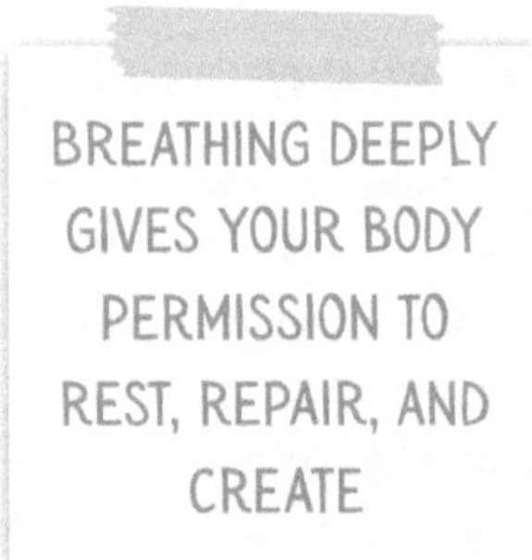

1. BELLY BREATHING (A.K.A., DIAPHRAGM BREATHING)

This is your foundation, the kind of breathing your body was built for, even if modern life trained it out of you. It shifts you out of panic mode and into calm, repair, and fertile territory.

How to Do It:

Sit or lie down comfortably.

Place one hand on your chest and the other on your belly.

Breathe in through your nose and feel your belly rise (not your chest).

Feel your belly drop as you gently exhale through your mouth.

Do this exercise for 5 to 10 minutes a day. Before bedtime is a great time.

Why It Works:

It lowers stress hormones, increases blood flow to your reproductive organs, and helps your body feel safe enough to do what it was designed to do.

2. BIG EXHALES

This is your reset button. If you've been shallow breathing all day or need a quick refresh, this gets the stale air out and the good stuff in.

How to Do It:

Take a big inhale through your nose, filling your lungs.

Exhale forcefully through your mouth, using your core to push every bit of air out.

Repeat 10 times.

Why It Works:

Fully emptying your lungs makes room for fresh oxygen. That boost helps your cells function better, and when your cells are thriving, your fertility has a much better shot.

3. 4-7-8 BREATHING

This one's a nervous system reset on demand. It's simple, powerful, and amazing for anxiety or winding down at night.

How to Do It:

Inhale through your nose for 4 counts.

Hold for 7 counts.

Exhale through your mouth for 8 counts.

Repeat for 4 to 6 cycles.

Why It Works:

It lowers cortisol, slows your heart rate, and helps your body relax. The more your system feels safe and regulated, the more it opens the door to conception.

WHEN YOUR BODY STARTS CRAVING SOMETHING THAT FEELS THIS CALMING, THIS GROUNDING, THIS GOOD, THAT'S YOUR SIGN YOU'RE BREATHING NEW LIFE INTO YOUR BODY

THE EVERYDAY BREATH PLAN

To make these exercises part of your daily life:

- Start small. Set aside 1 or 2 minutes a day to practice a technique. Then build up to 5 minutes.
- Pair it. Connect your breathing exercises to something you already do so you don't forget. Make them part of your morning or evening routine, before a meal, when getting in the car after work, or as a "requirement" before scrolling social media. Or you can pair it with the next step in this process, which we'll discuss in the next section, "Brain Breaks for Baby Makes."
- Track your progress. Pay attention to how your energy, mood, and even your menstrual cycle shift over time.

I have a feeling these few minutes of breathing will start to grow on you. Once you feel the difference from fuller breaths and better oxygen flow, it might become your favorite part of the day. And **when your body starts craving something that feels this calming, this grounding, and this good, it's a sign that you're breathing new life into your body.**

Before heading to the next section...

If you'd like the link to the videos that teach deep, intentional breathing, just scan the QR code.

BRAIN BREAKS FOR BABY MAKES

THE TYPE-A TURNAROUND

I had a client, Ashley, who used to call herself "Triple A" because she was so much more than "Type A." Before working with me, she and her husband admitted something that's more common than anyone wants to say out loud: even though they wanted a baby more than anything, they had no idea how they'd actually fit one into their already jam-packed lives.

Ashley did everything "triple well" with triple the intensity. Work, family, social commitments, workouts. If it could be optimized, she was on it. And guess which reproductive issue she had? The one that also tends to overdo everything: PCOS.

Ashley came to me as a private IVF client, and while I worked on securing her next doctor and making sure she would receive the right protocol with precise execution, I had her start with the foundational work, which we now call the Survive to Thrive Protocol and the Spirit Protocol.

The difference was night and day.

Before working together, Ashley had made only two blastocysts, and her doctor didn't think they looked great. They transferred them anyway so they wouldn't go to waste, but both transfers failed. After we worked together, she made eight beautiful blastocysts, and on the very first transfer from that cycle, she got pregnant and stayed pregnant.

When I later invited Ashley to share her story with my current clients, she didn't focus on the science or the IVF protocol at all. Instead, she talked about how the Survive to Thrive Protocol and the Spirit Protocol had completely changed her life! She finally had time for her husband and their growing family. She felt calmer, happier, and more present. Her days felt good again. She had more energy than ever, and both her career and personal life began to thrive.

Ashley didn't only get the baby she dreamed of; she got a life she loves.

If you are trying to prove to your brain that it's safe to get and stay pregnant, you have to show it that you're not already maxed out.

Now, how do you do that when you *are* maxed out and can't exactly quit your job or put life on hold? You simply need to pause (not stop) and give your brain a break.

If you're anything like me, you're constantly thinking and doing. It is actually hard for me to relax and do nothing because it feels like a waste of time—

time I could be using to be productive. But that constant go mode does not make me healthier or happier. It drains my energy and runs me down.

Here's the science. Your brain and body are in constant communication. When the brain senses you need to go, go, go, it shifts resources away from "nonessential" functions like fertility and goes into survival mode. That means your hormones, digestion, and sleep all take a hit as your body prioritizes simply getting through the day over creating life.

That's where short but powerful "brain breaks" come in. These intentional pauses are neurological resets. When you slow down even for a minute and focus on one thing at a time, you send a clear signal to your brain that you're safe. This activates your parasympathetic nervous system, the "rest and restore" mode, which supports hormone balance, better digestion, deeper sleep, and ultimately, fertility.

So what does that look like in real life? It's not about doing nothing. It's about doing *one* thing at a time: eating without scrolling, walking while focusing on one simple thing, like spotting the color pink, or breath focus without letting your to-do list start running in your head. **These small, consistent moments of presence teach your brain that it doesn't have to stay on high alert and that it is safe to conceive.**

THESE SMALL, CONSISTENT MOMENTS OF PRESENCE TEACH YOUR BRAIN THAT IT DOESN'T HAVE TO STAY ON HIGH ALERT AND THAT IT IS SAFE TO CONCEIVE

Okay, now it's time for the tactics. Here are a few simple ways to show your brain that you truly have the space, safety, and capacity to support another life.

THE DAILY "BRAIN BREAK" ROUTINE

Step 1: Choose Your Breathwork

Pick one of the breathing techniques from the previous section (Belly/Diaphragm Breathing, Big Exhales, or 4-7-8 Breathing) and practice it for **at least six breaths**. You can do this seated or lying down, with your feet up against the wall to help with circulation.

Then return to natural breathing for the rest of your break.

Step 2: Get Present

Close your eyes and go through your five senses. What do you...

- *Hear* at this moment?
- *Smell* at this moment?
- *Feel* at this moment?
- *See* at this moment?
- *Taste* at this moment?

When I get to "feel," I like to start at the top of my head and travel down through my body, noticing any sensations along the way.

This exercise grounds you in the present moment, shifting your focus from everything swirling in your mind to what's happening in your body *right now*.

Step 3: Customize Your Calm

From here, you can decide how to spend the remainder of your brain break.

Options include:

- Continuing with natural breaths
- Revisiting your five senses a few times to stay grounded and present
- Choosing a calming or empowering mantra, such as "I am healthy and so blessed to be so fertile"
- Saying a prayer or sending a moment of gratitude to someone or something

Once you've built the habit of taking one-to-five-minute brain breaks and you're ready for deeper healing at the cellular level, guided mindfulness and meditation can take things further by reducing stress and rebalancing key hormones.

Guided mindfulness practices like body scans, breathing exercises, or guided meditations help you stay present and break the pattern of overdoing (usually when trying to take care of everyone else). These techniques have been shown to lower cortisol—the main stress hormone that can disrupt ovulation, suppress progesterone, and interfere with implantation. Lowering cortisol helps restore a healthier balance of reproductive hormones like luteinizing hormone, estrogen, and progesterone, all of which are essential for ovulation, egg maturation, uterine lining development, and maintaining early pregnancy.

MEDITATION

Meditation, especially silent or mantra-based practices, goes even deeper by helping your brain shift out of chronic survival mode. Studies show it can raise DHEA levels (a hormone that supports ovarian health and egg quality), improve regulation of gonadotropin-releasing hormone, and support the pituitary's release of luteinizing and follicle-stimulating hormones, key players in follicle development and ovulation. Meditation can also lower prolactin, which is a hormone that, in excess, can interfere with fertility.

Beyond hormones, both meditation and mindfulness can reduce inflammation, improve blood flow to reproductive organs, and support mitochondrial health (your body's energy factories) in both eggs and sperm. All of this helps create an internal environment that's more welcoming for conception.

Whether you start with a short, guided mindfulness video or try a few minutes of silent meditation, even a small daily practice can calm your nervous system, shift hormonal patterns, and signal to your body that it's safe and ready to create new life.

Now, let's talk about meditation for a minute. I often hear people say they can't meditate because they can't turn their thoughts off. But the goal isn't to turn your thoughts off. If that were possible, you'd probably be unconscious. Meditation is simply noticing when your mind wanders and gently bringing it back to the present.

What usually gets in the way is that people expect to be good at something they've just started, instead of allowing themselves to practice and get a little better each time. Feeling unfocused is actually part of the process. Over time, those scattered moments get shorter, the calm moments grow, and those are the moments when your body does its deepest healing.

When I meditate consistently, it feels like I've taken half a Valium. I don't feel "out of it," but I feel focused, clear, and calm.

It's easy to slip out of practicing meditation and convince yourself there's something more important to do. This happens to me. All. The. Time. That's why I recommend starting small with five minutes of "brain breaks" to build the habit, then adding a minute or two each week until you reach fifteen or twenty minutes. Once you feel how good it is, you won't want to skip it. It simply feels too good not to do.

Before heading to the next section...

If you'd like the link to the course that I took on how to meditate (for busy professionals) and some of the other mindset and meditation tools that I find helpful, just scan the QR code.

MOVE TO CONCEIVE: TINY STEPS, BIG IMPACT

MAKE WALKING WORK FOR YOU

How relaxing is a walk outside surrounded by nature? You get to see everything growing around you, breathe in fresh air, and feel your shoulders drop two inches. Realistically, do you have time to take a long, peaceful walk in nature during the day, especially if you work? Usually not. My job gives me flexibility since everything I do is virtual and my clients are all over the world, but I'm still glued to a screen most of the day.

Hitting ten thousand steps felt like one more impossible thing on my already ridiculous "healthy habits" list. Meanwhile, my husband, Brian, who's an executive health coach, was always reminding me how much I was sitting. He gets nervous if you're not eating enough (especially protein) or moving enough. I call him my "protein and push-up pusher."

Then I found my solution: a walking pad with an adjustable incline. It's basically a treadmill without handrails, and I paired it with my adjustable standing desk. Now, while I'm talking to my team, checking emails, and yes, even while I'm writing this book, I'm walking. The only time I sit is during client calls.

And here's my little secret: I live in athletic gear all day but throw on a blazer for calls, so I still look professional. I do the same thing for podcasts, too. It's my version of "business on top, casual on the bottom" that I call "business on top, cardio on the bottom."

The walking pad is my hack for easily hitting 12,000 steps a day without it feeling like another thing to check off the list. Unlike so many gadgets I've wasted money on in the name of healthy habits, my standing desk and walking pad have been worth every penny.

(Okay, this non-sponsored commercial is officially over!)

Dr. Marcia and I shared the same brilliant business coach, Taylor Welch, and we were all on a call when she hit us in the face with this fact:

"Genes don't cause disease; they express your choices."

It stopped me in my tracks... (well, on my walking pad track!)

Dr. Marcia said that while you might have inherited certain genetic tendencies, your daily choices—what you eat, how you sleep, how you manage stress, and yes, how you move—determine whether those genes stay quiet or become active troublemakers.

Movement is one of the most powerful ways to influence your cellular health and, in turn, your fertility. The way you move signals your body to repair, regenerate, and function at its best. When it comes to supporting your cells, which are the building blocks of everything from hormone production to egg and sperm health, three types of movement stand out: **walking, stretching, and weightlifting**. These are not only exercises to keep your butt from blending into the back of your knees (anyone else?); they are movements that help your body thrive on every level.

In the following sections, we will explore how each of these forms of movement plays a unique role in cellular health and fertility and how to make them a natural, energizing part of your routine. You will see how the simple things you are learning in this Survival Protocol section can keep you from turning on the disease genes that could prevent you from living a long, healthy, pain-free life, or more immediately, from kissing your baby sooner.

Walking: Turning Healthy Genes On and Disease Genes Off

Walking is one of the tools that could help signal to your genes, *Hey, don't turn on those bad ones, please!* It is such a simple habit that feels good and can really impact your overall health and wellness, and... (say it with me) therefore your fertility!

Simply walking can do some pretty impressive things behind the scenes. Research suggests that regular movement may positively influence gene expression patterns associated with inflammation and cellular repair. Walking also supports autoimmune health by settling an overactive immune system and easing the chronic inflammation that could get in the way of conception and overall wellness.

Here's the nerdy part about how it could help your body and your future family:

Walking and Autoimmune Health: Many women struggling with infertility also deal with autoimmune conditions like Hashimoto's. Walking helps stimulate lymphatic circulation, which matters because your lymphatic system relies on muscle movement, not the heart, to move waste out of the body. When lymph flow improves, detox pathways work more efficiently, which could help calm immune flare-ups. Walking has also been shown to lower inflammatory markers and support a more balanced immune response. The result is a body that feels less reactive and more resilient.

Walking for Hormone Health: Your hormones run the show when it comes to fertility and energy. Walking helps lower cortisol, the stress hormone that signals your body to prioritize survival over reproduction. When cortisol stays elevated, ovulation and implantation can suffer. Walking also improves insulin sensitivity, which supports blood sugar balance and is especially important for women with PCOS. Add in the natural endorphin boost, and you get better mood stability and more consistent hormonal signaling.

Walking and Your Reproductive System: Unlike intense workouts that can add more stress, walking is restorative. It increases blood flow to your ovaries and uterus, delivering oxygen and nutrients where they are needed most. It helps reduce oxidative stress, which protects egg and sperm quality. On a cellular level, walking supports mitochondrial function, meaning your cells have more usable energy. And since reproduction is energy-expensive, that matters.

STRETCHING TO SUPPORT YOUR CELLS AND CYCLES

Stretching might seem like a small thing, but it's one of the simplest ways to keep your body ready for everything life (and motherhood) throws at you. It's not only about flexibility or feeling good in the moment, though I think it feels really good. Stretching can help your cells, organs, and reproductive system work better, too.

Think of stretching like a quick tune-up for your body:

- **Improves Blood Flow:** It gets blood flowing, delivering oxygen and nutrients where they're needed most, including your ovaries, uterus, and every other cell involved in creating life.
- **Releases Tension:** It melts away the tension that keeps your body locked up and stuck in stress mode, calming your nervous system.
- **Activates Rest-and-Restore:** It activates your parasympathetic nervous system, shifting you out of survival mode

so hormones like cortisol, estrogen, and progesterone can stay in the healthy ranges needed for regular cycles and conception.
- **Supports Detox and Immunity:** It helps your lymphatic system flush out waste, reduce inflammation, and support your immune system, key pieces of a body that's truly ready for a baby.

Personally, I now stretch often since realizing how much flexibility I've lost over the years. I used to be able to drop into the splits both ways without a second thought. Now, I think about how staying flexible will help me move easily as I get older. I always say to my kids, "Flexible bends and stiff breaks," when I urge them to stretch with me (they *still* don't!). I plan to be the eighty-year-old still touching her toes, rocking Pilates, and having solo dance parties in the kitchen!

So stay flexible and ready to dance by stretching every day!

GROUNDING WHILE STANDING OR STRETCHING

Grounding is the practice of making direct contact with the earth, most often by walking barefoot on grass, sand, or soil. Some research suggests that direct contact with the earth may allow free electrons to enter the body, which could help neutralize free radicals, lower inflammation, and support a calmer nervous system. While the research is still emerging, the proposed mechanism is simple: less oxidative stress and a more regulated stress response. Some small studies suggest grounding may help regulate cortisol rhythms and improve sleep quality, likely by supporting nervous system balance and lowering inflammation.

I also like to think of grounding as sending your brain a clear signal: you are safe. And when your brain feels safe, it is far more willing to move your body out of survival mode and into restoration and creation mode.

Because I love stacking habits, I stand or walk barefoot in my backyard when I am on phone calls with friends or family, or I do my morning stretches on the grass so my hands and feet can make contact. I am usually listening to something inspiring at the same time. Three wins, one block of time.

WEIGHTLIFTING FOR FERTILE STRENGTH AND RESILIENCE

Weightlifting is often overlooked in fertility conversations and, honestly, in women's health in general, but its benefits are undeniable. It is one of the most powerful ways to support your cells, hormones, and overall health. As I mentioned, after Mila was born, I worked with a friend who is an integrative medicine doctor and learned that my testosterone was so low it was almost undetectable. Her recommendation? Start lifting weights.

The number one reason I hear most women avoid lifting is that they worry about getting bulky. But that's not something you need to stress about. First, building real muscle takes serious work. Trust me, I've watched my husband and my son, who are athletes, do it, and it involves eating so much food it's almost nauseating to witness. Second, what you might be calling "bulk" is often temporary inflammation from muscle recovery. When you start lifting, your muscles hold a bit more fluid as they repair and strengthen. If you keep going and fuel your body with real, whole foods, that puffiness will fade. What's left is a strong, lean, and less inflamed body that looks and feels amazing.

Here's how weightlifting supports your body and fertility:

- **Hormonal Balance:** Resistance training increases key hormones like growth hormone and testosterone (yes, women need some too), which are essential for egg development and ovulation.
- **Insulin Sensitivity:** Strength training improves how your body uses insulin, helping regulate blood sugar. This is crucial if you have PCOS, since insulin resistance can throw off ovulation and hormone balance.
- **Mitochondrial Activation:** Remember the formula: we need energy to create. Weightlifting boosts mitochondrial function, giving your cells more energy to support healthy eggs, sperm, implantation, and early embryo development.
- **Anti-Inflammatory Effects:** Lifting reduces chronic inflammation by calming your immune system, which is critical since inflammation can interfere with egg and sperm quality and embryo implantation.
- **Bone and Muscle Strength:** Strong bones and muscles help support your body during pregnancy, reduce injury risk, and help you stay strong, confident, and vibrant no matter where life takes you.

To be clear, when we're building a baby-ready body, we don't want to overdo heavy weight training. The goal is to direct your energy toward creating and growing healthy eggs and embryos, not repairing and building big muscles.

Start with simple bodyweight moves like lunges, squats, planks, push-ups, and core work. You can find plenty of great trainers on YouTube who demonstrate proper form, which is far more important than the amount of weight you lift. When you're not in treatment or at a point in your cycle where pregnancy might be possible, you can slowly add more weight to build strength.

Always check in with your medical professional about your specific situation. But in general, a practitioner who understands how movement supports blood flow, energy, cellular health, and hormone balance should encourage you to stay active while trying to conceive. Remember that many doctors haven't studied these connections in detail, so you may need to advocate for yourself when it comes to staying active in a way that truly supports your fertility.

DETOX TO DIAPERS: CLEANSE YOUR WAY TO CONCEPTION

WHAT EVEN THE BEST PROTOCOLS MISS

I have worked with women facing every mental and physical challenge. I have worked with women who struggle with depression, PTSD, and sleep deprivation due to their demanding professions, as well as those who suffer from premature ovarian failure or various other issues that impact nearly every organ system. Every time, I would brace myself for how impossible their journey might be… and then they would get pregnant with a healthy baby.

No matter the egg reserve, age, or lifestyle, it always seemed like the right Science Protocol could overcome almost any obstacle.

Then came a client who changed everything I believed.

She was healthy, with a beautiful egg reserve, but had not been successful in prior IVF cycles. Her protocol was completely wrong, and I knew I could fix it and get her doctor on board. With a new customized plan and exact execution, her next cycle looked perfect. Her follicles grew slowly and evenly, just the way I like to see them. By all accounts, it was her best egg retrieval yet.

THE RIGHT PROTOCOLS MEAN NOTHING IF YOUR BODY IS NOT PREPARED TO RECEIVE NEW LIFE

And then, out of fifteen eggs, none made embryos. I was stunned. I had missed nothing, yet it felt impossible. Determined to find answers, I worked with my functional medicine expert and ran evaluations we typically reserve for transfer prep. What we discovered defied all our initial results: she had dangerously high levels of certain toxins. She was then able to focus on clearing them, and on her very next retrieval, she produced three blastocysts. For context, in her previous five retrievals combined, she had only made four.

On her very first transfer after detoxing, she became and remained pregnant.

That experience taught me an invaluable lesson that I have discussed often in this book: nothing can force an embryo to be created, nor can anything force a pregnancy to happen or continue. **The right protocols mean nothing if your body is not prepared to receive new life.** The body has to know that it's okay and "safe" to have a baby.

Let's talk about toxins, the uninvited guests in your body that, when they build up, can quietly sabotage your plans for pregnancy.

There are physical toxins like metals, mold, chemicals, bacteria, and parasites. These are the things that overwhelm your system and force your body to work overtime to keep up.

But physical toxins don't stop there.

Over time, they often show up as what I call emotional toxins: that "mean girl" voice in your head that spirals into anger, anxiety, depression, or endless self-doubt. When your brain gets stuck in these loops, it flips your body into survival mode on repeat. And here's the important part: those mental and emotional patterns are often symptoms indicating underlying hormonal imbalances that can effectively be addressed.

Think about being quick to anger, which is commonly linked to estrogen dominance when detox pathways and liver clearance are sluggish. Or depression that manifests when your body is running low on key nutrients and minerals needed to properly function.

Now, having toxins is normal. Your body is beautifully designed to handle them through the liver, lymphatic system, and kidneys. But like a pool filter after a big storm, when the toxin load gets too heavy, bodily systems can't keep up. Detox pathways slow down, energy depletes, and your brain receives a clear message: *This is not the time to create life.*

Our goal isn't to eliminate every toxin; that's nearly impossible in the modern world. The goal is to lighten the load so your body can stay efficient, balanced, and out of survival mode. When that happens, your system finally has the space and energy to shift back into conception mode.

WHAT TOXIN OVERLOAD DOES

Toxins don't hang out harmlessly. They hijack your hormones, drain cellular energy, damage mitochondria (the batteries that power eggs and sperm), disrupt your gut microbiome, and trigger chronic inflammation. This chain reaction can derail ovulation, lower sperm quality, and make implantation harder by sending your body into survival mode instead of creation mode.

Alcohol and Energy Trade-Offs

Questions about drinking alcohol are some of the most common ones I get. And while I am all for balance, it is important to understand what alcohol actually does inside the body.

Alcohol is metabolized as a toxin, so your liver prioritizes breaking it down before focusing on other repair work in the body.

When you drink, energy and resources are redirected away from egg development, hormone balance, cellular repair, and sperm production. Survival always comes before reproduction, so detox takes the lead.

As we age, this process becomes more energy-demanding. The same drink your body handled easily in your twenties can take longer and require greater metabolic effort to clear. If your goal is pregnancy, especially over forty, we want your body signaling abundance, not diverting energy to constant cleanup.

You can still enjoy a drink occasionally, but it should not be something you are doing very often if pregnancy is the goal.

When you understand the energy trade-off, you get to decide intentionally instead of unknowingly pulling energy away from healing, hormone balance, and fertility.

SIGNS YOUR BODY IS OVERLOADED WITH TOXINS (YES, EVEN HIS)

Toxins don't always show up as something obvious. More often, they create subtle but persistent signals that your detox systems are overwhelmed and your body is working overtime to keep up. When that happens, energy gets pulled away from repair and reproduction.

Here are some common signs your toxic load may be too high:

Brain and Energy Clues

- Frequent headaches or brain fog
- Feeling exhausted, no matter how much you sleep
- Trouble concentrating or feeling mentally "off"

Skin and Inflammation Signals

- Acne, eczema, rashes, or unexplained skin flare-ups
- Puffiness or visible inflammation
- Slower recovery from workouts or injuries

Gut and Detox Clues

- Bloating, constipation, or digestive discomfort
- Feeling worse after eating certain foods
- A history of antibiotic use, gut infections, or IBS-type symptoms

Hormonal Red Flags

- Irregular cycles or intense PMS
- Mood swings that feel out of proportion
- For him: low libido, low testosterone, or hormonal imbalance

Fertility-Specific Signs

- Egg quality concerns despite "good" labs
- Sperm issues such as low count, poor motility, poor morphology, or high DNA fragmentation

Environmental Exposure History

- Past or current mold exposure
- Heavy metals or occupational toxin exposure
- Living in a constant "chemical soup" from plastics, pesticides, cleaners, and pollution

Other Male Signs

- Increased belly fat

- Hair thinning
- Irritability or low motivation

If several of these sound familiar, your body, or his, may be stuck in survival mode because detox pathways are overloaded. Lightening that load is often one of the fastest ways to shift back toward conception mode.

DAILY DETOX PRACTICES TO LIGHTEN THE LOAD

Did you know your lymphatic system needs *you* to move it? Otherwise, blood, energy, and cellular waste can become stagnant, and we all know what stagnant water creates. It becomes a breeding ground for bacteria and toxins. Your lymphatic system relies on your movement, breath, and muscle contractions to pump lymph fluid, flush out waste, and deliver nutrients throughout your body.

By doing small, intentional things to keep your lymphatic system moving, you create a steady, healthy flow of nutrients in and toxins out. This helps your body stay vibrant, balanced, and ready to create new life.

Throughout the Survive to Thrive Protocol, you have laid the groundwork for activating your body's natural detox processes. Now it is time to build on that momentum.

You don't need an extreme cleanse to feel better or prepare your body for pregnancy. Daily habits make the biggest difference, and they're simple enough to weave into your everyday life.

BY DOING SMALL, INTENTIONAL THINGS TO KEEP YOUR LYMPHATIC SYSTEM MOVING, YOU CREATE A STEADY, HEALTHY FLOW OF NUTRIENTS IN AND TOXINS OUT

- **Move Your Body:** We've already talked about this, but gentle, consistent movement helps boost lymphatic flow. Walking, yoga, dancing, jump squats, or bouncing on a mini trampoline for ten minutes a day can all get your lymph moving.
- **Dry Brushing:** Brushing your skin toward your heart is a simple, effective way to support lymphatic drainage and help your body detox.

- **Hydrate:** Drink half your body weight in ounces of water each day (about 80–100 ounces for most people) to flush toxins and boost energy.
- **Get Sunlight:** Aim for at least 15 minutes of early morning sunlight without sunglasses to regulate your circadian rhythm. This supports hormone balance and improves sleep, both key to your body's natural detox and fertility.
- **Prioritize Nutrition:** We covered this topic earlier, but to recap: eat whole foods and focus on cruciferous vegetables like broccoli, kale, and Brussels sprouts to support detox pathways. Include prebiotic foods like jicama, green bananas, or cooked and cooled potatoes to feed your gut.
- **Sweat It Out:** Regular exercise, infrared saunas, or Epsom salt baths can help your body release toxins through sweat.
- **Castor Oil:** Castor oil has been used traditionally to support gentle circulation and abdominal comfort, and some practitioners believe that castor oil packs encourage your body's natural detox pathways. Apply organic castor oil to your liver area (on the right side, under your ribs) using a soft cloth, cover it with a towel, and relax for 30–60 minutes.
- **Oral Care:** Swishing unrefined coconut oil (oil pulling) for 10–20 minutes daily can help detoxify and reduce inflammation. Thorough brushing and flossing *twice a day* lowers the risk of gum inflammation and keeps harmful bacteria out of your bloodstream.
- **Reduce Toxin Exposure:** Choose organic produce when possible to avoid pesticides. Use clean body products (check out EWG.org), ceramic or stainless steel pans instead of Teflon, and filtered water (I use the Berkey system). Avoid high-mercury fish like tuna, swordfish, and mahi-mahi; opt for safer choices like salmon. Watch out for BPA (bisphenol A) in cans, plastics, and to-go coffee lids.
- **Limit EMF Exposure:** Keep laptops and phones off your lap to reduce unnecessary electromagnetic field exposure.
- **Avoid Drugs:** Skip marijuana (which can contain heavy metals) and cocaine, which can directly harm sperm and future babies.
- **Fasting:** Give your body a break from digestion by fasting for 12 hours overnight, like finishing dinner by 7 p.m. and eating breakfast

at 7 a.m. This simple habit helps your body focus on repair and detoxification instead of constant digestion.

- **Consider Supplements:** For additional support, some functional medicine experts suggest 200 mg of R-lipoic acid daily and 500 to 1,000 mg of glutathione or NAC twice daily for about 10 days. Charcoal or clay binders can help bind and eliminate toxins for up to four weeks to help bind and eliminate toxins, but they should be taken away from vitamins and supplements, not while actively trying to conceive or during IVF treatment, and only when detox pathways are open. Think daily bowel movements and regular sweating.

DETOX PLANS

If you are interested in doing a formal detox two to three times a year, when you are not actively trying to conceive, it could help your body function more efficiently and free it of toxins that could disrupt your organ systems.

I highly recommend working with a talented functional medicine expert when considering which detox program would work best for you, but here are a few I've seen recommended.

Fasting: Longer fasts (16+ hours) can boost insulin sensitivity and support cellular repair, but keep them to your follicular phase (days 1–14) to avoid stressing your hormones and disrupting progesterone later in your cycle.

The Master Cleanse: This DIY cleanse has been around for decades. It involves drinking a mixture of water, lemon juice, maple syrup, and cayenne pepper for several days with no solid food. While it can help reduce bloating and give your digestion a much-needed break, it is low in nutrients and calories, which can stress your system, especially if you are already feeling depleted. If you're actively trying to conceive, I don't recommend it, but it could be an option to consider months before you plan to start trying.

Medical-Grade Detox: For a deeper reset, a formal detox program like the Thorne MediClear 10-day liver detox can help your body flush out heavy metals, chemicals, and excess hormones. Plan to wait at least 60 days after finishing before trying to conceive so both partners can start fresh.

WHEN (AND WHY) TO DETOX BEFORE BABY

The timing of a detox depends on the type you choose and when you plan to start trying to conceive or begin fertility treatments. For most daily detox habits like movement, hydration, nutrient-dense foods, and regular elimination, you don't need to leave space between those habits and starting treatment.

However, if you're using supplements or doing a formal detox program, it's best to wait about eight to twelve weeks after finishing before trying to conceive. Detox programs help loosen up toxins stored in your body, and that buffer period gives your system time to fully clear them.

It can be helpful to start a detox after heavy medication use, such as IVF drugs or vaccinations that cause a reaction, or after major events like pregnancy or breastfeeding (once nursing is complete). You might also benefit from a detox after pregnancy loss or if you're noticing signs of toxin overload in your body. A detox can also be a great reset after a stretch of time when healthy habits have slipped, like during the holidays or a busy season of travel.

Remember, detox only works if toxins can exit. Daily bowel movements and regular sweating are not optional during a detox phase.

REBUILDING ENERGY AFTER ILLNESS OR VACCINATION

When you get a vaccine or a serious illness that completely wipes you out, your body needs time to recover before jumping into fertility treatments. Vaccines do exactly what they are designed to do: train your immune system to recognize and fight infections. That training period can temporarily increase inflammation, fatigue, and immune activity, throwing your hormones and energy out of balance.

If your body is still focused on fighting or recovering, it simply may not have enough energy to also focus on growing a new life. And if it has to choose, it will always prioritize survival over reproduction. Your body knows that without your health, there can be no baby.

Once you are feeling better, the goal is to rebuild energy and support your mitochondria, the tiny powerhouses inside every cell. When your mitochondria are healthy, your body repairs more efficiently, inflammation settles, and hormones stabilize. That is the foundation your body needs before conception or fertility treatment.

How to Bounce Back Better

- Drink water like it is your full-time job. Add minerals or electrolytes to support cellular hydration and energy. I share the ones I use in the resources linked through the QR code at the end of this chapter.
- Support cellular recovery with supplements like NAD, CoQ10 with PQQ, and acetyl L-carnitine to help recharge your cells.
- Focus on whole foods only, especially antioxidant-rich options like berries, leafy greens, and colorful vegetables to calm inflammation.
- Use the daily detox practices outlined earlier to support your body's natural detox pathways.

When to Restart

The functional medicine expert on my team recommends waiting about three months after a vaccine, booster, or major illness before starting fertility treatments, and longer if you still do not feel fully like yourself.

(Yes, I totally blamed her there, so I don't have to be the bad guy!)

I know waiting can feel impossibly hard when you are eager to move forward. But if you are investing your time, money, and energy into conceiving, especially with treatments as demanding and expensive as IVF, you want your body thriving, not just surviving. Give yourself the time to work through the Survive to Thrive Protocol until you feel steady, recovered, and *energized* enough to create new life.

It really is worth the wait.

Now that you've built a foundation for health, and therefore fertility, by giving the body what it is designed to need, you've done the most important work first. With nourishment, sleep, movement, stress regulation, and detox support in place, your body has the resources it needs to function efficiently and effectively.

And how lucky are you to be learning these techniques now, before creating your family, so these habits can be passed down?

This work is not only about improving fertility. It supports a healthier pregnancy, lowers the risk of postpartum depression, and gives you a better chance of thriving through motherhood. Beyond that, it shapes the health of your future children and sets the tone for how they relate to their bodies.

These habits not only change *your* life. They create a ripple effect that supports generations to come.

CHAPTER 2 SUMMARY

- **Survive to Thrive Protocol:** Fertility improves when your body feels safe, supported, and well-resourced. This protocol moves you from protection mode to creation mode by stacking simple daily habits that build energy instead of draining it.
- **Food Without Fear:** Eat real food, and your health, wellness, and fertility will flourish. Whole foods lower inflammation, stabilize blood sugar, and fuel egg and sperm health, while restrictive diets trigger fear and shame that push your body into survival mode.
- **Restorative Sleep:** Sleep is your free fertility treatment. Deep, consistent sleep restores hormones, repairs cells, lowers stress, and gives your body the green light to create life.
- **Breathing for Balance:** Deep, intentional breathing shifts your nervous system out of fight-or-flight and into rest and repair. More oxygen, lower cortisol, and better blood flow help your body open the door to conception.
- **Brain Breaks:** Short pauses throughout the day retrain your brain to feel safe. These tiny moments of calm tell your body you have the space and capacity to support a pregnancy.
- **Movement That Supports Fertility:** Walking, stretching, and light strength training improve cellular energy, hormone balance, circulation, and inflammation without pushing your body into stress mode.
- **Detox Done Gently:** Daily detox habits help clear toxins, protect energy, and support hormones. The goal is not extreme cleansing but lightening the load so your body can thrive.

Before heading to the next section...

If you'd like links to the medical grade detox, minerals, and electrolytes I use, along with a daily routine checklist for restorative sleep, just scan the QR code

3. The Tests That Help Reveal Root Causes of Infertility

Quick note: What you're about to read is meant for education, not medical advice. Always check with your healthcare provider before adding or changing any supplements, medications, or treatments to make sure they're safe and the right fit for you.

Before we get started, be honest with me. Did you already learn and implement the Survive to Thrive and Spirit protocols to build your natural foundation for fertility? Or did you skip that step because you are impatient, like me, and jump straight into blood work and testing?

If it is the latter, I get you, because I am you. Just know that your blood work results likely will not reflect your true baseline if you did not do the "clean up" that almost everyone needs first.

Think of it like testing a pond. If the water is murky and full of debris, testing it right away only confirms what you already know: the debris needs to be cleared out *first* so you can get an accurate reading of what the pond actually needs to be healthy and balanced. That is exactly what the Survive to Thrive and Spirit protocols do. They are your cleanup crew, clearing the "debris" in your body that creates imbalances in your reproductive system.

Once that work is done, it is time to test the waters and look for clues about what might still be creating disruption in your system and making pregnancy a bit harder.

But for this, we are going to need professionals.

TRADITIONAL MEDICINE VS FUNCTIONAL MEDICINE EXPERTS

Traditional medicine and functional medicine are often framed as opposites, and while they do not always appreciate each other's approach to healing, they are quite complementary. Each is trained to answer a different question and offer a different type of solution, and once you understand the genius of both, you can better choose the right approach for your issue instead of expecting one system to do everything.

Traditional medical doctors are trained to diagnose disease and treat it efficiently. Their education focuses on identifying what is wrong and correcting it through medication, procedures, or surgery. This approach shines in emergencies, acute situations, and clearly defined medical problems, and it relies heavily on large clinical studies and established guidelines that tend to focus more on treatment than prevention.

Functional medicine practitioners, who are not always doctors but can be, are trained to understand how the body's systems work together and how imbalances build over time. Their focus is on prevention, optimization, and long-term support, especially in situations when symptoms are present but standard testing does not fully explain what is happening.

At its core, traditional medicine asks, "What is wrong, and how do we treat it?" while functional medicine asks, "Why is this happening in the first place?"

TRADITIONAL MEDICINE TRAINING TYPICALLY FOCUSES ON FIGURING OUT AND FIXING WHAT IS WRONG, WHILE FUNCTIONAL MEDICINE LOOKS FOR ROOT CAUSES OF THE ISSUE, OR WHY IT'S HAPPENING

These differences in training naturally shape how each approach shows up in practice, particularly in how providers test, interpret labs, and decide on next steps. Traditional medicine uses population-based reference ranges, so if a lab value falls within that range, it is considered normal. This type of data is incredibly helpful for diagnosing disease and determining when medical intervention is necessary. Functional medicine considers optimal ranges and interprets labs alongside symptoms, cycle patterns, energy levels, and lifestyle, recognizing that a number could be technically normal but still not ideal for optimized health and wellness.

The same contrast appears in testing. Traditional doctors tend to order a focused set of labs designed to diagnose or rule out major problems. Functional medicine practitioners often order broader panels to better understand why a number looks the way it does. Thyroid testing is a good example. In traditional medicine, screening often includes TSH, which shows how strongly the brain is signaling the thyroid to work. Functional medicine may use a fuller panel to assess how much hormone is available, how well it is being used, and whether other factors are influencing thyroid function.

How those results are handled is where the difference becomes most clear. If you are working with a traditional medicine provider and your labs are off, the goal is often to stabilize the issue, and medication is used to bring the system back into a safer range. Functional medicine examines the same results and focuses on what may be contributing to the imbalance in the first place, creating a plan that uses nutrition, minerals, supplements, and lifestyle changes to reduce the need for medication over time when appropriate.

In fertility, traditional medicine and functional medicine can be a powerful combination when both providers are skilled. The goal is not loyalty to one system. The goal is clarity, so you can use both approaches wisely and create the healthiest possible foundation for pregnancy and beyond.

FINDING THE RIGHT FUNCTIONAL MEDICINE EXPERT

In "Part 2: The Book on IVF," I go into detail about how to choose your IVF doctor. If you are considering hiring a functional medicine expert, here is a simple guide.

Functional medicine providers go by many names, including naturopath, integrative MD, functional medicine practitioner, or hormone specialist. Some are physicians, and some are not. What matters most is not the title but how they evaluate your case.

A good practitioner should meet the following criteria:

- They do not rely on expensive testing as the starting point. They can identify likely issues through your symptoms and history, then use labs to confirm and refine the plan.

- They give you a clear plan with milestones and an endpoint instead of an open-ended, never-ending process.
- You begin to see or feel changes within one to two months, such as better energy, more regular cycles, improved sleep, or fewer symptoms.

If nothing is shifting, or you feel worse, that is a sign the approach is not working, and I would reconsider continuing with that practitioner.

One of the functional medicine experts on my team recommends using the Institute for Functional Medicine website, IFM.org, to search for providers. Practitioners listed there have completed formal training through the Institute for Functional Medicine, which means they have standardized education in systems biology, root-cause analysis, and evidence-informed functional medicine principles.

Choosing the right practitioner can save you months, sometimes years, of spinning your wheels. And as you will learn in this book, do not stay with someone who is not delivering results simply because it feels convenient.

BLOOD TESTS THAT GET YOU WISE TO YOUR *WHYS*

These are not the typical fertility labs your traditional doctor usually runs. Those are covered in the Science Protocol section. This is the broader bloodwork that the functional medicine expert on my team often reviews when we are looking for hidden fertility clues.

These markers help explain how the body is actually functioning and, more importantly, *why* pregnancy may be harder than it should be. And **when you get wise to the *why*, you stop dealing with *what* it causes.**

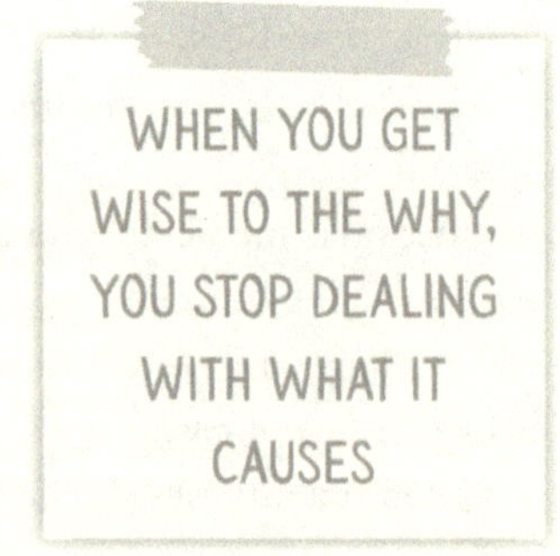

Complete Metabolic Panel (CMP): Checks blood sugar, kidney and liver function, and hydration. High glucose can indicate insulin resistance, which can impact ovulation and egg quality. If detox pathways aren't flowing well, hormones can build up and disrupt the cycle. Electrolytes matter, too, since they affect how cells respond to hormonal signals.

Lipid Panel: Hormones are made from fat. If cholesterol is too low, your body may struggle to make estrogen, progesterone, and testosterone. High LDL or triglycerides often indicate inflammation or insulin resistance, which can affect implantation and increase miscarriage risk.

Complete Blood Count (CBC): Low red blood cells or hemoglobin can reduce oxygen to your reproductive organs. White blood cell levels help detect inflammation or immune issues, both of which can interfere with egg quality and pregnancy.

Thyroid Panel: TSH (thyroid-stimulating hormone), free T4 (thyroxine), free T3 (triiodothyronine), reverse T3, thyroid antibodies, such as TPO (thyroid peroxidase), and binding proteins, such as TBG (thyroxine-binding globulin), give the full story. Your thyroid regulates ovulation, metabolism, and uterine lining development. If anything here is off, it can affect your entire cycle. High antibodies could point to an autoimmune issue like Hashimoto's, which is often overlooked but closely linked to fertility challenges.

Additional Markers:

- Vitamin D supports hormone balance, immune health, and implantation.
- Insulin helps uncover metabolic issues tied to PCOS or egg quality.
- Homocysteine reveals problems with detox and DNA protection in eggs and sperm.
- High-sensitivity CRP (hs-CRP) shows chronic inflammation that can block implantation or affect embryo development.

FUNCTIONAL MEDICINE LABS

When our functional medicine expert wants to get more specific, she might recommend specialty labs that give a deeper look into how your body is functioning. Here are some that she might recommend:

- HTMA (Hair Tissue Mineral Analysis) measures minerals, metals, and stress patterns.
- The Organic Acids Test (OAT) checks gut health, nutrient deficiencies, and detox function.

- GI mapping identifies infections, imbalances, and inflammation in the gut.
- Total Toxin Burden tracks specific environmental toxins in your system.
- The DUTCH Test gives a comprehensive look at hormone levels and how your body processes them.

Many of these tests can be done right at home, depending on your country or state. Most don't even require a blood draw.

The bad news? They're usually not covered by insurance, and the costs can add up quickly, especially when you include the analysis and treatment plans. That's why it's so important to work with someone who can get you these tests at cost, know how to interpret them correctly, and give you proper protocols to fix any issues quickly.

Before heading to the next section...

If you'd like the template for the blood tests my functional medicine expert recommends, along with the functional ranges and what high and low results could mean, just scan the QR code.

SUPPLEMENTS WITH A STRATEGY

A solid functional medicine expert should never lead with supplements. And supplementation should not be considered unless you've been committed to foundational work in the Survive to Thrive and Spirit protocols for about three months and then checked your blood work to see what your body actually needs.

From there, supplements can help you boost or balance your levels. Here are the three key times they can be the right kind of support:

1. **A deficiency nearly impossible to fix through diet.** For example, most of us need magnesium because the soil isn't as rich as it used to be, so it's much harder to get from food. And you don't want to be without magnesium. It's involved in over 300 essential biochemical reactions in the body, including muscle and nerve

function, blood sugar control, energy production, and hormone balance. Yet it's become one of the most common deficiencies.

2. I've also seen that the majority of my clients have a vitamin D deficiency, which could impact their immune system, hormone regulation, and even embryo implantation.

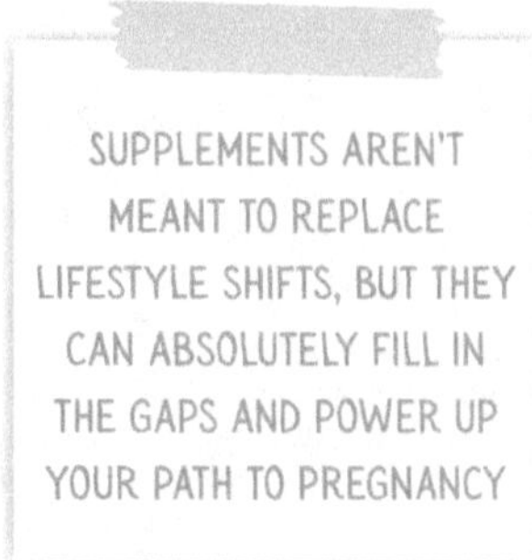

3. **For short-term boosts.** Sometimes your body needs a little help, like when you want more energy for cell production to support egg and sperm quality, or when you're traveling and need support for your immune system or digestion.
4. **For longer-term support.** Some supplements might be needed on a more ongoing basis to help manage chronic inflammation, support detoxification from environmental toxins, or maintain nutrient levels your body struggles to hold onto.

Supplements aren't meant to replace lifestyle shifts, but they can absolutely fill in the gaps and power up your path to pregnancy.

SUPPLEMENTS FOR "EVERYONE"

Getting blood work and knowing exactly where you are deficient is always ideal, but sometimes it is not possible. The functional medicine experts on my team compiled a list of supplements that almost everyone, male or female, could benefit from to boost overall health and fertility. These are the ones that help keep you on the right side of the Fertility Formula by getting more energy into your cells, clearing out toxins, and refilling what is missing, especially the vitamins and minerals most people are low in.

The following supplements we recommend may help you feel like a vibrant human again and improve the function of every cell, especially the ones you are most focused on right now: eggs and sperm.

SUPPLEMENTS FOR "EVERYONE"			
SUPPLEMENT	DESCRIPTION	DOSE	WHEN TO TAKE
MULTIVITAMIN OR PRENATAL	Look for methyl folate (not folic acid) and chelated minerals for better absorption.	As directed on the label	Daily through preconception and pregnancy
IMPORTANT NOTE: FOR THE REST OF THESE BELOW, YOUR MULTIVITAMIN OR PRENATAL MIGHT ALREADY INCLUDE SOME. CHECK YOUR LABEL AND COMPARE INGREDIENTS AND DOSES BEFORE ADDING ANYTHING NEW. NO NEED TO DOUBLE UP IF YOU'RE ALREADY COVERED.			
OMEGA-3 FATTY ACIDS (EPA + DHA)	Could support hormone balance, egg quality, and reduce inflammation. If it's fish oil, choose the triglyceride form.	500-900 mg	Daily through preconception and pregnancy
VITAMIN C	Could support detox, gut health, and progesterone production. Buffered or liposomal forms are gentler on the stomach.	1,000 mg	Daily during preconception only
ALPHA-LIPOIC ACID	Supports healthy mitochondria, which power your eggs and sperm.	100 mg	Daily during preconception only
VITAMIN D3 WITH K2	Supports immune health, hormone balance, and fertility. Most people are low, even in sunny climates. Functional medicine aims for 50-80 ng/mL (125-200 nmol/L) because "not deficient" isn't the same as optimal.	2,000-4,000 IU	Daily through preconception and pregnancy
ZINC (PICOLINATE)	Important for egg quality, implantation, and early embryo development. Pair with copper-rich foods to stay balanced.	15 mg	Daily during preconception only
MAGNESIUM (GLYCINATE OR MALATE)	One of the most common deficiencies, thanks to depleted soil, stress, and modern diets. Magnesium supports hormone balance, energy, and relaxation.	325-400 mg	Daily through preconception and pregnancy

SUPPLEMENTS THAT MAY HELP SPECIFIC FERTILITY CONCERNS

The following are not daily vitamins, but they could help with deeper issues that affect fertility: things like stress, inflammation, gut health, or sluggish detox pathways. These are often the underlying factors that lead to problems with egg and sperm quality. In some cases, the right supplement can give your body the support it needs to function the way it was designed to.

SUPPLEMENTS THAT MAY HELP SPECIFIC FERTILITY CONCERNS			
SUPPLEMENT	DESCRIPTION	DOSE	WHEN TO TAKE
ASHWAGANDHA (FEMALE)	An adaptogen that could help calm your stress response by supporting adrenal health. If you're always "on," wired at night, or feel like stress is running the show, this may help.	1 dropperful daily (liquid extract)	Daily during preconception only
ACETYL L-CARNITINE (FEMALE AND MALE)	Supports energy production and mitochondrial function, especially helpful if you eat little or no red meat.	500 mg	Daily during preconception only
ROYAL JELLY (FEMALE AND MALE)	A nutrient-rich bee product packed with vitamins, amino acids, and probiotics. Often used for egg quality, sperm quality, and hormone support. Avoid if you're allergic to bees.	1,000 mg	Daily during preconception only
PROBIOTICS (FEMALE AND MALE)	Especially helpful if you've used antibiotics recently or struggle with gut issues. Gut health plays a major role in hormone balance.	25 billion CFU	Daily during preconception only
MELATONIN (FEMALE AND MALE)	Supports sleep and acts as an antioxidant that may help protect eggs and sperm. If it makes you groggy, try a smaller dose or a slower-release form.	1-3 mg	1-3 months before egg retrieval
LIPOSOMAL GLUTATHIONE (FEMALE)	A master antioxidant that could protect eggs from oxidative stress. Some experts suggest pausing once pregnant to avoid overactivating detox pathways.	1 ml	Daily during preconception only
ARGININE (MALE)	Supports blood flow and may improve sperm production and quality.	1,400 mg	Daily

SUPPLEMENTS THAT REQUIRE TESTING BEFORE USE			
SUPPLEMENT	DESCRIPTION	DOSE	WHEN TO TAKE
IRON	Essential for red blood cell production and a healthy uterine lining, but too much can cause digestive issues or worse. Always test before supplementing.	Based on blood work	Daily through preconception and pregnancy
DHEA	Sometimes used to support ovarian function, especially for low responders or those with diminished ovarian reserve. Not everyone tolerates it well, so professional guidance is key.	Based on blood work	Daily during preconception only
IODINE	Important for thyroid and hormone balance, but too much or too little without testing can throw your thyroid off. Always confirm with lab results first.	Based on blood work	Daily through preconception and pregnancy

WHY MOST DOCTORS DON'T "DO" SUPPLEMENTS

Doctors are smart to be cautious about recommending supplements.

First, as we've talked about, doctors won't recommend something they weren't trained in. Second, the supplement industry isn't regulated the way pharmaceuticals are. That means what's on the label isn't always what's in the bottle. Doctors worry supplements could interfere with your treatment plan or even make things worse.

Not all supplements are created equal. Some cheaper versions are packed with fillers or low-quality ingredients that can actually make you less healthy. **When supplements are of low quality, your body spends more time cleaning them up than using them.**

You want professional-grade brands with high-quality ingredients to avoid toxic fillers and improve absorption. Otherwise, you could be spending time and money on products that either make you feel worse or that your body can barely use at all.

TRUSTED SUPPLEMENT SOURCE

It's not just the brand that matters. Where you buy supplements can help you or hurt you. If you're shopping on Amazon, only buy directly from the brand or a verified seller. Some third-party sellers have been caught refilling name-brand supplement bottles with other ingredients and affixing fake labels. If your bottle arrives with a sticker label instead of a printed label, send it back immediately.

> Through our professional credentials, my husband and I have access to a reputable wholesale platform for practitioner-grade supplements. I am happy to share that resource with you. You'll find the link in our online resources. Feel free to share it with anyone you know who could benefit from professional-grade supplements at a discount!
>
> Our dispensary includes the specific protocols that the functional medicine experts on my team recommend for different fertility stages, like before an egg retrieval, after a transfer, once pregnant, and beyond. It also includes protocols for common issues like stress, sleep, and gut health, though you can use it to purchase any supplements you need. (I even buy supplements here for my kids.)
>
> If swallowing pills is an issue, you'll be glad to know that many professional-grade supplements also come in powder, liquid, or gummy form. (Friendly warning, though: powdered supplements without added flavorings can taste absolutely awful. I'm not talking mildly unpleasant; I mean truly, shockingly disgusting. You've been warned!)

THE HEALTH YOU BUILD, THE LEGACY YOU SHAPE

Congratulations! You've officially completed the Survive to Thrive Protocol playbook!

As I've emphasized throughout this section, the goal is to move slowly and build these practices into your days until they stop feeling like a checklist and start feeling like your normal way of living. My hope is that once you feel the powerful effects of these simple, though not always easy, habits, you won't want to go back.

And when you do slip, because you are human, you will already know exactly what to do to return to balance.

These are the habits I have consistently seen create the most meaningful, *positive* outcomes. And they do not only support fertility. They support a lifetime of feeling strong, clear, and pain-free.

I turned fifty this year, and while perimenopause can be unpredictable with cycles, moods, and even how you look, I feel really good most of the time because I still practice this protocol. I'm strong and unusually flexible for my age because I personally practice what I shared in the previous section titled "Move to Conceive: Tiny Steps, Big Impact." Have I mentioned I can still do the splits after a good stretch or two tequila sodas with lime cocktails... whichever comes first?

Anxiety still creeps in, but I have learned that how long it lingers is often within my control. When I implement the practices in the previous sections, "*Juuust Breeeeeeathe*" and "Brain Breaks for Baby Makes," my anxiety drops dramatically and sometimes disappears altogether.

I am also about to repeat all of the bloodwork I mentioned in the section "The Tests That Help Reveal Root Causes of Infertility" because these are not just fertility strategies. They are health strategies, and I cannot make smart decisions about optimizing my health without data.

WHAT YOU CHOOSE TO DO TODAY BECOMES A GIFT, NOT JUST FOR YOURSELF, BUT FOR THE FUTURE FAMILY YOU'RE WORKING SO HARD TO CREATE

I hope this section inspired you to make these habits part of your life for fertility and for the long haul. When you do, you are not only protecting your own health, but you are influencing your family's health as well. As we learned, these habits may help reduce the activation of genes linked to chronic conditions over time. **What you choose to do today becomes a gift, not just for yourself, but for the future family you are working so hard to create.**

CHAPTER 3 SUMMARY

- **Test the Waters After You Clear the Pond:** Once you start feeling better with the Survive to Thrive basics, testing helps you find what might still be quietly disrupting your fertility. These tests are less about what is "wrong" and more about why it is happening.
- **Normal Is Not the Same as Optimal:** A lab result can be "normal" and still not be ideal for making a baby. Functional medicine looks at what is optimal for fertility and connects your numbers to your symptoms and goals.
- **The Why Changes Everything:** When you understand the root cause, you can sometimes avoid bigger interventions later. This is how you stop chasing symptoms and start fixing the actual issue.
- **Better Testing, Better Clues:** Broader bloodwork like CMP, lipids, CBC, a full thyroid panel, vitamin D, insulin, homocysteine, and hs CRP can reveal patterns around inflammation, detox, metabolism, and hormone function that basic fertility workups miss.
- **Specialty Labs Go Deeper:** Tests like HTMA, OAT, GI mapping, toxin panels, and DUTCH can help uncover mineral issues, gut infections, detox bottlenecks, hormone breakdown patterns, and hidden stress loads.
- **Choose the Right Practitioner:** A good functional medicine expert connects the dots, gives you a plan with milestones and a finish line, and helps you feel or see changes within a month or two.
- **Supplements Need a Strategy:** Supplements are not the first step. They work best after lifestyle foundations and bloodwork, when they fill true deficiencies, support short-term boosts, or help longer-term needs like inflammation and detox.
- **This Is Bigger Than Fertility:** The habits and insights you build here are not only for getting pregnant. They are for feeling better, staying healthier, and shaping a stronger future for you and your family.

Before heading to the next section...

If you'd like links and discounts to the supplements and detox programs I use and recommend for specific clients, just scan the QR code.

4. Spirit Protocol: Energy Alignment for Growth

For our purposes in this chapter, "Spirit" refers to your energy, your nervous system state, your vibration, or your level of consciousness in any given moment. I occasionally reference "God" as well, and though I personally believe we can access incredible strength from a Higher Power, feel free to swap that word out for whatever resonates with you. Lastly, I refer to babies as "she" for simplicity.

(Record screech!) *Wait—you just said "Spirit," "vibration," "consciousness," and "God." Um, can we skip this and get to the Science Protocol, the real stuff that will actually help me get and stay pregnant?*

I hear you. And with a lot of respect, and more than ten years working in infertility and IVF consulting, I need to say this clearly: this is the real stuff. This is science. And the belief that it's not could quietly keep you from kissing your baby sooner.

I know that it might feel confronting. But it's a pattern my success coach Steph and I have seen over and over again after working with hundreds of women.

Clients tend to fall into one of three camps: they fully embrace the Spirit Protocol from the start, they do it reluctantly, or they refuse to do it at all.

Steph has been with me from the very beginning. I lovingly call her "human Valium." She helps our clients create a calm sense of empowerment. They typically feel lighter and happier after working with her (*if* they choose to engage, which most do) and often are stunned by how much better they feel. While it's rare for someone to outright refuse the Spirit Protocol, it is incredibly obvious when they aren't doing it.

The women who refuse spiritual work are almost never the ones who move through their fertility journey easily or quickly. They tend to hold a firm belief that nothing will help, fixate on problems instead of addressing them, even when we clearly show them how, and overlook the progress they are making.

These clients often leave the program early and can be quite venomous about it, insisting our consulting was "worthless," "a failure," and something we should be "ashamed" of.

To date, this has happened maybe five times in ten years. And even though Steph and I usually see it coming, it still hurts. Not because of what they believe about the program but because, as you'll learn next, we recognize that it reflects what they believe about *themselves*.

And that belief is absolutely wrong.

My favorite stories come from the clients who approach the Spirit Protocol reluctantly, sometimes with a heavy dose of skepticism, and then end up giving it the most credit for turning their infertility journey around. You can hear many of these stories in the *Path to Parenthood* episodes on my podcast.

This reluctant but compliant approach shows up often with my UK clients, who initially think I'm a sweet, overly enthusiastic, slightly ridiculous American asking them to do very American things. And then later on, usually with minimal enthusiasm, they admit that it actually worked... and that I am not slightly but *completely* ridiculous. (And that belief is absolutely right!)

Do you remember the fruit tree graphic at the beginning of the book? The Survive to Thrive Protocol is the soil. This is where you cleared the weeds, replenished the nutrients, and strengthened the foundation for growth.

Now it is time to look at something just as important: alignment. That is the work we begin in the Spirit Protocol.

Alignment is what allows growth to happen with ease. A tree can have a strong seed and endless potential, but if it is not positioned to receive the right energy from the sun, it will struggle to grow and reproduce. When a tree is aligned with sunlight and nourishment, it grows and naturally produces fruit. When it is planted in constant shade or exposed to disruptive forces, growth slows or stops altogether.

The same is true for fertility.

As you learned with the Fertility Formula, reproduction requires sufficient energy and a lower toxin load. In the Survive to Thrive Protocol, you focused on restoring physical energy and reducing physical toxins.

The Spirit Protocol builds on that foundation by addressing another powerful source of energy: emotional energy.

Emotions are energy in motion. They move through your body and mind constantly, and they exist on a spectrum from high energy to very low energy. Some emotions generate energy and support growth, while others drain energy and make growth much harder.

From a biological standpoint, emotions are physiological events. Every emotional state triggers changes in brain chemistry, nervous system signaling, hormone output, and cellular energy use. Fear, shame, and guilt activate stress hormones like cortisol and adrenaline, pulling energy away from repair and reproduction. Love, peace, and joy activate the parasympathetic nervous system, improve blood flow, support hormone balance, and free up energy for growth. In other words, emotions directly influence how much usable energy your body has available at any given moment.

Low-energy emotional states feel exactly like what they are: exhausting, constricting, and draining. They can leave you feeling stuck, overwhelmed, numb, anxious, or depleted. When you live in these states for long periods of time, your body receives a clear biological message that you are in survival mode and that it is not safe to grow or create.

Based on what we've experienced in life, our nervous system learns which emotional states feel normal and therefore safe, even if they drain our energy. So even when we dislike how low-energy states feel, we may unconsciously stay aligned with them. They are familiar.

And we tend to attract and reinforce the same level of energy we carry inside. There is a saying that helped me understand this: *"Your outer world reflects your inner beliefs."* The energy you hold internally shapes what you notice, how you respond, and what you tolerate, including in your fertility journey. *Like finds like.*

If you don't like what you're seeing in your life, or if you feel consistently low on energy, overwhelmed, discouraged, or stuck, this section is here to help you consciously shift that pattern. This work is not only about more joy. It is about more usable energy, which, as we know, is essential for conception mode.

And if optimizing fertility is not motivation enough, here is another powerful reason to do this work: Children learn emotional tone before they learn language. This is not about guilt. It is about possibility. When you elevate your energy, you raise the emotional standard of your home. Your child gets to grow inside that steadiness, and you get to live there too.

So, are you ready for an emotional chiropractic adjustment?

Okay. Let's get growing.

LEVELS OF ENERGY ALIGNMENT

Have you ever had a conversation with someone where you're both speaking the same language, but it felt like you were not communicating at all?

I remember this vividly with a friend of mine, especially when I tried to compliment her. What came out of my mouth felt loving and supportive, but what she heard sounded negative or critical. So I clarified. Then she misinterpreted it again. I tried a third time, genuinely confused, wondering how we were missing each other so badly.

It felt like my words were going through some Willy Wonka–style machine in her brain, where kind thoughts went in, and rude comments came out on the other side. Wanting her to understand me, I kept pouring energy into explaining myself, trying to lift her up to the meaning of my words. But she kept pulling them down. Eventually, I stopped talking to her as much because constantly defending my intentions was exhausting.

Years later, I was introduced to Dr. David Hawkins's Map of Consciousness. Suddenly, what had been happening between my friend and me made perfect sense, and for the first time, I could actually visualize it.

Dr. Hawkins created a framework that explains how our internal emotional states exist at different energy levels. At the lower levels, perception is narrow, rigid, and defensive. As energy rises, perception becomes more open, flexible, and expansive. What finally clicked for me was this: when two people are operating from very different energy levels, understanding each other becomes incredibly difficult.

I like to think of it as living on different floors of an apartment building. Someone in the basement can speak clearly to another person in the basement. But if you're on the second floor, their words may sound muffled, distorted, or incomplete. You might hear something, but if you try to interpret what they're saying, you're likely to misunderstand it.

Dr. Hawkins represented this concept using a cone-shaped map that includes numbers, colors, and emotional states, arranged from low to high. Each level carries its own emotional tone and shapes perception, behavior, and decision-making.

Building on his work, I created what I call the *Levels of Energy Alignment*. I expanded the concept to include visuals such as states of matter and the kinds of physical energy each emotional state tends to generate or drain. If you're a visual learner, this chart is designed to help you see what different emotional energies look like and feel how they operate in your body.

This concept is where alignment becomes visible, practical, and something you can work with directly.

As we walk through my version of the chart, I'll show you how different emotional energy states can influence your experience of your fertility journey, your body, and even your relationships. Then we'll move into simple, practical exercises to help you identify the energy you naturally align with now and how to begin shifting toward higher-energy states that support growth, ease, and conception.

This is where awareness turns into real change.

LEVELS OF ENERGY ALIGNMENT

ENERGY LEVEL	EMOTIONAL STATE (ENERGY IN MOTION)	COLOR	STATE OF MATTER	FELT EXPERIENCE	GROWTH CAPACITY
13	ENLIGHTENMENT	VIOLET		UNTOUCHABLE	UNLIMITED
10-12	LOVE, JOY, PEACE	PURPLE		FREE	EXPANSIVE
7-9	WILLINGNESS, ACCEPTANCE, REASON	BLUE		RESILIENT	EVOLVING
6	NEUTRALITY	GREEN		FLEXIBLE	SHIFTING
4-5	PRIDE, COURAGE	YELLOW		MOTIVATION	STRUGGLING
3	ANGER	ORANGE		FRUSTRATION	STALLED
0-2	SHAME, GUILT, FEAR	RED		HEAVY, BREAKABLE	UNAVAILABLE

COLD AS ICE: SHAME, GUILT, AND FEAR

At the bottom of the scale are shame, guilt, and fear. This is the lowest energy state, represented by solid matter. It feels heavy and breakable, and from a biological standpoint, growth is unavailable here.

This state is where the nervous system is locked into survival mode. Energy is conserved, circulation narrows, inflammation rises, and reproduction is deprioritized.

This is where I lived during the hardest seasons of my fertility journey. I blamed myself and Brian for everything I thought we were doing wrong (i.e., guilt). Each failed transfer reinforced the fear that I would never be a mom, or never be a mom again, and that somehow it was my fault and therefore deserved (i.e., shame). The energy was heavy. Brittle. Breakable.

But solid matter doesn't stay solid forever.

With enough heat and movement, it begins to change.

FRACTURING THE SOLID: ANGER, PRIDE, AND COURAGE

As energy rises, we move up on the Alignment chart from shame and fear into anger, then into pride and courage. These states are still uncomfortable, but they're different in an important way. You're no longer collapsed and frozen; there is movement here.

Anger actually carries more energy than fear. It creates pressure. It cracks what was once solid. I often think of the term "hothead" when I picture this level of energy. The heat creates movement.

That's why frustration can feel strangely empowering. It wakes you up. It mobilizes you. Where fear freezes, anger pushes back. For example, **feeling *angry* about the cost, time, or effort IVF requires often feels more energized than feeling *ashamed* that you need it.**

> FEELING ANGRY ABOUT THE COST, TIME, OR EFFORT IVF REQUIRES OFTEN FEELS MORE ENERGIZED THAN FEELING ASHAMED THAT YOU NEED IT

As pride and courage come online, even more momentum returns. Motivation starts to build. Growth is still a struggle here, but it's no longer stalled. The body is beginning to re-engage, and for the first time in a while, forward movement feels possible.

LIQUIDITY: NEUTRALITY AND FLEXIBILITY

Next on the Alignment chart is neutrality, represented by liquid. This is where the nervous system starts to regulate, and the felt experience shifts from rigid to flexible.

Here, events stop being labeled as good or bad. They simply are. That may sound subtle, but biologically, it's powerful. Neutrality prevents unnecessary energy drain. Your body is no longer burning precious fuel reacting to every stimulus as a threat, which frees up energy for conception mode.

For example, when a retrieval doesn't create the number of embryos you expected, the emotion of neutrality sounds like this: *This is what happened. I don't know what it means yet. Tell me more.* In other words, you're neutral;

you're not joyful, nor are you spiraling down into the basement of fear and shame.

RISING INTO MOTION: WILLINGNESS, ACCEPTANCE, AND REASON

As energy continues to rise, we enter emotions of willingness, acceptance, and reason. This is a liquid–gas state where resilience builds, and it becomes easier to align with higher-energy states as you evolve with the information you choose to learn.

Instead of reacting, you are evaluating. You take in new information, and, based on what you know to be true, you are willing to adjust.

You begin asking better questions and making clearer decisions that are grounded in facts and understanding, not driven by intrusive fear.

Here, setbacks still hurt, and sad things are still sad, but they no longer knock the energy out of you, leaving you defeated and exhausted. After a failed transfer, acceptance might sound like: *I did what I could. Nothing had to be perfect. This was not the right child at the right time.*

Then reason steps in. You understand that while this may not have been the right child at the right time, there are still productive questions to ask. *Is it reasonable to consider a different protocol? Should a diagnostic test be discussed now to ensure nothing is blocking implantation?*

When you are in this energetic state, you are no longer stuck in blame or panic. You are engaged, curious, and empowered to make thoughtful next steps without draining yourself in the process.

EXPANDED AND FREE: LOVE, JOY, AND PEACE

From there, you rise into love and peace. At this level on the Alignment chart, you'll see that energy expands so fully that it takes on a "gaseous state," where the body receives a powerful signal of safety, allowing hormones to regulate more easily, inflammation to quiet, and energy to become abundant and available to create your baby.

This is not about loving *everything*, especially something like your infertility or IVF journey, but about freedom. Freedom from outcomes controlling your emotional state.

Here, you may genuinely love your life even if your baby isn't in it yet, because you know something deeply and steadily true: nothing external gets to dictate what you feel internally. Love, joy, and peace are no longer conditional.

There's an important myth I need to dismantle. People who live in love, joy, and peace are often dismissed as ignorant. There's even a saying: "ignorance is bliss." But if you understood the biology of love, joy, and peace, you would quickly see what I believe to be true: anyone who can genuinely live in these states consistently is a genius. They have cracked one of life's most complicated puzzles: how to be genuinely happy.

Here's why most people try and fail at this game.

First, biology. Your brain is wired for fear, not happiness. Its primary job is to keep you alive, which means staying alert, scanning for danger, and preparing for worst-case scenarios, not cultivating peace or joy.

Second, the world around you. You're surrounded by millions of people who have never tried to solve this puzzle or who tried and decided it was too hard, so they stopped. Many of them will unconsciously try to pull you back down to where they live because, as the saying goes, misery loves company.

Third, it takes far more work and effort than most people are willing to put in. Choosing to live here is not for the weak. It requires doing something many people avoid at all costs: showing your authentic self.

I know this might sound like a tangent, and it is, but stay with me.

I think of living in love, joy, and peace as living in the energy we were born with before life started shaping us.

Over time, life adds layers of protection. Fear, shame, and survival strategies develop in response to experiences that once required them. Those strategies can be helpful early on, but as they accumulate, they become heavy, and that weight slowly pulls us down the Levels of Energy Alignment scale.

Choosing love, joy, and peace means doing the tedious, uncomfortable work of chipping away at the clutter that no longer serves you until you return to the authentic, energized, happy soul you were born as. That process exposes the real you, which can feel uncomfortable and surprisingly hard to maintain. It requires fiercely protecting your authentic self and your energy from people, environments, and narratives that want to pile the clutter right back on top of you.

> If you choose to do the work that allows your natural energy to consistently live in love, joy, and peace, it can feel lonely at first. It may seem like more people are against you than with you.
>
> But the ones who are with you will be among the strongest, most resilient, and most self-aware humans you will ever meet. They expand your energy instead of draining it, and they help you create what once felt impossible.
>
> That is very good company to keep.

UNTOUCHABLE: ENLIGHTENMENT

At the very top of the emotional states on the Alignment scale is enlightenment. This is not just a gaseous state but a shift beyond physical matter, more like radiant energy than substance. It cannot be contained because it is not something you hold. It is something you become.

From a biological standpoint, such an existence would be the ultimate state of safety and unlimited energy.

Although I don't teach about this level because, frankly, I have never lived there, from what I understand, enlightenment requires complete detachment from outcomes—a state in which your inner peace remains steady no matter what happens. (That is not me. I care deeply and am strongly attached to results.)

So while enlightenment exists on the map, it's not the destination I'm guiding you toward. And more importantly, you don't need to be anywhere near enlightened to create life. You simply need enough safety in your body and enough available energy for creation to happen.

And unlike enlightenment, that is very attainable.

WHEN INFERTILITY TRIGGERS SURVIVAL MODE

I bet you know that the absolute worst thing someone can say to you is, "Just relax. The reason you're not getting pregnant is that you're too stressed." I remember those obnoxious conversations, and if you've read the introduction, you know exactly how I used to respond to that comment.

Well, I'm about to tell you something even more obnoxious. You might want to throw this book across the room after you hear it. But hear me out.

Ready?

Are you sure?

Here it goes.

Your infertility might be causing you so much heartache and pain that your brain has started associating pregnancy with danger. And when your brain senses danger, it switches to survival mode —the opposite of conception mode. That means prolonged infertility can actually create more infertility.

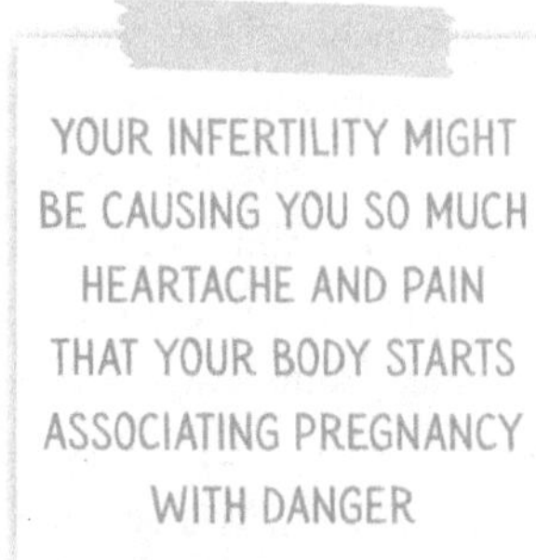

Ugh. That was hard to say.

In the previous section, we discussed how the brain is the boss of your fertility, how it prioritizes energy for survival over conception, and how chronic stressors can keep the body stuck in survival mode.

Here's another important layer.

Your brain is wired for fear. Fear is a survival tool. When you're afraid, you become hyperaware. And when you're hyperaware, you're less likely to do something life-threatening. It's why you can blissfully watch an ocean sunset one moment and suddenly imagine how a shark would definitely eat you if you stepped into that water. When that jolt breaks your calm, picture your brain cheering itself on: *Boom. Kept you alive again. You're welcome.*

This built-in alarm system, known as negativity bias, has been hardwired into our brains since humans existed. The problem is that it cannot distinguish between a true life-threatening danger and modern stressors, like a friend casually mentioning how easy it was for them to get pregnant... twice.

Just because your brain is wired for fear doesn't mean you're doomed to live in it. You already have real challenges to navigate. You do not need your mind piling imagined worst-case scenarios on top of an already exhausting fertility journey.

As we move through this chapter, we are going to work toward a few powerful shifts.

The first shift is helping you feel both free and in control during your family-building journey. Freedom comes from knowing what you can control and putting your energy there. The first step is learning to tell the difference.

The second shift is transforming your relationship with your fertility journey. Even if your path to parenthood has been long and full of disappointment, there *is* a way to shift from shame, fear, and anger toward acceptance, clarity, and even peace. Does that mean you'll never find yourself in a puddle of tears the next time your period shows up? No. You'll probably still cry your eyes out. But you may bounce back faster, with more resilience and less self-blame.

The third shift is teaching you how to stop your fear-based brain from spiraling into catastrophic worst-case scenarios. It's time to become the boss of the current boss: your brain. You've been taking orders from her for far too long. And while she means well, she's operating from an outdated script. It's time to confront her kindly and then gently shut her down.

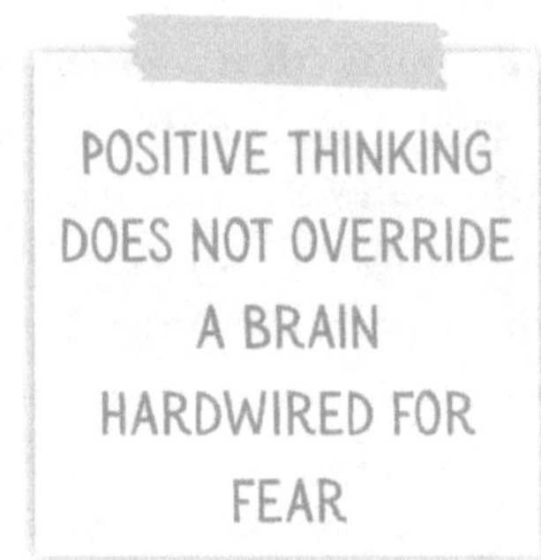

And as we work through these shifts, especially the uncomfortable parts you cannot control, I'm *not* going to ask you to surrender or free-fall without a net. I'm going to give you tools to create safety and stability even in uncertainty.

Let's be very clear. This is not "think positive and positive things will happen." **Positive thinking does not override a brain hardwired for fear.** If anything, it adds guilt, because now you're beating yourself up for not being positive enough on top of already feeling devastated and frustrated about your fertility struggles.

What *does* work is something far more practical and far more compassionate, and it's where we'll start: making choices.

EXERCISE: YOUR CHOICES BRING YOUR CHILD CLOSER

Every choice you make either moves you closer to or further from your dreams. And the best part is that you are in control of those choices.

In this section, we explore the powerful decisions that can help shape your energy, your focus, and your family. This is about stepping out of the feeling that life is happening to you and realizing you can be the one making it happen.

Whether it's choosing to become a mom, loving your child unconditionally (*Wait, what?* ... Hang on, I'll explain.), or deciding where you direct your precious energy, every decision shapes your experience. These choices put you back in the driver's seat and align you with what you want most.

When I went through my own journey, I didn't know any of what I'm about to share with you until after my kids were born. Looking back, I don't think I would have become the shell of myself that I was by the end of my journey if I'd known then what I know now. And I would have been able to love my children unconditionally from the very start.

You have the opportunity to move through this journey in a healthier way, one that allows you to love both the family you're creating and yourself in a real, wholehearted way. That is a gift I wish I'd had, and I'm genuinely excited for you to live it.

Choice No. 1: Choose Happiness, Even Without a Child

But wait, Tasha... How I feel right now is temporary, right? Once I have the family of my dreams, I won't be so sad or stressed. I'll be free and flying high like a kite until I reach Cloud Nine, where I'll be forever with my baby... right?

(Cue the awkward teeth emoji: 😬)

I used to think the same thing. I believed that once my heartbreaking fertility journey was over and I was holding my baby, I would finally be out of infertility jail and happy. But that wasn't my experience. In fact, my anxiety, shame, and fear tightened their grip *after* I had children.

Why? Because **your stressors don't disappear when you have a baby. They multiply.** Your brain's job is to keep you alive, and once there's a tiny human with zero survival skills depending on you, your brain starts clocking double shifts to keep you both safe.

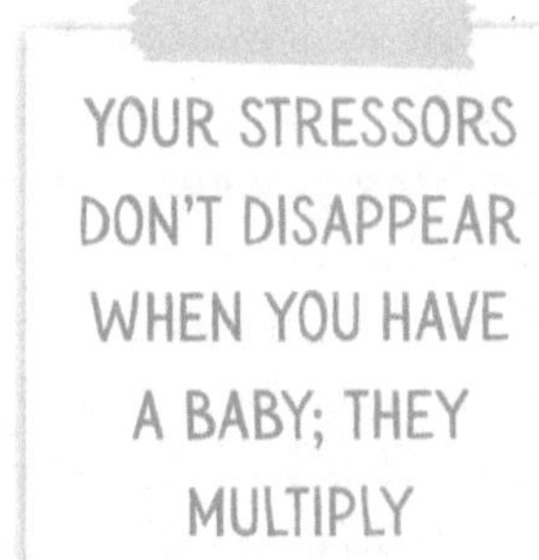

The fear you feel now doesn't vanish; it evolves into a constant stream of *what-if* thoughts about your baby. The shame and guilt you carried for not "doing everything right" during infertility often stick around, and as you begin questioning every parenting decision, it often grows.

That feeling of being "less than" because getting pregnant was hard? It can explode when you start comparing your baby, your parenting, and your life to everyone else's. (Trust me, you have not seen competitive chaos until you've witnessed preschool holiday performances.)

You might think you're immune to all of that. I thought I was too. But I didn't understand how my fear-based brain worked.

I thought I was unhappy because of my prolonged infertility and IVF. I was living through something deeply hard and genuinely traumatic. It wasn't fair that something that takes others a few minutes lying down was taking me years of procedures, tens of thousands of dollars, and endless uncertainty.

But the truth is, I wasn't lacking happiness because of infertility alone. I was unhappy because I allowed my fear-based brain, or as I call her, the "mean girl" living in my head, to run the show.

I hadn't yet understood that happiness wasn't going to magically appear on the other side of this journey unless I learned how to cultivate it internally. External things, even beautiful ones like children, can spark moments of happiness, but they don't sustain it. And when happiness fades, we often start searching for the next thing to give it back to us.

YOU CAN CHOOSE HAPPINESS IN SPITE OF INFERTILITY WHEN YOU UNDERSTAND THAT HAPPINESS IS A CHOICE AND AN INSIDE JOB, NOT SOMETHING YOU EARN THROUGH EXTERNAL ACHIEVEMENTS

That becomes a never-ending cycle of looking outside yourself for happiness, not finding it, and then feeling even worse because you believe you failed to find it.

You don't have to choose unhappiness because your fertility journey is hard. **You can choose happiness in spite of infertility when you understand that happiness is a choice and an inside job, not something you earn through external achievements.**

This does not mean pretending everything is fine or forcing toxic positivity. It means recognizing that you didn't choose this hardship, but you *do* get to choose how you move through it.

You can stay stuck in *Why me?* Or you can shift to *This is awful, and I will be okay. So what's next?*

That question: *What's next?* is powerful. It moves you from helplessness into action. It turns struggle into strength.

And here's the bigger picture. I'm certain this infertility journey will not be the hardest thing you face in your life. Hard seasons do not stop once you have children.

EVERY TRULY INSPIRING PERSON I KNOW HAS LIVED THROUGH CHALLENGES THAT SHOULD HAVE FLATTENED THEM, BUT THEY ROSE ANYWAY. AND YOU CAN TOO, IF YOU CHOOSE

Extraordinary lives are built in hard

seasons. If you're anything like me, you are
not here for an ordinary life. You are here for one filled with depth, meaning, and real joy.

Every truly inspiring person I know has lived through challenges that should have flattened them, but they rose anyway. And you can too, if you choose. If it were easy, everyone would have one.

The way you move through this season shapes who you become. An extraordinary fertility journey can shape an extraordinary parent and, ultimately, an extraordinary family. One created by someone strong enough to grow through hard things instead of being defined by them.

Just as important, it is shaped by someone who learns to choose happiness from the inside out. Not because life is easy or everything goes as planned, but because joy becomes a practiced skill rather than a reward for finally getting what you want.

When you build that happiness now, you don't only arrive at motherhood with a baby in your arms. You arrive with peace, resilience, and the ability to truly love the life you worked so hard to create.

Choice No. 2: Choose To Become A Mom

This looks like an easy one, right? You might be thinking, *Done. Next!*

But don't move on yet, because we often forget that some of our choices around becoming a mom are limited. And if you don't recognize what you can and cannot control, you could spend a lot of energy on things you can't control, end up with fertility fatigue, and run out of energy before creating the family of your dreams.

For years, I tried to control how I would become a mom by planning every step. But my path to parenthood was nothing like I had planned. I planned to get pregnant naturally, but I did IVF. I planned to do one egg retrieval for all my kids, but I ended up doing nine. I planned for my first transfer to work, but it ended in a short-lived pregnancy. I planned for the rest of my pregnancies to happen

YOU WILL BE A MOM, OR A MOM AGAIN, BECAUSE YOU'VE CHOSEN TO BE. BUT YOU DON'T GET TO CHOOSE EXACTLY WHEN OR HOW IT HAPPENS OR WHO SHOWS UP, SO STOP WASTING YOUR ENERGY TRYING TO quickly, but they took a total of five years. I planned for three kids, two years apart. I have two kids, five years apart.

My plans were just that: *my* plans. But they weren't necessarily the *right* plans. In my usual control-fanatic ways, I seemed to have forgotten that having a child isn't a solo endeavor. There are other people involved: your partner, if you have one, your child, and God, who is as invested in this story as you are, even when it doesn't feel that way.

During the five years it took me to create my family, there's one thing I wish someone had told me, one sentence that could have saved me from spiraling into anxiety attacks for the first time in my life: **"You will be a mom, or a mom again, because you've chosen to be. But you don't get to choose exactly when or how it happens or who shows up, so stop wasting your energy trying to."**

If being a mom feels right in your heart, if thinking about it makes you feel lighter, happier, or more at peace, then it's for you. Your desire to be a mom is valid, powerful, and right. It's bigger than logic; it's divine.

But becoming a mom isn't only about you. It's about opening yourself to the mystery of how your child will arrive, when they decide the time is right, and who they will be.

The coolest part? Watching who shows up when you let them.

My kids could not be more different. And with each of them, in their own unique way, I've had to check my ego at the door and let them be exactly who they are. Not the way I would have planned it, not what feels most natural to me, but in a way that's completely and unmistakably their own. (And let's be honest, that isn't easy, because if they did things my way, they'd obviously be right all the time.)

But seriously, by stepping back and letting them be who they are, as long as it's respectful to themselves and others, we've built a relationship where I'm learning about life from them as much as I'm trying to teach them about it.

To be clear, my instinct to control is still very much alive. Their lives (okay, my life) would be so much easier if they always listened to me. But then I remember thinking my own mom knew *absolutely nothing*. And later, when I went to college, I realized she was basically right about everything.

The gift of this journey is discovering that your child wasn't meant to fit into your vision but to expand it in ways you never saw coming. When you choose to become a mom, you're not choosing the timing, the path, or the personality that shows up. You're choosing to guide, love, and support a human being as they grow into who they are meant to be.

THE GIFT OF THIS JOURNEY IS DISCOVERING THAT YOUR CHILD WASN'T MEANT TO FIT INTO YOUR VISION, BUT TO EXPAND IT IN WAYS YOU NEVER SAW COMING

Choice No. 3: Choose to Love Your Child Unconditionally, Today and Always

You might be thinking, *Why on earth is she asking me to choose to love my child unconditionally? Of course I will!*

I thought the same thing. But there was one big reason I unknowingly withheld unconditional love from my children: I was afraid of getting hurt.

At the beginning of this book, I shared my journey of getting pregnant, but I didn't share how I felt once I actually got pregnant after going through round after round of IVF. With Hudson, after experiencing a biochemical pregnancy before him, I held back my excitement for a long time. *You never know,* I kept thinking. And I had proof that I was being "smart" not to get too attached to this pregnancy—proof in the form of heavy bleeding at nineteen weeks and hospital bed rest at twenty-six weeks due to complete placenta previa. The doctors were preparing for an early delivery that, statistically, probably wouldn't end well for us.

Hudson's pregnancy wasn't filled with unconditional love for him. It was filled with fear and constant prayers that he'd stay inside until my scheduled C-section at thirty-six weeks.

And he did. And *then* I loved him.

Then came Mila, who, as you know, took seven additional egg retrievals and eight embryo transfers over three years. As I mentioned before, I had spent so long wanting her, not getting her, and feeling beaten down by the grueling IVF process that, when I finally got pregnant, I was numb.

I felt... nothing.

And that realization breaks my heart.

I'm crying while writing this because it's so painful to admit how much love my kids missed out on because I had forgotten how strong I was and let my fear-based brain take over. It told me it was safer to guard my heart than to risk hurting it, which meant I subconsciously chose to love my children only if they were born healthy.

And I don't want that for your children or for you.

You get to choose to love your child unconditionally right now, in whatever form they are in. You might think, *But they're in no form at all yet, so I don't have to.* But that's not true.

Your child already exists.

Science nerd alert: Newton's first law of thermodynamics states that energy cannot be created or destroyed; it can only be transferred from one form to another. That means your child's energy is already here, waiting for the right time and form to join you.

And what is their energy on the Levels of Energy Alignment scale? You already know the answer: love. The more aligned you are with love, the more aligned you are with them.

So what does loving your child today actually look like? Often, it starts with letting go of thoughts, even the quiet ones, like

- *I will love my child only if they stay for about forty weeks and are born healthy.*
- *I will love my child if they show up how, when, and who I expect them to be.*
- *I will love my child if they carry my (or our) genetics.*

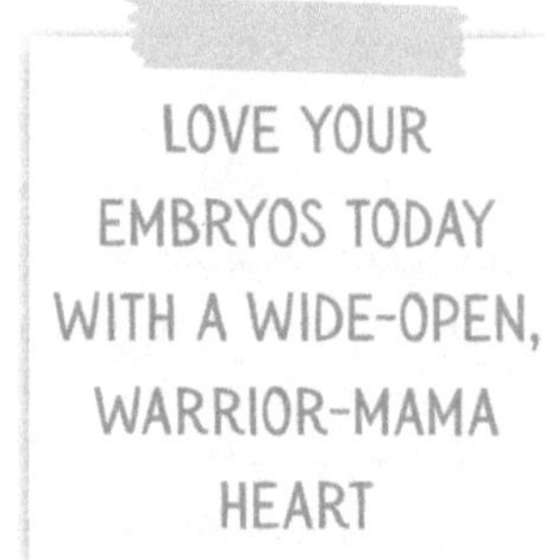

Instead of fearing your embryos or pregnancy like I did, I'm challenging you to do something I didn't know how to do at the time: **love your embryos today with a wide-open, warrior-mama heart.**

This doesn't mean it won't hurt if your child doesn't show up, stays only a short time, or arrives in a way you didn't plan. It hurts deeply.

But you are strong enough to go through it, and you will be okay. How do I know? Because look at what you've already been through. Not only did you survive, but you also became stronger, wiser, and more resilient than ever.

Use that strength. Use that love. The kind that says, *You are welcome in my life exactly as you are, on your terms. I am your mom. I will be okay no matter what. And I am not afraid to love you today and always.*

Choice No. 4: Choose To Love Yourself (*Did You Just Roll Your Eyes At Me?*)

Okay, before you brace yourself for a cheesy self-help moment, let me say I get it, and I promise that's not where this is going. Hear me out, because this one hit me like a brick to the face.

I always knew I'd be the most loving mom when my kids arrived. And I am. Some might even call it "a bit much," and they're not wrong. I smother my kids with (slightly aggressive) hugs and kisses; I smell them often (not a typo), and they know when I say "eyes," it means to look me in the eyes for three seconds, which resets my soul. (Pro tip: start this at birth so they grow up thinking it's normal.)

Do I love them so much it hurts? Absolutely. Am I slightly obsessed with them? Yes.

So, of course, they'll learn to love themselves, right? How could they not, with all the love I'm pouring into them?

Then I read Brené Brown's *The Gifts of Imperfection*. She writes:

You can't teach a child how to love themselves if you don't love yourself... We cannot give our children what we don't have. **Where we are on our journey of living and loving with our whole hearts is a much stronger indicator of parenting success than anything we can learn from how-to books.**

WHERE WE ARE ON OUR JOURNEY OF LIVING AND LOVING WITH OUR WHOLE HEARTS IS A MUCH STRONGER INDICATOR OF PARENTING SUCCESS THAN ANYTHING WE CAN LEARN FROM HOW-TO BOOKS
-BRENÉ BROWN

When I first read that line, *"We cannot give our children what we don't have,"* it stopped me in my tracks. I started crying and had to put the book down. Because here's the thing: if I couldn't model love for myself, how could my kids ever learn to love themselves?

And the truth was, I didn't love myself.

If I had, I wouldn't have spoken to myself with constant judgment, disappointment, and shame. It was relentless, especially when I looked in the mirror, pointed out everything I could be doing better, or replayed every "mistake" I convinced myself I would have avoided if I were smarter.

Now, I wasn't sitting in front of them, pointing out my flaws. I was always careful about what I said in front of them. But you can't fake energy. Kids have superpowers when it comes to sensing it. Don't even try to fool them.

When I realized my kids were learning from me, it hit me that they weren't seeing their own perfectly imperfect and unique qualities, and that I'd be the reason they would learn to dim their light. Everything changed for me that day. I chose to start seeing myself as the extraordinary human God made me to be.

IF YOU WANT YOUR CHILDREN TO RECOGNIZE AND CELEBRATE THEIR OWN UNIQUE GIFTS, QUIRKS, AND APPEARANCE, YOU HAVE TO MODEL IT FIRST

Next, I realized I was doing the same thing with my husband, focusing on what he could do better rather than the millions of things he was already doing right (see the following callout box).

By seeing and celebrating our strengths, we teach our kids to focus on their gifts rather than their flaws, and to do the same for their future partners. These two mindset shifts were monumental gifts to my children.

But let me tell you, these shifts don't happen overnight. Like anything else that brings authentic peace, love, and joy, it takes time, effort, and a whole lot of practice. But **if you want your children to recognize and celebrate their own unique gifts, quirks, and appearance, you have to model it first.**

I Finally Chose to Love My Husband

Once I started giving myself grace and seeing myself as beautifully human, I made another decision: I would truly love Brian.

Up until that point, I thought I loved him. But do you really treat someone the way I was treating him if you love them? Just like I realized with myself, I would never speak to someone I loved with the kind of constant criticism I directed at him.

The same harsh inner critic that showed up to pick apart my own shortcomings was also speaking to my husband.

Like with myself, I focused only on what he was doing wrong. And let me tell you, the list was long. I had a highlight reel of his greatest hits always ready to play.

- He chews so loudly, I'm convinced he needs mouth surgery.
- He hangs his hoodies on the outside of the closet door, right next to perfectly good hooks inside the closet that he literally has to pass to hang the hoodie.
- He mumbles so much, and I got so sick of asking, "What?" a million times a day that I trained myself to only ask yes-or-no questions. Somehow, he still answers with "mhhh, suh, ah." (Um, WHAT?!)

While I very much still notice these things, I don't experience them the same way anymore.

Beyond doing the deeper work of learning how to truly love myself, two things helped me make a huge shift. First, when I feel annoyed with him, I remind myself that he is a human having a human experience and doing the best he can, and so am I. I know I also have *a couple* of flaws, so why would I expect him not to? Second, when I catch myself being critical, I immediately list ten things he is doing right, so those become the dominant thoughts I hold about him.

I like to say that Brian and I have been together for over twenty-two years, and I have unconditionally loved him for four. Because of the work I did on myself, I finally allowed myself to fully trust him, fully be vulnerable with him, and fully receive his love while loving him back. Our imperfectly beautiful marriage has taken work, *really hard work*, and it has been worth every bit of the noise he makes while eating cereal.

Choice No. 5: Choose To Protect Your Energy

My first anxiety attack hit during IVF, right in the middle of the infamous "two-week wait" (which is really more like nine days). If you haven't done IVF, once the embryo is transferred, you basically do nothing but wait to see if you're pregnant... and overanalyze everything.

One night, lying in bed, I suddenly couldn't breathe. I wasn't even thinking about anything stressful. I was simply trying to sleep, but my body had other plans. It had reached its breaking point and started screaming. At the time, I blamed the progesterone, even though that made no sense. This wasn't my first transfer. It was probably my seventh or eighth, and this reaction had never happened before.

Looking back, the cause is painfully obvious. For nine days, I poured all my energy into trying to control the uncontrollable. Every bite of food (*Should I eat this or not?*). Every twinge (*Is that implantation or gas?*). Every hour felt like two hundred as I counted down to the blood test. I did everything humanly possible to make this pregnancy last, even though the outcome was never mine to control. My body finally gave out and short-circuited into panic.

If your goal is to thrive, not simply barely survive, protecting your energy isn't optional. And there are three simple (but not always easy) steps you can start today.

Step 1: Know the Difference Between What You Can and Can't Control

When it comes to conception, whether you're doing fertility treatments or not, there's a clear point when nothing you do will improve or ruin that embryo's chances to stick and stay.

I remember working with a client two days before her embryo transfer. She asked, "What's next? What else should I do?" We had spent the previous month preparing her body and mind to be receptive to pregnancy and confirming her protocol with her doctor.

So I told her, "Unless you're planning to drink bleach, nothing you do or don't do will change the results. You've done everything you can control, and nothing needs to be perfect either."

Three things there. First, the drinking bleach comment was me trying to be funny (and yes, I usually get a half-laugh half the time). The second part was to remind her that we had already done the work and covered everything we could control, thoroughly and correctly. The third part was for my fellow perfectionists. She had done enough, and we aim for "better than before," not "perfect."

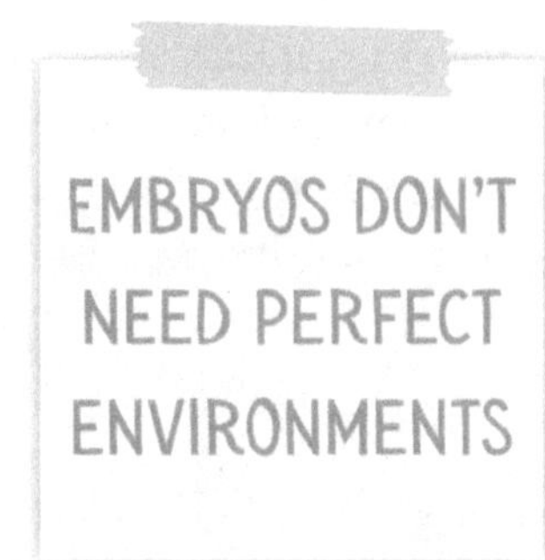

We'll talk much more about this issue in "Part 2: The Book on IVF," but **embryos don't need perfect environments.** They can stick and thrive in all kinds of conditions. And there's no such thing as a perfect environment anyway. I've often seen small, strategic changes create big improvements in fertility. That's why many of my clients preparing for IVF end up getting pregnant naturally. When you adjust your body enough on the right side of the Fertility Formula and have enough energy, your body knows it's safe to make a baby.

Step 2: Be Intentional About Where You Put Your Energy

After you understand what you can and can't control, choose to feed your senses with things that give you energy instead of draining it.

In the next section, we'll do an exercise called "Let's Get High Together" to help you identify what lifts you up.

What are you choosing? Are you doom-scrolling fertility blogs and feeling more confused and defeated? Are you on social media comparing yourself to everyone with the "perfect" family and sinking into shame? Do you watch the news and feel your whole body tense with stress?

If so, stop.

If it feels like an energy drain, it is. Instead, choose things that give you energy, make you smile, or better yet, make you laugh. (Anything with Melissa McCarthy or Will Ferrell usually works for me.)

Don't let other people's chaos, like depressing news or toxic social accounts, rob you of your precious energy. Their mess can drain you, and choosing to pour energy into things that deplete you could be the very reason you don't create the family of your dreams.

And I'm not being dramatic here. I've found that the number one reason people stop building their families isn't time or money; it's fertility fatigue. That's my term for when someone spends so long fighting heartbreak and exhaustion that the weight of it finally pins them down and they no longer have the *energy* to get back up.

Your energy is precious, Mama. It's the main ingredient in the Fertility Formula, and it's limited. Protect it fiercely.

DELEGATING WHAT YOU CAN'T CONTROL TAKES COURAGE AND WISDOM, AND IT'S NOT ALWAYS EASY

Step 3: Delegate What You Can't Control

"Let it go" and "surrender" never made sense to a control-loving DIYer like me. But you know what does? Delegation.

And you can assign those tasks to different people. When it comes to whether an embryo will stick and stay, I have the perfect person: your child. Let them know how much you want them to arrive, and let them know that no matter what they choose, it will be okay.

Other good "whos" include trusted professionals who can help you overcome recurring issues or obstacles, and good "whats" include divine guidance. We'll talk more about harnessing your superpower with your higher power in the next section, but for now, remember this: understanding that God will always make the right plans for you and accepting that you might not fully understand them while they're unfolding can bring you so much peace.

Delegating what you can't control takes courage and wisdom, and it's not always easy. But what you get in return is the right "person" for the job, because if it's something beyond your control, it's not meant for you to handle. And the reward for that trust is more energy.

For a long time, my life felt like a series of confusing twists, with incredible blessings woven in alongside heartbreaking, painful, exhausting obstacles. I used to look back and think it was unfair. I didn't believe I deserved the hardships I was given.

But now I see it clearly. It was a curated training ground.

Moving through hard things, surviving them, and coming out stronger and much wiser quietly prepared me for the work I do today. None of it felt purposeful at the time. But every challenge sharpened me, stretched me, and built a level of resilience I didn't know I would need.

My mission is to reduce infertility, pregnancy loss, and unnecessary IVF by helping women make each attempt more successful. This kind of work hasn't been done before. And because of that, it requires courage, persistence, and sustained energy over long periods of uncertainty.

I didn't plan this life. The version of adulthood I imagined in my twenties was simpler, more comfortable, and far easier. And yes, there are still moments when I wonder what it would be like to walk away from this mission and begin that smaller, easier version of life.

But the experiences I've had were too costly, too formative, and too influential to ignore now. The mission is too clear, and the cost of not finishing it is far too high. Walking away would mean wasting everything that qualified me to be here. And the truth is, this work gives me energy.

When I think about you, I feel energized and deeply grateful. You are the reason I keep building, refining, and pushing forward, because I know these tools can fundamentally change your fertility journey and help you kiss your baby sooner.

I didn't choose my past, but because of what I've lived, learned, and survived, I now know I am bold enough, strong enough, and *becoming* confident enough to lead a mission this big. I didn't plan for any of it, but I will succeed because I've *chosen* to accept it.

Choice No. 6: Choose Growth Over Regret

If the first big energy drainer is worrying about every possible "what if" in the future, the second is getting stuck in a "shoulda, woulda, coulda" mindset about the past.

Too often, we replay the past and beat ourselves up for what we did or didn't do, convinced that if we had made different choices, everything would be better. But those "mistakes" you're holding onto weren't mistakes at all. They were lessons that taught you what you need to succeed in the future.

You are exactly where you're supposed to be right now because this is where you are. Even if it's not where you planned to be, this is the right part of your journey and the right time. The moments leading up to this one aren't mistakes; they're part of what brought you here.

Of course, there's one exception. If you learn something but don't use it, keep doing what you were doing, or let past experiences keep you stuck, then, to me, that's a mistake. But if you've grown, gained insight, and started moving differently (even if you're still figuring it out), those lessons are investments with huge returns.

> YOU ARE EXACTLY WHERE YOU'RE SUPPOSED TO BE RIGHT NOW BECAUSE THIS IS WHERE YOU ARE

And yes, some of those lessons come at a high price. But anything truly valuable does. The more you've invested, the greater its worth.

You get to decide how you see your past. You can let it weigh you down, keeping you stuck in regret and shame, or you can choose to see it as something that adds value to your wisdom and strength.

Once you choose the latter, the key is in the new story you tell yourself, the way you choose to see what happened.

Here are some common regrets I hear and how you can reframe them if you choose to:

Typical Regret #1: "If only I had started trying to get pregnant earlier instead of waiting until I had the right partner or financial situation."

Reframe: Choosing to wait for the right situation was an act of love for your child. Bringing a child into the wrong relationship or an unstable situation would not have been fair to them, and it would have cost you deeply as well. You chose wisdom over urgency, and that is something to be proud of.

Typical Regret #2: "If only I hadn't wasted time and money on IUIs before moving to IVF."

Reframe: Trying IUI was a calculated decision, just like IVF. You're assuming IVF would have worked sooner, but you don't actually know that. Those same months could have been spent in failed IVF cycles, leaving you in the same place, only more exhausted and with fewer resources. You made the best decision you could with the information you had at the time.

Typical Regret #3: "If I had known about this protocol or issue sooner, I wouldn't have had a pregnancy loss."

Reframe: Your child did what was right for *their* journey by staying only a short time. What was best for them may not have been what was best for you, and that truth is painful. But when we choose to become a parent, we are also choosing to allow our child to arrive how, when, for how long, and as who they are meant to be.

So when you look back at your past, instead of thinking, *What did I do wrong?* or *Why me?* Ask yourself:

- *What did I learn?*
- *How did this prepare me for where I am now?*
- *How have my life and my skills improved because of what I learned?*

If you're asking these questions about your fertility journey and you're still in it, they might feel impossible to answer right now, and that's okay. But give it time. I believe that one day your struggles will make sense and reveal their purpose in beautiful ways you can't imagine today.

For now, remember this: your past could be a wealth of resources, not a series of regrets. It holds the lessons that make you stronger, wiser, and more prepared for what's next... if you choose to see it that way.

EXERCISE: KNOW YOUR NOW AND YOUR WHY

Now that you've seen how the Levels of Energy Alignment work, from the heavy, frozen energy of shame at the bottom to the light, open feeling of freedom at the top, let's figure out where your inner world naturally hangs out. This helps you set a baseline for where you are now so you can get clear on where you want to go. It also gives you a few simple ways to start shifting things.

Step 1: Tune In

Grab a piece of paper and answer the following questions. Spread them out on the paper so you have eight lines between each of them. This is helpful when you get to Step 2.

1. How would you describe your natural energy using the words from the scale?
2. Where do you want to be?
3. Would you like to choose to become that person today?

Step 2: Get Motivated

Like in the Survive to Thrive Protocol, when we ask why, we get wise. You're much more likely to reach your goal when you have a meaningful reason behind it. Without one, a goal becomes another annoying task on your list that you don't actually want to do.

This step helps you get clear on the *why* behind wanting to raise your energy level.

On the first line below each of your answers to the three questions, write the word "why." These are your *why lines*.

- On the first line, answer *why* you picked your response to each question.
- On the second line, answer *why* you wrote what you did on the first line.
- On the third line, answer *why* you wrote what you did on the second.

Keep going all the way through eight lines.

Don't overthink it. Write the first thing that comes to mind. But don't stop at three or five. Keep going until you hit *eight* lines. The first few answers are usually surface-level. The last few tend to reveal the truth that actually moves you.

Your *why* on line eight is the one that could finally give you the motivation to shift your default emotional state and change how you experience life.

Why does that matter?

(Here comes the mom guilt!) Children mirror your behavior, especially if you're the same-sex parent. If you're constantly operating from fear, anger, or anxiety, you'll unconsciously pull your child from their naturally high-energy emotions of love, joy, and peace into that same emotional state and make it their baseline, too. This isn't because you're a bad parent, but rather because that's how energy functions.

Let's break that cycle of low-energy living for our bodies, our fertility, and our children.

And instead... Let's get high together.

EXERCISE: LET'S GET HIGH TOGETHER

Now that you have motivation for where you want to be, let's get some real data on what's lifting you up and what's dragging you down.

This exercise helps you spot the habits and choices that already give you energy and make you feel light, happy, and free. Just as importantly, it shows you what's cluttering your energy and pulling you into the lower vibes that drain you and leave you feeling heavy, cranky, and exhausted.

By the end, you'll have a snapshot of what gets you "high" and what gets you "low" so you can choose how to spend your energy more wisely. And for the things you have to do (like checking emails, my personal mood killer), you'll know where to set stronger boundaries or build better systems.

Step 1: Energy Audit

Grab a pen and paper, a journal, or your phone's Notes app. For the next two weeks, you'll track your actions and how they make you feel.

After each activity or interaction, use the scale from the Levels of Energy Alignment graphic, listed again below, to describe how you felt during and after that experience by noting your Emotional State and your Energy Level.

For example:

- Walks outside: Acceptance (8), Love (10), Peace (12)
- Talking to someone who really knows and loves you: Reason (9), Love (10)
- Your diet: Neutrality (6) when balanced, but maybe Fear (2) before the bite, and Shame (0) after, if you're deep in restrictive eating
- Reading this book: Neutrality (5) if you're open but undecided, Reason (9) if the information is making sense
- Online research on infertility: Fear (2)
- Scrolling social media or online support groups: Can swing from Shame (0) to Love (10) depending on the content

LEVELS OF ENERGY ALIGNMENT

ENERGY LEVEL	EMOTIONAL STATE (ENERGY IN MOTION)	COLOR	STATE OF MATTER	FELT EXPERIENCE	GROWTH CAPACITY
13	ENLIGHTENMENT	VIOLET		UNTOUCHABLE	UNLIMITED
10-12	LOVE, JOY, PEACE	PURPLE		FREE	EXPANSIVE
7-9	WILLINGNESS, ACCEPTANCE, REASON	BLUE		RESILIENT	EVOLVING
6	NEUTRALITY	GREEN		FLEXIBLE	SHIFTING
4-5	PRIDE, COURAGE	YELLOW		MOTIVATION	STRUGGLING
3	ANGER	ORANGE		FRUSTRATION	STALLED
0-2	SHAME, GUILT, FEAR	RED		HEAVY, BREAKABLE	UNAVAILABLE

Step 2: Reflect, Evaluate, Take Action

Once you've built your list, figure out what needs to stay, go, shift, or be replaced.

Ask yourself:

- *What activities or people give me energy? How can I bring more of that into my life?*
- *Which ones deplete me? Do I have to keep doing it, or can I create a better system for it or set a boundary around it?*

Step 3: How "High" Are You?

Let's find out how high you get throughout your day (yup, the jokes will keep coming until this section is done). Get the average by adding up the total number of activities with their assigned number and then dividing the total number by the number of activities you tracked. The result is your current state of natural energy.

Step 4: Get High as a Kite

Now set a goal to raise it by 10 percent over the next two weeks. Did my overachievers hear that? *Just 10 percent.* Slow, steady shifts are what actually stick. They rewire your patterns without burning you out.

Repeat the tracking a few weeks later, this time for one week, with the intention of raising your average by another 10 percent until you're getting closer to your natural, desired state.

A few reminders as you do this work:

- Have grace and compassion for yourself. Defying the gravitational pull of fear and shame is hard work.
- Bouncing around the scale based on what's happening in your life is completely normal.
- Celebrate even the tiniest upward shift. You are rising up!

Okay, so now you know what to do when you want to get really high for the day (I promise that is the last joke about it).

But there is *one* thing that will block your ability to rise, no matter how much work you've done: a lack of boundaries.

EXERCISE: BOUNDARIES AS THE NEW PRENATAL

I believe people-pleasing is one of the most overlooked blocks to fertility. When you give and give without pause, you drain your precious energy. And when you constantly push down your own emotions to keep others comfortable, those emotions don't disappear. They get stored.

Think of it this way: those unexpressed emotions take up space in your body. Space that could otherwise be used for growth and creation. When your system is already crowded with resentment, guilt, or unspoken frustration, there's very little room left for a baby to grow.

And that's exactly how it feels when you carry the weight of heavy emotions inside.

Want to know the most common profession among my clients? Nurses. Right behind that? Teachers and other service-based professionals.

It's not a coincidence that these kind, purpose-driven women who have been trained to give endlessly and get back very little in return, who show up no matter how empty their tank is, are also the ones struggling to conceive. They're exhausted. Their bodies have nothing left to give.

And it's also not a coincidence that these women are drawn to working with me. I'm a recovering people-pleaser too. For years, I would rather suffer all day than make someone else uncomfortable. I'd bite my tongue, keep the peace, and tell myself it was fine because I was strong enough to handle it.

And honestly? I still catch myself doing it.

Learning to set and stick with boundaries is one of the most important things you can do, not only for your health but also for the family you're trying to build. **Boundaries aren't walls; they're doors. They let the right people and energy in, and they keep the draining, unhelpful stuff out.**

BOUNDARIES AREN'T WALLS; THEY'RE DOORS. THEY LET THE RIGHT PEOPLE AND ENERGY IN, AND THEY KEEP THE DRAINING, UNHELPFUL STUFF OUT

Setting them now, before parenthood, is a necessity. There will always be energy suckers and over-askers. If you don't know how to protect your energy, it will keep getting used up by everyone else. And as we've learned about modeling, you'll pass the same people-pleasing patterns to your kids.

So what does this look like in real life?

Maybe there's someone who constantly drains you. You don't have to cut them out completely, but could you see them less often, change when or how you interact, suggest meeting in a group instead of one-on-one, or build in activities that are actually fun?

Think board games that keep your brain engaged, like my favorite, Rummikub. Or games that make you laugh. Put on upbeat music. Give your brain something positive to focus on. Choose things that make it hard to stay in a bad mood while doing them.

This way, you are not avoiding them. You are managing the energy in the room.

Or maybe there's something you do at work that's not your job. Ask yourself, *is this actually mine, or do I do it because I do it best?* If it's not yours, delegate it, train someone (and then train them again and again until they get it or until you realize they never will and need to be replaced), or let someone else do it, even if it's not perfect. Your energy is too valuable to waste on tasks you resent.

Here's a big one: how many times has someone offered to help, and you said no so you wouldn't be a burden? You can change this through practice: start saying yes. No, not "yes," but "YES!" If someone offers, trust that they meant it, and if they didn't, that's their issue to handle, not yours.

And here's the flip side: how many times has someone asked you to do something that has nothing to do with your current goals or invited you somewhere you already know will drain you, and you still said yes because you didn't want to hurt their feelings?

You have to practice saying yes to receiving help and no to always being the one who gives it. And yes, you will be terrible at it at first. Trust me.

Here are a few things that help.

First: Give yourself a "pause phrase" so you don't have to say yes or no on the spot. It can be something as simple as, "Let me check a few things and get back to you." That buys you time to actually choose, instead of defaulting to people-pleasing.

Second: Follow up at a later time with, "I'm not available." And no, you're not being dishonest. Your time might actually be available, but your *energy* is not available for that task, event, or obligation.

Things to remember:

When you do say yes out of habit (not if... when), you are allowed to go back an hour later, or even the next day, and change your answer. Try: "I totally forgot I had something else I need to handle, so I'm going to have to pass. If anything changes, I'll let you know." You don't need to overexplain. You're not on trial. But if the person is extra pushy, it is good to say you are doing something (and use it as a reminder that pushy people drain your energy, so you need even stronger boundaries).

When you do say yes and instantly regret it, don't beat yourself up for "having no boundaries again." Instead, notice what it feels like in your body when your energy gets hijacked. Then practice what you wish you would've said instead, and give yourself grace. Lots and lots of it. I believe that people-pleasing is an addiction. It soothes the fear of not being loved, not being chosen, and not being enough. And for most of us, that pattern has been building for decades.

So yes, what I'm asking you to do is challenging.

Will it feel uncomfortable to receive when you're used to being the giver? Absolutely. But that discomfort means you're changing and growing, and that's a beautiful thing.

Now that we've started clearing space with the people around you, it's time to talk about the one critic who's the loudest, rudest, closest to you, and hardest to escape.

She's the "mean girl" living in your head.

EXERCISE: TAMING THE MEAN GIRL LIVING IN YOUR HEAD

What Shame Sounds Like in Real Time

I used to have the meanest "mean girl" living in my head, and during my fertility journey, she got especially nasty.

It was my *eighth* egg retrieval at my third clinic, and I was being forced to attend an IVF orientation. An orientation where they explain what an egg retrieval is and how to give yourself shots. (Seriously?)

I tried reasoning with the admin, but she kept repeating that it was mandatory. So I walked in with my arms crossed like I was auditioning for the role of "most unamused human alive." I slumped in my chair and clenched my jaw. Everyone else looked so excited to be there. Happy couples showing off their color-coded binders, proud and organized with their medical records. My eyes rolled so hard in the back of my head I thought they might get stuck.

And then came the questions. The rookie couples, asking rookie questions.

I sat there with a smirk, thinking, *Ugh, you are all so naïve. Just wait. IVF doesn't work.*

That's when the "mean girl" in my head chimed in, and do you want to know what she said?

Oh no, Tasha, you're wrong. IVF does work… it just doesn't work for you. (Gut punch. Gasp. Ouch.)

She wasn't done.

You are the naïve one here, not them. You are the idiot doing IVF for the eighth time, thinking that it's going to magically work. You're actually a joke at this point, and everyone feels sorry for you.

My very next thought was, *You're right.*

I sat up straight, held my breath, and tried with everything in me not to cry.

Most of us have a "mean girl" living in our heads.

She runs the show with fear-based thoughts and worst-case scenarios, pointing out every possible flaw or failure as if she's protecting you. But what she's really doing is keeping you stuck in the lowest Levels of Energy Alignment—heavy, constricted emotional states like fear, shame, and guilt. And as you now know, those states are biologically incompatible with growth and creation.

So how did she get here? Who invited her?

She was built during times in your past when fear and self-criticism felt necessary to stay safe. She is the scared you who learned to survive hard things by staying hypervigilant. The problem is, she never got the update that you grew up. She's still using the same outdated protection strategy she's always used: fear and shame.

To be clear, she's not the enemy. She's trying to help. She just doesn't know how to help in a way that supports growth.

The goal isn't to kick her out... because you can't. The goal is to change your relationship with her and rewrite the script she's been running on repeat.

When *you*, the grounded, capable woman you are today, take the lead and show her that you're safe and back it up with real proof, those heavy, stuck emotions can start to move. Energy rises. Your nervous system regulates. And your body shifts out of survival mode and back toward growth.

The next exercise is called "Taming the Mean Girl Living in Your Head" (also known as "Taming the A-Hole in Your Head," for my mixed audiences), and it has two parts.

First, you'll learn how to help emotions move up the Levels of Energy Alignment, clearing out the low-energy states that have been cluttering space your body needs for growth and creation.

Second, you'll begin gently rewiring your fear-based brain. This is where your strong adult self steps in to reassure that younger version of you that she doesn't need to run the show anymore, and you'll show her the evidence.

This is one of my favorite exercises to practice and to teach. It blends somatic experiencing, EMRes® techniques, and a few of my own tools that I've seen create powerful shifts. It's one of the first real steps in clearing emotional and physical space for your baby.

And before we start, I want to say this again: your child is so lucky to have you as their mom. I truly mean it.

Step 1: Ground Yourself

Close your eyes.

Go through your five senses one by one:

- What do you see (even with eyes closed)?
- What do you hear?
- What do you taste?
- What do you feel (on your skin or supporting your body)?
- What do you smell?

Take your time. Go into the details.

Why this matters: Getting present to one thing is like closing all the tabs on your computer. It allows for better focus and calm almost immediately.

Step 2: Find the Feeling

Keep your eyes closed and scan your body. Where do you feel the emotion showing up? Maybe it's in your throat, chest, stomach, or somewhere else.

Once you find it, describe it like this:

- What material is it? (Metal, liquid, stone?)
- What shape is it? (Round, sharp, spiky?)
- How big is it? (A pebble? A golf ball? Bigger?)

Why this matters: Emotions don't float around; they land in the body. We want to find them and move them along so they stop cluttering things up. When you locate the sensation and describe what it looks and feels like, you'll notice when that look or feel starts to change. That shift is your cue that the emotion is moving out, the decluttering process in action.

Step 3: Stay With It

Focus on that physical feeling. Don't try to change it in any way. Simply be with it.

After a minute or two (or more, depending on how long it has been cluttered up), the look or shape of it typically starts to shift.

Once the sensation has faded (give it some time), scan your body to see if another emotion is showing up. If it is, repeat the process with that one too.

Why this matters: Instead of shoving down and ignoring the emotion, hoping it goes away, we are doing the opposite. We are giving it our full and undivided attention. Awareness allows the typically ice-cold, hard, and stuck emotion at the bottom of the Levels of Energy Alignment to begin to warm up and become more fluid. You are not only decluttering your body of those emotions but also training your brain to understand that you can fully feel the emotion and still be safe.

Step 4: Talk to Her

Most emotions come down to one of two things: feeling unsafe or feeling shame. Feeling unsafe might show up as anxiety, needing control, or feeling on edge. Shame might sound like *I'm not good enough, I don't deserve this,* or *Something is wrong with me.* There might be other emotions too, but these two tend to be the biggest ones underneath it all.

Ask yourself: *Has this emotion been a pattern for most of my life? Do I remember where it started?* Remember the girl inside of you who first felt it. Picture your younger self at the age when you first picked up these fears and patterns.

Now, imagine her in the room with you, where you can have a real conversation.

And, in the most loving way, tell her what's true:

- "What happened was not fair; it was wrong, and it was not your fault. I know you know that, but I had to say it again."
- "You are saying these hurtful things because you are scared, but you don't have to be afraid anymore. What happened was a long time ago, and we've grown up and into something incredible. Look at us now! Aren't you proud? We're strong, resilient, and resourceful, and honestly, we should be a lot more messed up than we are (wink). Seriously, though, we can handle anything."
- "I've got you. Always. I'm here now, I'm in control, and we're doing great."
- If you have a relationship with God, invite that presence in too: "God has always been there for us and always will be, and I have proof." Then share that proof with her.

Why this matters: So many of these patterns, especially how our brains respond to danger, were built by a younger version of you who didn't feel safe or protected. Those old responses became familiar and easy for your brain to follow, even decades later. To truly rewire your brain, you need to give it new experiences and new paths to take. When you consistently choose the path of safety, compassion, and love, your brain learns to guide your body there instead of straight into stress. Over time, that becomes the new well-worn path your mind automatically takes when fear or shame shows up.

Tips for Success:

- Do this exercise often, especially at the beginning. It builds emotional resilience and helps clear out the stuff you didn't even realize you were carrying.
- Keep a journal or notes on your phone to track what comes up, what shifts, and any patterns you start to notice. You might find a few repeat offenders.
- Share your experience with someone you trust. Someone who knows the real you. Saying it out loud may help you continue to move the emotion out of your body instead of keeping it shoved inside. It could also remind you that you're deeply loved and never as alone as you think.

When I first tried this, I felt like I needed to do it every fifteen minutes. That alone was eye-opening. I hadn't realized how anxious I really was until I finally gave those feelings a place to land. I even kept a little cheat sheet of the steps so I wouldn't forget what to do or say next. Before long, it became second nature.

These days, when I'm feeling really anxious, I go through all the steps again. But sometimes, I do a shortcut. If a thought is really harsh or something I absolutely don't want to invite in, I say, "Reverse... reverse." It's my way of taking it back.

Or if it's the mean girl inside, slipping into her old habits, I keep it simple. When she starts up, I say, "Nope. That's not true." She backs off right away. Sometimes she even agrees with me. (She's such a pushover!)

Before heading to the next section...

If you'd like to download the worksheets for the exercises I shared and get details on the video series I created on mindset for my Mamas, just scan the QR code.

FINDING SUPERPOWER IN THE HIGHER POWER

We're going to talk about God next. If the topic makes you uncomfortable, you're welcome to skip this section. But I gently invite you to lean into that discomfort. Progress often comes from being willing to get uncomfortable.

OMG, GOD!

A little background: I've always believed in God, and I've always prayed. I grew up Catholic but didn't get much out of Mass. Going was simply what you did… So I did it.

During my fertility journey, I prayed to saints and even wore medals around my neck. But I wasn't really connected to them. It felt more like pleading—another thing to try that couldn't hurt, right?

As an adult, I explored all kinds of spiritual practices and read plenty of books. My favorite connection, other than God, was with angels. Guardian angels and archangels felt like having a loving, supportive network of superheroes helping me, guiding me, protecting me, and cheering me on. (And my angels, by the way, have a *wicked* sense of humor.)

But I never really *studied* God until recently. I met someone in a business group who had a strong relationship with God. At first, I thought it was kind of weird (okay, really weird, to be honest). But I was curious. I told this person, "I don't get your relationship with God. It's different."

After talking for a while, he said, "If you want to understand my relationship with God, you need to do three things."

- Pray daily. (Check! Was already doing this.)
- Find a church. (Okay, I will go a couple of times to check the box.)
- Read the Bible. (What?! Ugh!!! Noooooo!)

My first thought? *I shouldn't have asked.* I didn't have time to read the Bible, and half the words didn't even make sense in the order they're written. I'm out.

But I had asked the question, and I got the answer. The ball was in my court. I could have ignored it, and I was tempted to. But that's not really my style because I don't believe in coincidences.

My second thought? *OMG, God, you are so annoying sometimes!!!*

At the end of 2023, I committed to reading the Bible. Well, sort of. My friend, Gina, told me about a podcast, *The Bible in a Year with Fr. Mike Schmitz*, that reads it to you in short bursts (and of course I sped it up) and then explains what it means.

Here's what stood out to me:

- Boy oh boy, there are some famous mindset and life coaches out there stealing content straight from the Bible.

- I liked the simplicity because I like to optimize everything. No more chasing modalities, rituals, or superstitious "reversing" practices. There's one main resource to reach out to for any need or issue: *The* Source. Nice and efficient.

- It made me feel both significant and insignificant at the same time. I know I've been carefully created for a magnificent purpose if I choose to live it. But I also know that my personal plans and desires are small in the *big* picture, and it's okay that I don't always understand plan.

- The world feels more incredible now, especially nature. Each night when I take my dog out to pee, I look up at the stars and say to God, "Hey, nice work!" (not kidding).

- I've also come to understand that terrible things can happen to me or to people I love, and somehow, they can still serve a purpose. That awareness makes me appreciate my billions of blessings even more.

- I've learned to measure everything by its energy (even Bible interpretations). If the energy behind it is love, I know it's from God. If it carries judgment or shame, that's from man.

Something else that is cool is that I feel like I have become my own "psychic." Since studying God and talking to God more, my intuition has gotten even stronger. I can ask a question and get an immediate answer. And how do I know that it is actually coming from God and not me? That is easy: it's never the answers I want to hear! It's frustrating and kind of funny at the same time. Since I'm stubborn, I'll go back the next day and ask the same question, hoping for a different answer. But the answer is always the same. Or sometimes, I get silence, which feels like God saying, "We've already talked about this. I'm not doing this again." (Spicy, right?!)

PEOPLE WHO LIVE IN GENUINE PEACE USUALLY HAVE A STRONG RELATIONSHIP WITH THEIR SOURCE

I'm not saying you should do what I did or try anything that doesn't feel right for you. I'm sharing what I learned while researching happiness and peace, and how this experience brought more calm into my life. It also led me to a really good, small church full of incredible humans. I'm sure there's someone a little off hiding in the crowd, but it's been over two years, and I still haven't found them.

And maybe the biggest change of all, especially for someone like me who tends to like to control a teeny, tiny bit, is that I actually feel less in control but somehow much freer and at peace. I think that's God's idea of having a sense of humor.

Over the years, I've explored many mindset practices and healing modalities out there. I've always been fascinated by how people find peace. Anytime I meet someone who radiates real calm and grounded happiness, I want to know their secret. And the more I asked, the more I noticed a clear pattern: **people who live in genuine peace usually have a strong relationship with their Source.**

Some call it God. Some call it the universe, angels, or energy. The language varies, but the common thread is the same. They believe something greater than themselves is guiding them, supporting them, and working on their behalf. And because of that belief, they tap into a level of strength and energy that feels almost like a superpower.

I often think of this connection as something even beyond enlightenment on the Levels of Energy Alignment chart. Humans may touch enlightenment at times, but Source exists beyond human limitation. And choosing a real relationship with Source requires you to rise into higher energy to connect. But here's the beautiful part: once you do, Source does the heavy lifting. With that partnership, you're lifted higher than you could ever climb on your own.

In many ways, partnering with a higher power is an energetic shortcut. It makes it easier to rise through the Levels of Energy Alignment and access states like acceptance, reason, love, joy, and peace. You're no longer relying solely on your own limited reserves. You're drawing from something far bigger.

And yes, science backs this up. People who feel connected to a Higher Power consistently show lower stress levels, steadier nervous system regulation, and stronger immune function. But beyond the data, there's something harder to measure and easier to feel. They carry a calm confidence that no supplement, therapy session, or mindset tool can create on its own. It's the peace that comes from knowing you're connected to a Source of unlimited energy, support, and love that wants to work *with* you.

So if you're exhausted, stuck in lower emotional states, and feeling like you've been doing this alone... And if the idea of a higher power gives you even a flicker of relief or energy simply thinking about it, maybe it's time to explore a Source that resonates with you. It could be the missing piece to finding the peace you've been searching for.

BUT WAIT, DOES GOD WANT YOU TO HAVE A BABY?

I actually did a whole podcast on this in Episode 55. When I hear a client who has a strong relationship with God say, "I don't think God wants me to have a baby," I want to slam a buzzer like I'm on a game show and yell, "False!"

Instead, I ask, "Why do you want a baby?" They talk about family, love, connection, and legacy. Then I intentionally lift the energy and say, half joking and very lovingly, "Okay, just making sure this isn't a 'Brave New World' plan to create an army of beautiful humans."

Once we're in a lighter, higher-energy space, I move into reason and ask, "Does this feel right in your heart?"

When they inevitably say yes, I explain it this way: "Your desire for a child is rooted in love, and that's the same energy God uses to guide us. If this desire is in your heart, it's because God placed it there, and **God wouldn't put something in your heart that wasn't meant for you."**

And then, because I can't help myself, I usually add, "Plus, God wants more believers. If you believe, chances are your children will too. That's one more follower. Everyone wins!"

I mean... that makes sense, right?

CHAPTER 4 SUMMARY

- **Spirit Protocol Is Not "Woo," It's Biology:** Your nervous system state and emotional energy influence hormones, inflammation, and how much usable energy your body has available for growth, which makes this real science, not fluff.
- **Alignment Determines Whether Growth Feels Easy or Hard:** Like a fruit tree aligned with sunlight, fertility responds best when your internal energy is aligned with emotions that support growth, rather than staying stuck in survival mode.
- **Your Internal Reflects Your External:** The energy you carry internally tends to shape what you notice, tolerate, and find in the world around you.
- **Levels of Energy Alignment:** Emotional states exist on an energy spectrum that directly influences your health and, therefore, fertility. As energy rises from shame and fear into anger, neutrality, acceptance, reason, and eventually love, joy, and peace, your system moves from frozen survival into flexibility, strength, and creation. Higher energy is not denial or blissful ignorance. It is disciplined, intentional, and biologically supportive of growth.
- **Infertility Can Train Your Brain to Fear Pregnancy:** When heartbreak stacks up, your brain could start associating pregnancy with danger, reinforcing survival mode unless you interrupt the pattern.
- **Choices Create Emotional Momentum:** Choosing happiness, motherhood, unconditional love for your child, love for yourself, protecting your energy, and growth over regret builds a steadier internal home for creation.
- **Energy Audits Turn "Vibes" Into Data:** Tracking what lifts you and what drains you gives you a clear map for where to set boundaries and where to add more of what brings you back to yourself.
- **Boundaries Are the New Prenatal:** People-pleasing and emotional swallowing store heavy energy in the body, and boundaries protect the exact resource on which fertility depends most.

- **Taming the Mean Girl Rewires Survival Mode:** By locating emotions in the body and helping them move instead of staying stuck, and by rewriting the fear-based script your brain has been running on repeat, you shift from an inner critic that drains you to an inner voice that supports safety, growth, and resilience.
- **Superpowers with Your Higher Power:** Whether you call it God, Source, or something else, building a relationship with a Higher Power could act like an energetic shortcut. That connection makes it easier to access high-energy, growth-promoting emotional states like love, joy, and peace that support fertility and help you create anything meaningful in your life.

If This Lit Something Up in You

If your spirit feels low on the Levels of Energy Alignment and you know you're ready for deeper work, look for details on the video series I offer called Conscious Creation: Elevating Your Mindset. It includes additional exercises designed to help shift your energy into higher states, with the goal of showing you how to genuinely love your life today while still building what matters most to you, whether that's your family, your career, your relationships, or your connection with yourself.

This isn't surface-level mindset work. It's a full energy reset.
It's the same process I used to calm my own anxiety-prone, fear-based brain while building a business, creating a strong and meaningful marriage, raising an extraordinary family, and to be at peace but always striving for more as I step into the second half of my life.

If you refuse to let your past or present dictate how you feel or what you're capable of creating, I believe you'll love this video series.
You can learn more by scanning the QR code.

5. Science Protocol: The Diagnostic Deep Dive

Ready to get nerdy with me? Welcome to the Science Protocol. This is where we start working alongside your medical team, whether that's a fertility doctor, OB/GYN, or another specialist, to uncover the clues behind your fertility and figure out your next best steps.

If you've been following along, the Surviving to Thriving Protocol in the first chapter was all about building a solid foundation. We focused on key nutrients and minerals, restorative sleep, brain breaks, meditation, and movement: everything that helps balance hormones and pulls you out of survival mode. Then, in the Spirit Protocol, we cleared out the mental and emotional clutter that can drain your energy and mess with your hormones.

Now that your system has received more support, it's time to examine what your numbers are indicating.

In this section, we'll cover:

- The baseline tests that show whether egg and sperm can meet, fertilize, and grow in the uterus
- Bloodwork and functional labs that reveal what's really driving reproductive issues
- The fertility roadblocks that show up when your body is stuck in survival mode and what to bring up with your doctor to actually start solving them

This part of the process helps you see whether all the pieces for conception are in place and whether they're in good enough shape to make pregnancy more likely. When you understand how your body works and how to spot what's missing, you'll have better, more productive conversations with your care team.

CONCEPTION 101: THE REAL REQUIREMENTS FOR GETTING PREGNANT

Before we get into the tests, let's do a quick crash course in sex ed so everything makes more sense.

I'm guessing you know how babies are made. (If not... you'll need a very different book, and as much as I love you, you might want to hold off on parenting plans until you've got the mechanics down.)

What I really mean is understanding the ingredients needed for conception. Based on the questions I get from followers, a lot of people don't actually know all the parts and players involved.

Making a baby is incredible, a true miracle, and it takes more than having eggs and sperm. There are several checkpoints that need to be working together. When everything lines up, pregnancy can happen. When one thing is off, it can make the process harder. That's why walking through the steps helps you troubleshoot before you're even officially "trying."

- **Sperm:** For natural conception, we're talking around 39 million and up. Yep, your health teacher lied. It definitely doesn't take "just one."
- **Eggs:** At least one *mature* egg needs to develop and be ready to ovulate.
- **A successful meetup:** That means:
    - Ovulation is occurring, and a mature egg is released from the follicle.
    - Fallopian tubes are open and able to pick up and transport the egg.
    - Cervical mucus becomes thin and sperm-friendly at the right time.
    - Sperm survive the vaginal environment, pass through the cervix, and reach the egg in the fallopian tube.

- **Fertilization:** The egg and sperm meet and successfully combine.
- **A welcoming uterus:** A healthy, receptive lining that can support implantation and pregnancy.
- **A strong cervix:** One that stays closed and supportive throughout pregnancy until delivery.

Alright, class is over! Now let's look at the tests that can help uncover what might be getting in the way.

DIAGNOSTIC DEEP DIVE: UNCOVER YOUR FERTILITY MYSTERY

This next section walks you through the key tests that can help reveal what's working and what might need some help at each major checkpoint in the baby-making process.

Some are blood tests, some are diagnostic procedures, and some you can actually do yourself. They may not always explain *why* something is happening, but they're incredibly useful for spotting *what* needs attention.

Tests are marked "Mom," "Dad," or "Both" so you know who they're for, whether that role is filled by you, your partner, or someone helping make this baby possible.

MALE FERTILITY TESTING: UNDERSTANDING SPERM HEALTH (DAD)

You've probably heard that it starts with the egg, but we're flipping that. We're starting with the sperm. It's wild how many couples struggling to conceive haven't tested the male partner.

Even if you already know there are fertility challenges, understanding your partner's sperm health is crucial for mapping out your next steps.

Take my experience: after almost a year of trying naturally, we found out Brian had a low sperm count. That meant natural conception and IUI weren't even options, and IVF was the only path if we wanted to use both our genetics. If we'd known that from the start, I could have spared myself a year of obsessive research, meticulous charting, and unnecessary stress.

Remember, sperm are half the equation. And if there's a structural issue, like a varicocele (a swollen vein in the scrotum that can overheat the testicles and mess with sperm production), you want to catch it early and decide whether surgery makes sense.

I've worked with couples where years of failed IVF might have been avoided if the varicocele had been handled upfront. No one wants to reach the point where her biological clock is blaring and the fear of never having a baby starts to settle in. And the unspoken frustration: *What if he had gotten the varicocele fixed... would we have a family by now?* starts to stick.

The foundational work you learned in the Survive to Thrive and Spirit protocols can be game-changing for male fertility. Reducing inflammation, balancing hormones, and supporting overall health create the environment sperm need to thrive. But once you have the results of a semen analysis and DNA fragmentation test, you can get even more specific with lifestyle, nutrition, and supplementation.

That's why we're starting here, with the male-only testing that's too often skipped but could impact creating the family of your dreams.

SEMEN ANALYSIS (DAD)

A semen analysis gives a snapshot of overall sperm health. It evaluates how many sperm are being produced, how well they move, how they are shaped, and whether the environment they live in supports fertilization. This test should be done early, even when the focus has been placed on the female partner. Male factors are common and often easier to improve than most people expect.

What this test evaluates:

- Sperm count, which reflects overall sperm production
- Motility, which shows how well sperm move and how many are swimming forward
- Morphology, which looks at sperm shape and structure
- Volume, which measures how much semen is produced
- pH, which reflects how supportive the semen environment is for sperm survival

How to Test

The test requires a semen sample, usually collected through masturbation at a fertility clinic or lab. Some labs allow at-home collection, but timing is important, and samples must be delivered quickly to ensure accuracy.

When to Test

There is no specific timing required. Most doctors recommend two to five days of abstinence beforehand for the most accurate results. Longer abstinence is not better and can actually worsen motility.

Target Ranges

Reference ranges vary slightly by lab, but generally healthy values include:

- Sperm count of at least 15 million per milliliter or 39 million per ejaculation
- Motility of at least 40% moving sperm
- Morphology with at least 4% normally shaped sperm
- Volume of at least 1.5 milliliters
- pH between 7.2 and 8.0

Possible Causes of Low or Abnormal Results

- Hormone imbalances, such as low testosterone
- Chronic stress and poor sleep
- Inflammation or infection
- Varicocele, enlarged veins around the testicle
- Heat exposure from laptops, hot tubs, or saunas
- Nutrient deficiencies
- Smoking, weed, alcohol, or other recreational drugs
- Toxin exposure from food, water, or personal care products

Possible Solutions to Discuss With Your Doctor

- Survive to Thrive Protocol to support hormone balance, reduce inflammation, and improve sperm production
- Evaluation and treatment of hormone imbalances, if present
- Assessment and treatment of infection or inflammation
- Review of medications, supplements, and environmental exposures that could impact sperm
- Medical or procedural options, such as Clomid or varicocele repair when appropriate

Questions for Your Doctor Based on Results

- Which specific markers in my semen analysis are most concerning, and why?
- What do you think is driving these abnormalities?
- What additional testing would help clarify the root cause?
- What changes should we prioritize first, and for how long?
- When should we retest to see if interventions are working?
- At what point would medical treatment be recommended?

If Results Look Normal, But Pregnancy Isn't Happening

A normal semen analysis does not always mean healthy sperm. Some sperm look fine on paper but struggle to fertilize an egg or carry healthy DNA. If pregnancy is not happening despite normal results, it is time to look deeper rather than assuming bad luck.

Questions to Ask Your Doctor if Results Look Normal

- Could sperm DNA fragmentation be contributing?
- Would oxidative stress testing give us more insight?
- Are we good candidates for natural conception or timed cycles?
- Are there additional male-factor tests we have not explored yet?

DNA FRAGMENTATION TESTING (DAD)

DNA fragmentation testing looks at how damaged the sperm's DNA is. This is more important than most people realize. Even when sperm count, motility, and morphology look normal, damaged DNA can still interfere with embryo development and increase the risk of miscarriage. This test goes a layer deeper than a basic semen analysis and gives clearer insight into the genetic quality of the sperm.

What this test evaluates:

- The percentage of sperm with damaged or broken DNA
- Overall sperm genetic integrity
- Potential risk factors for poor embryo development or pregnancy loss

How to Test

The test is done using a sperm sample, typically collected at a fertility clinic or specialized lab. The sample is analyzed using specific assays designed to detect DNA damage. Your doctor will review the results and discuss next steps.

When to Test

This test is especially helpful if:

- Semen analysis results are normal, but pregnancy is not happening
- There have been multiple failed IVF or ICSI cycles
- There is a history of recurrent pregnancy loss
- You want a deeper look at sperm quality before starting IVF or ICSI

Target Ranges

While ranges can vary slightly by lab, general guidelines include:

- DNA fragmentation under 15% is considered optimal

- Levels between 15 and 30% may reduce fertility potential
- Levels above 30% are associated with significantly reduced outcomes

Lower is always better when it comes to DNA fragmentation.

Possible Causes of High DNA Fragmentation

- Oxidative stress
- Chronic inflammation
- Poor sleep or high stress
- Smoking, weed, alcohol, or recreational drugs
- Environmental toxin exposure
- Varicocele
- Infections or untreated medical conditions
- Advanced paternal age

Possible Solutions to Discuss With Your Doctor

- Survive to Thrive Protocol to reduce oxidative stress, improve cellular repair, and support sperm DNA integrity
- Identification and treatment of infections or inflammation
- Evaluation and treatment of varicocele, if present
- Review of medications and environmental exposures
- Targeted antioxidant or medical support when appropriate and guided by testing

Questions for Your Doctor Based on Results

- What do you believe is contributing most to my DNA fragmentation levels?
- Should we evaluate for infection, inflammation, hormones, or varicocele?
- What interventions do you recommend prioritizing first?
- How long should we implement changes before retesting?

- How do these results impact our chances with natural conception versus IVF or ICSI?

MENSTRUAL CYCLE (MOM)

Restore the Cycle, Then Build the Baby

When Sophia, a 44-year-old woman with PCOS, came to me, she had already started her own version of the Survive to Thrive Protocol and was seeing amazing results. Her doctors had told her that only medication, like birth control, could regulate her 47-day cycles. But she trusted her instincts and believed that what I call "lifestyle vitamins" could make a difference in her fertility.

And she was right. Her 47-day cycles shifted into a textbook 28-day cycle. Her PCOS symptoms eased. Her hormone levels, which doctors had called hopeless, started to look more like those of a woman ten years younger. Even her AMH, a number most doctors treat as fixed, moved back into the normal range.

With her natural fertility restored, Sophia set her sights on IVF. Up until then, she had endured five failed IVF cycles. Each round had chipped away at her body, her spirit, and her hope. Every doctor gave her the same line: "You're 44. This is the best you are going to get."

But Sophia's gut told her otherwise. She knew the answers she needed weren't online, so she reached out to me.

With her body already in conception mode and with me guiding her on the right IVF protocol to discuss with her doctor, her very next cycle produced four beautiful blastocysts in one round. Compare that to her previous four rounds, which had given her only one blastocyst total.

On her first transfer, she got pregnant.

And the rewards from her work kept on coming.

Her pregnancy was so smooth that her OB/GYN kept asking if she was sure she had used her own eggs and not a donor's. Sophia proudly said yes. Her doctor even called it "the pregnancy of a 34-year-old." There were no typical issues that come with a high-risk label or gestational diabetes, even though it ran in her family.

Sophia's story proves that when you blend smart science with real healing, IVF does not have to feel like a battle. Pregnancy does not have to feel fragile. Motherhood does not have to start in survival mode.

You get to create from calm, clarity, and confidence… and kiss your baby sooner.

What if I told you your cycle is supposed to feel like almost nothing? No racing to the bathroom to avoid bleeding through your pants. No spotting between periods. No cycles that are too short or too long. No cramping, back pain, clots, headaches, or intense PMS. Simply a mild, manageable period that comes and goes without drama.

Many women are told that unpredictable, painful, and disruptive menstrual cycles are "normal" and are often casually given birth control to manage the symptoms. While these experiences may be common, they are not signs of a normally functioning reproductive system. They are signals that something is a bit off and needs attention, not only for fertility but also for overall health, quality of life, and long-term wellness.

Many factors can influence your menstrual cycle, depending on the patterns and symptoms you're seeing. The sections below will help you understand what's normal, what different symptoms could mean, and which questions to bring to your doctor when something doesn't feel right.

Learning how to read and understand your menstrual cycle can improve how you feel every single month of your life and can also play a powerful role in improving pregnancy outcomes.

How to Track and Evaluate

- Track cycle length from day one of bleeding to the day before your next period starts for several months

Target Ranges

- An ideal cycle length is 28 days. That said, a consistent cycle between 26 and 32 days is still considered healthy.
- Clear signs of ovulation each cycle (we will discuss this next)
- Period lasting 4 to 5 days of moderate flow and no clots
- PMS that is mild or minimal

What a Shorter Follicular Phase Could Mean

The follicular phase runs from the start of your period to ovulation and is your egg's prep time. If it's too short, your body might be rushing egg development, which could affect maturity. That doesn't always mean poor-quality eggs, but if you're struggling to conceive and have short cycles, it's worth investigating.

Questions to Ask Your Doctor:

- Could a short follicular phase affect my egg quality or fertility?
- Can we do an ultrasound to see how my follicles are developing?
- What options would you recommend to support this phase?

What a Shorter Luteal Phase Could Mean

The luteal phase continues from ovulation to your next period. This is your progesterone window, when your body builds a thick, supportive lining for a possible pregnancy. If it's too short, it could point to low progesterone, which makes implantation harder.

Even if the egg is strong, it needs enough time in a stable, welcoming environment to settle in and grow. If that window closes too soon, it simply does not get the chance.

Questions to Ask Your Doctor:

- Can we track my progesterone levels after ovulation through the end of my cycle?
- What could help lengthen and support this phase?

What a Long Menstrual Cycle Could Mean

Cycles longer than 32 days may point to delayed ovulation. Your body may be taking longer to mature a follicle, or it may signal something like PCOS. If your cycle runs long consistently, it's time to dig deeper.

Questions to Ask Your Doctor:

- What could be causing these longer cycles?
- Is PCOS a possibility?
- Can we track my follicle growth and hormone levels?

- What other tests would help us figure this out?

What No Cycle Could Mean

No period (amenorrhea) is your body yelling for help. It's not something to fix with birth control and move on from—it's a sign that something bigger is off. It could be stress, under-eating, intense workouts, thyroid issues, PCOS, or low ovarian reserve. The silence is a message. Time to listen.

Questions to Ask Your Doctor:

- Why do you think I'm not getting a period?
- What testing could give us real answers?
- What are our next steps based on those results?

What Heavy or Painful Periods Could Mean

This could be a sign of endometriosis, polyps, fibroids, or hormone imbalance, such as high estrogen or low progesterone.

Questions to Ask Your Doctor:

- Could this be endo, fibroids, polyps, or hormone-related?
- What tests would help us find out?
- What treatments target the root cause?

What Blood Clots in Your Period Could Mean

Clots may indicate that your uterus isn't shedding its lining efficiently. High estrogen or uterine abnormalities like fibroids or polyps could be the issue.

Questions to Ask Your Doctor:

- What could be causing these clots?
- Are there any scans or tests that would help confirm it?

What Severe PMS or Cramping Could Mean

PMS symptoms like mood swings, fatigue, bloating, and irritability often signal hormone imbalance. Painful cramps may mean prostaglandin levels are too high. Prostaglandins are inflammatory chemicals that tell the uterus to contract. When there are too many, those contractions can become stronger and more painful than they should be.

Questions to Ask Your Doctor:

- Could high prostaglandins or hormone shifts be behind my symptoms?
- Can we track my estrogen and progesterone across the cycle?
- What could help bring my hormones back into balance?

OVULATION AND LH SURGE TESTING (MOM)

Ovulation is the moment your ovary releases an egg, and the window for fertilization opens. When ovulation occurs too early, the follicles that contain the eggs may grow too quickly. That can limit the egg's maturity and hardiness for fertilization. Early ovulation can also shorten the time estrogen has to rise, which is needed to properly build the uterine lining for implantation.

When ovulation happens too late, the body often struggles to mature an egg efficiently. The egg may take too long to develop, which can throw off hormone signals and affect the rest of the cycle.

When ovulation is inconsistent or not happening at all, getting pregnant becomes much harder and sometimes not possible. Ovulation and LH surge testing help us see whether ovulation is actually happening, when it's happening, and how strong that signal really is.

How to Test

Use at-home ovulation predictor kits to detect the surge in luteinizing hormone, or LH, which typically happens about 24 to 36 hours before ovulation. Here's an insider tip: use non-digital ovulation kits that show two lines, rather than digital tests that give a smiley face or a yes/no result. I prefer the two-line tests because you can actually see LH rising as the second line gets darker over a few days. Digital tests can be inconsistent, and this simple switch has helped many of my clients understand their cycles much more clearly.

Track cervical mucus as well. Right before ovulation, it often becomes clear, slippery, and stretchy.

If ovulation predictor kits are leaving you confused, you could discuss bloodwork and ultrasound monitoring with your doctor throughout the cycle to confirm whether ovulation occurred and on which cycle day.

Specifically:

- Bloodwork on cycle days 2 to 4 to assess baseline FSH, LH, estrogen, and sometimes AMH
- Ultrasound monitoring in the follicular phase to track egg development and estrogen response
- Bloodwork around ovulation when LH patterns are unclear
- Bloodwork 5 to 7 days after ovulation to assess progesterone production

This approach helps determine whether ovulation is happening, whether it is occurring too early or too late, and whether hormone levels after ovulation are strong enough to support implantation.

When to Test

If you're just getting started, begin testing around cycle day 7. That may feel early since most people ovulate between days 12 and 16, but it helps catch early ovulation patterns. After tracking for a couple of months, you should have a good sense of your usual ovulation window. From there, start testing about two days before that window when you want to confirm ovulation.

If you're trying to conceive or going through IVF, continue tracking ovulation each month and keep notes. This information should guide conversations with your doctor and help inform decisions about treatments or medications that could support you.

Target Ranges

- Ovulation occurs around cycle day 14 +/- 2 days

- An LH surge is typically reflected by LH levels of 15 mIU/mL or higher
- A period 12 to 14 days later
- Progesterone levels of 3 ng/mL or higher, measured 5 to 7 days after ovulation, confirm ovulation and implantation support

What Early Ovulation Could Mean

Ovulating too early, typically before cycle day 11, can mean the egg didn't have enough time to fully mature. Eggs that mature too quickly may be less resilient and can struggle with fertilization or healthy embryo development. This can happen when FSH is higher than ideal, which is often linked to diminished ovarian reserve, or when stress signals push the body to ovulate too soon.

Early ovulation can also affect the uterine lining. Estrogen needs time to rise in order to thicken the lining. When ovulation happens too early, that window can be shortened, leaving the lining too thin to support implantation.

Questions to Ask Your Doctor if You Ovulate Early:

- Could my eggs be maturing too quickly? How can we check?
- Would an ultrasound to measure follicle size before ovulation help?
- Can we check my uterine lining near ovulation to see if it's ready for implantation?
- Are my progesterone levels strong enough after ovulation?

What Late Ovulation Could Mean

Late ovulation (after day 16) isn't always a problem, but depending on the cause, it can impact both egg quality and lining receptivity.

If estrogen is too low beforehand, the lining may not build up well.

When ovulation is delayed, estrogen can act on the uterine lining for too long, causing it to get thick and overgrown. Without enough progesterone stepping in at the right time, the lining may not become the cozy, supportive environment an embryo needs to implant.

Questions to Ask Your Doctor if You Ovulate Late:

- Could this be linked to PCOS, thyroid issues, or something else? What tests can confirm?
- Are my estrogen and progesterone levels where they need to be before and after ovulation?
- Can we check my lining near ovulation to make sure it's implantation-ready?

What No Ovulation Could Mean (Anovulation)

If you're not ovulating at all, your body isn't releasing an egg, so pregnancy isn't possible. Signs of anovulation include irregular cycles, skipped periods, or consistently negative Ovulation Predictor Kits.

Possible Causes of Anovulation:

- PCOS (often with high LH, irregular or absent ovulation)
- Thyroid dysfunction
- High prolactin levels
- Nutrient deficiencies, chronic stress, or over-exercising
- Low ovarian reserve

Questions to Ask Your Doctor if You're Not Ovulating:

- Could PCOS, thyroid, or prolactin be the cause? What tests can confirm?
- Should I check my AMH or FSH to look at ovarian reserve?
- Is there a way to support natural ovulation before jumping to medication?

ANTRAL FOLLICLE COUNT (AFC) (MOM)

Now that we know whether you have a healthy menstrual cycle, we can look at the other factors necessary for you to successfully conceive, starting with how many eggs you produce each month. To do this, we can perform an antral follicle count (AFC), a transvaginal ultrasound that gives a snapshot of how many follicles are hanging out in your ovaries. Since each follicle holds an immature egg, this test helps estimate your ovarian reserve—basically how many eggs you might have left.

When to Test

This test is best done between cycle days 2 and 4, before your body starts gearing up for ovulation.

Target Results

I hesitate to give a strict target for follicle count because I've seen successful outcomes across a wide range. Some of my clients have one or two follicles growing, while others have over thirty.

A high AFC (20+) is often seen as a major advantage, but it's not always that simple. In some cases, especially with PCOS or other hormone imbalances, a high count means lots of follicles, but many aren't maturing properly. The most common IVF client I work with is someone who produces plenty of eggs but ends up with few embryos, or few healthy ones, developing.

But with the right protocol, timing, and execution, my clients have doubled or even tripled the number of embryos they've created.

If you're trying to conceive naturally, it can also help to work with a practitioner who tracks how many days your follicles have to grow before ovulation and how large they're getting. That kind of data gives you clearer insight into what your body might need to create healthy embryos.

Questions to Discuss With Your Doctor if AFC Is on the Lower End:

- How do my AFC results compare to my age, AMH, and FSH levels? Are they consistent with a lower egg reserve?
- If so, what could be causing the lower AFC? Could the lower AFC for my age be due to endometriosis?
- Would you recommend any medications to help support my AFC? I have heard that starting with either Clomid or letrozole could be an option, but what do you think?

- Are there any other medications that you would recommend?

Questions to Discuss With Your Doctor if AFC Is on the Higher End:

- How do my AFC results compare to my age, AMH, and FSH levels?
- Is there other testing that could uncover if I have PCOS or not?
- Would it be helpful to track my follicles and lining in a natural cycle to see how they are growing and the size they are at ovulation?

HYSTEROSALINGOGRAM (HSG) (MOM)

An HSG is a test that checks whether your fallopian tubes are open so your egg can actually meet sperm. If the tubes are blocked, natural conception isn't possible. This is a key test if you're trying to conceive naturally or if previous testing suggests potential tubal issues.

An HSG can also show fluid in or around the fallopian tubes. If fluid is present, especially inside a tube, it could indicate a hydrosalpinx, meaning the tube is blocked and filled with fluid. That fluid can leak back into the uterus and make implantation less likely. It can also signal prior infection, inflammation, or scar tissue. This condition is important to address before trying naturally or moving forward with IVF.

When to Test

HSG is usually done shortly after your period ends, around cycle days 5 to 10, when your uterine lining is thinnest. That timing helps give the clearest image without anything getting in the way.

Now here's something you'll be glad you knew ahead of time. Check with your doctor first, but I usually suggest taking three Tylenol about 30 minutes before the procedure. It will not make it painless, but it could take the edge off and make the whole thing more manageable.

Target Results

Both tubes are open and clear, with no fluid buildup. If the dye flows freely through both tubes and spills into the abdominal cavity without delay or pooling, you are good to go.

What to Do If the Results Aren't Ideal

If one or both tubes appear blocked, here's what to consider:

- Sometimes a blockage is just a temporary spasm. Your doctor may suggest repeating the test to confirm.
- If the blockage seems real, follow-up testing such as a sonohysterogram or laparoscopy can provide more detail, depending on what else is going on.
- If fluid is seen in a tube, especially consistent with hydrosalpinx, this is important to address. That fluid can flow back into the uterus and lower implantation rates. In IVF cycles, many doctors recommend removing or clipping the affected tube before transfer to improve outcomes.
- Some blockages can be treated, but fallopian tubes are incredibly tiny and delicate. Surgery to open them is not always effective or recommended.

In many cases, I suggest exploring pelvic floor physical therapy or seeing a specialist in fertility-focused abdominal massage. Some practitioners have had success improving blockages this way. If both tubes are fully closed and conservative approaches have not helped, IVF might be the most efficient path forward.

Questions to Discuss With Your Doctor if Your Results Aren't Ideal:

- Could this be a temporary spasm, or is there a true blockage?
- Should we repeat the HSG or use a different method to confirm?
- Is there any fluid in the tubes, and if so, does it look like hydrosalpinx?

- If fluid is present, how could it affect natural conception or IVF outcomes?
- Are there any procedures or therapies you've seen that actually improve tubal function?

TESTS FOR THE UTERINE LINING (MOM)

Think of your uterine lining as the ultimate welcome mat for a fertilized egg. Each cycle, your body builds it up to create a soft, nutrient-rich place where an embryo can settle in and stay.

Most people know a thin lining can make implantation harder. But a lining that's too thick can be problematic, too. Like in Goldilocks, your lining can't be too thin or too thick. It needs to be *just right.*

I've had many clients who have been told anything over 14 millimeters is no big deal. I disagree. In my experience, once the lining creeps past 14 mm, implantation rarely works.

Thickness isn't the only factor. You also want to know if there's inflammation, infection, fluid, a growth, or a blockage that could interfere with implantation. These issues don't always show up on a basic ultrasound, and they often go unchecked even after months, sometimes years, of failed implantations, biochemical pregnancies, or early losses.

In this section, we'll walk through the tests that uncover what's really going on with your lining. We're looking for:

- The right thickness at the right time
- A healthy, receptive environment
- Nothing standing in the way of your embryo implanting and staying

Because your uterus isn't only a landing pad. It's the nest that needs to support a pregnancy for the next nine months.

LINING THICKNESS

When to Test

The best time to check lining thickness is right before or after ovulation. A transvaginal ultrasound can measure the thickness and show the pattern. Both of these give clues about whether your lining is receptive.

Target Results:

- I personally like to see 8–13 mm.
- A trilaminar (triple stripe) pattern is a great sign of receptivity.

If Your Uterine Lining Is Too Thin

This could be from low estrogen, poor blood flow, uterine scarring (like from a D&C), or general hormonal issues. Outside of the Survive to Thrive and Spirit protocols, focus on improving blood flow and nourishment to help it grow and become more receptive. Here are some ideas to discuss with your doctor:

Supplements That Could Help:

- L-Arginine (1000 mg twice per day): supports uterine blood flow
- Vitamin E (400 IU twice per day): supports endometrial health
- Baby aspirin: may boost circulation, but use caution if you also take Vitamin E due to blood thinning

Lifestyle and Circulation Boosters:

- Red light therapy or hyperbaric oxygen: promote oxygen delivery
- Pelvic floor therapy or fertility massage (Mayan or Mercier): support circulation
- Phytoestrogenic foods: flaxseeds, red clover, royal jelly, maca
- Herbal teas: red raspberry leaf (2–3 cups a day)
- Acupuncture: supports hormone regulation and blood flow
- Castor oil packs: promote healthy pelvic circulation

Questions to Ask Your Doctor if Your Lining Is Too Thin:

- Could my estrogen levels be too low? Should we check it?
- If I don't tolerate estrogen well, could letrozole help build my lining instead?
- Could my past procedure or scarring be affecting my uterus?

If Your Uterine Lining Is Too Thick

If your uterine lining is too thick, it could be due to estrogen dominance, polyps, or uterine hyperplasia, where excess estrogen causes the lining to build up abnormally. Focus on reducing inflammation and supporting estrogen balance.

Hormone-Supporting Steps:

- Anti-inflammatory foods: whole foods, especially cruciferous vegetables, turmeric, and wild blueberries
- Liver support: milk thistle, dandelion root, broccoli sprouts

Questions to Ask Your Doctor if Your Lining Is Too Thick:

- Could I be estrogen-dominant? If it is possible:
    - Should we test my estrogen and progesterone in the luteal phase?
    - Would progesterone help balance my estrogen levels?
- Should we check for polyps or hyperplasia with an ultrasound or hysteroscopy?

ENDOMETRIAL BIOPSY

When it comes to uncovering sneaky issues that can block implantation, two tests top my list: a hysteroscopy and an endometrial biopsy. Hysteroscopy gives you a direct view of the uterine cavity to spot anything physically obstructing it, such as a polyp, fluid, or scar tissue. The biopsy, on the other hand, gives you a behind-the-scenes look at what you can't see, specifically inflammation or infection that could quietly prevent implantation.

The main thing we're checking for is chronic endometritis, a low-grade, lingering inflammation in the uterine lining. It doesn't always come with symptoms, but it can absolutely impact embryo success.

The key test here is the CD138 plasma cell stain, which identifies plasma cells, your immune system's "smoke signal" for inflammation. If they're present, that's your red flag to treat before any transfer or fertility treatment. It's the fastest, most affordable way to confirm if inflammation is there.

Then there are the molecular tests:

- EMMA (Endometrial Microbiome Metagenomic Analysis) examines the overall bacterial balance in the uterus, assessing whether the environment is mostly healthy, Lactobacillus-dominant, or disrupted.
- ALICE (Analysis of Infectious Chronic Endometritis) digs deeper to identify which bacteria might be causing inflammation, even when plasma cells aren't visible yet.

In short:

- To confirm infection or inflammation, start with CD138.
- To find out what's causing it, use ALICE.
- To see the full microbial ecosystem, consider EMMA.

Most women only need the CD138 test. But if inflammation or failed transfers keep happening, or you want to be sure nothing within your control could block implantation, ALICE and EMMA can offer the extra detail needed to address the root cause before trying again.

When to Test

An endometrial biopsy is usually done between cycle days 5 and 14: after your period but before your lining gets too thick.

Pro tip: If you're already scheduled for a hysteroscopy, ask your doctor to do the biopsy during the same appointment.

What the Results Could Mean For a CD138 Plasma Stain:

- Normal: No plasma cells found, no chronic endometritis.
- Abnormal: Plasma cells are present, which means inflammation is affecting implantation.

What the Results Could Mean for EMMA/ALICE:

- **Low Lactobacillus:** Not enough of the good bacteria to support a healthy uterine environment
- **Harmful bacteria:** A sign that infection could be blocking implantation or causing inflammation

What to Do If the Biopsy Comes Back Abnormal:

- If your CD138 plasma stain is abnormal (plasma cells found):
  - The first step is usually a 10- to 14-day course of antibiotics.
  - After treatment, your doctor may recommend a repeat biopsy to confirm the infection is gone. I personally prefer a repeat biopsy so you know for sure it has cleared. Chronic endometritis sometimes requires a different antibiotic if a second round of treatment is needed.
- If your ALICE test is abnormal (specific harmful bacteria found):
  - Your doctor may prescribe a targeted antibiotic based on which bacteria were identified.
  - After treatment, follow up with vaginal and oral probiotics to restore balance.
- If your EMMA test is abnormal (low Lactobacillus or bacterial imbalance):
  - Focus on rebuilding a healthy uterine microbiome with high-quality probiotics, both oral and vaginal.
  - Supporting gut and immune health with anti-inflammatory foods and prebiotic fiber can also help maintain long-term balance of beneficial bacteria.

Questions to Ask Your Doctor If the Biopsy Comes Back Abnormal:

- What's the treatment plan to clear the infection?
- Can we repeat the biopsy afterward to make sure it's resolved?
- What do you think about EMMA or ALICE testing based on what we already know, or can we move forward without them?

SALINE SONOGRAM (SALINE INFUSION ULTRASOUND)

Think of a saline sonogram (also called a saline infusion ultrasound or sonohysterogram) as a way to inspect your uterus from the outside. It gives you a clear view inside the uterus to spot anything that might be getting in the way of implantation. Unlike a regular ultrasound, this test uses sterile saline to gently fill the uterine cavity during an in-office scan. The fluid opens up the space enough to highlight things like fibroids, polyps, or an irregular shape that could make it harder for pregnancy to take hold.

When to Test

The best window is right after your period but before ovulation, usually between cycle days 5 and 12. Your uterine lining is still thin, which helps the view. And since you haven't ovulated yet, there's no risk of disrupting a potential pregnancy.

What the Results Could Mean

What you want to see: a smooth, open uterine cavity with nothing blocking the view.

What might show up:

- Fibroids or polyps: Benign growths that take up space and may interfere with implantation
- Scar tissue (Asherman's syndrome): Adhesions that can thin the lining or make it patchy
- Septate or irregular-shaped uterus: Structural issues that can lower chances of implantation or raise miscarriage risk

- Fluid in the uterus: A possible sign of infection, inflammation, or a blocked tube

What to Do If the Ultrasound Comes Back Abnormal

Here's what to consider depending on what shows up.

Polyps or Fibroids

If they're small and not invading the cavity, your doctor may suggest leaving them alone. But if this is the only abnormal finding and you've been struggling to conceive or stay pregnant, it's worth a closer look. Polyps are usually easy to remove. Fibroids are trickier. Removal has to go deep enough to get the root, which can temporarily reduce blood flow to the ovaries. If you're over forty or have a low egg count, it's often best to create embryos first and save fibroid surgery for later so you don't lose precious time during recovery.

Scar Tissue or Adhesions (Including Asherman's Syndrome)

Not every saline sonogram will catch scar tissue, since technique and equipment play a role. If any adhesions or areas of scarring are seen or suspected, a hysteroscopy is usually the next step to confirm and remove them. In some cases, when the scarring is extensive and the uterine walls stick together, it is called Asherman's syndrome. Even mild scar tissue can interfere with implantation, so clearing it can make a big difference.

Uterine Septum or Irregular Shape

If the shape looks off, surgery might be needed to correct it. There's also a strong link between a uterine septum and endometriosis, so if one is found, ask your doctor whether endometriosis testing makes sense.

Fluid in the Uterus

This could mean inflammation, infection, or a blocked fallopian tube, allowing fluid to leak back in. A hysteroscopy may be needed to get a closer look before moving forward with trying to conceive.

Questions to Ask Your Doctor If the Ultrasound Comes Back Abnormal:

- If I have polyps, would removing them improve my chances of implantation?
- If I have fibroids, do they need to be removed, or could we move forward without surgery?
    - At what point do fibroids become worth removing, even if we're not sure they're the cause?
    - How could fibroid removal affect blood flow to my ovaries and my recovery timeline?
    - If I'm doing IVF, should we create embryos before scheduling fibroid surgery?
- If a uterine septum is found, should we also consider that I might have endometriosis?
- What could be causing fluid in my uterus?
    - Could this be a sign of endometriosis?
    - What's the next step to treat it?
- If everything looks normal but I've been trying for over a year, is a hysteroscopy still worth doing to double-check?

SURGICAL HYSTEROSCOPY

If you've been trying to conceive for years and still don't have answers, a surgical hysteroscopy might be the test that finally gives you clarity. Unlike a saline ultrasound, which looks inside the uterus from the outside, a hysteroscopy uses a small camera to go directly inside your uterus and inspect every detail up close.

I strongly recommend this test, especially if you've had past surgeries, a C-section, a D&C, a "normal" saline ultrasound but still no implantation, or any history of miscarriage. It can detect features that a saline ultrasound might miss, such as Cesarean scar defects, scar tissue, or subtle uterine abnormalities that could be blocking implantation.

A saline ultrasound can be helpful, but it's only as good as the technician and the equipment. It might miss thin bands of scar tissue or small pockets of fluid, like hydrosalpinx, that can interfere with implantation. A hysteroscopy gives you a direct view from the inside. It's far less subjective and much more precise.

This isn't a test you want anyone doing. If your doctor finds polyps, scar tissue, or thickened lining during the procedure, you want someone who can remove it with fertility in mind. Taking out too much could make it hard to rebuild your lining, and in rare cases, the lining may not fully regenerate. That's the worst-case scenario, but it's important to choose your surgeon wisely.

This procedure is typically done under anesthesia, and for good reason. It can be extremely painful without it. Your cervix wasn't designed for equipment to pass through it. Some doctors offer to do it while you're awake, but I don't recommend it. If something is found, you'll want to be under anesthesia so your doctor can remove it safely and comfortably.

It's a bit more effort than a saline ultrasound, but that extra step could uncover what every other test has missed and finally explain why implantation hasn't been happening. I even think of a hysteroscopy as "paving the way" for pregnancy. Literally. Even when the doctor finds nothing, that light sweep of the lining leaves behind a fresh, receptive surface. Think of it as dermabrasion for your uterus.

When to Test

A hysteroscopy is typically done after your period but before ovulation, usually between cycle days 6 and 12. That's when your lining is thin enough for clear visibility.

During that cycle, you should not try to conceive naturally or plan an embryo transfer. The following month is usually fine, depending on what was found and whether any tissue was removed.

What the Results Could Mean

Normal: A smooth, clear uterine cavity with no obstructions.

Possible findings:

- Fibroids or polyps: Growths that may interfere with implantation
- Scar tissue or adhesions (including Asherman's syndrome): Can prevent proper lining development
- Uterine septum or abnormal shape: May lower implantation chances or increase miscarriage risk

- Fluid in the uterus: May indicate inflammation, infection, or hydrosalpinx
- Cesarean scar defect (isthmocele): A weak spot that can trap fluid or affect implantation

What to Do If the Hysteroscopy Finds an Issue

Polyps or Fibroids

Small polyps are usually easy to remove and may be worth addressing if they're the only issue. Fibroids can be trickier. Ideally, they're removed at the root, but recovery can temporarily reduce blood flow to the ovaries. If you're over forty or have low ovarian reserve, you may want to create embryos first to preserve your timeline before surgery.

Scar Tissue or Adhesions (Including Asherman's Syndrome)

A hysteroscopy is one of the best tools for diagnosing and removing scar tissue. Clearing these adhesions can often restore a healthy lining and improve implantation success.

Uterine Septum or Structural Issues

A uterine septum can interfere with implantation and increase miscarriage risk. If one is found, surgery may help. It's also smart to ask about testing for endometriosis, since the two often co-occur.

Fluid in the Uterus

Whether caused by hydrosalpinx, infection, or inflammation, fluid can disrupt implantation. Further testing may be needed before moving forward with conception.

Cesarean Scar Defect (Isthmocele)

This weak spot from a prior C-section can trap fluid or interfere with embryo attachment. In some cases, surgical repair is necessary to restore a healthy uterine surface.

Questions to Ask Your Doctor If the Hysteroscopy Finds Something:

- What do you recommend for next steps based on what you found?
- If fibroids are present, do they need to be removed now, or can we proceed without surgery?
  - At what point do fibroids become a likely barrier to pregnancy?
  - If fibroids are removed, how could that affect ovarian blood flow and recovery time?
  - If I'm doing IVF, should I create embryos before any surgery?
- If a uterine septum is found, should we also consider that I might have endometriosis?
- What could be causing fluid in my uterus?
  - Could this be a sign of endometriosis?
  - What's the next step to treat it?

MRI

An MRI (magnetic resonance imaging) provides detailed images of your pelvic organs, including the uterus, ovaries, and surrounding tissues. Unlike an ultrasound, which can miss subtle issues, an MRI provides a much clearer picture.

I often recommend an MRI if there's suspicion of endometriosis or adenomyosis before jumping to laparoscopy. I think of endometriosis as vines that can twist around your reproductive organs, wrapping tightly and restricting function. MRI imaging helps reveal where those "vines" might be growing and which organs they're affecting.

While a laparoscopy is still the only way to officially confirm endometriosis or remove it, an MRI can often detect signs of both endometriosis and adenomyosis. Adenomyosis, which occurs when uterine lining tissue burrows into the muscle wall of the uterus, can't usually be confirmed with hysteroscopy, but an MRI can visualize it clearly through characteristic patterns like a thickened uterine wall or small cysts inside the muscle layer.

In short, an MRI can often give enough information to help decide whether surgery is even necessary.

When to Test

An MRI is worth considering when something feels off, but standard tests keep saying everything looks "normal." If you're dealing with pelvic pain, heavy or painful periods, unexplained infertility, or bowel or bladder issues that flare with your cycle, an MRI can help uncover what's going on beneath the surface.

What the Results Could Mean

A normal MRI should show a clean, healthy uterus with no abnormal thickening, cysts, or shadows.

If adenomyosis is present, the MRI may show a thickened junctional zone (the layer between the uterine lining and muscle wall).

If endometriosis is present, it can reveal:

- Endometriomas (ovarian cysts filled with old blood)
- Signs of deep infiltrating endometriosis (when endometrial-like tissue starts growing into or around organs such as the bowel or bladder)

What to Do If the MRI Finds an Issue

If signs of adenomyosis or endometriosis show up, your next steps depend on your symptoms and fertility goals.

Treatment often focuses on calming inflammation while protecting fertility. Hormonal options such as birth control or GnRH medications (Lupron, Orilissa, Synarel, or Zoladex) can reduce estrogen, which fuels both adenomyosis and endometriosis. These medications temporarily put the ovaries into "sleep mode," giving the uterus and surrounding tissues a break to recover.

If you want to go beyond medication alone, this is where the protocols come in. The Survive to Thrive Protocol focuses on lowering inflammation through food, stress reduction, sleep, and strategic supplementation. The Spirit Protocol supports emotional regulation and nervous system balance, which also play a role in uterine health and implantation.

Together, these approaches work on the environment, not just the infection, so you are not only treating the issue but also strengthening the foundation.

Surgery is sometimes needed for more severe adenomyosis, but if fertility preservation is the goal, make sure the plan includes a uterine-sparing procedure such as an adenomyomectomy, not a hysterectomy.

For endometriosis, surgery is the only way to officially diagnose and remove the lesions. The most effective approach is excision surgery, which removes the disease at its root rather than burning the surface (which is called ablation). Some surgeons use robotic-assisted laparoscopy, which can offer enhanced precision and visualization. In experienced hands, this approach may help preserve healthy tissue and surrounding organs, which is especially important when fertility is a priority. That said, a highly skilled laparoscopic surgeon may achieve similar results without robotics.

Questions to Ask Your Doctor If the MRI Finds an Issue:

- Do you recommend any additional testing, or is this result satisfactory enough to move forward?
- What are my treatment options, and how do they align with my fertility goals?
    - If Surgery Is Recommended:
        - Who do you recommend I use for this procedure?
        - Will you use excision or ablation?
        - Will these findings impact my IVF success or fertility outlook?

LAPAROSCOPY

A laparoscopy is a surgical procedure that gives your doctor a full view of your pelvic cavity. Unlike ultrasounds or even a hysteroscopy, which stays focused on the inside of the uterus, a laparoscopy looks outside the uterus at your ovaries, fallopian tubes, and surrounding pelvic organs. Small incisions are made so a tiny camera can explore what's really going on. It's the only way to officially diagnose endometriosis and to identify and treat pelvic scar tissue or structural issues that could interfere with egg pickup, tubal function, or even implantation.

Endometriosis happens when tissue similar to the uterine lining grows outside the uterus. That tissue doesn't belong there, and it can cause inflammation, pain, bloating, and fertility issues. Over time, it can also lead to adhesions, which are bands of scar tissue that stick organs together. When ovaries or fallopian tubes are pulled out of place or restricted, egg pickup can become harder, even if ovulation is happening normally.

Adenomyosis is similar, but instead of growing outside the uterus, the tissue burrows into the muscle wall, often leading to heavy or painful periods and a chronically swollen uterus. While laparoscopy can sometimes reveal signs that suggest adenomyosis, like an enlarged or irregular-looking uterus, it can't confirm it. MRI is the best tool for officially diagnosing adenomyosis.

I don't usually recommend laparoscopy as a first step. But if you're dealing with intense periods, clotting, painful sex, bowel issues, unexplained infertility, or if you feel like something isn't right and it's affecting your quality of life, it may be time to consider it. That said, I often start with an MRI. It's noninvasive and can pick up signs of endometriosis, adenomyosis, blocked tubes, or scar tissue, giving you more clarity about whether surgery is worth pursuing.

When I walk clients through this decision, I always start with one key question: how much is this impacting your day-to-day life? If symptoms are manageable and you're not in the middle of IVF, we may try medication to reduce inflammation and manage pain. But if you've had failed embryo transfers, persistent symptoms, or feel like you're running out of answers, a laparoscopy might finally give you the clarity and relief you've been missing.

When to Test

Laparoscopy doesn't need to happen on an exact day of your cycle, but most doctors prefer to do it in the first half, after your period ends and before ovulation, to avoid any early pregnancy risk.

Consider laparoscopy if:

- You have severe endometriosis symptoms that affect quality of life.
- You've had multiple unexplained failed IVF cycles.
- Your MRI or hysteroscopy suggests adhesions, blocked tubes, or hydrosalpinx.

What the Results Could Mean

A clear laparoscopy means no visible endometriosis, scar tissue, tube problems, or structural interference affecting egg pickup or implantation.

If something is found, it might include:

- Endometriosis ranging from small spots to more aggressive lesions that affect organs
- Adhesions that pull or trap ovaries and fallopian tubes, which could interfere with egg pickup or normal tubal movement
- Blocked tubes, which prevent the sperm and egg from meeting
- Hydrosalpinx, a fluid-filled tube that can lower implantation success, needs to be addressed before transfer

What to Do If Laparoscopy Finds an Issue

If your doctor confirms endometriosis, adhesions, or tubal damage, your next steps depend on the severity and your fertility goals. What matters most is that you're working with a surgeon who specializes in excision surgery, meaning they remove the root of the problem rather than burning the surface, while also preserving your fertility.

Some doctors recommend GnRH (gonadotropin-releasing hormone) medications like Lupron before or after surgery. These medications temporarily lower estrogen levels, which helps shrink lesions and reduce inflammation. It also gives your surgeon a clearer view during the procedure and may reduce regrowth afterward.

But here's the caution: if you're preparing for an egg retrieval, especially with lower ovarian reserve, long-term Lupron use can slow everything down to a stop. It puts your ovaries into a deep rest state that may take months to recover from, which could delay your IVF timeline.

If you're doing IVF, you might choose to create and freeze embryos before surgery. But if you're trying naturally and think surgery could be the missing piece, it may be better to skip ovarian suppression altogether.

Questions to Ask Your Doctor If Laparoscopy Finds an Issue:

- What exactly did you find, and how severe is it?
- How could these findings impact my fertility?
- What steps should I take after surgery to prevent endometriosis from coming back?

Remember, when you ask your doctor about functional medicine topics like lifestyle, nutrition, supplements, or holistic health remedies, that's not their specialty. Traditional doctors are trained to diagnose and treat with medicine or procedures, not to figure out why something is happening. Still, it's worth asking for their perspective so you can make informed choices and build a complete picture of your options.

GENETIC TESTING (BOTH)

Whether you've been trying to conceive for years or you've just started and want to avoid wasted time, genetic testing is a key step. Two important tests to consider are carrier screening and karyotype screening.

Carrier screening looks for inherited gene mutations that could affect your child if both partners carry the same condition. Karyotype screening evaluates the number and structure of your chromosomes to identify rearrangements that could impact embryo development or increase miscarriage risk.

Most IVF doctors check carrier screening early, but many wait to suggest karyotype testing until after multiple failed transfers or abnormal PGT (preimplantation genetic testing) results. PGT is helpful, but it is not perfect. If there is an underlying chromosomal issue, then you want to know about it sooner, not after several emotionally and financially draining cycles. That is why I recommend considering both tests upfront.

Only one partner needs to start with carrier screening. If that person is not a carrier, the other partner can usually skip testing. But both partners should complete karyotype screening, since chromosomal rearrangements can affect fertility even when you feel completely healthy.

CARRIER SCREENING (MOM OR DAD AT FIRST)

Carrier screening checks whether you carry inherited gene mutations that could be passed to your child if your partner carries the same condition. You can be completely healthy and still be a carrier. The concern only arises if both partners carry the same mutation.

This test is especially helpful before conception, but it can still provide clarity during fertility treatment or early pregnancy.

COMMON CONDITIONS INCLUDED ON MOST PANELS:

- **Cystic fibrosis (CF):** Affects lung and digestive function
- **Spinal muscular atrophy (SMA):** Causes progressive muscle weakness
- **Fragile X syndrome:** Can lead to intellectual disabilities and fertility issues
- **Sickle cell disease and thalassemia:** Blood disorders that affect oxygen transport
- **Tay-Sachs disease:** A neurodegenerative condition more common in certain ethnic groups
- **Other inherited conditions:** These vary by ethnic background and family history, so if you know of any that run in your family, mention them before testing to make sure they're included.

Quick story: when Brian and I did carrier screening, the genetic counselor asked if there was a family history of mental disorders. We both paused. Knowing our families, I asked, "Can you define mental disorders?" Once she did, we realized she wasn't talking about the "personality quirks" that run deep on both sides. We laughed hard. The genetic counselor did not.

(Moving on!)

When to Test

Carrier screening can be done at any time, but ideally before conception. If you're already pregnant or doing fertility treatments, it can still help you understand potential risks.

What the Results Could Mean:

- **Negative result:** You're not a carrier for anything tested, so your partner doesn't need to be screened.
- **Positive result:** You are a carrier, so your partner should be tested for the same mutation. If you're both carriers, there's a 25%

chance your child could inherit the condition. Genetic counseling can walk you through options.

Questions to Ask Your Doctor if You're a Carrier:

- How serious is this condition, and what would it mean for our child's health?
- Should we consider IVF with PGT-M (testing embryos for specific conditions) to reduce the risk?

KARYOTYPE SCREENING (BOTH)

Karyotype screening evaluates the number and structure of your chromosomes to identify rearrangements that may impact embryo development or increase miscarriage risk. These changes often do not affect your own health, which is why many people have no idea they carry them.

Although it is often suggested only after repeated losses or failed transfers, karyotype screening is a simple blood test that can be done early and may prevent unnecessary cycles.

When to Test

Anytime. But don't wait for multiple losses or failed transfers to be told it's finally time. This simple blood test can be done early and could save you time, money, and heartache.

What the Results Could Mean:

- **Normal result:** You have the expected 46 chromosomes in the correct arrangement. It's unlikely chromosomal issues are causing your fertility struggles.
- **Abnormal result:** You have a chromosomal abnormality that may impact embryo development or pregnancy. Possibilities include:
    - Balanced translocation: A piece of one chromosome has switched places with another. You may feel totally healthy, but

this can lead to embryos with too much or too little genetic material.
  - Unbalanced translocation: Extra or missing pieces of DNA, which can lead to implantation failure, miscarriage, or developmental issues
  - Aneuploidy: Missing or extra chromosomes, such as Turner syndrome (45,X) or Klinefelter syndrome (47,XXY), which can affect reproduction

Questions to Ask Your Doctor if Karyotype Testing Finds an Issue:

- How could this chromosomal issue affect our chances of a successful pregnancy and a healthy baby?
- Should we consider IVF with PGT-SR (testing for structural rearrangements) to help select embryos with balanced genetics?

ENDO, ADENO, FIBROIDS, AND PCOS (MOM)

With most of your diagnostic testing behind you, you and your doctor should now have a clearer picture of what might be making it harder to get or stay pregnant. Now it's time to understand what those clues actually mean and what to do about them.

This section focuses on the most common conditions I see in the women I work with. Some of this will overlap with what we covered earlier in the testing section, but here you'll find more details on how each condition impacts fertility, what treatment options may help, and the key questions to ask your doctor to be sure nothing is missed. Whether you're trying naturally or planning IVF, these insights will help you feel more confident and supported in addressing these common fertility challenges.

ENDOMETRIOSIS

Endometriosis happens when tissue similar to your uterine lining starts growing outside the uterus. Even though it's in the wrong place, this tissue still responds to your hormones each month, causing inflammation, pain, and sometimes scar tissue. For many women, it shows up as painful periods, heavy bleeding with clots, or deep pelvic pain that doesn't feel normal.

The problem isn't only the pain. The inflammation, scar tissue, or fluid buildup can make it harder for the egg and sperm to meet and can also interfere with implantation. If your periods are debilitating or you're living with ongoing pelvic pain, it's a strong sign that something deeper may be going on, and it's worth getting evaluated.

Tests to Confirm Endometriosis

Imaging, like ultrasounds or MRIs, can sometimes detect larger lesions or ovarian cysts, but to know for sure, a laparoscopy is required. You can revisit the earlier sections in this book for more details on both tests. As a general rule, I usually recommend that my clients discuss an MRI with their doctor before moving to a laparoscopy, especially if the goal is simply to confirm or rule out endometriosis.

What Treatment Plans Are Available if You Have Endometriosis

The first step is the Survive to Thrive Protocol. Reducing inflammation and balancing your hormones is the foundation of long-term reproductive health. It also helps ensure that if endometriosis is removed, it stays gone.

If you're trying to conceive naturally, talk to your doctor about medications that help regulate or suppress estrogen levels since estrogen fuels endometriosis. Doing so can help shrink tissue, reduce inflammation, and make your uterus more receptive.

For moderate or severe cases, laparoscopic excision surgery may be needed. This is the preferred method for removing endometriosis lesions and improving your chances of pregnancy. The skill of your surgeon is crucial. Look for someone who specializes in fertility-preserving excision rather than ablation, which often misses deeper disease.

If you're pursuing IVF and endometriosis is suspected or confirmed, your doctor may recommend skipping a fresh transfer and using a suppression protocol with a frozen embryo transfer instead. This approach quiets your hormones for several weeks or months, reducing inflammation and giving your uterus a clean slate. In the embryo transfer section of this book, we'll go deeper into specific protocols to discuss with your doctor if endometriosis is part of your picture.

Questions to Discuss with Your Doctor if You Suspect Endometriosis:

- Could I start with an MRI to check for signs of endometriosis?
- What medications would you recommend to help with conception and implantation while managing inflammation?
- If I need IVF, would a suppression protocol improve my transfer success?
- Should I meet with a surgeon who specializes in excision if surgery might be needed?

ADENOMYOSIS

Adenomyosis happens when tissue from the uterine lining starts growing into the muscular wall of the uterus. This can cause the uterus to enlarge, feel tender, and sometimes change shape. It often leads to very heavy, painful periods and persistent pelvic discomfort that doesn't seem to let up. Over time, the inflammation and structural changes make it harder for fertilization and implantation to happen. If you're experiencing intense cramping, heavy bleeding, or pelvic pain that never fully goes away, it's important to get checked.

How Is Adenomyosis Different from Endometriosis

When I first started researching these two conditions, I couldn't understand why the treatments sounded so similar. If you're feeling that same confusion, here's the simple version. Both conditions involve tissue growing where it shouldn't and are heavily influenced by estrogen, but they affect fertility in different ways.

Endometriosis grows outside the uterus, leading to inflammation, adhesions, and sometimes blocked fallopian tubes. Treatment usually focuses on reducing estrogen and removing the misplaced tissue. Adenomyosis, on the other hand, happens inside the uterine muscle. The tissue burrows into the wall, causing swelling and inflammation, and creating a uterine environment less welcoming to implantation. In this case, it's less about completely shutting down estrogen and more about keeping it steady while supporting progesterone to calm inflammation and restore function.

Tests to Confirm Adenomyosis

Ultrasounds or MRIs are the best ways to identify adenomyosis. They can show a thickened or irregular uterine wall, which is often a key sign. For more details on these tests, revisit the sections on MRI, hysteroscopy, and laparoscopy in this book.

What Treatment Plans Are Available if You Have Adenomyosis

Like with endometriosis, the first step is the Survive to Thrive Protocol. It's the foundation for lowering inflammation, balancing hormones, and creating a healthier reproductive environment.

If you're trying to conceive naturally, talk to your doctor about strategies that help regulate estrogen and support progesterone. That combination can calm the uterus, normalize cycles, and increase the likelihood of implantation.

For IVF, adenomyosis often requires skipping a fresh transfer and using a suppression protocol before a frozen transfer, similar to how endometriosis is managed. Your doctor may recommend quieting your hormones for several weeks to reduce inflammation and reset the uterine environment. Once the uterus is calm, medication is used to carefully rebuild the lining in a more receptive, balanced way. This approach can greatly improve implantation and pregnancy outcomes.

In more advanced cases where medication isn't enough, a surgery called an adenomyomectomy may be considered. This procedure removes the affected tissue while preserving the uterus. It's typically an option only when the adenomyosis is limited to one area and should be done by an experienced surgeon, but for the right patient, it can improve both symptoms and fertility.

Questions to Discuss with Your Doctor if Adenomyosis is Suspected:

- Which imaging test would give us the clearest picture of what's happening with my uterus?

- What treatment options could help reduce symptoms and improve my chances of conceiving naturally?
- If I need IVF, would a suppression protocol improve my implantation rates?
- Should I consider surgery if my symptoms are severe or not improving with medication?

FIBROIDS

Fibroids are noncancerous growths in the uterus that can cause heavy bleeding, irregular cycles, and sometimes make it harder to get pregnant. Their impact depends on their size and location. Some fibroids are harmless and don't need any intervention, while others can distort the uterus, block the fallopian tubes, or interfere with implantation. If you're dealing with heavy, unpredictable periods, bloating that makes you feel like you swallowed a balloon, or unexplained fertility struggles, fibroids could be part of the picture.

Tests to Confirm Fibroids:

- An ultrasound is the first and most common test for spotting fibroids, helping to determine their size, number, and location.
- A saline infusion sonogram (SIS) uses fluid to expand the uterus, which makes smaller or hard-to-see fibroids easier to detect.
- A hysteroscopy allows your doctor to use a tiny camera to look inside the uterus for fibroids that could interfere with implantation.
- An MRI provides the most detailed view and is especially useful if surgery is being considered or if adenomyosis is also suspected.

What Treatment Plans Are Available if You Have Fibroids

The first step is the Survive to Thrive Protocol. Lowering inflammation and balancing your hormones can help slow fibroid growth and ease symptoms. Fibroids thrive on estrogen, so supporting your body in maintaining steady hormone levels is key.

If you're trying to conceive naturally, talk to your doctor about medications that can help regulate hormones and minimize fibroid growth. Some treatments work by lowering estrogen, while others focus on supporting progesterone to help bring balance.

For fibroids that are directly affecting conception or implantation, surgical removal (myomectomy) may be needed. Unlike a hysterectomy, this procedure removes the fibroids while preserving the uterus. The right surgical approach depends on where your fibroids are located.

- A hysteroscopic myomectomy is best for fibroids inside the uterine cavity that interfere with implantation. It's minimally invasive and has a quick recovery.
- A laparoscopic or robotic myomectomy is used for fibroids in the uterine wall or on the outer surface. It's still a fertility-preserving surgery but requires more recovery time.

If you're planning IVF, fibroids inside the uterus or distorting its shape may need to be removed before transfer to give you the best chance at implantation.

Whether fibroid surgery is the right move and when to do it depends entirely on your individual situation. There's no single rule that fits everyone. If you're doing IVF and fibroids are affecting implantation, one strategy is to complete your egg retrievals first and freeze enough embryos to create your family before surgery. This protects your ovarian reserve since recovery can temporarily reduce blood flow to the ovaries and, in some cases, lower AMH or antral follicle count.

However, if your fibroids are clearly blocking pregnancy or interfering with the uterine cavity, surgery first might be the better choice. The best plan depends on your fibroid size, location, ovarian reserve, age, and fertility goals.

Questions to Discuss with Your Doctor if Fibroids are Suspected:

- Do I need an MRI or saline infusion sonogram to get a clearer picture of my fibroids?
- Are my fibroids affecting my fertility, or can we safely monitor them for now?
- If surgery is needed, which type of myomectomy would best preserve my uterus?

- Are there any medications that could help manage fibroid growth while I'm trying to conceive?

PCOS (POLYCYSTIC OVARY SYNDROME)

PCOS can show up in many different ways and not always how you'd expect. You might have irregular or missing periods, signs of insulin resistance like intense carb cravings or blood sugar crashes, or unexplained weight gain. You may also have higher levels of androgens such as testosterone, DHEA-S, or androstenedione, which can lead to acne, coarse hair growth on the face, chest, or abdomen, and thinning hair on the scalp.

Then there's what's known as "lean PCOS." In this case, your AMH and follicle count may be high, but your hormone balance is still off enough to interfere with ovulation. You might still get regular periods, and your labs might even look normal at first glance. But if ovulation isn't being tracked closely, it's easy to miss that your body isn't actually releasing an egg.

And just because you're bleeding regularly doesn't mean you're ovulating. It's completely possible for your body to go through the motions of a cycle without releasing an egg. These are all signs that PCOS might be disrupting ovulation, which is essential for egg and sperm to actually meet.

Tests to Confirm PCOS

PCOS is diagnosed based on a combination of symptoms and by ruling out other conditions. There's no single test that can confirm it, but there are key clues your doctor will look for. Blood work helps measure hormones like LH (luteinizing hormone), FSH (follicle-stimulating hormone), testosterone, DHEA-S (dehydroepiandrosterone sulfate), fasting insulin, and glucose. These results reveal how your body is handling hormones and blood sugar.

An ultrasound can show multiple small follicles on the ovaries, often described as a "string of pearls." But not everyone with PCOS has this pattern, and not everyone with this pattern has PCOS. Your cycle history also provides important context. If your periods are irregular or missing altogether, that's an important clue that your hormones aren't coordinating the way they should.

What Treatment Plans Are Available if You Have PCOS

The main goal for healing PCOS is to improve insulin sensitivity, lower inflammation, and bring hormones back into rhythm. The best place to start is the Survive to Thrive Protocol. Because PCOS is often tied to insulin resistance, stabilizing blood sugar is the most powerful way to restore ovulation. That means eating meals that combine protein, healthy fats, and fiber, and not going too long without food, so your blood sugar doesn't crash.

Exercise also plays a huge role. Strength training and walking, the kind of movement I outline in the Survive to Thrive Protocol, help your muscles use glucose more efficiently and improve insulin function. A short walk after meals can make a real difference.

Don't underestimate stress and sleep either. High cortisol from lack of sleep or constant stress makes insulin resistance worse. Prioritizing rest, sleep hygiene, and simple relaxation practices can help rebalance hormones naturally. When insulin is working properly, testosterone levels drop, ovulation becomes more consistent, and your cycle starts regulating itself again.

Targeted supplements like inositol, magnesium, and berberine can also support insulin balance and hormone regulation. If you're trying naturally, talk to your doctor about ovulation-supporting medications. Letrozole (Femara) is often the best first-line option since it tends to be more effective than Clomid for PCOS-related ovulation issues. Clomid can still work, but it's less helpful when insulin resistance is the main cause. Metformin may also be prescribed to help regulate blood sugar and support ovulation.

IVF Considerations for PCOS

I'll cover this in much more detail in "Part 2: The Book on IVF," but PCOS and IVF can work beautifully together when done right. When I start working with a client who has PCOS or a high follicle count, I get excited because their egg-to-embryo ratio can dramatically improve with the right approach. These cases respond incredibly well when the protocol and execution are customized, which is what I do!

The challenge is that many IVF protocols aren't designed for someone with PCOS. The standard cookie-cutter approach (see "'Okay' IVF" in Part 2) often leads to uneven follicle growth, where only a few eggs reach maturity at the right time. Even worse, when the protocol doesn't account for a high follicle count, the risk of ovarian hyperstimulation syndrome (OHSS) skyrockets. OHSS isn't only uncomfortable; it can be dangerous and often results in poor-quality embryos.

I've seen PCOS clients go from four blastocysts to sixteen and from two to ten simply by working with the right doctor, using the right protocols, and carefully executing each step based on the results. When IVF is done correctly for PCOS, the results can be night and day.

Questions to Discuss with Your Doctor if PCOS is Suspected:

- Which blood tests should we run to confirm or rule out PCOS? Should we include testosterone, DHEA-S, androstenedione, LH, FSH, fasting insulin, and glucose?
- Would an ultrasound help us see if I have multiple small follicles or a "string of pearls" pattern?
- What's the best approach to get my cycles and ovulation back on track naturally?
- Should I consider letrozole, metformin, or another medication to help trigger ovulation?
- If I need IVF, how will you adjust the protocol to prevent overstimulation and improve embryo quality?

CERVIX CHECK: THE UNSUNG HERO OF A STRONG PREGNANCY (MOM)

Your cervix is like a protective gate, strong enough to hold space for new life and smart enough to open when the time is right. But if it's weakened or scarred, it may not offer the support a growing pregnancy needs. Sometimes it can even make conception harder by blocking sperm from getting where they need to go. You can check all of this ahead of time so you're protecting both the beginning and the future of your pregnancy.

When to Test

If any of this sounds familiar, it's worth having your cervix checked before trying to conceive:

- A second-trimester loss or preterm labor in the past
- Cervical procedures like a LEEP, cone biopsy, or multiple D&Cs
- Unusually light or irregular periods
- Trouble getting pregnant without a clear reason

How to Test It

There are a few simple ways your doctor can assess your cervix:

- A transvaginal ultrasound to measure cervical length
- An HSG, or saline sonohysterogram, to check for scar tissue or blockages
- A manual exam to see how firm and closed your cervix feels

What the Results Could Mean

Here's what you want to see:

- Cervical length over 25 mm (2.5 cm)
- Closed and firm cervix unless you're in labor
- No scarring or blockages getting in the way of sperm

Options When the Cervix Needs Help:

- Short or weak cervix: Progesterone support or a cerclage (stitching it closed early in pregnancy) can help keep everything secure.
- Scar tissue blocking sperm: A minor procedure may open the pathway. If not, bypassing the cervix with IUI might be the best route.
- Chronic inflammation: Test and treat for infections, support healthy cervical mucus, and don't overlook the impact of gut and vaginal health.

Questions to Ask Your Doctor:

- Is my cervical length strong enough to hold a pregnancy?

- Do I have any scarring that could make it harder to conceive?
- Should I plan for a cerclage if I get pregnant?
- Would progesterone support be helpful for my cervix?
- If there's a partial blockage, what are my options for getting sperm where it needs to go?

Now that you understand the structure, it's time to look at the chemistry. Next up, we'll break down your bloodwork to see how your hormones are communicating and what they're revealing about your fertility story.

Before heading to the next section...

If you'd like printable charts to take to your doctor, space to write down your results, and more, just scan the QR code.

BLOOD WORK BREAKDOWN: DECODE YOUR FERTILITY CHEMISTRY

Now that you've confirmed everything physically checks out, it's time to look at your fertility chemistry. Hormones can make or break your chances, and sometimes the biggest roadblock to pregnancy is an imbalance that hasn't been fully addressed yet.

These blood tests give you a deeper look at your ovarian function, egg reserve, and hormonal rhythm. Some of these are probably already on your doctor's radar, especially for establishing a baseline of your egg supply. But this list goes a little deeper. I recommend doing these after your imaging and structural testing, or at least alongside them. Too often, bloodwork is prioritized before confirming that everything structurally looks good, leading to wasted time and ineffective treatments.

Here's the encouraging part: your results aren't permanent. These numbers reflect both your genetics and your environment, which means you have more influence over them than you've likely been told. I've seen women lower high FSH, raise low AMH, and get their cycles back on track, all without medication, by following the Survive to Thrive and Spirit protocols for a few consistent months.

If you're doing IVF, keep this in mind. Hormone levels like FSH, AMH, estradiol, and progesterone, along with AFC, cycle length, and BMI, should all help guide your protocol design. We'll walk through how in "Part 2: The Book on IVF," where you'll learn what these numbers mean for your protocol choices and how to use them to your advantage.

But first, let's look at what each hormone does, when to test it, and what to do if your results fall outside the ideal range.

FOLLICLE-STIMULATING HORMONE (FSH): THE FOLLICLE-STARTING HORMONE (MOM)

FSH is produced by your pituitary gland and acts like a wake-up call for your ovaries. It tells them it's time to start growing follicles, which are the sacs that hold your eggs. It's one of the key hormones that gets your body ready for ovulation.

When your FSH is in a healthy range, your follicles develop steadily and predictably. If FSH is too high, it can mean there are fewer eggs available or that they're maturing too quickly, which can affect egg quality. If it's too low, it could mean your brain isn't sending a strong enough signal to your ovaries to get things started. That often happens with hypothalamic amenorrhea, a condition caused by stress, under-eating, or over-exercising that throws off your hormonal communication and pauses ovulation.

When to Test

Test FSH on cycle days 2 to 4 to get the most accurate read on your ovarian reserve and brain-to-ovary communication. It's best to test it alongside estradiol, since high estradiol can sometimes suppress FSH and make results look lower than they really are.

Target Ranges

Target levels should be below 10 mIU/mL on cycle day 3, with the optimal range around 6–8 mIU/mL.

What Low FSH Could Mean

Very low FSH levels (below 1 to 2 mIU/mL) could mean your pituitary isn't giving your ovaries the signal they need. Without that signal, ovulation may not happen, and periods may be irregular or missing altogether. This often points to a communication breakdown between the brain and ovaries, sometimes caused by stress, under-eating, or over-exercising. In these cases, your doctor might suggest ovulation induction medications such as Clomid or letrozole to help stimulate egg development. GnRH therapy, or gonadotropin-releasing hormone therapy, can also be used in two ways: either to help restart ovulation or to temporarily quiet the ovaries before IVF with medications. To support your body's natural signaling and hormonal balance, the Survive to Thrive Protocol can be especially helpful, as it focuses on improving energy balance, lowering stress, and rebuilding the hormonal communication that keeps your cycle on track.

Questions to Ask Your Doctor if FSH Is Low:

- Could my low FSH mean I have hypothalamic amenorrhea?
- Would GnRH therapy help restart ovulation?
- If I'm not ovulating, what medications do you recommend to help? What do you think about Clomid, Letrozole, or injectable medications?
- Should we test for other hormone imbalances like PCOS or thyroid issues?
- Can we track my cycles to confirm if and when I'm ovulating?

What High FSH Could Mean

High FSH (above 10 mIU/mL on days 1-4) means your ovaries are working extra hard to recruit follicles. It's often a sign of diminished ovarian reserve, where fewer eggs are available and the body compensates by pushing harder. But rapid follicle growth can lead to eggs that mature too quickly and don't fertilize or grow into embryos well.

In this case, the goal is to calm the ovaries and slow follicle development so the eggs have enough time to mature. Some doctors use priming after ovulation to help regulate the next cycle. Depending on your exact FSH level, your doctor might recommend estrogen, norethisterone (Aygestin), or combination birth control priming.

Questions to Ask Your Doctor if FSH Is High:

- Could my high FSH be making my follicles grow too quickly and affecting egg quality?
- What medications would you recommend to help lower it?
- Should we retest next month to see if my FSH is fluctuating?
- Can we check AMH, antral follicle count, or estradiol to get a fuller picture?

How FSH Fits Into Your Precise Protocol for IVF

FSH is one of the key hormone inputs I use to help determine the precise IVF protocol my clients discuss with their doctor. I'll go into more detail about which priming medications to consider in "Part 2: The Book on IVF."

I also created software that walks you through what my research shows your protocol should look like based on your exact and unique inputs.

Go to the QR code for more details on "*Your Perfect Protocol for IVF*."

ESTRADIOL: THE ESTROGEN THAT BUILDS THE FOUNDATION (MOM)

Estradiol (E2) is the main form of estrogen your ovaries produce. It's a key player in follicular development, ovulation, and getting your uterine lining ready for implantation. In short, when estradiol is in its happy place, it creates a welcoming environment for ovulation and embryo implantation. But if it's off, either too high or too low, it can throw your cycle out of whack and make conceiving a real challenge.

When to Test

It's a good idea to test estradiol (E2) on cycle days 2 to 4, ideally along with FSH.

Target levels for estradiol on cycle day 3 are typically 25–80 pg/mL, with the lower end of that spectrum preferred if FSH is also normal.

As follicles grow, they produce estrogen. The more follicles you have, the higher your estradiol climbs. A ballpark estimate is about 200 pg/mL per mature follicle before ovulation. That's why someone doing IVF with only a few follicles might see estradiol around 400 pg/mL at trigger, while someone with a high follicle count could hit 3,000 pg/mL or more.

If estradiol gets above 3,000 pg/mL, especially during IVF, your doctor should start thinking about Ovarian Hyperstimulation Syndrome (OHSS) prevention strategies.

What Low Estradiol Levels Could Mean

Low estradiol can mean your ovaries aren't producing enough estrogen to support ovulation or thicken your uterine lining, which can lead to irregular cycles, a thin lining, or difficulty sustaining a pregnancy. Common causes include diminished ovarian reserve (DOR), premature ovarian insufficiency (POI), hypothalamic amenorrhea (often related to stress, overexercising, or under-eating), or estrogen-suppressing medications. If your estradiol is too low, your doctor might suggest estrogen support through patches or pills to help build your uterine lining and support follicle growth, or ovulation medications like letrozole or Clomid to naturally boost estrogen by stimulating follicle development.

Questions to Ask Your Doctor if Estradiol Is Low:

- Does my low estradiol mean I'm not ovulating, and should I track it?
- Could low estrogen be affecting my lining and implantation chances? Can we check my uterus lining around ovulation?
- Would you recommend medications to increase my estrogen?

What High Estradiol Levels Could Mean

High estradiol at the start of your cycle can reveal important clues about how your ovaries are functioning. It might suppress FSH, which can hide a low ovarian reserve, signal that a lead follicle is growing too early, or point to a functional ovarian cyst.

For those doing IVF, high estrogen early in the cycle can sometimes result from recent estrogen priming. But if your estradiol is high without priming, your doctor might recommend an ultrasound to check for cysts or a dominant follicle, closer cycle monitoring, or even postponing stimulation to avoid starting with a lead follicle already developing. They may also recommend adjusting the next cycle's medications to prevent elevated estrogen and early follicle recruitment.

Questions to Ask Your Doctor if Estradiol Is High:

- Could high estrogen mean I have a cyst or a lead follicle already?
- Should we wait to start meds or pause and consider a different approach next cycle that first reduces estrogen?

LUTEINIZING HORMONE (LH): THE OVULATION TRIGGER (MOM)

LH is the hormone that gives your ovary the final push to release a mature egg. It works alongside FSH to help follicles grow, but when the time is right, LH surges and signals ovulation. If LH is too low, that surge may never happen, and ovulation can stall. If it's too high, it can confuse the whole process and impact egg quality.

When to Test LH

You can check LH multiple times in the first half of your cycle to see how things are progressing. If you usually ovulate around day 14, testing on day 3 gives you a helpful baseline. Then test again around days 12–15 to catch the surge that tells you ovulation is near. If you want extra confirmation that you actually ovulated, a test on day 16 or 17 can help, but most of the time, a progesterone test between days 21 and 23 will give you a clearer answer.

Target Ranges

Target levels should be under 7 mIU/mL on day 3. A mid-cycle surge typically starts around 15 mIU/mL and can climb well above 25, depending on your unique pattern.

What Low LH Could Mean

Low LH often means ovulation isn't happening or at least not reliably. Your brain might not be sending a strong enough signal, so your follicles don't mature fully and your eggs don't develop the way they should. The condition is common in cases like hypothalamic amenorrhea, where stress, under-eating, or intense workouts disrupt hormone signals. It can also happen if your pituitary needs a reset, especially after long-term birth control.

If your LH is low, your doctor might suggest medications like Clomid or letrozole to stimulate follicle growth, or an hCG trigger shot to mimic an LH surge and support ovulation. Supporting your body's natural signaling through proper nutrition, rest, and hormonal balance, like what's outlined in the Survive to Thrive Protocol, can also help your body feel safe enough to ovulate on its own.

Questions to Ask Your Doctor if LH Is Low:

- What could low LH be doing to my ovulation and egg development?
- Are we sure I'm ovulating, or should we track things more closely?
- Would Clomid or Letrozole, with or without an hCG trigger shot, make sense for me?

What High LH Could Mean

If your LH is high on day 3, and especially if it's higher than your FSH, it might be a sign of PCOS. In PCOS, LH doesn't follow the normal surge pattern. It stays high, which sends mixed messages to the ovaries. That can lead to delayed or skipped ovulation, lower-quality eggs, and higher androgens. If you've also got acne, irregular cycles, or unwanted hair growth, this might be your missing clue.

When LH is high, the goal is to quiet the system so your ovaries respond more normally. Your doctor might recommend metformin if insulin resistance is part of the picture, since it can help bring LH down, or a low-dose gonadotropin protocol to keep follicle growth steady without overstimulation. More frequent ultrasounds can also help ensure follicles aren't developing or ovulating too early.

Questions to Ask Your Doctor if LH Is High:

- Could this be PCOS, and should we check my androgens to know for sure?
- Are there treatments that could bring LH down and improve ovulation?
- Should we test for insulin resistance?
- Can we track my follicles more closely so we don't miss ovulation?

ANTI-MÜLLERIAN HORMONE (AMH): THE OVARIAN RESERVE MARKER (MOM)

AMH is made by the small follicles in your ovaries and gives you a general sense of how many eggs you might have left. It doesn't measure egg quality, but it does show how your ovaries might respond to fertility treatment. Think of it as a headcount, not a quality check.

When to Test

AMH can be tested on any day of your cycle, as levels usually remain steady throughout the month.

Target Ranges

Target levels should fall between 1.0 and 4.0 ng/mL.

What Low AMH Could Mean

If your AMH is below 1.0, it indicates a low ovarian reserve. That doesn't mean you can't get pregnant, but it may mean fewer eggs to work with. AMH naturally declines with age, but it can also drop early from stress, autoimmune issues, prior ovarian surgery, or premature ovarian insufficiency.

If your AMH is low, your doctor might suggest medications like Clomid, Letrozole, or low-dose injectables to help stimulate ovulation, as well as a transvaginal ultrasound to check your antral follicle count and confirm how many eggs are in play. It's also worth exploring possible root causes for the drop, especially if your number seems low for your age.

Questions to Ask Your Doctor if AMH Is Low:

- Are there medications that could help boost my chances of ovulating or conceiving naturally?
- Could we do an ultrasound to check how many follicles I'm working with this cycle?
- Could we check my AMH again in a couple of months to see if this is a true number versus a lab error?
- Could anything be causing my AMH to drop faster than it should?

What High AMH Could Mean

If your AMH is over 4.0, it could be a sign of PCOS. This usually means your ovaries have many small follicles that aren't maturing and ovulating as they should. It might sound like a good thing to have more eggs, but when they get stuck at an early stage of development, it can disrupt hormone balance and ovulation. High AMH can also raise your risk of overstimulation during fertility treatments if medication isn't carefully managed.

When AMH is high due to PCOS, the focus is on helping your body ovulate regularly and keeping hormones balanced. Your doctor might recommend metformin, a medication that helps improve insulin sensitivity, if insulin resistance is part of the picture, or a low-dose IVF protocol to prevent overstimulation and keep follicle growth steady. Supporting blood sugar balance, managing stress, and incorporating gentle movement can also help restore hormonal rhythm.

Questions to Ask Your Doctor if AMH Is High:

- Could this be PCOS, and should we test my androgens to know for sure?
- Are there medications that can help regulate my hormones and support ovulation?
- Should we check for insulin resistance, and what would treatment look like if I have it?
- How can we track my follicles to make sure they're actually maturing each cycle?

PROGESTERONE: THE PREGNANCY HORMONE (MOM)

Progesterone is made after ovulation by the corpus luteum, which forms from the follicle once it releases an egg. That leftover structure turns into a temporary hormone factory, producing progesterone to thicken your uterine lining and prepare it for implantation. If that lining isn't built well enough or doesn't stay that way, it becomes harder for a pregnancy to stick. Later in pregnancy, the placenta takes over progesterone production, but in the early stages, it's all up to your ovaries.

When to Test

Progesterone is usually tested in the mid-luteal phase, about 5–9 days after ovulation, to confirm that ovulation has happened and that your body is making enough of the hormone to support implantation. If you're pregnant, progesterone levels may also be tracked in the first trimester to ensure they're rising properly.

If you're doing IVF, talk with your doctor about checking progesterone levels the day before your embryo transfer and weekly afterward. This is covered in detail in "Part 2: The Book on IVF," in the section on embryo transfers.

Target Ranges

Target levels should be between 10 and 20 ng/mL in the mid-luteal phase. In early pregnancy, the ideal range is typically 11-44 ng/mL. For IVF clients, I like to see progesterone around 20 ng/mL the day before transfer, about 30 ng/mL one week later, and roughly 40 ng/mL at the pregnancy test, continuing to rise as early pregnancy progresses.

What Low Progesterone Could Mean

If your progesterone is under 10 ng/mL in the luteal phase, it could mean your body isn't making enough to support a healthy lining or early pregnancy. That can be tied to luteal phase deficiency, irregular ovulation, or hormone imbalances such as PCOS. Stress, poor nutrition, or thyroid issues can also play a role.

Low progesterone can lead to implantation issues, early miscarriage, or cycles where ovulation doesn't occur. Your doctor might suggest progesterone supplements (oral, vaginal, or injectable), medications like Clomid or letrozole to improve ovulation quality, or testing for thyroid and other hormonal imbalances. Supporting overall hormone health through nutrition, rest, and stress balance, like in the Survive to Thrive Protocol, can also help.

Questions to Ask Your Doctor if You Have Low Progesterone:

- What might be causing my low progesterone, and how could that affect my chances of getting or staying pregnant?
- Would progesterone support help me, and which form would be best?
- Should we look into thyroid function, PCOS, or other hormone patterns to get a better picture?

What High Progesterone Could Mean

High progesterone in a non-pregnant cycle isn't common, but it can happen. Sometimes it's linked to fertility medications or ovarian cysts. It can also occur if your adrenal glands are overproducing hormones due to adrenal hyperplasia.

When progesterone is too high, it may affect how well the uterine lining responds and can throw off implantation timing. Your doctor may recommend an ultrasound to check for cysts or adjust your medication protocol if you're undergoing treatment. If it's not related to medication, you know what to do... yes, the Survive to Thrive Protocol!

Questions to Ask Your Doctor if You Have High Progesterone:

- Could this be from cysts, medications, or another hormone imbalance?
- Is high progesterone affecting my chances of implantation?
- Would an ultrasound help us understand what's going on?
- Are there treatments that could help bring my levels back into a better range?

- How should we track my hormones moving forward so we can adjust if needed?

TESTOSTERONE: THE FERTILITY-FUELING HORMONE (MOM)

Testosterone isn't just a male hormone. Women need it too, just in smaller amounts. It helps your follicles grow, supports egg development, boosts libido, and keeps your energy steady. When testosterone is in balance, your cycle runs smoothly and your body stays primed for ovulation. When it's off, it can quietly throw off everything from your mood to your fertility.

When to Test

Test on cycle days 2 to 4, ideally alongside DHEA-S and SHBG (sex hormone-binding globulin), since those help show how testosterone is being used in your body.

Target Levels

Total testosterone should typically fall between 15 and 70 ng/dL for women, though this can vary by lab.

What Low Testosterone Could Mean

Too little testosterone can lead to low drive, fatigue, and weak ovulation signals. Low levels make it harder for follicles to mature and for ovulation to occur. You might notice low energy, decreased libido, or slower recovery after workouts. This can happen from overtraining, under-eating, chronic stress, or certain medications like birth control.

If levels are low, your doctor may also check adrenal health (that's the fancy name for how your body handles stress) and DHEA-S levels since they're closely linked. If those results come back off balance, your first move is to get consistent with the Survive to Thrive Protocol, which can often help restore harmony naturally.

Questions to Ask Your Doctor if You Have Low Testosterone:

- Could low testosterone be affecting my ovulation or egg development?
- Should we test DHEA-S or SHBG to understand what's really going on?
- Could my stress levels, exercise routine, or medications be playing a role?
- How can I safely support my hormones without overcorrecting?

What High Testosterone Could Mean

Too much testosterone can disrupt ovulation and point toward PCOS or other androgen-related issues. It can block ovulation, increase facial or body hair growth, and cause acne. In IVF, high androgens can also affect how your ovaries respond to stimulation.

If testosterone is high, your doctor may check for insulin resistance, since high insulin levels can drive androgen levels up. Treatment could include medications like metformin or inositol supplements, along with nutrition and lifestyle strategies to support blood sugar balance and hormone regulation.

Questions to Ask Your Doctor if You Have High Testosterone:

- Could this be related to PCOS or insulin resistance?
- Should we test my insulin, glucose, or androgen levels to confirm?
- What can we do to bring my testosterone back into balance naturally?
- How might high testosterone affect my ovulation or IVF results?

TESTOSTERONE: THE SPERM-STRENGTHENING HORMONE (DAD)

Testosterone is the engine behind sperm production, libido, and energy. It drives the creation and maturation of sperm in the testes and helps maintain overall reproductive health. When testosterone is in a healthy range, it supports not only fertility but also mood, stamina, and muscle mass—all signs that the body is functioning at its best.

When to Test

Men can test testosterone at any time of day, but levels are usually highest in the morning, so an early-morning blood draw gives the most accurate reading. Testing both *total* and *free* testosterone helps show how much is available for the body to use. It's also smart to check LH (luteinizing hormone), FSH (follicle-stimulating hormone), and prolactin at the same time to see how the brain and testes are communicating.

Target Levels

Optimal total testosterone typically ranges from 400 to 900 ng/dL, while free testosterone should fall between 9 and 30 pg/mL. Every lab is a little different, but what's important is how these numbers fit with energy, libido, and sperm health, not simply what's "in range."

What Low Testosterone Could Mean

Low testosterone can lead to low sperm count, reduced libido, fatigue, and even mood changes. It might come from chronic stress, excess weight, sleep issues, certain medications, or long-term alcohol or steroid use. Sometimes, it's related to a condition called hypogonadism, where the testes don't make enough testosterone.

If levels are low, your doctor might explore lifestyle shifts, nutrition, or supplements to improve hormone balance naturally. In some cases, medications like Clomid (clomiphene citrate) can be used to signal the body to make more testosterone without shutting down sperm production, unlike direct testosterone replacement, which can lower sperm count.

Questions to Ask Your Doctor if Testosterone Is Low:

- What do you think could be causing my low testosterone?
- Should we check my LH, FSH, and prolactin to see if my brain is sending the right signals?

- Would Clomid or another medication help boost natural testosterone without harming sperm production?
- Could lifestyle changes like improving sleep, nutrition, or reducing alcohol help bring levels back up?

What High Testosterone Could Mean

High testosterone isn't always good news. If it's from natural production, it usually means everything's working well. But if it's from external testosterone use or anabolic steroids, sperm production can drop sharply because the body stops signaling the testes to make sperm. Over time, that can cause testicular shrinkage and fertility issues.

If levels are very high and there's no supplementation, your doctor might check for adrenal or testicular concerns, since both can rarely produce excess testosterone.

Questions to Ask Your Doctor if Testosterone Is High:

- Could my high testosterone be from supplements or medications I'm taking?
- Is this affecting my sperm production or fertility potential?
- Should we check my adrenal function or other hormone levels to rule out an imbalance?
- What's the safest way to maintain healthy testosterone levels while protecting sperm quality?

PROLACTIN: THE NURTURING HORMONE (MOM)

Prolactin is made by your pituitary gland and is best known for helping with breast milk production. But when levels get too high, it can interfere with your reproductive hormones and disrupt ovulation. It's one of those sneaky hormones that can quietly affect fertility without clear symptoms until your cycle starts changing.

When to Test

If your cycles are irregular or you're having trouble getting pregnant, prolactin is worth checking. It should be tested early in the morning with a fasting blood draw, since stress, poor sleep, or even mild stimulation, such as a quick workout or even a hug, can cause temporary spikes. There's no specific cycle day required for testing.

Target Ranges

Prolactin levels should be under 25 ng/mL. That generally indicates healthy pituitary function and regular ovulation.

What Low Prolactin Means

Low prolactin is rare and usually poses no concern for fertility. If it comes back low, it's still worth mentioning to your doctor, but it often doesn't require treatment or follow-up.

Questions to Ask Your Doctor if Prolactin Is Low:

- Is my low prolactin something that needs attention, or could it be a one-time result?
- Could it be connected to anything else going on with my hormones?
- Should we repeat the test or do any follow-up lab work to be safe?

What High Prolactin Means

High prolactin, also called hyperprolactinemia, can block the signals your brain sends to trigger ovulation. It can lower FSH and LH levels, preventing normal ovulation. Common causes include small pituitary tumors (usually benign and treatable), thyroid dysfunction, certain medications, chronic stress, or other health conditions.

If your prolactin levels are high, your doctor will likely want to identify the cause and treat it so your hormonal signals and cycles can normalize.

Questions to Ask Your Doctor if Prolactin Is High:

- What could be causing my elevated prolactin levels?
- Should we check for thyroid issues or a small pituitary tumor?
- Are there medications that could help lower prolactin, like cabergoline or bromocriptine, and would they make sense for me?
- How will we know when my prolactin levels are back in a healthy range?

RH FACTOR: THE COMPATIBILITY CHECK (MOM AND POSSIBLY DAD)

The Rh factor is a protein found on red blood cells. Most people have it, which makes them Rh positive. If you don't, you're Rh negative. This doesn't affect your ability to get pregnant, but it can influence how your body responds during and after pregnancy, especially if your baby is Rh positive and you're not.

Rh factor is one of the first things checked when you start fertility treatment or prenatal care. Most clinics, OBs, and midwives test it automatically, and you only need to check it once since your Rh status never changes.

When to Test

Rh factor is typically tested early. If you're doing IVF, your clinic will likely check it as part of your initial lab work. If you're trying naturally, it's usually tested at your first prenatal appointment. Again, this is a one-time test since your Rh type doesn't change.

Here's how it works:

Who gets tested first? You do. The person carrying the pregnancy is always tested first.

If you're Rh positive: You're in the clear. Your body already recognizes the Rh protein, so even if your baby is Rh positive, there's no conflict.

If you're Rh negative: Your partner should be tested next.

- If your partner is also Rh negative: There's no issue. The baby will be Rh negative, too.

- If your partner is Rh positive: There's a chance the baby could be Rh positive. If the baby's blood mixes with yours, your immune system could create antibodies against it. That's where Rhogam comes in. It's a simple shot given around 28 weeks of pregnancy and again after birth if the baby is Rh positive. It prevents your body from developing antibodies that could affect future pregnancies.

What It Means if You're Rh Negative

If you're Rh negative, your immune system may view Rh-positive blood as foreign. This becomes important if your baby or embryo is Rh-positive because even a small amount of blood mixing during pregnancy, miscarriage, egg retrieval, or embryo transfer could trigger antibody formation. These antibodies usually don't cause issues in a first pregnancy, but they can pose serious risks in later ones by attacking an Rh-positive baby's red blood cells.

That's why early testing and prevention matter. A Rhogam shot can stop that immune reaction before it starts. Most fertility clinics will protect you early if there's any risk of Rh incompatibility.

Questions to Ask Your Doctor if You're Rh Negative:

- Should we test my partner to check Rh status?
- Will I need a Rhogam shot during or after pregnancy?
- Can we check whether I've already developed Rh antibodies?
- Do we need to take any special precautions for IVF or embryo transfer?

HOW ACCURATE ARE THESE BLOOD TESTS?

Most hormone and ultrasound tests are highly reliable, but none are perfect. Bloodwork results can vary depending on how the sample is handled. If a sample sits too long before testing or isn't properly brought to room temperature after freezing, results can shift slightly. Occasional lab or reporting errors can happen, too.

If something seems far off from what's expected or doesn't match past results, it's always okay to repeat the test the next month. And if this is your first round of testing, review the results with your doctor to make sure they make sense for your age, cycle history, and overall fertility picture.

TEMPORARY CHANGES TO YOUR HORMONES, UTERINE LINING, AND MENSTRUAL CYCLE

I once worked with a client who came to me in tears. She'd been told she had diminished ovarian reserve and needed to start IVF right away. She was young, overwhelmed, and determined to do IVF only once, so she hired me to make sure it worked. As we talked, I found out she'd had fibroid surgery three months earlier.

That detail shifted the entire plan.

Instead of rushing into treatment, I built her a recovery protocol to give her body the time and support it needed to heal. Guess what it included? You got it! It was a customized version of the Survive to Thrive Protocol and the Spirit Protocol you've already learned about.

She followed it, and within a few months, her hormone levels started moving in the direction we like to see, and she got pregnant naturally.

I've seen surgery, inflammation, travel, and viral illnesses completely throw off hormones, affect the uterine lining, and make cycles unpredictable. I've also seen these same disruptions lead to disappointing IVF results when recovery wasn't prioritized. While the body can sometimes recalibrate on its own, waiting and hoping that it will fix itself in a few months isn't a plan. The smarter approach is to support healing as quickly and completely as possible.

Here are some of the most common reasons your hormones or menstrual cycle might be temporarily off:

- **Significant stress:** Emotional or physical stress can disrupt the hypothalamus, the part of your brain that controls hormone release, which can delay or even block ovulation.
- **Rapid weight changes:** Gaining or losing weight quickly can alter hormone production and affect your cycle.
- **Intense exercise:** Too much high-intensity training can suppress ovulation and reduce progesterone. Your body sees it as a survival challenge, not a good time to conceive.
- **Surgery:** Especially procedures for fibroids or endometriosis, which can cause temporary inflammation, disrupt blood flow to the

uterus, and interfere with normal hormonal signaling. Recovery support helps bring balance back and restore healthy function.

- **Travel or jet lag:** Changing time zones and sleep patterns can throw off your circadian rhythm, which affects hormone timing and cycle regularity.
- **Medications:** Steroids, antipsychotics, and even some allergy medications can disrupt hormone signals and interfere with ovulation.
- **Recent illness or recovery:** Whether it's the flu, COVID-19, or another virus, your body may pause ovulation while it focuses on healing. It can also happen with long recoveries or lingering inflammation.
- **Vaccines:** Some vaccines can trigger a short-term immune response that temporarily shifts hormone levels and your cycle. It's usually a reset, not a setback.
- **Dietary deficiencies:** Not getting enough fats, proteins, or key nutrients can lower hormone production and disrupt your cycle.
- **Environmental toxins:** Exposure to things like BPA, phthalates, or other hormone disruptors can create short-term changes in hormone balance.
- **Sleep disruption:** Poor or irregular sleep patterns can throw off cortisol and melatonin, both of which influence reproductive hormones.
- **Weaning off hormonal treatments:** Stopping birth control, IVF meds, or hormone therapy for PCOS can cause a temporary hormone rollercoaster while your body recalibrates.
- **Smoking or frequent heavy alcohol use:** Either can interfere with hormone production and contribute to irregular cycles.
- **Short-term thyroid changes:** Temporary shifts in thyroid function, whether overactive or underactive, can affect ovulation and bleeding patterns.
- **Breastfeeding or recently stopping:** As prolactin levels drop and hormones adjust after weaning, your cycle may take time to normalize again.

If you've experienced any of these and your hormone levels are heading in the wrong direction, don't panic. Your body is capable of incredible recovery when given the right support. By focusing on recovery and using the Survive to Thrive and Spirit protocols, those levels can return to where they were... or even improve.

These protocols don't only help you feel better or speed up healing; they remind your body how to function at its best and create the conditions where pregnancy becomes not only possible but also more likely.

CHAPTER 5 SUMMARY

- **Structure Comes Before Strategy:** This chapter walks through the physical checkpoints required for pregnancy so you can confirm that sperm, eggs, tubes, uterus, cervix, and timing are actually set up to work together.
- **Sperm Is Half the Equation:** Male fertility testing is prioritized early because sperm issues are common, often overlooked, and frequently easier to improve than most people expect.
- **Your Cycle Is Your Loudest Signal:** Cycle length, ovulation timing, bleeding patterns, and symptoms act like a monthly report card showing how well your hormones and ovaries are communicating.
- **Ovulation Quality Matters More Than Timing:** Confirming whether ovulation is occurring, when it occurs, and how strong the hormonal signals are provides critical insight into egg maturity and implantation potential.
- **The Uterus Must Be Ready to Receive:** Lining thickness, inflammation, infection, scarring, polyps, fibroids, and uterine shape are evaluated to be sure the uterus is a safe, welcoming place for an embryo to implant and stay.
- **Genetics Can Quietly Change the Game:** Carrier screening and karyotype testing help rule out inherited and chromosomal issues that could cause repeated losses, failed transfers, or poor embryo development.
- **Endo, Adeno, Fibroids, and PCOS Leave Clues:** Common conditions are broken down so you can recognize their patterns, understand how they affect fertility, and ask better questions about diagnosis and treatment.
- **Bloodwork Decodes the Chemistry Behind the Structure:** Hormones like FSH, estradiol, LH, AMH, progesterone, testosterone, and prolactin reveal how your brain, ovaries, and uterus are communicating and where support is needed.
- **Knowledge Turns You Into a Partner in Care:** By understanding what each test means and what to discuss with your

doctor, you move from a passive patient to an informed decision-maker with a clear plan forward.

Before heading to the next section...

If you'd like printable charts of the bloodwork list to take to your doctor, space to write down your results, and more, just scan the QR code.

6. Paths to Parenthood (Let's Get You Knocked Up!)

You've uncovered as much as you possibly can about your fertility mystery. You've tackled the root issues, confirmed that all the necessary parts are in place, and ruled out anything major that could get in the way.

Now it's go-time. Whether you're trying naturally, using timed intercourse, or heading toward IUI or IVF, the goal is the same: help the egg and sperm meet, fertilize, and implant under the best possible conditions to give you the highest shot at pregnancy.

This chapter is all about your choices for conception, what you need in order to consider each option, and strategies to make that path as successful as possible.

One quick note before we dive in: when it comes to IVF, that's a whole different beautiful beast. The strategies, protocols, and execution are what I'm most often hired to help with because IVF success comes down to strategy and timing, and that's what I've spent more than ten years perfecting. Some people come to me hoping to avoid IVF altogether, and others need support navigating the emotional side of the process, but most reach out for help getting IVF to finally work.

So I'll touch on it briefly here so you can see how IVF fits into the bigger picture of your fertility options, but the next section of this book, "Part 2: The Book on IVF," is where we'll go deep into exactly how to make it work for you.

PLAIN OL' SEX

Let's keep this simple. This is the no-intervention option, just smart timing and letting nature do its thing. You're using your body's natural signals to guide when to have sex so the egg and sperm have the best shot at meeting.

WHEN TO CONSIDER IT

This approach works best when everything is functioning as it should. Ovulation is regular, tubes are open, sperm are healthy, and there are no major roadblocks on either side.

CONCEPTION CHECKLIST

✓ Healthy sperm count (at least 39 million)
✓ At least one mature egg
✓ Ovulation is happening naturally
✓ Cervix opens at the right time
✓ Sperm can swim through the cervix
✓ Clear, open fallopian tubes
✓ Egg and sperm can fertilize
✓ Uterine lining is healthy and receptive
✓ Cervix is strong enough to stay closed during pregnancy

STRATEGY FOR SUCCESS

Use ovulation test strips with two lines (not the digital smiley-face kind) and start testing around day 9 or 10 if you typically ovulate around day 14. If your cycle is shorter, start around cycle day 7. Once that second line starts to show up, even faintly, it's time to have sex every other day. Keep going until the line fades. There's no need to chart temperatures or inspect your cervix like a science project. Every-other-day timing keeps sperm quality high and stress levels low.

TIMED INTERCOURSE

Sometimes your body needs a nudge. Timed intercourse uses medication to help build follicles and support more predictable ovulation, then strategically times intercourse to align with your most fertile window. It's a way to optimize your chances while still staying in the natural conception zone.

WHEN TO CONSIDER IT

This option is best for those who need support with follicle growth or ovulation but have everything else functioning well: open tubes, healthy sperm, and a receptive uterine lining. It's often a first step when cycles are irregular or when an IVF cycle isn't strong enough to move forward, but you still want to give pregnancy a real shot.

CONCEPTION CHECKLIST

✓ Healthy sperm count (at least 39 million)
✓ At least one mature egg (with or without medication)
✓ Cervix opens at the right time
✓ Sperm can swim through the cervix
✓ Clear, open fallopian tubes
✓ Egg and sperm can fertilize
✓ Uterine lining is healthy and receptive
✓ Body is in conception mode, not survival mode
✓ Cervix is strong enough to stay closed during pregnancy

SUPPORT THIS TREATMENT PROVIDES

These are the areas this treatment helps strengthen so your body can do what it's meant to do more effectively:

✓ Follicle growth is supported to help eggs grow and mature properly
✓ Ovulation is supported or induced with medication and a trigger shot

STRATEGY FOR SUCCESS

Your doctor may recommend medications that support follicle growth and ovulation, such as Clomid or letrozole, or low doses of gonadotropins such as Gonal F, Follistim, or Menopur, followed by a trigger shot to time ovulation precisely.

The trigger also helps the egg mature and supports early progesterone production, which prepares the uterine lining.

Once ovulation is confirmed, you'll time sex during your fertile window to boost your chances of conception. Tracking is key. Your doctor should be monitoring hormone levels such as estrogen, progesterone, and LH, checking follicular growth, confirming ovulation, and assessing the uterine lining. This data helps you see what's working, what isn't, and what to adjust before, during, and after ovulation, and then again a week later, so you're not only trying, you're learning.

IUI (INTRAUTERINE INSEMINATION)

IUI is a procedure where washed sperm is placed directly into the uterus to help it reach the egg more easily. By bypassing the cervix and getting sperm closer to the fallopian tubes, it removes a few natural obstacles, but the sperm still need to swim and fertilize the egg on their own. Because timing is so critical, this process is closely monitored to catch ovulation at the right moment.

WHEN TO CONSIDER IT

IUI is often the next step when timed intercourse isn't getting the job done, whether there's a mild male factor, cervical mucus issues, or you want to give sperm a bit of a head start. It's a great option when ovulation is happening naturally or with support, sperm count is slightly low but still workable, and everything else, tubes, lining, and egg quality, looks good. It's also commonly used after failed timed intercourse cycles or as a less intensive step before IVF.

CONCEPTION CHECKLIST

✔ Sperm count is workable (at least 5 million per mL post-wash)
✔ At least one mature egg (usually supported with medication)

✓ Clear, open fallopian tubes
✓ Egg and sperm can fertilize
✓ Uterine lining is healthy and receptive
✓ Body is in conception mode, not survival mode
✓ Cervix is strong enough to stay closed during pregnancy

SUPPORT THIS TREATMENT PROVIDES

These are the areas this treatment helps support or enhance to make conception more likely:

✓ Ovulation is supported with a trigger shot
✓ Cervix is bypassed, so mucus and sperm entry aren't barriers
✓ Multiple eggs can grow and mature with or without medication support

STRATEGY FOR SUCCESS

Your doctor may recommend medications that support follicle growth and ovulation, such as Clomid or letrozole, or low doses of gonadotropins such as Gonal-F, Follistim, or Menopur, followed by a trigger shot to time ovulation precisely.

The trigger also helps the egg mature and supports early progesterone production, which prepares the uterine lining.

The ideal timing for IUI is the day before ovulation. Since sperm can survive for a few days, but the egg only lasts about 12 to 24 hours, some clinics recommend back-to-back inseminations to boost your odds of success.

Your doctor should track hormone levels, follicle size, ovulation timing, uterine lining development, and progesterone on the day of the IUI, one week after, and again near your pregnancy test. If IUI doesn't work, this information gives you and your doctor valuable insight into what happened and how to improve the next round.

IVF (IN-VITRO FERTILIZATION)

IVF is a process where your ovaries are given medication that acts like fuel for egg development, helping more of the eggs you already have grow and mature enough to be fertilized. Once they're ready, those eggs are retrieved from the ovaries and fertilized in the lab, either by surrounding them with sperm to let fertilization happen naturally or with ICSI (intracytoplasmic sperm injection), where an embryologist selects a healthy sperm and injects it directly into the egg to encourage fertilization. The embryos that develop are then transferred into the uterus.

WHEN TO CONSIDER IT

IVF is often the best or only option when certain roadblocks to conception are in the way, such as severe male factor infertility, blocked or missing fallopian tubes, or fertilization challenges that other methods can't solve. It's also an excellent choice when timed intercourse or IUI hasn't worked (after completing the Survive to Thrive and Spirit protocols, of course). IVF also makes it possible to genetically test embryos to help prevent passing on specific conditions.

CONCEPTION CHECKLIST

✔ At least one mature egg (usually supported with medication)
✔ Sperm capable of fertilization (with or without ICSI)
✔ Egg and sperm can fertilize naturally or with lab support
✔ Uterine lining is healthy and receptive
✔ Body is in conception mode, not survival mode
✔ Cervix is strong enough to stay closed during pregnancy

SUPPORT THIS TREATMENT PROVIDES

✔ Helps multiple eggs mature with medication support
✔ Fertilization can be assisted with ICSI if needed
✔ Can bypass blocked tubes, cervical issues, or poor sperm parameters
✔ Embryos can be genetically tested for certain conditions
✔ Embryos can be frozen and transferred later when the uterus is most receptive

STRATEGY FOR SUCCESS

There are so many that I dedicated half of an entire book to them in Part 2! Here's a summary: Whether you have a low egg count or a high one, if your protocol isn't designed around your actual numbers and your doctor isn't making real-time adjustments during stimulation to optimize results (for example, if you know your retrieval date before you even start stimulation medications), you risk wasting eggs, embryos, a load of money, and precious time.

CONCLUSION TO PART 1: THE BOOK ON FERTILITY

CHOOSING WHAT WORKS FOR YOU

"Part 1: The Book on Fertility" is officially complete! Congratulations on reaching this moment!!

You've just learned how to become the healthiest, most naturally fertile version of yourself. Whether you get pregnant with or without treatment, your body and mind are now primed for an easier pregnancy, smoother delivery, faster recovery, and a stronger postpartum experience. You've also learned how to create lifelong health for both you and your family. Yes, that means you can all age more easily and better, too. This is truly generational work.

Okay, next up is "Part 2: The Book on IVF."

If IVF is part of your path, I got you. I *really* got you. This isn't just my jam; it's my zone of genius. You're about to step into IVF with more knowledge and confidence than you ever thought was possible before picking up this book. And by the end, you'll practically have "MD in IVF" after your name for "Mama Director."

Let's get growing!

CHAPTER 6 SUMMARY

- **This is the Action Chapter:** After all the testing, healing, and groundwork, this chapter is about choosing your path to parenthood.
- **Every Path Has Requirements:** Whether it's sex, timed intercourse, IUI, or IVF, success depends on the same basics. Healthy sperm, a mature egg, good timing, open pathways, and a receptive uterus.
- **Plain Ol' Sex Still Needs Strategy:** Natural conception works best when ovulation is predictable and timing is smart.
- **Timed Intercourse Adds Precision:** When ovulation needs help, medication and monitoring turn random cycles into clear opportunities.
- **IUI Gives Sperm a Head Start:** By bypassing the cervix and tightening timing, IUI helps when sperm or timing is the weak link.
- **IVF is a Tool:** IVF solves specific roadblocks, but success still comes down to protocol and execution.
- **One Size Never Fits All:** The right path depends on your data, not age, timelines, or clinic defaults.
- **Learning Matters Even When It Doesn't Work:** Each cycle should give you answers, not just another attempt.
- **Your Body Sets the Ceiling:** No matter the method, conception works best when your body is in creation mode, not survival mode.

Before heading to the next section...

If you'd like to see what my recommendations for your IVF protocol could look like using the software, Your Perfect Protocols for IVF, so you can discuss them with your doctor, scan the QR code.

Part Two
The Book on IVF

7. IVF Success: Get Pregnant Without Getting F—ed

The Story Behind IVF Uncovered: Let's clear one thing up. Doing nine egg retrievals and ten embryo transfers didn't qualify me to consult. And honestly, if someone says to you, "I've done ten rounds of IVF and want to give you advice," please run.

What it did qualify me for was knowing exactly what it feels like to give everything you have and still walk away empty-handed... for years. Knowing the hollow ache of having "everything" but not the one thing that matters most: your family. And knowing what it feels like to be in "infertility jail," trapped by the pressure, feeling like a shell of my former self, obsessively researching anything that might help me finally meet my baby.

I never thought this would be my life's work. It was someone else's idea. In 2016, Mila was two years old, and I sat down with a career consultant named Sarah Walton.

After a bunch of questions, she said with total confidence, "You should be a fertility coach."

I giggled nervously, wondering how I would tell her what I really thought: *that's ridiculous*. Instead, I smiled and said politely, "That's not a thing." She smiled right back and told me, just as politely, to make it one.

At the time, I had two tiny humans, a full-time job, and exactly zero extra time.

Six days later, I was laid off. New CEO. Big restructure. I remember thinking, *Okay, God... that was subtle.*

So I went all in and started building what would become The Fertilities Unite Project. Or "The FU Project," which, yes, was a nod to my inner dialogue during most of my five-year IVF journey.

In the beginning, I did what most fertility coaches do now: I supported my clients through their journey, helping them advocate for better care with their medical team, mindset work, and holistic health practices.

Then, in 2018, one of my clients began working with Dr. Debra Minjarez, a brilliant, double-board-certified reproductive endocrinologist who had served as medical director at multiple top clinics. She had the best results, and her approach was the most unique and logical I had ever seen.

When she was still practicing (sadly, she's no longer taking patients), I kept sending more and more clients her way. Her results spoke for themselves.

I've worked closely with other incredible doctors, too, but Dr. Minjarez was on another level. She knows so much and cares so deeply. She didn't just create and carry out customized protocols with precision; she ensured the entire team, including the embryologist, was aligned and doing everything possible to optimize success.

In 2021, I started writing a version of this book because I knew this information could not stay locked behind private consulting. Women needed access to how fertility and IVF actually work, how protocols should be built based on biology, and how to advocate for themselves with clarity and confidence.

But there was one problem. How could I help women figure out what their precise protocol should be without me needing to be present?

That question led to the software. By inputting hormone levels and key data, women receive a report with protocol considerations to discuss with their doctor, from priming meds and stimulation dosing to antagonist and trigger timing.

From there, I built a calculator to execute the protocol precisely and expanded our mindset and functional medicine tools so women could get guidance specific to their symptoms, bloodwork, and energy needs without having to hire individual experts.

With all of these pieces working together, I believe we can succeed at a much-needed mission: to reduce infertility, prevent more pregnancy losses, and improve IVF success worldwide.

And we are on our way. Today, we support clients in over 15 countries, with Kenya being the newest addition!

If you believe in this mission too, I have one big favor to ask. Please share this book, even your own copy, and leave a review. Reviews are how women find it when they are searching for answers.

When you share, you help reduce infertility and pregnancy loss rates, lower the number of IVF treatments needed, and increase the success rate of every IVF cycle worldwide.

I would be so grateful to have your help. I cannot do this alone. So let's get this into the hands of the mamas still waiting to kiss their baby sooner.

Ah, that double entendre never gets old for me. I giggle every time.

But really, how do you make sure you don't get f-ed in the IVF process but still get pregnant? You level up. That's exactly what we're about to do. No more hours (or let's be honest, months) scrolling through endless internet rabbit holes only to find yourself lost like Alice. This is the information that will help you have real, strategic conversations with your doctor about your IVF protocol and how it's actually being executed.

You're probably exhausted from learning, researching, and trying to piece together what actually works so you can finally see success or avoid failed IVF altogether. But this should feel different. As of this writing, you cannot find such information anywhere else. No one else has gathered IVF success strategies from not just one or two doctors but from thousands of protocols across the best and worst clinics around the world and distilled them into a repeatable formula. Our formula includes specific protocols and execution guidance based on your unique biology, organized in a way that finally makes sense to you, the patient.

I know I've said this before, but it's worth repeating: I am not a doctor. And that is exactly what makes this information so powerful. I didn't learn this in school or pull it solely from research papers. What I'm sharing isn't limited by clinic policies or standard IVF playbooks. It's not about what should work in theory but about what I've *seen* work, over and over again, in real IVF cycles with real outcomes.

You should expect to hear things from your doctor that don't always align with what I say, especially if you haven't had success with IVF yet. And that's one of the biggest points of this book.

Of course, always follow your doctor's medical guidance. But if your results aren't improving and what you're learning here looks very different from your current plan, that's your sign that there is still hope and strategy waiting for you, and it may be time to get a second opinion.

My goal for you is simple: **take 100 percent responsibility for your IVF treatments, but not 100 percent of the blame.** And the only way to do that is to know exactly what will make your IVF as successful as possible and accept nothing less.

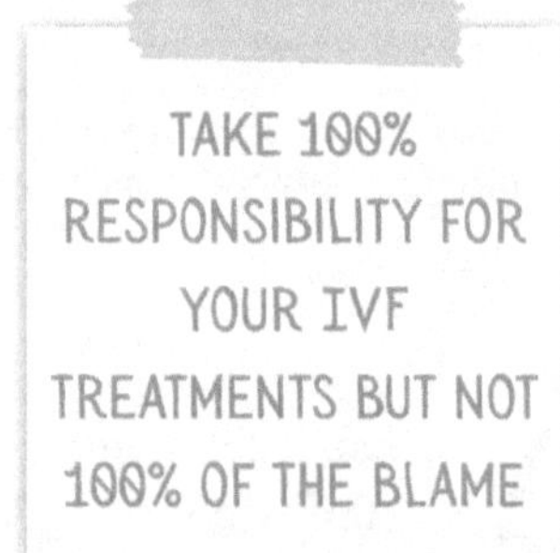

IVF'S INCONVENIENT TRUTHS

Let's start with what most IVF patients don't see, or try really hard not to see: the inconvenient truths. I'm not sharing these to make you afraid of IVF, but to wake you up and help you see things clearly from the start. So many women walk into IVF believing that something this scientific and advanced has to work the first time. Then the wind gets knocked out of them when it doesn't. And then it doesn't again. And again. Until one day they realize they haven't taken a full breath in years.

But it doesn't have to be this way. When you go into IVF with your eyes wide open, you can better protect your time, money, egg reserve, and the energy you pour into it.

After we walk through the inconvenient truths, I'll share what my experience has taught me so you know exactly how to protect yourself from that "gut punch" before it happens.

By the end of this journey, I don't want you barely breathing or standing there numb, waiting for the next hit and too used to the pain to even flinch. I want you taking big, full, confident breaths, feeling strong, clear, and steady, knowing exactly what you can control to help you create the family and life of your dreams.

Okay, you might want to brace yourself *just* for this first one...

INCONVENIENT TRUTH: THE SYSTEM PROFITS FROM MORE *TREATMENTS*

(Ouch!)

I know, I know, I'm sorry, but we must address the elephant in the stirrups. While IVF is an incredible opportunity to help your body do what it was made to do so you can finally create your family, it is also a *very lucrative business*. That doesn't make it bad; it just means your clinic and you might have different definitions of success.

Let's start with some stats that make me throw up a little in my mouth.

The average IVF patient in the U.S. spends over $53,000 on treatment, and only 27 percent have full insurance coverage. That doesn't even include lost income from time off work, travel costs, or the long list of extras. One cycle alone averages $23,474, and most people go through about 2.7 of them.

And remember from the introduction to this book, when I paid out of pocket for my first IVF round, my clinic charged me around $20,000. The very next cycle, once insurance kicked in, they billed the insurance company $11,000.

They charged me more than they charged a multibillion-dollar insurance company.

It felt like finding out my boyfriend had been cheating on me.

There are absolutely IVF *doctors* who are in this work for the mission rather than the money. But I personally don't know of any IVF *clinic owners* or *partners* who are. I have a hard time believing any board meeting with investors kicks off with, "So, how can we lower our per-patient revenue this quarter and have each patient do fewer treatments?"

I could be wrong, but when investors or business partners are involved, the goal often becomes simple: maximize per-patient revenue and profits.

And what's the most profitable model? One that keeps you coming back. More cycles. More medications. More add-ons. More of everything.

What Experience Has Taught Me: You Are 100 percent Responsible for Your Family-Building Journey

You are the CEO of your family, and no one cares about it or the costs that come with it (and I am not just talking financial) as much as you do.

So instead of being afraid of your doctor, afraid to ask questions, afraid to come across as difficult, or worried they will compromise your treatments if you are annoying to them, shift your focus. **Be less afraid of upsetting your doctor and more afraid of wasting your time, money, energy, and egg reserve on a process that never leads you to your baby.**

Here, you will learn the real factors that drive IVF success and the strategies that help you overcome setbacks, drawn from data and experience with the most brilliant IVF doctors in the world. I will also teach you how to *respectfully* and *effectively* have conversations with your doctor about strategy and decisions that impact your results.

> BE LESS AFRAID OF UPSETTING YOUR DOCTOR AND MORE AFRAID OF WASTING YOUR TIME, MONEY, ENERGY, AND EGG RESERVE ON A PROCESS THAT NEVER LEADS YOU TO YOUR BABY

But first, you need to accept that if you are walking into a business to hire a service, it is up to you to protect your investment.

Once you understand that their definition of success may not match yours, you put on your CEO hat and find the doctor whose mission aligns with your own.

INCONVENIENT TRUTH: WHEN IT COMES TO IVF, THE ODDS FAVOR THE HOUSE

I have never liked how the doctor decides what to share with you about your IVF treatments and results. It feels a little like Vegas: what happens in the embryology lab stays in the embryology lab. It is completely up to the doctor whether anything gets documented and how much they choose to explain.

That lack of transparency works in their favor. The less they share, the less they are held accountable. The less they explain, the fewer questions they get from you.

If they make a mistake, they do not have to tell you. And if they do not tell you, they probably avoided a lawsuit.

When IVF fails, I have rarely heard a doctor explain what could have been done differently or better to increase the chances of success. Instead, it often lands on the easiest target: the woman and her body. And too often, she believes it.

In IVF, there is a significant risk for the patient and a significant reward for the clinic. The clinic gains no matter what, while you might lose everything. And that is exactly why, when it comes to IVF, the odds favor the house.

What Experience Has Taught Me: Strategy Always Beats Luck

I always tell my clients, "While I will never guarantee a pregnancy, I am certain that with a couple of strategic changes, you could see a huge improvement in your results."

If I can say that without even seeing their monitoring reports, it is because they have already told me about major red flags, such as something in their protocol or its execution that's working against them. Once I review the monitoring reports, I can precisely pinpoint what could have improved the success rates.

Sometimes it's the wrong priming, the wrong dose from the start, no adjustments when hormone levels call for it, lack of monitoring, the wrong trigger timing or medication, or even lab issues that only become clear once we look at fertilization and embryo growth.

While there will always be information patients are not allowed to see, learning how to read and interpret your own data gives you power. It helps you ask smarter, more strategic questions that open better conversations and lead to stronger outcomes.

That is exactly what this book will teach you. You will learn to spot red flags in your IVF treatment and shift from a passive patient to an active partner in your care. You will learn how to play the IVF game with strategy instead of luck and finally stack the odds in your favor.

INCONVENIENT TRUTH: IVF'S DEFINITION OF "SUCCESS" WOULD BE A FAILURE ANYWHERE ELSE

IVF success rates that actually result in a baby in your arms are far lower than most patients realize.

The chart below shows the average IVF success rates per round for egg retrievals using your own eggs, embryo transfers using your own eggs, and embryo transfers using donor eggs. These rates come directly from the Centers for Disease Control and Prevention (CDC.gov) and represent live births per attempt, not positive pregnancy tests. In other words, a cycle only counts as "successful" if it ends with a baby.

The second part of the chart shows how many retrievals or transfers it actually takes to reach a 99 percent chance of live birth. For example, with a 52.6 percent success rate per attempt, your cumulative chances rise to 77.6 percent after two tries, 89.4 percent after three, and 99 percent after about six.

Here are the success rates by age and treatment type:

EGG RETRIEVALS NEEDED FOR 99% CUMULATIVE SUCCESS (OWN EGGS)

Source: CDC.gov, 2022 reporting year

Age Range	Success Rate Per Retrieval	Retrievals Needed
Under 35	52.6%	~6
35-37	39.7%	~9
38-40	26.1%	~15
Over 40	9.4%	~47

EMBRYO TRANSFERS NEEDED FOR 99% CUMULATIVE SUCCESS (OWN EGGS)

Age Range	Success Rate Per Transfer	Transfers Needed
Under 35	49.1%	~7
35-37	46.0%	~7
38-40	41.1%	~9
Over 40	25.4%	~16

EMBRYO TRANSFERS WITH DONOR EGGS (ANY AGE)

Age Range	Success Rate Per Transfer	Transfers Needed
Any	52.0%	~6

In any other field, this level of "success" would be a big, flashing red flag with "*FAIL*" written all over it. But in IVF, you're trained to feel lucky to fall within these numbers.

What Experience Has Taught Me: We Don't Follow the Numbers, We Follow the Plan

While the national average shows it can take up to six embryo transfers to have a baby, even for the youngest patients or those using donor eggs, for years now, my clients' average has stayed between 1.3 and 1.5 transfers. That includes women under 35, over 40, with endometriosis, PCOS, or multiple failed cycles behind them.

How does that happen? Strategy.

When you build a plan for egg retrievals and embryo transfers based on your unique biology and use real data from your own cycles, your chances of success could rise dramatically. And yes, that is exactly what this book will teach you to do.

Now that you see how the system works, you move differently. You put on your CEO hat. You stop hoping blindly and start building strategically. We don't expose the system to be cynical. We do it so we can do IVF better and make success more repeatable.

IVF GLOW-UP: FROM "OKAY" TO OPTIMIZED IVF

I remember my client telling me that her doctor, at a very prominent clinic, said, "Your IVF protocol doesn't really matter. We're just looking for that one good egg." Meaning, whether they give you high or low doses of medication, use this drug or that one, or start in the follicular or mid-luteal phase, the results will be the same because it's all just a numbers game to find that one good egg.

I can confidently say I fully and completely disagree. Protocols matter *a lot*.

They can influence how many follicles show up from the start, how many actually grow, how evenly they grow, how fast they grow, and how many are strong enough to make it to the embryo stage.

So if you're hearing any version of that myth, you're probably at a clinic that does "okay" IVF, not optimized IVF, and that's your cue to smile politely, gather your things, and head for the door.

"OKAY" IVF FOR EGG RETRIEVALS

"Okay" IVF is what I call the standard, one-size-fits-*none* approach. It's what happens when protocols are handed out like templates with your name filled in at the top but not built around your biology.

Here's what a typical "okay" IVF protocol looks like:

- Birth control for three weeks, starting on day one of your period
- 300 units of FSH medication, such as Gonal-F or Follistim
- 150 units of Menopur or Meriofert
- An antagonist such as Cetrotide or Ganirelix
- Nine days or less of stimulation medication before the trigger shot
- Trigger with Ovidrel, providing 6,500 IU of hCG

I've seen this protocol used for women with 2 follicles and women with 22. I've seen it used with both low and high AMH and FSH. Each of those profiles requires a specific protocol and execution of it to get the best results possible.

Here's the typical execution of "okay" IVF:

- The medication dose stays the same no matter how your follicles are growing, or worse, it's increased toward the end, which often causes some follicles to grow too fast while others lag behind.
- Monitoring feels more like something to check off a list rather than real data being used to make smart, strategic adjustments.
- The egg retrieval date is already set before you start medication.
- Communication is minimal at best and usually limited to you and your nurse.
- Your doctor isn't running the show or making protocol changes. Your nurse is, which turns "okay" IVF into "oh hell no" IVF.
- And when it doesn't work, the "solution" isn't a new strategy, but to crank up the meds even more or repeat the same protocol with a Lupron flare.

The typical result I see with "okay" IVF.

Follicles often grow at very different rates. A few reach the right size for fertilization (more on those ranges to come), but most don't. So, when only a couple of embryos are created, the conclusion is usually "poor egg quality."

And even when "okay" IVF does lead to embryos, many turn out to be "unhealthy."

Wait, did I just say that a protocol could increase the number of genetically healthy embryos? Yes! I have case studies to prove it. Remember, when embryos are tested, you're not actually testing the cells that make up the fetus itself. And if the cells around it are "exhausted" from being blasted with medications, they may start replicating abnormally.

Other times, the issue isn't uneven growth but low response. You do a full round, end up with no embryos to transfer, and hear, "Well, we gave you max meds, and you're still not responding, so you probably need donor eggs."

Now, egg donation is an incredible option for the right time and the right person. But about 60-70 percent of my clients were told they needed donor eggs, yet fewer than 5 percent actually ended up using them.

This isn't a small difference, and it isn't a coincidence. It should make anyone pause before concluding their body is broken or that donor eggs are the only option.

OPTIMIZED IVF FOR EGG RETRIEVALS

Let's talk about "optimized" IVF. Whoo hoo!

When IVF is optimized, your protocol is built around your biology, adjusted based on real-time results, and supported by an exceptional lab. That's when your real potential becomes visible, not because things are being done "right," but because they're being done precisely.

This approach starts with you and evolves using the data your body provides during treatment.

After nearly a decade of studying IVF protocols and outcomes, I've seen what the most successful IVF doctors actually do to create plans that work for the individual sitting in front of them.

Here are the key inputs they focus on and how each one helps fine-tune your plan:

YOUR KEY INPUTS AND HOW THEY DETERMINE YOUR IVF PROTOCOL	
KEY INPUT	**HOW IT GUIDES YOUR PROTOCOL**
AGE	Trigger timing
YOUR MENSTRUAL CYCLE	Priming strategy: medication type and duration
ANTRAL FOLLICLE COUNT (AFC)	Priming strategy: medication type and duration Trigger shot medication
ANTI-MÜLLERIAN HORMONE (AMH)	Priming strategy: medication type and duration Trigger shot medication
FOLLICLE-STIMULATING HORMONE (FSH)	Priming strategy: medication type and duration
BODY MASS INDEX (BMI)	Stimulation medication dosing
YOUR HISTORY	Narrows medication options based on past response and outcomes

What you should expect from a doctor who's doing optimized IVF:

- A protocol built around your actual data, not averages or clinic scheduling
- Medication doses that change when your body gives new information, not after the cycle is already over
- A doctor who is actively involved, reviewing results and making decisions in real time, not delegating strategy to a checklist or nurse

Optimized IVF doesn't guarantee a baby. Nothing does. But it does remove a lot of unnecessary guesswork and wasted cycles. While I will never promise success, I am very clear about this: **when IVF is done strategically, you protect your time, your money, and your egg reserve** instead of burning through them.

WHEN IVF IS DONE STRATEGICALLY, YOU PROTECT YOUR TIME, YOUR MONEY, AND YOUR EGG RESERVE

This approach is often the difference between creating your family and being told you "ran out of options" when the real issue was how the process was handled.

WHY CLINICS MIGHT PICK "OKAY" IVF OVER OPTIMIZED IVF

I recently spoke with a woman who was at a very famous and wildly expensive clinic. She had a strong follicle count and should have had great success with IVF, but that's not what happened. Her first round gave her zero blastocysts. Her second round gave her seven, but only one was genetically normal. The clinic told her she probably had major egg quality issues and needed to keep doing more retrievals to find the good ones.

I felt sick hearing about her cookie-cutter protocol from start to finish and how both she and the clinic blamed her for the poor results.

And then I couldn't help but wonder if the clinic's approach was part of a larger strategy. The shockingly poor outcome from the first round knocked her down. That slight bump in the second round gave her just enough hope to hook her for another.

Instead of *one* well-designed, appropriately timed retrieval, they could bill her for *three* overpriced ones.

I truly believe she could have seen success with one egg retrieval, because this was my usual consulting client: plenty of eggs and few to no embryos.

When she mentioned my name to her doctor, he said something like, "Oh, I know Tasha. Don't bother working with her. She would agree with everything I'm already doing." So she felt confident there was no need to hire me because her doctor was already planning to do what I would have recommended.

The truth is, I've taken plenty of clients away from that doctor and sent them to others in the same area who actually do optimized IVF from the start. So I think he's officially afraid of me. Or really tired of me.

(Either way, I get it. And honestly, I kind of like it. It makes me feel like a big mama bear protecting her little mamas. *Rooooaaaar!*)

So, the multi-billion-dollar question is this: why aren't more doctors doing optimized IVF?

Without being inside every clinic, here's what years of consulting have shown me:

1. **No Research Papers.** Some clinics follow a "no trials, no try" approach, which is frustrating. Anyone in medicine knows how flawed, biased, and expensive research can be. The ones funding the studies are often the ones making the most money from them. I believe too many doctors miss out on progress by ignoring unresearched, yet effective, methods that their more successful peers are using every day.
2. **Hands Are Tied.** Some doctors aren't free to choose the best protocol for each patient. They work for big fertility networks, and those networks set the rules. Switching things up takes time, paperwork, and often approval from people who aren't even treating the patients.
3. **Limited Exposure.** Doctors who have only worked at one clinic may never see how others approach IVF differently or more effectively. Ideally, clinics would share best practices that actually work, but I haven't seen that happen much.
4. **"If It Ain't Broke..."** I can see how, from a clinic's point of view, their process doesn't look broken. So why change it? The way IVF is commonly done is profitable, predictable, and produces success rates that sit comfortably at the national average.

But from my perspective, **as someone who has been a patient and now works in this field, IVF as both a process and an industry is broken.**

AS SOMEONE WHO HAS BEEN A PATIENT AND NOW WORKS IN THIS FIELD, IVF AS BOTH A PROCESS AND AN INDUSTRY IS BROKEN

I think of IVF as the road we all travel to reach the same destination: having a baby. But that road is full of massive potholes. Cycle after cycle, as we drive over them, our "cars"—our bodies—take the hit. Eventually, the car breaks down. And when it does, the road points the finger at the car.

No. It wasn't the car. It was the potholes!

Fix the potholes, and the car runs the way it was designed to. Fix IVF protocols and success standards, and many bodies will too.

Right now, the system allows those potholes to stay, and the damage gets written off as "statistics."

WHAT DOES A SUCCESSFUL ROUND OF IVF LOOK LIKE?

The definition of "success" with IVF is all over the place, so I want to show you what I believe actually counts as success.

Yes, having a baby is the ultimate goal. But a baby doesn't automatically mean their IVF was successful. It means the goal was reached, but not necessarily that the path there was efficient, strategic, or something worth repeating.

When I got pregnant with my son Hudson, it was after my second egg retrieval. I had around fifteen eggs retrieved in each of the first two rounds but ended up with only two decent-looking day-3 embryos each time ("day-3" referring to embryos that have been growing in the lab for three days). Both times, those embryos were transferred fresh. The second round worked, and that was Hudson.

However, looking back, that wasn't successful IVF.

At 33, with fifteen eggs retrieved, I should have had around *seven* day-3 embryos per round. Not two. That means across those two cycles, it was possible for me to have fourteen or more day-3 embryos instead of four, with plenty on ice for when I was ready for baby number two.

You already know what happened next: I went back to that clinic for baby number two and got the same results across three additional rounds, with no positive pregnancy outcomes at all.

If I had seen then that those cycles were never actually successful and that my results could have been so much better, I could have saved myself a lot of time, money, egg reserve, and sanity.

Let me give you another example.

I once spoke with a woman who wasn't working with me, but she wanted to know why her second retrieval didn't work when her first "successful" round gave her two blastocysts. I asked for her full numbers.

Here's what she told me:

First round: 22 eggs retrieved → 12 mature → 4 fertilized → 2 blastocysts → 1 normal embryo

Second round: Same egg count → *zero* blastocysts

She had hoped for the same results the second time. I had to explain that neither round was truly successful. With twenty-two eggs, the results should have been stronger. That kind of drop-off in embryo development usually points to uneven follicle growth caused by incorrect medication dosing from the start or by not adjusting the dosing appropriately as follicle sizes and hormone levels change, not egg quality.

THE TRUE ART IN ART (ASSISTED REPRODUCTIVE TECHNOLOGY) IS EVEN AND STEADY FOLLICLE GROWTH, NOT TOO FAST AND NOT TOO SLOW

The true art of ART (assisted reproductive technology) is even and steady follicle growth, not too fast and not too slow. When that happens, it is a sign you have the right doctor, the right lab, and a truly successful cycle.

Here's what I look for in a well-optimized IVF cycle:

- Antral Follicle Count (AFC) → Eggs Retrieved: *at least* 80%
- Eggs Retrieved → Mature & Fertilized: *at least* 80%
- Eggs Fertilized → Day-3 Embryos: *at least* 80%
- Day-3 Embryos → Blastocysts: varies by age, but could be 50% or more

So if someone has 22 eggs retrieved, here's what would ideally be seen on the conservative side:

18 mature → 14 fertilized → 11 day-3 embryos → 6+ blastocysts (depending on age)

And yes, you can *beat* these numbers.

WHEN A PROTOCOL IS BUILT SPECIFICALLY FOR THE PATIENT AND EXECUTED CORRECTLY, OUTCOMES CAN LOOK DRAMATICALLY DIFFERENT

The following case studies from some of my clients show the difference between IVF that meets the national average and IVF that is truly optimized.

The goal here isn't to impress you with numbers but to help you see patterns. **When a protocol is built specifically for the patient and executed correctly, outcomes can look dramatically different.**

CLIENT SUCCESS STUDY 1

Age	34 years old
PCOS	Yes
AFC	21 follicles
AMH	2.86 ng/mL
FSH	5.47 mIU/mL

	BEFORE OPTIMIZATION	AFTER OPTIMIZATION
EGGS RETRIEVED	21	25
MATURE EGGS	7	18
FERTILIZED EGGS	2	12
BLASTOCYSTS	2	10
GENETIC TESTING	Yes	Yes
NORMALS	2	7

CLIENT SUCCESS STUDY 2

Age	35 years old
PCOS	No
AFC	9 follicles
AMH	0.9 ng/mL
FSH	8.0 mIU/mL

	BEFORE OPTIMIZATION	AFTER OPTIMIZATION
EGGS RETRIEVED	7	7
FERTILIZED EGGS	7	7
BLASTOCYSTS	2	5
GENETIC TESTING	Yes	No
NORMALS	1	No genetic testing. First transfer resulted in success

CLIENT SUCCESS STUDY 3

Age	33 years old
PCOS	No
AFC	29 follicles
AMH	3.3 ng/mL
FSH	6 mIU/mL

	BEFORE OPTIMIZATION	AFTER OPTIMIZATION
EGGS RETRIEVED	10	10
MATURE EGGS	8	6
FERTILIZED EGGS	5	7
BLASTOCYSTS	2	5
GENETIC TESTING	Yes (1 normal)	No genetic testing. First transfer resulted in success.

CLIENT SUCCESS STUDY 4

Age	32 years old
PCOS	No
AFC	4 follicles
AMH	0.33 ng/mL
FSH	18 mIU/mL

	BEFORE OPTIMIZATION	AFTER OPTIMIZATION
EGGS RETRIEVED	4	4
FERTILIZED EGGS	4	3
BLASTOCYSTS	1	3
GENETIC TESTING	Yes	Yes
NORMALS	1 Day 7	1 Day 5, 1 Day 6, 1 Low-Level Mosaic

CLIENT SUCCESS STUDY 5

Age	40 years old
PCOS	No
AFC	3 follicles
AMH	0.2 ng/mL
FSH	6.4 mIU/mL

	BEFORE OPTIMIZATION	AFTER OPTIMIZATION
EGGS RETRIEVED	4 (across eight egg retrievals)	1
FERTILIZED EGGS	4 (across eight egg retrievals)	1
DAY 3 EMBRYOS	0	1
GENETIC TESTING	NA	NA
NORMALS	NA	Frozen transfer of her single day 3 embryo was successful

CLIENT SUCCESS STUDY 6

Age	38 years old
PCOS	No
AFC	13 follicles
AMH	4.4 ng/mL
FSH	2.4 mIU/mL

	BEFORE OPTIMIZATION	AFTER OPTIMIZATION
EGGS RETRIEVED	19	27
FERTILIZED EGGS	19	22
BLASTOCYSTS	4	11
GENETIC TESTING	YES	YES but only 4
NORMALS	3	4 of the 4 tested were normal. 6 left untested

Sexy, right?

When it comes to embryo transfers, instead of egg retrievals, my definition of success depends on a few key factors:

- Whether we are transferring day-3 embryos or blastocysts
- If the embryo is tested or untested
- How many embryos are transferred

- What is the age of both the eggs and the sperm

Because of that, I do not use a fixed success rate the way I do for egg retrievals. My rule is simple. If you have had a failed transfer, we do not keep repeating the same protocol and assume the embryo is the problem.

I have an entire chapter on maximizing embryo transfers where I share exactly how I prepare my clients, the kinds of conversations I encourage them to have with their doctor, and the success rates that can happen once preparation is done correctly.

Overall, when you understand what real success in IVF should look like, you know what you should expect. And if your results look very different, that is your sign that something needs to change, whether it is your protocol, execution, medical team, or sometimes all three.

I remember saying to someone recently, "I know you are 42 years old, but that protocol was never going to work for you." She had been beating herself up over her age, full of fear that her body would not allow her to have this baby. Hearing her say that her poor results were her fault because of her age broke my heart. **I wish every woman doing IVF knew that while age can make success more challenging, it's the protocol that decides whether you have a chance at all.**

OWN THE PROCESS. CHANGE THE OUTCOME.

I WISH EVERY WOMAN DOING IVF KNEW THAT WHILE AGE CAN MAKE SUCCESS MORE CHALLENGING, IT'S THE PROTOCOL THAT DECIDES WHETHER YOU HAVE A CHANCE AT ALL

(If you have your phone nearby, open YouTube and play "Try Everything" by Shakira. Skip the ad... unless it's one of mine... and then once the music starts, read this section!)

My ten rounds of IVF were 100 percent my responsibility. But I had the same issue that I hear from almost every new client: "I didn't know what I didn't know."

I kept saying yes to cycles that repeated the same protocol and yielded the same disappointing results. I ignored red flags because I was scared and desperate. I focused so hard on the end goal that I didn't stop to question the process that clearly wasn't working.

I was doing my best. I read *everything*, asked questions, and tried to advocate for myself. But the information I truly needed, the kind that could have helped IVF actually work for me, was nowhere to be found.

Now it's available—you're reading it here. And that's what makes Part 2 of this book so exciting because, once you read it, you are never going to have to say, "I don't know" when it comes to making decisions about your IVF journey.

My goal is simple. I want to help you get the outcome you want without wasting cycles, money, or energy on a plan that was never going to work for you.

I actually do believe IVF can be a numbers game. But not in the "just keep trying and hope one sticks" kind of way. **In optimized IVF, you work the numbers by adjusting what you can control and stacking the odds in your favor.**

IN OPTIMIZED IVF, YOU WORK THE NUMBERS BY ADJUSTING WHAT YOU CAN CONTROL AND STACKING THE ODDS IN YOUR FAVOR

I didn't know any of this when I started. And I truly believe that's why it took nine egg retrievals and ten transfers to have my two kids. But you? You get to do better. And that lights me up.

In Part 2 of this book, you'll learn:

- What brilliant IVF doctors are doing differently
- How to avoid cookie-cutter protocols
- What matters with meds, timing, and strategy
- How to choose the right doctor for you
- What to expect during egg retrievals and how to respond afterward
- How to avoid the most common IVF mistakes
- What it actually takes to make embryo transfers work

So you can stop:

- Searching the internet at 2 a.m. for answers
- Following strategies meant for someone else
- Feeling blindsided after every failed cycle
- Second-guessing every decision
- Wondering if you should be doing more and more
- Worrying that you might never be a mom or a mom again

This information took me almost ten years to learn, test, and turn into something teachable. But it's here! And once you understand how IVF really works and what to expect from exceptional care, that clarity leads to confidence. You stop feeling like you're riding in the back of a flatbed truck with your life savings flying out the back. Instead, you're in the driver's seat. Calm. Cool. In control.

Now, unlike what the Shakira song says, you're not going to "try everything." You're going to try the *key* things that will bring your gorgeous babies into this world.

And here's what excites me most: if everyone doing IVF reads this book, then every IVF patient will go through the process more educated, supported, and strategic.

We *can* change the success rates of egg retrievals and transfers worldwide. This might be more than a book on IVF... The outcome could be an infertility revolution!

(Okay, okay, I know. I went too far again... but fertility can happen! Are you in this with me?)

Your first order of business: put this book down, replay the song, and get up and dance!

CHAPTER 7 SUMMARY

- **Adopt the "CEO" Mindset:** Take full responsibility for managing your treatment and protecting your investment; don't be afraid to ask "annoying" questions to avoid wasting time and egg reserve.
- **Identify Business Misalignment:** Recognize that clinics are lucrative businesses; their definition of success (maximizing revenue) may not always align with yours (getting pregnant in the fewest cycles possible).
- **Demand Optimized vs. "Okay" IVF:** Reject "one-size-fits-none" templates. Optimized IVF requires a protocol built on your specific hormone data, adjusted in real time by a doctor, not a nurse.
- **Challenge the "Poor Egg Quality" Myth:** Failed cycles are often blamed on the woman's age or eggs when the real culprit is a poorly timed or executed protocol that causes uneven follicle growth.
- **The 80% Efficiency Rule:** Aim for a "successful funnel" where you retain at least 80% of your count at each stage: from follicles to eggs and from eggs to fertilized embryos.
- **Strategy Over Luck:** Success isn't just a numbers game. You can stack the odds in your favor by ensuring the "art" of your cycle—even, steady follicle growth—is prioritized by the lab and doctor.
- **Monitor the "Vegas" Lab:** Since clinics rarely volunteer information on their own mistakes, you must learn to interpret your own monitoring reports to hold the medical team accountable.

8. Precise Protocols for Egg Retrievals

Last month, I found something I had been hoping to see for nearly a decade. No, it wasn't a flat lower stomach (how dare you). It was my medical record.

I was cleaning out old emails to free up space when I spotted the massive file of my IVF medical records that I had sent to my fourth clinic. For years, I had thought about how cool it would be to personally analyze my own IVF cycles the same way I do for my clients, but I assumed there was no way to get them back.

There they were, sitting in my inbox like a time capsule, waiting to be opened.

I printed them out and reviewed them as if I were prepping for a client call. And sure enough, the patterns lined up with what I had long suspected based on my confusing results, especially for someone my age with strong follicle counts and what they always called "perfect fertility."

My protocols followed "okay" IVF formulas instead of being optimized. Not surprisingly, I ended up with very few embryos because my follicles consistently grew unevenly.

Even before seeing my protocols, I knew it wasn't my egg quality, no matter how many times I was told otherwise. Not because I was young, but because it never felt right. And then I was proven correct when, as I shared before, my fourth doctor suggested embryo testing to confirm that my eggs were causing the failures. But at my oldest age and doing IVF and genetic testing of the embryos for the first time, both embryos I made were genetically normal.

Was that a coincidence? Maybe. Do I believe it was? Absolutely not.

I fully believe I could have avoided nine retrievals and ten transfers if I had known then what I know now. But as I've said before, I wouldn't change a thing.

My path to parenthood was humbling, hollowing, and heartbreaking. But it was mine for an important purpose. It gave me the clarity to see what's broken, the grit to challenge it, and the fire to rebuild a smarter, kinder way forward for every woman coming behind me.

IVF VS NATURAL CONCEPTION

To understand how IVF medications are meant to help, it's important to first understand what IVF is actually trying to do. This comparison between natural conception and IVF shows you exactly what IVF can support and what it can't override.

IVF Doesn't Create More Follicles. In both natural conception and IVF, your body is working with the same follicle supply. The difference is how many follicles get the signal to grow.

In a natural cycle, your brain sends hormone signals to select one or two "alpha" follicles. There's a limited amount of "food," so only the alphas get fed and mature while the rest are reabsorbed. Typically, one egg is released during ovulation.

In IVF, stimulation medication doesn't make new follicles appear. It simply gives more of your existing follicles the "food" they need to grow, allowing more than only the alphas to mature.

IVF Can't Make Fertilization Happen. Once eggs are retrieved, the next step is fertilization. In natural conception, sperm meets egg in the fallopian tube. In IVF, sperm are either added to the eggs in a dish or injected directly into them using Intracytoplasmic Sperm Injection (ICSI).

This can help overcome barriers like a tough outer shell on the egg, but if the egg and sperm aren't healthy or compatible, fertilization still won't occur. IVF can assist the meeting, but it can't force the outcome.

IVF Can't Make Embryos Grow. In natural conception, embryos develop in the best environment possible: the body. In IVF, embryos grow in a lab.

Even in excellent labs, no environment can fully replicate the uterus. IVF also cannot protect against lab errors, media issues, or human mistakes. Embryo development still depends on cellular health and proper conditions.

IVF Can't Make Implantation Happen. In a natural cycle, the embryo finds its way to the uterine lining and implants if conditions are right. In IVF, the embryo is placed directly into the uterus, but nothing forces implantation.

Hormones, timing, immune balance, and overall health will determine if the body accepts the embryo.

IVF Can't Guarantee Pregnancy. In both natural conception and IVF, nothing can force a pregnancy. Staying pregnant depends on hormone balance, cell health, and genetics, and IVF doesn't override any of that.

I HOPE YOU ARE SURPRISED BY HOW LITTLE IVF ACTUALLY CREATES CONCEPTION. IT'S FAR MORE NATURAL THAN PEOPLE REALIZE

I hope you are surprised by how little IVF actually *creates* conception. It's far more natural than people realize.

Next up, I'll walk through the main categories of medication used in most IVF treatment plans: priming meds, stimulation meds, antagonists, and the trigger shot, so you can see how each medication supports different data points and decisions.

PRIMING: CALMING THE CHAOS BEFORE STIMULATION BEGINS

In the section above, you saw how follicle development works naturally versus with IVF. So what does priming actually do? Ideally, it stops the alpha follicles from jumping ahead before your doctor is ready to hand out the "food," a.k.a., stimulation meds. That pause gives more follicles a real shot at growing into mature eggs.

Priming is like giving your ovaries a nap. While they are resting, they cannot respond to early hormone signals. Then, when the nap is over and it is time for stimulation medications, the goal is for all of the follicles to wake up and start growing together at the same rate.

Here is where things can go sideways.

Sometimes priming is too strong. Instead of a "nap," your ovaries fall into a full-on "coma." When it is time to stimulate, they are still groggy. The doctor notes the slow growth and prescribes more stimulation medication to try to "wake them up."

More stimulation meds do not only mean more money. They can also lead to uneven follicle growth, which means fewer follicles in the ideal size range will become embryos. This is how someone with a higher egg reserve can still end up with poor embryo results.

MEDICATIONS AND TIMING FOR PRIMING

Typical medications used for priming include combination birth control pills, norethisterone or Aygestin, and estradiol, which is estrogen. Lupron is occasionally used, but it is less common for priming than the other options.

Priming medications exist on a spectrum. Some are more suppressive than others, and that suppression can increase based on when the medication is started in the cycle and how long it is used.

The chart below shows the most common priming medications, listed from most to least suppressive, along with how timing and duration can affect their level of suppression.

PRIMING MEDICATIONS FROM MOST TO LEAST SUPPRESSION			
PRIMING MEDICATION	**CYCLE START**	**LENGTH**	**LEVEL OF SUPPRESSION**
COMBINATION BIRTH CONTROL (OCP) + LUPRON	OCP on cycle day 1-3, then add Lupron 7 days later	21+ days	Highest
LONG LUPRON PROTOCOL	5-7 days after LH surge	15+ days	Very High
OCP (FOLLICULAR, 15+ DAYS)	Cycle day 1-3	15+ days	Very High
OCP (FOLLICULAR, 8-14 DAYS)	Cycle day 1-3	8-14 days	High
OCP (LUTEAL)	5-10 days after LH surge	7-10 days	Moderate to High
NORETHISTERONE / AYGESTIN (LUTEAL)	5 days after LH surge	7-10 days	Moderate
ESTRADIOL (LUTEAL ESTROGEN PRIMING)	5 days after LH surge	Until period begins	Light
NO PRIMING / STRAIGHT START	Follicular phase (cycle day 1-3) or mid-luteal (5-7 days after LH surge)	–	None

Note: The last five strategies listed are the ones I tend to recommend most to my clients. Talk to your doctor about starting with the least suppressive priming option first. I've seen cycles with no priming lead to more even follicular growth than those that used it. And I've seen stronger priming, meant to help even things out, end up doing the opposite.

SITUATIONS THAT MAY CALL FOR PRIMING

When I built the IVF protocol software that designs medication plans based on patient data, priming formulas took the longest to create and ended up being the most complex part of the entire system. That is because priming decisions are influenced by multiple factors such as hormone levels, cycle length, and follicle counts. This is where IVF shifts from simply okay to truly optimized, because the right priming depends on your biology, not a default plan.

But in many clinics, scheduling comes into play. When retrieval dates are fixed, priming medication choices often narrow quickly. Combination birth control is commonly used because it makes timing predictable, not because it is always the best option for your ovaries. Some patients should not be on birth control at all, yet it becomes non-negotiable when a clinic can only perform retrievals on certain days.

When the calendar drives the plan, the length of priming that best suits your biology may also be compromised. It may be too short or too long because you must have your egg retrieval on a specific date instead of responding to real-time feedback from your body.

The chart below breaks down common reasons priming is used, when it may help, and what to watch for, so you can have a more informed and confident discussion with your doctor.

PRIMING CONSIDERATIONS TO DISCUSS WITH YOUR DOCTOR		
WHEN PRIMING MAY HELP	**WHY PRIMING MIGHT HELP**	**NOTES**
PCOS	Slows early follicle growth when cycles are irregular and many follicles are recruited. More common with high AFC or AMH 3.0 ng/mL or higher.	Not all PCOS patients need priming. If cycles are regular and stimulation starts after ovulation with a mid luteal start, ask if priming is necessary.
HIGH BASELINE FSH	Lowers FSH and prevents early dominant follicles when day 2 or 3 FSH is over 10 IU per mL.	Aim for controlled slowing, not over suppression. Higher FSH often means fewer but more sensitive eggs. Use the least suppressive option that works. Consider checking FSH one to two days before stopping priming.
CLINIC SCHEDULING	Used by some clinics to fit retrievals into their calendar rather than your biology.	Too long can cause over suppression, fewer mature follicles, and higher costs. Too short may limit benefit.
HIGH AFC (30+)	Reduces active follicles at baseline and lowers OHSS risk, even when many eggs are retrieved.	The goal is balance. Strong yield without pushing the ovaries too hard.
DOCTOR PREFERENCE	Some clinics prescribe the same priming protocol to nearly everyone.	One size fits none protocols rarely give the best results. There should be a clear, measurable goal for priming.
SHORT CYCLES	Extends follicle growth time when ovulation occurs before day 11, supporting egg maturity.	Typically done in the luteal phase to lengthen the follicular phase.
HIGH BASELINE ESTROGEN	Lowers estrogen before stimulation and prevents lead follicles from jumping ahead.	High baseline estrogen can trigger early ovulation, uneven growth, low egg maturity, and poorer embryo development.

When it comes to understanding outcomes and pinpointing what part of a protocol could be adjusted to improve results, especially getting follicles to grow evenly, we pay close attention to *when* follicular growth becomes uneven.

If follicles look even at the *start* of stimulation, *priming* likely did its job. If things go off track *later*, the issue is more often tied to the dosing and execution of the *stimulation* medication.

You will learn how to spot this when we break down how to read your monitoring reports. (So much good stuff ahead!)

SIGNS THAT YOUR PRIMING PROTOCOL WAS SUCCESSFUL

- Your AFC before priming is similar after priming, unless suppression was intentional to reduce OHSS risk.
- Follicles start growing evenly once stimulation begins, without one or two racing ahead.
- If baseline FSH was high, priming brought it down without shutting the ovaries down.
- Estrogen levels at baseline are in a favorable range to start stimulation, not pushed too high or too low.
- Stimulation meds work steadily, without needing rapid dose increases to get the ovaries to respond.

STIMULATION: HIT THE PRECISE DOSE AND TIMING

Stimulation medications are essentially the "food" for your eggs. They provide the energy your follicles need to grow, and like food, the amount matters. Too little, and growth can stall. Too much, and things can get chaotic. The goal is to give enough fuel so your follicles grow steadily and together.

Designing a stimulation protocol is a dynamic process based on what your body is doing in real time. This is why following a cookie-cutter protocol or one that worked for someone else rarely yields the best results for *you*.

Which medications you start with, the doses used, when stimulation begins, whether adjustments are made along the way, and when medications are stopped all influence whether you reach the goal of creating strong, healthy embryos.

There are several key elements that shape how stimulation medications are chosen, started, adjusted, and stopped. Below is an overview of the main factors that influence a stimulation protocol and how those decisions are typically made.

WHAT SHAPES A STIMULATION PROTOCOL	
STRATEGY ELEMENT	**WHAT GUIDES THE DECISION**
MEDICATIONS USED	Doctor's training and preferences, access to specific medications, your history with each medication, age, certain medical conditions, and whether the cycle is fresh or frozen
STARTING DOSE	Antral follicle count combined with AMH
START TIMING	Priming needs, with typical start dates between cycle day 1 and 4 in the follicular phase or about 4 to 6 days after the LH surge in the luteal phase
LENGTH OF STIMULATION AND TRIGGER CRITERIA	Doctor's training and preferences, clinic scheduling limitations, avoidance of issues like OHSS, follicle sizes and hormone levels at monitoring appointments, and overall response to stimulation
ADJUSTMENTS DURING STIMULATION	Estrogen trends, follicle size distribution, days on medication, and target goals for trigger

MEDICATIONS FOR STIMULATION

Stimulation medications give your ovaries the signals they need to grow follicles. While brand names vary, these medications fall into a few main categories based on the hormones they provide.

The most common options include:

Pills

- Clomiphene or Clomid
- Letrozole or Femara

Injectables

- Follicle Stimulating Hormone (FSH): Gonal-F, Follistim
- Luteinizing Hormone or LH-Acting Medications: Menopur, Low-dose chorionic gonadotropin, including Pregnyl

Note: The medications listed here are the most commonly used in the United

States. If your medication has a different brand name, look it up to see which category it falls under.
Also, some medications contain both FSH and LH and are listed under the category they are most commonly associated with, or both are included when appropriate.

When you factor in medication type, combinations, doses, start timing, adjustments, and total days on stimulation, all guided by your individual data, the number of possible protocols is huge.

Knowing there is that much variability can feel overwhelming at first, but I encourage you to see it as empowering, especially if you have been placed on the same or very similar protocol over and over without getting the results you expected and were told there was nothing else to try, like I was. There *are* other strategies that could improve embryo development.

I include real client examples in this section below so you can see how these differences play out in real life.

Once the medications are chosen, dosing becomes the next critical piece, and it plays a major role in how your cycle unfolds.

DOSING OF STIMULATION MEDICATIONS STRATEGY

While many of these decisions really come down to your individual response and what your labs and ultrasounds are showing along the way, there are strategies I consistently prefer because I have seen them support better embryo development, and others I tend to avoid because they often do the opposite.

When I talk about stimulation dosing, I am referring to the total units per day of injectable medications, including both FSH and LH. To calculate your total daily dose, you simply add up everything you take in a single day.

For example, if you take 150 units of FSH and 150 units of LH on the same day, that equals 300 total units.

Clomid and letrozole are dosed differently. Clomid is typically prescribed between 50 and 150 mg, and letrozole is usually prescribed between 2.5 and 7.5 mg, not international units like injectables.

While this is not a direct or exact conversion, I still think of these pills as contributing to the overall stimulation load. In my framework, milligrams of Clomid are added to the total the same way injectable units are, and 2.5 mg of letrozole is roughly equivalent to about 75 units of an injectable.

For example, 150 units of FSH, 150 units of LH, and 50 mg of Clomid would equal 350 total units. Or, 150 units of FSH, 150 units of LH, and 2.5 mg of letrozole would equal 375 total units.

Again, this is *not an exact translation*, but it is the framework I use to help a client think through total stimulation load and have more informed conversations with their doctor.

The next thing to establish is the language around dosing. You will often hear terms like "mini stim" or "max dosing," but those labels are subjective. What one clinic calls low, another may call standard. So, while it is important to understand how your doctor defines these terms if they are suggested, here is how I define them:

IVF STIMULATION DOSE CATEGORIES	
HIGH-STIM / MAX DOSING	More than 450 total units of FSH and LH
STANDARD DOSING	375 to 450 total units
MINI-STIM / LOW DOSING	150 to 300 total units
NATURAL IVF	Just a pill (Clomid or Letrozole) plus 75-100 units of FSH or LH

The protocol I see most often and the one I described in detail in the section "'Okay' IVF for Egg Retrievals" uses the high end of standard dosing, usually around 450 total units, regardless of antral follicle count. These cycles are typically designed for quick growth, meaning 8 to 9 days on stimulation medications before trigger.

From what I have seen over and over, the most successful egg retrievals usually start a little lower than standard dosing, often around 375 total units, depending on the number of follicles present at baseline.

Not all doctors agree with this data. Many clients have told me their doctors insist that starting under 450 total units and reducing the medication at any point could result in fewer follicles growing. I strongly disagree.

The following are real client examples showing how lower (but not too low!) dosing, combined with strategic adjustments in dosing and timing, could dramatically improve embryo development rates.

Client Example One:

Protocol A
Total daily dose: 450 units
Eggs retrieved: 21
Blastocysts created: 2
Protocol B
Total daily dose: 225 units
Start timing adjusted
Eggs retrieved: 25
Blastocysts created: 10

Client Example Two:

Protocol A
Total daily dose: 450 units
No dosing adjustments
Eggs retrieved: 13
Blastocysts created: 5
Embryo development: 2 were normal day 7 embryos
Normal embryo rate: 40%
Protocol B
Starting dose: 375 units
Dosing strategically changed during stimulation based on results
Eggs retrieved: 21
Blastocysts created: 4
Embryo development: 3 were normal day 6 embryos
Normal embryo rate: 75%

Note: Even though the egg-to-blastocyst ratio was lower with Protocol B, the outcomes that actually matter improved. Normal embryos increased from 40 to 75 percent, and development shifted from 7 blastocysts to day 6 embryos, which are associated with higher live birth rates.

Client Example Three:

Protocol A
Total daily dose: 450 units plus Clomid
No adjustments
Eggs retrieved: 7
Blastocysts created: 2
Protocol B
Total daily dose: 225 units
Start timing adjusted
Eggs retrieved: 7
Blastocysts created: 5

Note: Even though the follicle and egg count stayed the same, blastocyst development increased by 150 percent!

On the other hand, starting too low can also backfire. When dosing is insufficient, only a few follicles respond early, and others join later. This staggered growth often leads to uneven follicle sizes and poorer embryo development.

As I mentioned previously: **Assisted Reproductive Technology (ART) is an art form... almost like a dance. When every move responds to your body's lead, the result can be a beautiful masterpiece worth admiring.**

ASSISTED REPRODUCTIVE TECHNOLOGY (ART) IS AN ART FORM... ALMOST LIKE A DANCE. WHEN EVERY MOVE RESPONDS TO YOUR BODY'S LEAD, THE RESULT CAN BE A BEAUTIFUL MASTERPIECE WORTH ADMIRING

STRATEGIES FOR STIMULATION PROTOCOLS BASED ON BODY MASS INDEX (BMI)

If your BMI is over 25 due to enlarged fat cells rather than muscle mass, you may need slightly higher doses of medication, often around 75 additional units. Fat tissue can interfere with the absorption of medications. One option to discuss with your doctor is using intramuscular injections, which can improve absorption without automatically increasing the dose.

On the other end of the spectrum, if your BMI is 18.5 or lower, or you have irregular or absent cycles, a history of over-exercising, or disordered eating, hypothalamic amenorrhea may be part of the picture. In these cases, LH-focused stimulation strategies often lead to a better response. I also tend to see that clients with a BMI under 18.5 often have higher AMH and antral follicle counts, which makes starting dose and estrogen-guided adjustments especially important for successful outcomes.

TIMING OF STIMULATION MEDICATION STRATEGY

Over the years, I've watched a very prominent clinic move further away from individualized care. As private investor involvement has increased, protocol customization has steadily decreased. Despite this shift, the clinic maintains a stellar reputation, and I often find myself practicing my poker face when people excitedly mention they are patients there.

The newest trend I have seen at this clinic is starting stimulation medications as late as cycle day 6 or 7. That is well past what most clinics would consider an appropriate start to the follicular phase, typically no later than cycle day 4. In these instances, I always encourage my clients to ask their clinical team for the specific rationale behind that timing. When a doctor at that clinic answers my client, the response is that the start of the stimulation medication did not matter because the patient was staying on estrogen, and the estrogen is holding back hormones and follicle growth.

(Buzzer sound!) Getting your period means ovarian activity has already begun. That is the activity. If estrogen were strong enough to stop your ovaries from making decisions, you would not have gotten your period in the first place. By the time bleeding starts, follicles are already responding to rising signals and beginning to organize.

When a nurse at that clinic answers my client's question, the reason given is that there was no availability in the operating room on the day the clinic wanted to schedule the egg retrieval. I appreciate the honesty, but I find that unacceptable. Taking on as many patients as possible, charging premium prices, and then being unable to properly execute IVF for each individual patient is not patient-first care.

I had one client at this clinic who was started on stimulation medications on cycle day 6. She retrieved seven eggs, which resulted in two blastocysts. I helped her prepare better questions for her doctor, including whether starting stimulation on cycle day 2 made more sense for her, along with changes to dosing and medication selection.

Her very next retrieval also produced seven eggs. This time, those eggs resulted in five blastocysts.

This is why I am so passionate about sharing what I have learned over the last decade. Once you know the red flags to look for and what best practices actually look like, famous doctor and clinic names stop impressing you. Discernment takes its place, helping you see whether a clinic's practices and protocols are truly designed to help you build your family.

Stimulation medications are typically started either in the menstrual or early follicular phase, usually around cycle days 1 to 3, or in the middle of the luteal phase, about 4 to 6 days after the LH surge.

CYCLE DAY STARTS FOR STIMULATION MEDICATION		
START PHASE	STANDARD START TIME	IF LOW OVARIAN RESERVE OR HIGH FSH
FOLLICULAR PHASE	Cycle Days 2 to 3	Start on Cycle Day 1
LUTEAL PHASE	Four to Six Days After LH Surge	Start Around Four Days After Ovulation

When starting stimulation medications in the follicular phase, the ideal timing is cycle days 1 to 3. In cases of lower ovarian reserve or higher FSH, stimulation is often started on cycle day 1, as follicle activity may already be underway.

Starting stimulation after cycle day 3 increases the risk of uneven follicle growth. By cycle day 4, the ovaries have had more time to organize on their own, and adding medication at that point often means some follicles are already pulling ahead. For that reason, cycle day 4 is generally the last day I would like to see stimulation start in the follicular phase, and even then, only in very specific situations worth discussing.

When stimulation medications are started in the luteal phase, the typical timing is about 4 to 6 days after the LH surge. If ovarian reserve is low or FSH is elevated, stimulation is often started closer to 4 days after the LH surge for the same reason. The ovaries tend to signal earlier and benefit from earlier support.

Using that same flexibility, a luteal start can sometimes be extended to day 7 after the LH surge if needed, but that would be the latest point at which I would want to see you begin taking stimulation medications.

Dual Stimulation: Two Starts in One Cycle

A mid-luteal start should not be confused with a "dual stim" protocol. Dual stimulation involves using stimulation medications in the follicular phase, completing an egg retrieval, and then restarting stimulation medications about five days later for a second retrieval in the same cycle.

From what I have seen, this approach rarely produces strong results for both retrievals. More often, one retrieval goes well, and the other does not.

When the first retrieval is successful and the second is not, my interpretation is that the body may simply be exhausted by the time the second stimulation begins. When the second, mid-luteal retrieval is the successful one and the first, follicular retrieval is not, I believe it often reflects that the initial follicular start was not well aligned with the body's hormone signals. In those cases, the medications and the trigger from the first attempt may act as a kind of reset, allowing hormone levels to settle into a more supportive pattern for the second stimulation.

Overall, if the first retrieval in the follicular phase is successful, I tend to see that as a sign that the protocol was likely a good fit for you. In those situations, it often makes more sense to wait a couple of weeks before starting again and then use the hormone levels from the baseline of that successful cycle as your reference point.

The goal is to look at apples-to-apples. Matching the same cycle day starts, medications, and dosing as closely as possible gives you the best chance of repeating a good outcome.

I go into this in more detail later on, in a section called "Round Two Retrieval: Pause or Play?"

LENGTH OF STIMULATION MEDICATION STRATEGIES

If we go back to how natural conception and IVF are actually similar, the ideal length of stimulation meds starts to make a lot more sense. In a natural cycle, eggs usually grow for about 11 to 13 days before the LH surge kicks in, and ovulation follows around cycle day 12 to 14. When that growth window is shorter than about 11 days, eggs often do not have enough time to fully mature. When it drags on much longer, it is usually a sign that something hormonal is off.

Those same patterns show up in successful egg retrieval cycles. But when I review monitoring reports from unsuccessful IVF rounds, I often see the opposite. Follicles race to 20 mm or larger in 8 or 9 days before the trigger shot. When growth happens that fast, I am rarely surprised to see uneven follicles at trigger and weaker embryo development afterward.

The goal of stimulation meds is to give your eggs enough time to mature without keeping them on medication so long that they grow too big and basically run out of gas before they ever get the chance to become embryos.

With that said, the number of days on stimulation meds cannot be decided in isolation. It must line up with follicle size, estrogen, progesterone, and LH levels. Any one of those can shorten or lengthen how long you stay on meds. I will walk through ideal hormone ranges and how they guide trigger timing in the trigger shot section, since trigger timing ultimately determines stimulation length.

For now, here is a solid general target for most people: **follicles usually need about 11 ± 1 days on stimulation meds, with roughly 80 percent of follicles measuring 17 to 19 mm ± 1 mm at trigger.**

FOLLICLES USUALLY NEED ABOUT 11 ± 1 DAYS ON STIMULATION MEDS, WITH ROUGHLY 80 PERCENT OF FOLLICLES MEASURING 17 TO 19 MM ± 1 MM AT TRIGGER

Getting there without overgrowing follicles often means easing up on medication in the back half of stimulation, assuming dosing started in the right place. The goal is slower, steadier growth, not slamming the gas pedal the whole way.

That is why, **when it comes to dosing and growth rates, I like to say, "Low and slow is the way to go."**

WHEN IT COMES TO DOSING AND GROWTH RATES, I LIKE TO SAY "LOW AND SLOW IS THE WAY TO GO"

On the flip side, being on stimulation meds for too long can also cause issues. It is less common, but when it does occur, it is usually tied to overly suppressive priming or diminished ovarian reserve, in which follicles are simply slower to wake up and respond.

Here are some factors that can lengthen or shorten the time on stimulation medication:

- **Priming protocol.** High suppression priming protocols could create that "coma" we discussed and slow the growth of the follicles.

- **Start date of stimulation.** A mid-luteal start often lengthens stimulation time, while a follicular start may shorten it.
- **Starting dose and dose adjustments.** High dosing without adjustments can shorten stimulation time, while very low dosing can extend it. And keep in mind, both too high and too low often lead to uneven follicle growth, which is linked to poorer embryo development.
- **Type of medications used.** Lupron flare protocols and human growth hormone could speed up growth.
- **How well medications are adjusted**. Adjustments made at the right time help keep growth steady instead of rushed or stalled.

SIGNS THAT YOUR STIMULATION PROTOCOL WAS SUCCESSFUL:

- Even follicle growth from start to finish, with ~80% of follicles growing within 4 mm of each other
- About 11 ± 1 days of stimulation with roughly 80% of follicles measuring 17-19 mm (± 1 mm)
- Around 80% of the follicles seen at the baseline ultrasound respond to medication and continue growing throughout stimulation
- About 80% of those follicles are successfully retrieved
- Strong fertilization rates
- Healthy embryo development

Before heading to the next section...

If you'd like to see whether you fit the profile for a follicular or mid-luteal start, and identify your ideal starting dose for stimulation medications, scan the QR code and look for Your Perfect Protocol for IVF.

OVULATION SUPPRESSOR: STOP THE SURGE

Once stimulation medication gets your follicles growing, your body's next natural move is to ovulate those eggs. In a natural cycle, that's exactly what we want. The eggs break free from their follicle walls, head down the fallopian tubes, and wait for sperm.

In IVF, that same process is a problem. If you ovulate before retrieval, those eggs are gone, and your doctor cannot get them back. That is why the ovulation suppressors join the party. Its job is to hold off the LH surge, the signal your body uses to release the eggs, until your follicles have reached the size your doctor believes gives you the best chance for mature, fertilizable eggs that could grow into beautiful embryos.

MEDICATIONS FOR OVULATION SUPPRESSORS

Most patients in IVF use GnRH antagonists, commonly called "antagonists" for short. In the U.S., the most prescribed are Cetrotide or Ganirelix. Their job is simple but critical: keep LH from surging too soon.

Another option is medroxyprogesterone acetate, sold under the brand name Provera. Research shows that starting Provera alongside stimulation meds in IVF cycles for women with a good ovarian reserve could also block the LH surge. This approach is most often used in women who respond quickly to the stimulation medication and may be considered for patients who have ovulated early with a standard GnRH antagonist. This option is worth discussing with your doctor if either situation applies to you.

TIMING OF THE ANTAGONIST

Your doctor may start the antagonist in one of two ways: either on a set day in the cycle, called a "fixed start," or based on follicular growth, called a "flexible start."

If your doctor uses a fixed start, your antagonist will likely begin after 5 to 6 days of stimulation meds. For a flexible start, you will likely start the antagonist once the lead follicle reaches around 14 mm.

Timing of the antagonist should ultimately be determined by what is happening with your results, but here are some reasons why timing might shift:

- If you have a lower egg reserve or are prone to early ovulation
- If you have a very high egg reserve and may be at risk for OHSS

Once the antagonist starts, it is taken daily until the trigger shot.

Here is a chart that shows the standard timing for starting an antagonist, along with common adjustments to discuss with your doctor based on ovulation risk and OHSS risk:

ANTAGONIST START TIMING IN IVF

SITUATION	START TIME TO DISCUSS WITH DOCTOR	GOALS
STANDARD PROTOCOL	After 5 to 6 days of stimulation or when a follicle reaches 14 mm	Standard prevention of early ovulation
LOW EGG RESERVE OR EARLY OVULATION RISK	Around 10 to 11 mm or days 3 to 4 of stimulation	Prevents early ovulation in fast responders
HIGH EGG RESERVE OR OHSS RISK	When estrogen rises faster than expected	Reduces risk of OHSS and hormonal overload

STRATEGIES FOR ANTAGONIST PROTOCOLS

If you have ovulated early in a past cycle, even while using an ovulation suppressor, this is something to plan for with your doctor so it does not happen again.

If you are not sure whether you ovulate early or you suspect it may have happened before, here are strategies worth discussing with your doctor:

- Checking LH levels more frequently during stimulation and daily as you get close to the trigger shot
- Doing an ultrasound right before retrieval to confirm follicles are not already empty, because there is no point in proceeding if ovulation has already occurred

If early ovulation has clearly happened to you in the past, more proactive adjustments may be appropriate:

- Switching from a GnRH antagonist like Ganirelix or Cetrotide to a progestin such as Provera

- Using an extended Clomid protocol, where Clomiphene is taken during stimulation along with a once-daily antagonist
- Adding the antagonist a few days into the priming phase
- Starting the antagonist earlier in stimulation and taking it twice daily instead of once
- Adding a late afternoon ultrasound on trigger day, the day before retrieval, or the day of the egg retrieval, to confirm the eggs are still inside the follicles
- Scheduling retrieval at 34 to 35.5 hours after the trigger shot, instead of the standard 36

This level of monitoring may not be offered by your IVF team, but it is worth advocating for. Yes, it can mean extra blood draws to check LH and additional ultrasounds if levels start rising, but there is no good reason a clinic should not accommodate reasonable monitoring when thousands, and sometimes tens of thousands, of dollars and so much more is on the line.

Making the assumption that you didn't ovulate early, and then finding out you did after a demanding egg retrieval, is an extremely costly mistake... and I'm not just talking financially.

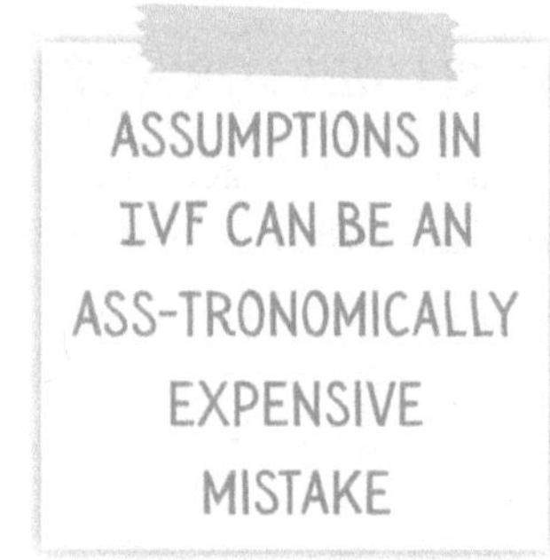

Some women come to me for consulting after this has already happened. For their next retrieval, they want a second set of eyes on the execution of their IVF treatments so they can better protect their investment. It is one of the most heartbreaking situations to hear about because it is so preventable.

This is why I say **assumptions in IVF can be an ass-tronomically expensive mistake.**

SIGNS THAT YOUR ANTAGONIST PROTOCOL WAS SUCCESSFUL

- LH levels remain low and stable throughout stimulation and do not spike as you approach the trigger shot.
- No follicles ovulate before retrieval.

- Follicles remain intact on ultrasound right up until the trigger and, if checked, before retrieval.
- Egg yield at retrieval closely matches the number of mature follicles seen on your final monitoring scan.

TRIGGER: GETTING THE TIMING RIGHT

In natural conception, a surge of LH is what tells the ovary it is time to ovulate. In IVF, the trigger shot is designed to act like that LH surge, starting the same chain reaction.

Once the trigger shot is given, the eggs begin their final changes. They loosen from the follicular walls that have been protecting them and restart the maturation process inside the egg itself. Up until this point, the eggs are essentially paused in a stage called meiosis. The trigger wakes them up and gets them ready to accept chromosomes from the sperm and create new DNA. When they reach this stage, they are considered mature, and only mature eggs can be fertilized.

Your doctor's goal is very specific. The trigger needs to give the eggs enough time to mature and loosen from the follicle, but not so much time that they fully ovulate and leave the ovary. Retrieval is then timed to catch the eggs in that narrow window, after they are ready but before they slip away and become impossible to retrieve.

MEDICATIONS FOR TRIGGER SHOTS

The most common trigger shots use human chorionic gonadotropin, or hCG. It comes in a few different forms and brands. Ovidrel is a lab-made version, while Pregnyl and Novarel are urine-derived hCG collected from pregnant women and then purified and processed into medication.

In some cases, your doctor may use Lupron on its own, combine it with hCG, or even add FSH. The exact trigger medication and dose are usually based on your follicle count on the day of the trigger, your estrogen levels, and your doctor's clinical preference.

If you are given a choice between brands, choose the least expensive option. For example, with an hCG trigger, the powdered version that you mix with 1 cc of liquid is often the lowest cost and works as well as the pre-filled syringe brand-name versions.

DOSING FOR TRIGGER SHOTS STRATEGY

Your trigger medication and dosing should be guided by your data, including your AMH, follicle count, estrogen levels leading up to the trigger, and how your eggs have responded to past triggers.

In general, if your AMH is under 2.0 ng/mL, your estrogen is under 3,000 pg/mL, your follicle count is under 20 and sometimes even up to 30 when estrogen is still under 3,000, and you do not have a history of ovarian hyperstimulation syndrome, your doctor will likely recommend an hCG trigger with or without Lupron.

If you have had low egg maturation in the past and fit into the above category, your doctor will likely want to increase the hCG dose to 10,000 IU or more, with or without Lupron. And for high follicle counts that have a risk of OHSS, your doctor will likely have you avoid hCG altogether.

Here is a chart with strategies for trigger shot medications and dosing to discuss with your doctor based on your specific biology:

STRATEGIES FOR TRIGGER SHOT PROTOCOL

SITUATION	STRATEGIES TO DISCUSS WITH YOUR DOCTOR	NOTES
AMH under 2.0 ng/mL Estrogen under 3,000 pg/mL Follicle count under 20 (up to 30 if estrogen still under 3,000) No history of OHSS	hCG 5,000-20,000 IU or hCG + Lupron	Supports ovulation and egg maturation
History of low egg maturation (and you fit into the criteria above)	Higher hCG dose (10,000+ IU) or hCG 5,000 IU + Lupron	May help improve egg maturation
AMH over 2.0 ng/mL Estrogen over 3,000 pg/mL Follicle count over 20 History or symptoms of OHSS	Lupron-only trigger	Adding 5,000 IU + of hCG could cause severe pain, OHSS, poor retrieval, and few or no embryos. FSH might also be included if Lupron alone doesn't complete LH surge.
Irregular periods and/or hypothalamic issues (BMI under 18.5, eating disorder, overexercise)	Avoid Lupron-only trigger	May not respond to Lupron trigger
Naturally low LH early in cycle (under 5 mIU/mL on days 1-4)	Avoid Lupron-only trigger	May not respond to Lupron trigger

TIMING OF THE TRIGGER SHOT

Timing the trigger shot is about finding the window where eggs are most likely to be mature and strong, without pushing them *past their peak*. This decision is typically based on follicle size, how long they have been growing, and hormone levels. When these pieces align, the trigger supports better egg maturation and stronger embryo development.

Target Follicle Size for Mature Eggs

The trigger shot should be given on the day follicles are most likely to contain mature eggs. Follicles 13 mm or larger *can* contain eggs, but they are usually *not* mature enough to fertilize until at least 15 mm. Follicles larger than 21 mm are often past their peak and less likely to produce healthy embryos.

Age can further guide the ideal follicle size at trigger. Here is what I have seen work best for follicle size ranges based on age:

TARGET FOLLICLE SIZE BY AGE AT TRIGGER

AGE	FOLLICLE SIZE ON THE DAY OF THE TRIGGER SHOT
35 and younger	18 to 21 mm ± 1 mm
36 to 42	17 to 19 mm ± 1 mm
43 and older	16 to 17 mm ± 1 mm

When Hormones Guide Trigger Timing

The main hormones that help guide trigger shot timing are estrogen, progesterone, and LH.

Most of the time, I use estrogen to help decide whether it is worth discussing dosing changes with your doctor. But estrogen can also play a role in trigger timing, especially when you have very few follicles or a lot of them.

When there are only one to three follicles growing, estrogen helps confirm whether those follicles are likely ready. A common goal is around 200 pg/mL of estrogen per follicle. That said, size matters! If you have one follicle that is already about 20 mm, but estrogen is still *under* 200 pg/mL, most doctors will trigger anyway. At that size, the follicle is starting to get past its peak, and follicles that get too big often do not turn into healthy embryos.

If that same follicle is closer to 17 or 18 mm and estrogen is still below 200 pg/mL, there is usually a little more room to wait. In that case, stimulation may continue for another day to let estrogen, which signals egg maturity, rise without letting the follicle get too big.

On the other end of the spectrum are very high follicle counts. This usually means 30 or more follicles near the time of the trigger shot. Here, the goal shifts to protecting you from OHSS.

The risk of OHSS goes up when estrogen climbs over 3,000 pg/mL. If you hit an estrogen level above 3,000 pg/mL by day eight of stimulation or earlier, many doctors will trigger sooner than planned, even if most follicles are not yet in the ideal size range. This helps reduce the risk of a ruined cycle and extreme pain for you afterward.

LH and progesterone can also help guide the timing of the trigger because they signal when your body may be preparing to ovulate. If LH rises to spikes well above 5 IU/L and approaches the 10 IU/L range, your doctor will likely be concerned that ovulation may be occurring. In that situation, a trigger shot may be needed sooner rather than later, or possibly not at all if the LH surge happened, in order to salvage any follicles that still can be saved. For this reason, it is important for LH to be checked in the back half of stimulation medications until the trigger shot.

Progesterone levels near 1.5 ng/mL are another signal that the LH surge and ovulation may be approaching. If it rises quickly and exceeds 3.0 ng/mL, ovulation may have already happened, and that will be an issue for a successful egg retrieval. Progesterone is usually checked at each monitoring visit, but it is especially important to track it closely in the later days of stimulation and leading up to the trigger shot.

Fast-growing follicles, fast-rising estrogen, early ovulation, and OHSS are often preventable with the right priming strategy, starting doses, medication adjustments earlier in the cycle, and proper monitoring, which we will cover in the section on executing egg retrieval. But when it does start happening, trigger timing and medication have to be adjusted in real time to match what your body is doing. When you see these signs starting or already in motion, it is best to talk with your doctor right away to give yourself the best chance of saving the cycle.

And if these hormones are not being checked and follicles are missing at retrieval without a clear explanation, you may have solved that mystery.

Picking the Power Pack

Once follicles are growing, the next step is deciding which ones you are actually going to build the cycle around. This is where dosing, time on stimulation meds, follicle size, follicle count, hormone levels, and trigger timing all come together.

Though some uneven growth of the follicles is expected, "Power Pack" is the name I give to the 80 percent of follicles that are all within 4 mm of each other during stimulation. When your medications, dosing, and administration are done correctly, creating a strong Power Pack is absolutely possible.

The Power Pack will have a lead follicle. This is not always the biggest follicle your ovaries are measuring. It is the largest follicle that is surrounded by several others close in size. For example, if you have ten follicles, one measuring 20 mm and the other nine between 14 and 16 mm, the Power Pack is the 14 to 16 mm group. In that case, the lead follicle in the Power Pack is 16 mm, and that is the size your doctor will likely plan trigger timing around.

When There Is No Clear Power Pack

If you get close to the trigger shot and do not have about 80 percent of follicles within 4 mm of each other, my strategy for deciding which follicles are most likely to become embryos shifts to follicle size relative to the number of days on stimulation.

For example, if you have two follicles already in the ideal range, around 17 to 19 mm ± 1 mm after about 11 days of stimulation, and two smaller follicles sitting around 10 to 12 mm, I would hope the doctor chooses the first group. If those same follicle sizes are present but it has only been 8 days since stimulation started, I would hope the doctor continues stimulation for another couple of days and aims for the second group.

As a reminder, a chart in the section above outlines ideal trigger sizes by age for more specific guidance.

Lower Ovarian Reserve Considerations

While it is often acceptable to sacrifice a true lead follicle to do what is best for the group, this becomes an issue when ovarian reserve is lower. If you have three follicles, each follicle represents a large percentage of the total. That makes even growth and protecting the Power Pack the top priority.

If growth is uneven and your alpha follicle consistently grows too quickly, only to be sacrificed for one of the other two, it points to a protocol and execution issue that needs to be addressed.

If you are in the middle of a round of IVF and you have a few follicles growing unevenly, here is a strategy to consider: discuss timed intercourse or intrauterine insemination (IUI) with your doctor instead. This can save on medications, money, and emotional energy when an egg retrieval is unlikely to yield more than one usable embryo, and changing the strategy for the next egg retrieval could give all three follicles a chance to develop into embryos.

Why "No Eggs Left Behind" Backfires

One strategy I really do not like to see is the "no eggs left behind" approach. This is when the doctor tries to retrieve eggs from both large and small follicles. I appreciate the intention, but this strategy often backfires because the size gap between those follicles is rarely within 4 mm.

What I see happen next is predictable. The larger follicles get too big and are no longer viable, while the smaller follicles still do not grow large enough to fertilize and develop into embryos. The result is usually zero embryos, followed by the explanation that, with a low egg reserve, there must be an egg quality issue. In my opinion, the real issue was execution decisions that could never work well, despite the egg count.

One More Dose Too Many

I also see cycles fall apart when follicle sizes are ideal on trigger day, but very high doses of stimulation medication are still given alongside the trigger shot.

If you have PCOS, a dose of FSH as part of the trigger can be appropriate, and that is different. What I am talking about here is continuing full stimulation medications on trigger day, even though follicle size is already ideal.

The exact approach always depends on your current biology, hormone results, and past outcomes. But in general, if follicle sizes are *ideal* on the day of the trigger shot, they do not need to grow more. They just need to go and get ready for the big day.

Timing of Egg Retrieval After the Trigger Shot

You can calculate the timing of your egg retrieval by counting how many hours have passed from when you took the trigger shot to when the retrieval actually happens. Keep in mind, the time you arrive at the clinic or hospital is not the same as the retrieval time. Your retrieval officially starts once you are in the operating room, under anesthesia, and the team is ready to go.

Egg retrievals are typically scheduled for about 36 hours after the trigger shot. For example, if your trigger shot was at 10 p.m. on Wednesday, your egg retrieval should begin around 10 a.m. on Friday.

If you have a lower ovarian reserve, are known to ovulate early, or if it looks like you might, there are two important steps to discuss with your doctor. First, ask for an ultrasound before anesthesia on the day of retrieval to confirm you have not ovulated early. This needs to be planned in advance so the right equipment and time are available. Second, your doctor may consider scheduling the retrieval a bit earlier, around 34 or 35 hours after the trigger shot.

In some cases, scheduling an egg retrieval closer to 37 hours after the trigger shot may be considered, especially if there is a history of low egg maturation. That timing does make me a bit nervous, but if this is something your doctor has experience with and has seen success from, that is an important context.

If retrieval occurs after more than 37 hours and eggs are missing, it is possible that some eggs have already left the follicles and are traveling down the fallopian tubes, making them impossible to retrieve. In that situation, the late timing of the egg retrieval is likely the reason those eggs were missed.

SIGNS THAT YOUR TRIGGER SHOT PROTOCOL WAS SUCCESSFUL

- Your progesterone is over 3.0 ng/mL, and your LH is over 15 mIU/mL (specifically for Lupron-only trigger shots) the day after the trigger shot. If you are using hCG, levels should be around 25+ mIU/mL.

- None of the follicles ovulated out before the retrieval.
- The doctor was able to retrieve all of the eggs in the follicles because they had loosened enough from the follicular walls.
- Egg maturation rate was 80% of the follicles retrieved (though the execution of the stimulation medications could influence this as well).

CHAPTER 8 SUMMARY

- **Priming Sets the Tone for the Entire Cycle:** Priming helps support even follicle growth, giving more follicles a fair shot at becoming strong eggs and embryos. In optimized IVF, priming is chosen based on your biology, not the clinic's schedule.
- **Stimulation Thrives on Responsiveness:** IVF works best when stimulation doses and timing respond to real-time feedback from your body. Strategic adjustments throughout help follicles grow steadily and together, which supports stronger embryo development.
- **Ideal Conditions for Embryo Development:** When about 80% of follicles grow within 4 mm of each other over roughly 11 ± 1 days, embryo development is often more consistent and reliable.
- **Ovulation Suppressors Safeguard Your Progress:** Antagonists play a key role in protecting eggs from ovulating too soon. Monitoring LH closely, especially later in stimulation, helps preserve cycles and outcomes.
- **Trigger Timing Maximizes Egg Maturity:** Well-timed triggers support egg maturation without letting ovulation sneak in early. Follicle size, days on stimulation, and hormone trends guide this decision.

Before we move on...

Let's check in. How are you feeling? Are you keeping up, or starting to feel a little overloaded?

If you're doing great, keep that momentum going! (And don't forget to scan the QR code to grab the resources for this chapter.)

However, if you're feeling a bit lost, remember: feeling overwhelmed by your treatment options is common, but knowing how to navigate them is not. If you're unsure which protocols to discuss, hesitant about challenging a provider's suggestions, or simply wish someone could help you manage the "big picture," you don't have to figure this out on your own. There is a way to bridge that gap.

Simply use the QR code below to schedule a conversation that could change your entire perspective on this journey. You don't have to do this alone; there are talented professionals who have spent years mastering these complexities so that you don't have to.

(Oh, and if it wasn't clear, that talented professional I know who is talented is me. Oh, it was clear? Very obvious? Ok, cool... cool.)

9. Decisions Before Retrieval

Now that you understand the medications and strategies behind optimized IVF, there are a few important decisions to think through before you choose your doctor. This chapter walks you through those decisions and shows how I help my clients weigh the options in a way that feels aligned with their family-building goals.

By the end of this chapter, it would be helpful to have a general sense of what you might want to do for each of these choices. Not because everything has to be set in stone, but because your preferences should help guide which doctor or clinic you partner with. Some clinics require certain decisions, and if you're unsure which option you would choose, but a clinic only allows one path, that might not be the right clinic for you.

For example, if you want to freeze embryos on day 3 instead of growing them to the blastocyst stage, you need to find a clinic that works with day-3 embryos and is willing to do a frozen transfer with them.

THERE IS A BIG DIFFERENCE BETWEEN WHAT COULD HAPPEN IN THEORY AND WHAT YOUR DOCTOR HAS REPEATEDLY SEEN HAPPEN IN PRACTICE

Once you are clear on your preferences, I do think it is valuable to hear your doctor's perspective, especially when their recommendations are based on what they have seen play out repeatedly with their own patients. **There is a big difference between what *could* happen in theory and what your doctor has *repeatedly seen* happen in practice.**

So let's walk through the decisions you get to choose before an egg retrieval. And yes, we are starting with the one that carries the most debate, pressure, and confusion for patients, and the one I work through most often with clients: genetic testing.

Is Genetic Testing Costing You a Baby?

I once worked with a client who had been through multiple egg retrievals. Every time, she ended up with two blastocysts. And every time she tested them, both came back abnormal.

She was exhausted. Mentally, physically, and financially. She was on the edge of giving up on IVF and on building her family altogether.

So I said something that made her eyes bug out of her head.

"Maybe you should stop testing your embryos."

She stared at me like I had suggested growing embryos in a mason jar on the windowsill.

She didn't say what she was thinking, so I said it for her. "You want to test because you're afraid of having a genetically abnormal child, right?"

"Yes," she said, visibly relieved.

"But you tried naturally first, right? And you did IUI?"

"Yes."

"And that was the same egg and sperm you're using now?"

That's when she paused. You could see the moment it clicked.

IVF does not cause genetic abnormalities. It does not change egg quality. It does not increase your odds of having a child with a genetic condition. IVF simply gives more of your existing eggs the opportunity to mature, fertilize, and develop into embryos.

So if you are doing multiple egg retrievals, getting to the blastocyst stage, testing, and not getting normal embryos, I want you to seriously consider changing the protocol, changing the lab, or stopping testing altogether.

I think I know why most people want to test, so let's address another elephant in the stirrups.

Worldwide, the chance of a pregnancy affected by a genetic condition compatible with life, such as Down syndrome, is about 0.1 percent at age 30, around 0.3 percent at age 35, and about 1 percent by age 40. It is not until age 45 and older that the risk rises closer to 3–5 percent.

In my work since 2016, I have had only one client get pregnant with a child with Down syndrome. She conceived naturally while waiting to start IVF in her mid-40s.

Of course, it is *possible*, but unlikely. And it's certainly not common.

What I hear far too often from clients is that genetic testing is framed as protection against a very high risk. It's as if choosing not to test means you are likely to have a genetically abnormal child.

That simply is not supported by real-world numbers.

I love genetic testing as a strategy when it truly protects your health, your embryos, and your family. And we will get into that next.

GENETIC ABNORMALITIES HAVE NOT INCREASED ALONGSIDE IVF USE. BUT TESTING RECOMMENDATIONS AND CLINIC REVENUE HAVE

What I do not love is the dramatic shift I have watched over the last decade, from very few patients being encouraged to test to now most being strongly pushed to do so. **Genetic abnormalities have not increased alongside IVF use. But testing recommendations and clinic revenue have.**

Whatever you choose, promise me this.

Make the decision that feels right for your family. Not the one driven by fear. Not the one forced by clinic policy. And not the one that keeps you stuck repeating cycles that drain you instead of moving you forward.

GENETIC TESTING OR NOT

Note: To keep things simple, all types of PGT (preimplantation genetic testing) are referred to as "genetic testing."

While this isn't the popular approach in IVF right now (although I do see the cool kids starting to change their ways), I no longer recommend genetic testing for *most* of my clients.

And that has been a big change in my recommendations from when I started consulting in 2016. Back then, I often encouraged clients to grow their embryos to the blastocyst stage and test them. But after years of watching real-life outcomes, I realized testing often gets in the way of the ultimate goal: a healthy baby as quickly as possible.

You might be thinking, *Whoa, whoa, whoa, Tasha. That's exactly what I want, too. How could skipping testing possibly help me get a healthy baby quicker?*

The short answer is that genetic testing is not completely accurate, no matter what your clinic says. You are not testing the actual fetal cells; you are testing the cells around them. And in my experience, the older a woman is, the more abnormal cells tend to show up.

On top of that, human error and lab variability play a role in results. Those factors are real, even if they are rarely discussed.

What matters most, though, is what I have seen repeatedly. Embryos, whether tested or not, usually fall into one of three categories. They do not implant at all. They implant briefly and stop developing within the first few weeks of a positive test. Or they grow into a healthy baby.

That pattern holds true for *well over 99 percent* of the pregnancies I have supported.

Because of this, I often see **clients who insist on genetic testing often take longer to have a healthy baby than those who choose to skip it.**

CLIENTS WHO INSIST ON GENETIC TESTING TAKE LONGER TO HAVE A HEALTHY BABY THAN THOSE WHO CHOOSE TO SKIP IT

Here is a more complete list of the reasons I changed my opinion about skipping genetic testing for some:

Miscarriages After Testing: I have seen clients transfer "genetically normal" embryos only to miscarry. When the fetal tissue was tested after, it showed a genetic abnormality like Trisomy. In other words, the original testing was wrong.

Healthy Babies Without Testing: As mentioned, I have worked with so many clients who tested embryos for years and received only "abnormal"

results. Then they stopped testing, transferred an untested embryo, and finally had their healthy child. Coincidence? Maybe. Do I believe that? Not at all.

Testing Accuracy Depends on People and Places: The results are only as reliable as the embryologist doing the biopsy and the lab analyzing it. I have seen clients go from getting only "abnormal" embryos to suddenly having all normal ones on their very next retrieval simply because they switched clinics or the clinic switched labs doing the testing.

Sampling Errors: Research shows the same embryo can test normal or abnormal depending on which cells are sampled. And, as you now know, those sampled cells are not the ones that become the baby.

Should-a-Would-a: Too often, new clients come to me regretting testing after creating all of their embryos that were labeled "abnormal." They wish they could transfer them, but most clinics will not. If you think you might end up in that situation, you may want to skip testing or consider a hybrid approach (see below).

Profit or Patient First: Testing often leads to more egg retrievals while you search for that "perfect" embryo. With an imperfect, subjective science (since what counts as abnormal can vary by clinic), plus fear-based messaging that you will regret not testing, this can easily become a very profitable business model. Do I think individual doctors are intentionally doing this? No. Do I think investor-backed clinics see the revenue opportunity? Yes.

And while I don't rely on research papers over what I have seen play out again and again in real life, the research on genetic testing has also become increasingly conflicting.

Some studies are used to support testing, while others raise serious questions about its accuracy and consistency. For example:

- A study by Tiegs et al. suggested that embryos labeled abnormal by a specific testing method did not result in live births, pointing to the idea that testing could be accurate under very controlled conditions.
- A large study by Bardos et al. found that different labs across the U.S. produced very different results when testing similar embryos. Interestingly, the labs that labeled more embryos as "normal" actually had higher live birth rates, suggesting that some clinics may be too strict and are potentially discarding embryos that could have resulted in healthy babies.

- Work from Gleicher and colleagues showed that embryos labeled abnormal were transferred and, in some cases, went on to become healthy babies. I would be curious to see the percentage of those embryos that implanted and remained past 10 weeks. From what I have seen clinically, that number is likely very small.
- A randomized trial published in the New England Journal of Medicine found no advantage to PGT-A over standard IVF when it came to live birth outcomes.

So while research always calls for more data before drawing firm conclusions, the pattern I see is clear. Genetic testing is inconsistent, highly lab-dependent, and not the fastest or most reliable path to a healthy baby, the way it is often marketed.

That said, this does not mean genetic testing is never the right choice. I *love* genetic testing when it is used *strategically*. So let's talk about those times next.

STRATEGIC WAYS TO INCLUDE GENETIC TESTING

- If you or your partner are carriers of known genetic conditions that you are trying to avoid passing on
- If you have more than four blastocysts on ice and want to reduce the number of transfers or avoid ending up with extra embryos (If you do not already have embryos frozen, you may want to consider the hybrid approach I outline below.)
- If you or your partner simply do not feel comfortable skipping testing (In my experience, it is often the male partner who insists on it) (I am not sure why, but I bet that could make a great psychology research project someday! I know, I am such a nerd.)
- If you are switching clinics and want to see if different lab conditions change your results
- If you are planning multiple retrievals, you might skip testing the first round but test later rounds once you have multiple untested blastocysts frozen

The key to accurate genetic testing results is making sure you are at a clinic with exceptional labs and embryologists. It is also important to know ahead of time if your clinic will transfer embryos labeled as abnormal or not.

What About Pregnancy Losses?

THE KEY TO ACCURATE GENETIC TESTING RESULTS IS MAKING SURE YOU ARE AT A CLINIC WITH EXCEPTIONAL LABS AND EMBRYOLOGISTS

You might be surprised that this isn't at the very top of my list for when to test embryos. That's because when a client has had even one pregnancy loss, my first instinct is usually to look somewhere else first.

This is where the functional medicine lens we talked about earlier can be incredibly helpful. I like to start with bloodwork for both partners, including genetic tests like karyotypes and Rh factor, along with a full panel to screen for deficiencies or imbalances that could interfere with staying pregnant. I also want to be sure the uterus has had the right diagnostic testing to rule out anything that could block a healthy pregnancy, especially an endometrial biopsy and a hysteroscopy. From there, we talk through medications to discuss with the doctor that could help support both getting pregnant and staying pregnant.

If I consistently saw pregnancy losses stop once embryos were genetically tested, I would feel very differently about this. But that's not what I see most of the time.

What I usually see instead is that **fixing root causes, adjusting medications around embryo transfer, and working with exceptional labs is what I see prevent pregnancy loss most often.**

FIXING ROOT CAUSES, ADJUSTING MEDICATIONS AROUND EMBRYO TRANSFER, AND WORKING WITH EXCEPTIONAL LABS IS WHAT I SEE PREVENT PREGNANCY LOSS MOST OFTEN

And by not relying solely on genetic testing, my clients often save tens of thousands of dollars by avoiding unnecessary egg retrievals and tests that were never going to fix the real issue in the first place.

HYBRID APPROACH TO GENETIC TESTING

One option I really like for clients who feel torn about genetic testing, especially when they are likely to create multiple embryos, is what I call a hybrid approach.

You freeze two or more of the *best-looking* blastocysts without testing them, and then you test the remaining embryos. The thinking here is that embryos with the strongest appearance are often more likely to be healthy, even though that is not always true.

If the tested embryos come back normal, that can give you more confidence that the untested ones are also likely healthy. And if the tested embryos all come back abnormal, you still have embryos on ice that look the strongest in terms of development and structure.

Not every clinic allows this approach, so it's important to ask your doctor early in the process.

If your clinic does not offer a hybrid option and you are planning more than one egg retrieval, there is another way to approach this. You could skip testing for the first retrieval that produces embryos, then decide whether to test embryos from a second retrieval based on how that first cycle went.

That way, if the second round does not produce any embryos labeled normal, you still have embryos frozen from the first cycle. And even though those embryos were not tested, it is very possible they are healthy, even if the second batch showed otherwise.

For many clients, this approach creates greater peace of mind and opportunities and options for success.

What if the results come back inconclusive?

Personally, I have never seen an embryo that was labeled inconclusive, then retested and called normal, go on to transfer successfully. I'm sure it has happened somewhere, but I haven't seen it in my own work, so I can't responsibly recommend it.

Re-testing means they are biopsied, frozen, thawed, biopsied again, refrozen, and then thawed once more for transfer. That is a lot of stress and potential damage to something incredibly delicate.

Embryos do best when they are disturbed as little as possible. Leaving them alone, minimizing manipulation, and protecting them from unnecessary handling simply gives them the best chance to survive and thrive in a lab environment that already involves a lot of human intervention.

Conversations to Have with Your Doctor About Genetic Testing

It is important to know how your doctor feels about testing your embryos and for you to be open to the conversation while also understanding the intention behind their recommendations. Start by asking how many of their specific patients undergo testing to get an idea of what they will likely recommend for you. You could even ask when scheduling your appointment and see if the receptionist knows.

Next, ask directly if they would recommend testing for you or not, and why.

If you are against testing, be strategic about how you bring it up so you do not trap your doctor into saying something that could trigger you. It is good for the doctor to know upfront how you feel, but I always encourage you to hear their perspective, too, if that feels right to you. One way to start the conversation could be, "I'm leaning toward skipping genetic testing, but I'd also like to understand your perspective. Before we get into details, could you let me know, yes or no, if you would still work with me if I choose not to test?"

I find that some doctors talk a lot without actually answering the question. They jump into statistics and stories when all you really need at first is a clear yes or no. Asking it this way, kindly but directly, makes sure you get the information you need.

Next, I would ask your doctor for their *own* data behind the recommendation. A great place to start is with this question: "How many of your patients who chose not to test embryos went on to have a pregnancy loss after 12 weeks? And how many of your patients who chose not to test embryos delivered a child with a genetic condition?"

And if that answer is more than 1 percent, or even more than one case in a single year, I would personally have a very hard time believing it because of what I've seen in my own work. But this question isn't about my experience. It's about understanding what *your* doctor has actually seen play out with their own patients.

Overall, whether to undergo genetic testing is a very personal decision, with many variables that go into making that choice. Most importantly, it needs to *feel* like the right choice for you.

DAY 3 VS. BLASTOCYST

My son was one of two day-3 embryos. These went in as a fresh transfer, and my daughter was one of two euploid (genetically normal) blastocysts (blasts) that went in as a frozen transfer. So, yes, **both day-3 and blastocyst, tested and untested, fresh and frozen transfers work!**

When deciding whether to grow the embryos to day three versus the blastocyst stage, here are some criteria to help you decide:

1. **Your Clinic's Policies:** Some clinics won't work with day-3 embryos. They may believe it saves patients from unnecessary expense and the heartbreak of a transfer that's unlikely to succeed. This can be true in some cases. However, for those who produce few embryos or whose day-3 embryos always fail to reach the blastocyst stage, working with day-3 embryos might be the only chance for success. And any doctors who work with day-3 embryos for transfer can tell you that success is very possible!

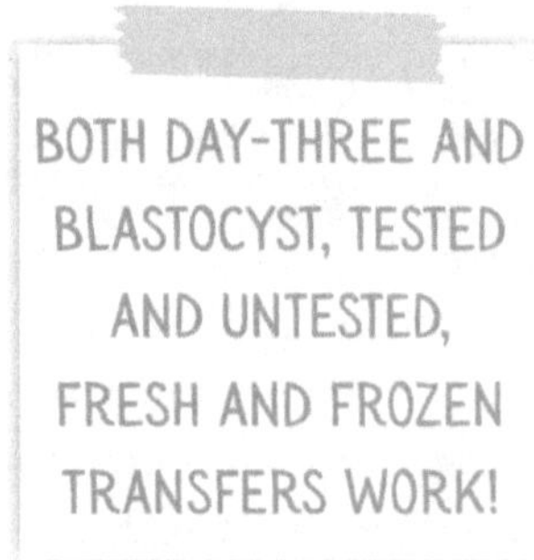

If you have diminished ovarian reserve (DOR) or your embryos consistently arrest between day 3 and the blastocyst stage, consider a clinic that is experienced and confident with day-3 embryos. Clinics that practice optimized IVF and respect the potential of day-3 embryos are often more successful with day-3 transfers.

2. **Genetic Testing Requires Blastocysts:** As of today, you can't effectively test day-3 embryos. If you want to do genetic testing, you need to grow the embryos to blasts.

3. **Number of Embryos and Strategy:** If you have four or more day-3 embryos and no history of embryos stopping between day 3 and the blastocyst stage, growing them to blasts is often reasonable.

Blending Methods: Hybrid IVF Strategies for Success

If you are planning multiple egg retrievals and have not had embryos make it to blasts before, one option is to freeze the first round as day-3 embryos and use those results to guide the next round. If that first retrieval yields more than four strong day-3 embryos, especially eight-cell or higher, you could consider growing embryos from the next round to blasts.

If it is your first IVF cycle and you do not yet know how your embryos behave, or if you planned to freeze at day 3 but now have more than four embryos progressing well, talk with your doctor about freezing up to four of the *best-looking* day-3 embryos and growing the remaining embryos to blasts.

There is nothing more defeating than investing the time, cost, and emotional weight of an egg retrieval, seeing healthy-looking day-3 embryos, and still ending up with nothing. Having embryos on ice creates options and opportunities for a healthy baby.

EGG PRESERVATION: THE 10 PERCENT YOU'RE TOLD... BUT THE 90 PERCENT THAT COUNTS

When 65 Eggs Are Not Enough to Make a Baby

I had a client freeze 65 eggs. Sixty-five. Not a typo. When she was ready to use them, out of 65 eggs, only 7 fertilized, resulting in one embryo that tested abnormal. She was stunned. She called me to consult on her next round of IVF that she had been confident she would never need.

That's an extreme story, but I hear similar versions of it all the time. Women freeze 10, 15, or even 20 eggs, thinking they've bought themselves an insurance policy for later. Then they come back ready to use them, and either no healthy embryos are made, or the very few embryos created fail to implant. They end up starting IVF again at a much older age, worried that their prime fertility window to make healthy embryos passed years ago.

My client had a very happy ending. On our very first round together, using the same clinic, she retrieved 35 eggs. This time, 27 were fertilized, and 19 made it to the blastocyst stage. Nineteen! Her first transfer was successful. She now has her baby girl and the option for many more siblings in the future.

When it comes to egg preservation, here's the part no one really tells you before you do it: **you don't do egg preservation to preserve eggs; you do it to create a baby.**

And those are two very different outcomes that require two very different protocols, technologies, expertise, and processes, with many steps in between.

Eggs are single cells, delicate, and fragile. The odds of each one surviving a freeze, then a thaw, then fertilization, then growing into an embryo, then freezing again, then thawing, and finally transferring are much lower than most people are told. And that makes sense. These little eggs have quite a journey to becoming a baby.

So when I see egg-freezing centers pop up with glossy ads like *"Just $4,000! Preserve your fertility!"* I want to scream, "Don't do it!" Because wherever you freeze your eggs, that lab owns them. And your eggs are only as good as the people and processes that handle them.

If you're considering egg preservation, here's how you can preserve your time, money, energy, and egg reserve... and give yourself a much better insurance policy:

- **Choose the best doctor.** Work with a clinic that focuses on quality over quantity and provides optimized IVF.
- **Choose the best lab with stats.** Find a lab with proven success in freezing and thawing eggs that actually go on to become babies, not only embryos.
- **Secure those eggs.** Make sure the clinic is stable enough to exist in 5 to 10 years. Get in writing what happens if they close. Who moves your eggs? Who pays for it? That should be clear before you sign anything.
- **Know your stats.** Keep checking your hormone levels, such as AMH, FSH, progesterone, estrogen, and AFC, so you're making decisions based on real-time data. And if those numbers start slipping, don't panic—pause. Get *whys* before you get worried. Figure out what's driving the change and fix that first.

While egg preservation is never a sure thing, when I work with clients using exceptional doctors and labs, I feel much more reassured that those tiny eggs could become embryos with the potential to grow into healthy babies.

FUTURE-PROOFING FERTILITY WITH A HYBRID PLAN

If you are preserving eggs and your data shows a low follicle count, low AMH, or rising FSH, or if you are about to undergo treatments that could impact fertility, like chemotherapy, and you do not have a partner yet but want children in the future, there is another option to consider. Freeze half of your eggs and fertilize the other half using a sperm donor to create embryos.

This is not an easy decision. It is complex, emotional, and more expensive. But if using your own eggs to build your future family is important to you, it's a way to secure embryos with your own eggs and learn sooner whether those eggs are likely to become embryos.

Fertilization and development tell you more than an egg count ever could. By creating embryos, you see how the lab performs and whether your eggs have the energy to grow and develop. Freezing eggs alone does not give you that insight.

If the results fall short, you find out sooner rather than later that you may need to adjust your protocol or even your clinic before investing more time, money, and emotional energy into egg preservation.

And when the timing is right, you will have embryos created from your youngest eggs, or eggs ready for fertilization, waiting for the moment you are ready to become a parent.

FRESH VS. FROZEN TRANSFERS

If embryos are transferred in the same cycle they were created, after fertilization and development to the embryo or blastocyst stage, this is called a fresh transfer.

If embryos are created, frozen, and transferred in a later cycle, this is called a frozen transfer.

Many clinics default to frozen transfers, but that does not mean a fresh transfer should be ruled out if you meet the criteria.

Sometimes the decision is made before the egg retrieval begins, such as when genetic testing is planned, certain procedures are happening before the transfer, or a suppression protocol is being used. Other times, the decision shifts based on real-time data.

For example, if you planned a fresh transfer but progesterone levels or lining measurements were not optimal at the time of the trigger shot, or if you became sick and developed a fever, it would usually make sense to pivot to a frozen transfer.

The reverse can also be true. If you planned a frozen transfer but there is no medical reason to delay, your hormone levels and lining look optimal, you feel well, and you are not experiencing significant bloating or pain after retrieval, your doctor may recommend moving forward with a fresh transfer.

Here are the times to discuss a fresh transfer with your doctor:

- You have a history of failed frozen transfers. But before assuming frozen is the problem, I would want to look closely at the protocols used and the root causes that may have driven those outcomes.
- You struggle to make day-3 embryos, or your embryos tend to look average in cell number or structure. In this case, putting them back into the body, nature's incubator, could be the better option.
- Your lab has not achieved strong success rates in thawing and transferring frozen embryos.
- You have multiple embryos and want to transfer one or two fresh embryos while freezing the rest.
- You struggle to build a thick lining, but at the time of the trigger, your lining and hormone levels look optimal.

Here are the times when I typically recommend a frozen transfer:

- You have a history of failed fresh transfers. Again, I would want to review the protocols and root causes before assuming a fresh transfer is the issue.
- You have a high follicle count, PCOS, or are prone to OHSS or have experienced it before.
- You have known inflammatory conditions such as endometriosis, silent endometriosis, fibroids, adenomyosis, or very heavy and painful periods and could benefit from calming estrogen activity first.
- You are currently in an inflammatory state, such as having active allergies, hives, or skin breakouts, or a recent virus or vaccine.

- Your hormone levels leading up to the trigger shot are not ideal. Progesterone is not below 1.5 ng/mL before the trigger, and the lining is not between 8 and 13 mm.
- Your lab does not have a high success rate in transferring fresh embryos.
- You need additional diagnostic testing, such as a hysteroscopy, saline ultrasound, laparoscopy, fibroid surgery, or endometrial biopsy.
- You plan to complete genetic testing.

Your doctor may also have a strong preference for one type of transfer based on where they see the most success. As long as there is no clear reason not to consider that approach and you feel comfortable with it, it often makes sense to move forward with the strategy your doctor is most confident executing.

IN IVF, THE "B" IN "PLAN B" OFTEN ENDS UP STANDING FOR "BEST"

At the end of the day, you can plan ahead, but the choice between a fresh or frozen transfer should be guided by real-time data whenever possible. **In IVF, the "B" in "plan B" often ends up standing for "best."**

CHAPTER 9 SUMMARY

- **Your Choices Shape Your Support Team:** Day-3 versus blastocyst, fresh versus frozen, genetic testing, and egg preservation are decisions to have an opinion on before solidifying your clinic. The choices you make before retrieval often determine which doctors, clinics, and strategies will truly support your goals and which ones will quietly limit them.
- **Genetic Testing Is Strategic, Not Mandatory:** Testing is not required for IVF success. When used without a strategy, it could actually slow the path to a healthy baby rather than speed it up.
- **Egg Freezing Is Not Always Insurance:** Freezing eggs without the right protocol, execution, and lab can create a false sense of security rather than real future family-building options.
- **Why Not Do Both:** Hybrid strategies combining testing, embryo stages, or preservation methods often increase flexibility, preserve options, and reduce regret when outcomes are unpredictable.
- **(Once Again) Data Drives Decisions:** Optimized IVF stays responsive to real-time data when choosing between fresh and frozen transfers, rather than locking you into a plan before your body and hormones have had their say.

10. Doctor Dating: Find Your Perfect IVF Doctor and Clinic

The Clinic Cliques: Cool Kids, Cults, and Celebrities

I find many of the doctors and clinics that people rave about are not actually great at IVF. I know that sounds harsh, and I truly wish it were different, because I want more doctors practicing optimized IVF.

But like every profession, there are a few exceptional ones, a lot of "okay" ones who call themselves exceptional online, and a handful who really should be doing something else.

And don't forget that IVF is a laboratory science. Exceptional doctors and embryologists working in exceptional labs, all under the same roof, are rare. You might get one or two, but finding all three together? That's gold.

Still, I see so many people get swept off their feet by three types of clinics: the cool kids, the cults, and the celebrities. Let's discuss each.

The cool kids: These are the clinics that were on top of the IVF industry decades ago and still get street cred for it. They haven't updated their protocols or their laboratories because they don't have to. They ride on their past reputations that never left them. It's like the people we all know who peaked in high school. Back then, they were "the shiz-nit" (FYI, that's an old person's way of saying "the shit"). And now it's painful to watch them retell the same old stories to people who don't know better.

The cult: You know those IG reels that say, "POV: when you've learned to filter your words but not your face"? That's me when I hear a certain clinic mentioned because it has a seemingly full-on cult following (and no, I will never name names). I wish they would quietly disappear, but instead, they're expanding locations. I personally have never seen a healthy pregnancy with any of their offices, and my clients who have used them have had several failed egg retrievals and/or transfers with beautiful-looking embryos. What is happening there? Could it be a coincidence that they are unusually unsuccessful only with my clients? Sure. Do I believe that? No. So I cannot bring myself to ever recommend this cult… I mean, clinic. And when I suggest to a new client that they switch clinics because of unusually poor results, they argue back like the clinic is their soulmate. (I swear, they must sprinkle something in the water because I cannot figure out how they get patients to defend poor results so fiercely.)

The celebrities: I talk to many new clients who tell me the name of their doctor and then wait for me to gasp in disbelief, as if they'd just told me Oprah had invited them to brunch in her Montecito garden.

These are the doctors who worked with a certain celebrity or have a popular podcast or YouTube channel. I usually hold a frozen smile while quickly assessing how much truth this new client can handle on our first call. And when they are ready, I share the hard news: their doctor is "eh" at best, and they are overpaying for an undeserved reputation.

Think about it. Most of the celebrities who shared their IVF journeys were famously *unsuccessful* for years before finally having a baby. So why would you ever want to use their doctor? And I understand that some doctors have a great social media presence or podcast and are very likable, but we want to pay for results, not ratings.

Overall, I am not impressed with a doctor or clinic because of a famous name, a celebrity they worked with, or a popular Instagram account or podcast. I am impressed by doctors who practice optimized IVF and work in exceptional labs run by exceptional embryologists, especially for cases like yours. And yes, that trifecta is hard to find, but it does exist.

In fact, when I pair a doctor with one of my clients, they have often never heard of the doctor or the clinic before.

So let's learn how to spot those rare exceptions or turn "eh" into "exceptional" by asking the right questions from the start so you can kiss your baby sooner.

Now that you have selected the eggs and sperm, it is time to find the final partners in building your family: your doctor and your clinic.

The doctor, the embryologist, and the lab are the major players in your IVF treatment.

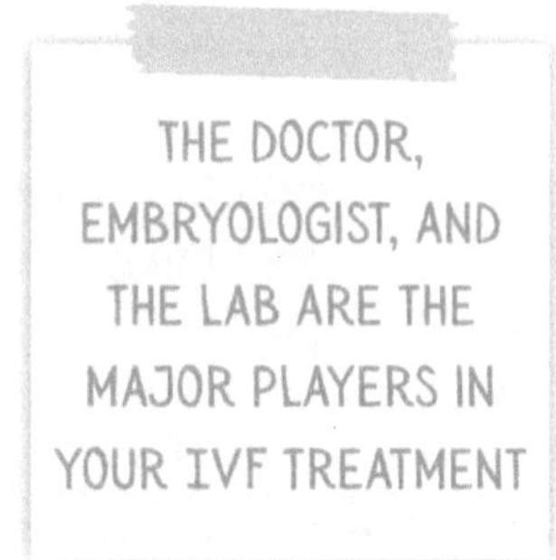

Your doctor sets the plan: the medications, the timing, the testing that gets done (or skipped), the dosages, and the overall execution of the protocol. They also handle key procedures like egg retrieval and embryo transfer. When you start with the right doctor, you give yourself the best chance to create healthy embryos and set yourself up for a successful pregnancy.

The embryologist is the one handling your eggs and embryos and guiding fertilization, freezing, and thawing. Their level of experience matters, and you want to know that senior embryologists are in the lab, since that indicates they have invested additional hours in advanced training.

And then there is the lab itself. **IVF is a laboratory science, and not all labs are created equal.** Everything from the equipment to the air filtration to the culture media affects whether embryos survive and thrive.

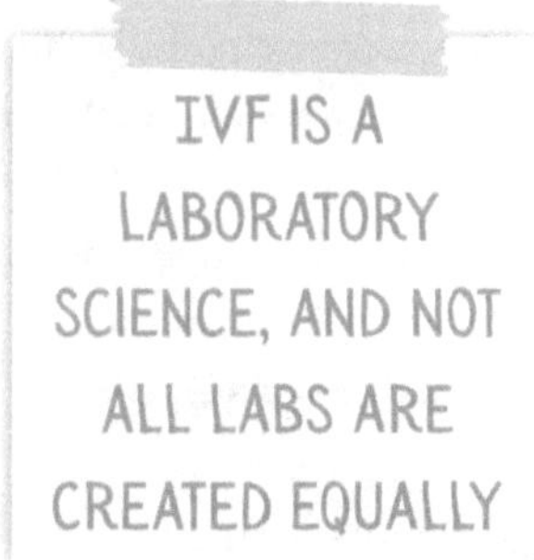

As you move through this section, you will learn how to choose the doctor and clinic that are the right fit for you. I also understand that sometimes there is no choice. Your doctor might be assigned to you based on location, insurance coverage, or government funding.

For those of you who do have options, this section will help you set yourself up with the right doctor from the start or find the next doctor if that is what you need.

PROFIT-FIRST VS. PATIENT-FIRST IVF

This is definitely a "do as I say, not as I do" topic when it comes to my energy around it.

Do you remember how shame sits at the very bottom of the Levels of Energy Alignment? When clinics unapologetically put profit before patients, when their bottom line or convenience takes priority over your outcome, even though you're paying them for results, I want to shame them... badly.

Which clinics? I'm far too polite to name them directly (translation: I do not want to get sued). But here's what I will say: if your clinic does any of the things below, they firmly fit into the "profit-first" category of IVF clinics, and we have a big problem.

So when I see clinics put profit before patients and my clients end up with "okay" IVF instead of optimized IVF while paying an extraordinary amount of money, or when I sit with my clients through the grief of failed cycles that could have been avoided, I cannot always rise above it like I ask you to do in Spirit Protocol.

Instead, I feel it deeply. And I usually get really angry. Then I sink even lower and think about how I want to publicly call out these clinics so no one else ends up there. (That's shame talking, FYI.) But I don't. Instead, I storm into Brian's home office, rant a little frantically about the latest clinic's nonsense that was passed off as "protocol," and throw in a few "Can you believe this?" comments, along with an "It's so gross" and a "How is this ok?!" before storming off to get back to work.

And yes, he *loves* it when I do that.

Anyway, my point is this: know whether you're working with a clinic that's profit-first or patient-first. That way, you can prepare for the limitations, set your expectations clearly from the start, or, better yet, choose a clinic that doesn't operate that way in the first place.

Here are some of the most common "profit-first" practices that undermine your IVF success rates:

- **Batching patients.** This is when everyone is put on the same schedule. It often involves medications like birth control that many patients shouldn't be using for priming. Even when birth control is appropriate, best practices for timing are usually ignored because the calendar is built around the clinic instead of your biology. So patients end up on it for too brief a time, too long, or at the completely wrong time.
- **Delaying stimulation meds.** I already mentioned this, but a very well-known clinic began pushing back the start of stimulation meds to fit in more patients with its limited operating room space. Compromising the ideal start day for stimulation

medication typically leads to uneven follicles and poor embryo development.

- **Minimal monitoring.** Some clinics check you once or twice during stims and then again near the trigger shot, with little if any hormone testing. It is impossible to optimize results without that data. So if your doctor isn't collecting it, it's basically like they're saying, "You get what you get, and you don't throw a fit... oh, and that will be $20,000." And now I *am* throwing a fit.
- **The clinic closed for the weekend.** Your body does not take weekends off, but some clinics do. There is no way to get the best results if your monitoring or trigger shot falls on a Thursday or Friday but needs to be rescheduled because the clinic is closed. And yes, when my clients go to clinics that close on weekends, the perfect trigger day somehow usually lands on a Thursday or Friday.
- **Quotas.** A doctor who used to work at a very famous clinic told me he was required to see sixty patients per hour. Sixty! If that were my quota, I would probably walk into the ultrasound room with sunglasses on to avoid eye contact, measure a few follicles (but not all) as quickly as possible instead of as accurately as possible, and rush out. That means the reports driving your next steps are probably incomplete or inaccurate, and the recommendations for adjustments will be off. Just kidding, those clinics don't do adjustments...duh! And you better not have a question, or you'll get the death stare or just be ignored.

(See, that was very judgey and shamey... I'd better end this section soon.)

- **MIA doctors.** If the only time you see your doctor is during the consultation and then they vanish, that's not acceptable, unless they were honest about it upfront. Many nurses are incredibly skilled, but they're not board-certified reproductive endocrinologists. That training takes years of extra investment. If nurses are making protocol calls, the cost should reflect that. But usually it doesn't, and without knowing their level of training, it's hard to fully trust their decisions. I've seen nurses give confusing or incorrect guidance, which is why consistent doctor oversight is non-negotiable.

- **Charging for questions.** This one makes me want to take my earrings off. You've already invested tens of thousands of dollars, with plenty of profit built in, so questions should be welcomed, not billed. Questions bring clarity, and clarity brings confidence that you're doing everything correctly and nothing is slipping through the cracks. The most important time to get answers is during an appointment for stimulation meds, yet that's often when access is most restricted. I can't tell you how many texts I get from clients asking me to clarify their medications, review instructions that are confusing, or answer questions because they can't get ahold of the doctor. And then I think about the women who don't have my number. What are they supposed to do? Guess? It's unacceptable.

Some things, like clinic closures, you cannot ask them to change (but you can change your mind as to whether you want to pay them for "okay" IVF). But others you can absolutely push back on. For example:

- Ask exactly how often you will be monitored and whether they can accommodate additional scans.
- Insist on starting stimulation on the right day of your cycle, or wait until the next month if proper timing isn't available.
- Ask how your presence and communication with your doctor work *during stimulation*, when questions are most urgent.
- And if they charge you to ask your doctor a question, that would be a deal breaker for me when choosing that doctor in the first place.

Understand that these practices are not typical of the best of the best IVF doctors I've witnessed. Take the GOAT (greatest of all time), Dr. Debra Minjarez, whose protocols and precision I studied closely. When she was practicing, she would never allow any of those profit-first practices because she only does optimized IVF and truly protects her patients' investment.

(And yes, if you can't tell, I have a bit of a girl crush on her. She's not only an incredible doctor but also one of the most amazing humans I've ever met. Even though we're friends, I completely fangirl over her. Honestly, she should be the president of IVF.)

THE BEST AND WORST FILTERS FOR CHOOSING A FERTILITY CLINIC

There are many ways women choose a clinic. Some rely on insurance coverage or referrals, while others focus on cost, location, online reviews, or published success rates. While each of these can offer useful information, they do not all deserve the same weight. Some filters give you meaningful insight into how a clinic truly operates, while others can quietly lead you astray.

In this section, I will walk you through the most common filters and show you which ones actually guide you toward a smart, confident decision and which ones you can safely ignore. The goal is simple: to help you choose a doctor and clinic that truly support building your family.

Insurance

Yes, always try to use your insurance if you have it. The only exception is if you are completely depleted physically, mentally, and emotionally and need to go with the most effective clinic regardless of coverage. That is rare, but when it happens, I support it 100 percent.

If you do have insurance, make sure you understand it completely.

Sometimes coverage is split between the male and female partner, which means you may have more benefits than you realize. And sometimes, when insurance lists a set amount for IVF coverage, it applies only to IVF-specific procedures, such as egg retrievals. The rest, including monitoring such as bloodwork, ultrasounds, and fertility medications, may be billed under your regular medical coverage. That can give you much more value than what first appears on paper.

And other times, coverage is split between "IVF" or "fertility"-specific charges and general charges. For example, I currently have a client who is a doctor, so she is very informed about how things should be covered and charged to insurance companies. She has limited IVF coverage, but her bloodwork and monitoring are covered by her regular insurance. Her clinic was refusing to bill the IVF charges separately from the bloodwork and ultrasound, but that is not allowed. She used the correct language, got her insurance company involved, and had them separate it.

Call your insurance company and ask:

- Do you have a patient advocate who can review my fertility coverage with me? (A patient advocate can walk you through the fine print, explain what is actually covered, and help you avoid surprise bills or missed benefits.)
- Does my coverage separate office expenses (like bloodwork and ultrasounds) from fertility medications and IVF procedures?
- Is there separate coverage for my partner or spouse?
- Do I need pre-authorization or pre-qualification? If so, what is the process, and how long does it usually take?

Once you understand your insurance fully, call the clinic and ask the receptionist whether they accept your insurance before setting up the consultation.

Pro tip 1: Always get a confirmation number at the end of your call. That way, if you need to call back or something gets mishandled, you won't have to start from scratch.

Pro tip 2: Use an AI tool to fully understand your insurance benefits. For example, if you want your bill broken into line items instead of bundled charges so you can use general insurance for specific services, you can upload your policy into the system. Then give your role (IVF patient), the context (writing an email), and the goal, such as getting monitoring and bloodwork covered using your insurance company's own language to improve approval and speed.

Referrals

The most useful referral is from someone with your biology who got pregnant quickly. So if you are getting a referral, only consider it if the person shares your similar profile: your age, AMH (anti-Müllerian hormone), FSH (follicle-stimulating hormone), AFC (antral follicle count), BMI (body mass index), and infertility factors. Otherwise, it shouldn't hold much weight.

Also, I would typically say to skip referrals from OB/GYNs or other professionals who often have friendly ties with IVF clinics. While it is illegal for clinics to pay for referrals, they can still offer gifts or put money into "marketing," which is really a softer way to reward them. (And no, I do not receive marketing money from the doctors or clinics I recommend to my clients. Although I once got an umbrella from a clinic, which, of course, made me immediately send them all my clients that year!)

Cost

You may not be able to sit down with the financial office before your first consultation, but you should at least be able to get a price list for treatments and add-ons. Having costs in hand before the consult helps you prepare smart questions and prevents unwelcome surprises later.

And remember what I mentioned in the callout box about "celebrity" doctors: just because they cost more does not mean they are better. In my experience, most clinics fall into a similar price range. If you see a clinic that is much higher or much lower, be cautious unless you know they have had incredible success with patients who share your exact profile.

From what I have seen, the higher-priced clinics are rarely worth the extra money, and the lower-priced clinics often make up for it in other ways. Usually, that means failed cycles that force you into multiple rounds, which end up costing you more in the long run.

Also, ask whether they offer bundled cycle discounts, refund programs, or partnerships with companies that provide IVF discounts or financial assistance. Sometimes there are options available that are not advertised, and it never hurts to ask.

Stats and Success Rates

Stats can be tricky to trust but also a useful resource. If I am not familiar with a clinic in the U.S., I start by checking CDC.gov for success rates. I prefer CDC.gov because reporting is mandated by law; every clinic must submit its data, and the numbers are independently verified and audited. The only drawback is that the data is usually a couple of years behind.

SART.org is another option, but not every clinic is a SART (Society for Assisted Reproductive Technology) member, and the data is self-reported before being processed. In my opinion, that leaves more room for bias than the CDC's numbers.

I often use hfea.gov.uk with my clients in the UK to review clinic statistics.

It is also important to know that some clinics exclude "research" patients from their reported success rates. You will know if this applies to you because you will be asked to sign a special consent form stating your cycle is part of a research study.

No statistics are perfect, and results can be skewed, but they are still a useful tool and one of many data points to consider.

Want to know my favorite stat to look at? Egg donor transfer success rates, because those cycles should be a layup unless the protocol or lab is weak.

I also pay close attention to clinics with a large number of cases and strong success rates in women over 40 using their own eggs for retrievals and transfers. That is the hardest population to get right and requires real strategic skill. If they successfully work with a high volume of women over 40 and their stats for that age range are well above the national average, I am usually impressed.

Location

Having an exceptional clinic nearby is a dream situation. But if your case is more complex or the local options are not strong, it is worth considering traveling.

Most people worry they will need to be away from their responsibilities for a month, but that is not the case. Typically, you only need to stay near the clinic for about seven to nine days for the egg retrieval and two to four days for the embryo transfer. The rest of the process can usually be done through outside monitoring at a local fertility clinic for bloodwork and ultrasounds. Of course, every clinic is different, so confirm what your clinic allows.

Traveling can feel inconvenient and expensive, but it is usually the opposite. For most, I see it as a short-term inconvenience for the ultimate cost-saving convenience: less IVF before holding your baby. **Nothing is more inconvenient or costly than another failed round of IVF that could have been avoided.**

NOTHING IS MORE INCONVENIENT OR COSTLY THAN ANOTHER FAILED ROUND OF IVF THAT COULD HAVE BEEN AVOIDED

Online Reviews

Using online reviews to choose a doctor is not something I have ever recommended. I don't see them as reliable because I know how they typically work. You either have businesses actively asking for reviews from clients as soon as they graduate with a successful pregnancy, or you have clinics that never ask for reviews at all, which means the only ones you see are from very unhappy patients who are the most motivated to tell their story.

However, if you insist on looking at reviews, there is a strategy to it.

Here are some tips for using online reviews wisely:

- Do not only focus on ratings. Read the actual reviews. Patterns matter most. If the same complaints or praises keep showing up, and they don't sound like one-off incidents or human error, pay attention.
- Check how many reviews there are. If a doctor has fewer than 100, a handful of strong opinions can easily skew the picture.
- Compare across multiple platforms. If the reviews line up across different sites, you are more likely to be seeing the real reputation of that doctor or clinic.

Those are some of the first filters to help you start narrowing things down. Once you've gathered that info, you'll probably have one or two doctors who stand out. Next, we'll talk about how to prepare for those conversations so you can feel clear, confident, and totally sure you've found the right fit.

PREPARE FOR THE CONSULTATION

Setting the Doctor (and Your Birthday!) Up for Success

By the time I dated Brian, I had already had a few boyfriends with whom I never spoke my mind. I would hold things in, get hurt, and repeat the cycle. So when Brian came along, I was ready to be upfront about my expectations rather than "cool" about everything. While it is true that I am easygoing with most things, there are some that will immediately set me off.

Take my birthday, for example. I don't care much about gifts because I typically get myself what I need. I love flowers, though some, like carnations, are offensive to me for some unknown reason. But there is one thing I do need: a card with a thoughtful note. That's what my mom and dad always did, and that's what makes me feel special. So early on, before my birthday, I told Brian that my only expectation was a card.

I wanted to set him up for success because I wanted to protect myself from disappointment. I knew that if I got no card, or a card with only "Happy Birthday! I love you!" scribbled inside, I would be hurt.

This is exactly what I want you to do in your fertility journey (and in life). Set people, and yourself, up for success by knowing what will make you happy or upset in a situation and communicating it. It is not kind or fair to know you have a trigger, say nothing, and then explode, or implode, when someone inevitably hits it.

That could look like saying to someone who always asks about your fertility journey, "I know you're excited to hear updates about our baby-making journey, so I wanted to share this: we're working on it, we're doing great, and I'll let you know when there's more news to share."

Or in a consultation with a new doctor, or after a failed cycle, starting with a "Before we begin" statement. For example: "Before we begin, I understand that egg donation is a great option for me, but I do not want to discuss that today. Is that possible?" This is especially important if egg donation, low AMH, or any other topic is triggering for you.

Another "before we begin" question could be, "I was planning on asking you specific questions about my past IVF rounds. How thoroughly did you review the previous monitoring reports so I know how much background I need to share?" This might feel direct, but it saves everyone time and unnecessary angst.

As I shared earlier, I learned this the hard way during my ninth egg retrieval. After gathering five years of records from three different clinics, I was asked, "So, how can I help you?" I felt all the blood drain from my body. I was crushed and stunned into silence. I had assumed he needed those records to review them, not as an activity for me to complete while waiting three months to speak with him.

Being clear about your expectations and asking about theirs is a win-win for everyone. You are protecting your peace and setting everyone around you up for success.

BEING CLEAR ABOUT YOUR EXPECTATIONS AND ASKING ABOUT THEIRS IS A WIN-WIN FOR EVERYONE. YOU ARE PROTECTING YOUR PEACE AND SETTING EVERYONE AROUND YOU UP FOR SUCCESS

And if you do set boundaries on the conversation and they get ignored, well, then you have my full blessing to walk over and flick them in the head while saying, "What [flick], did [flick], I [flick], say [flick]!" Then calmly sit back down.

Just kidding, don't do this because it's technically assault (but DM me if you actually do because I need to know you personally.)

Knowing what to expect in that first consult saves you time, energy, and a whole lot of disappointment.

When setting up the call, ask the staff if there is a cost for the consultation and what it will and will not include. Confirm the cost, whether any labs or ultrasounds are included, how long the consultation will last, and whether the doctor will review your records ahead of time and how thoroughly.

If the staff does not mention whether the doctor will review recommended protocols, let them know you plan to ask specific questions and confirm that the doctor will be prepared to answer them. For that, the doctor will need your bloodwork and previous monitoring reports (if applicable).

MATERIALS TO GATHER

The potential clinic will likely request all your medical records. Depending on how many rounds of IVF you have done, that could be a huge pile of paperwork. My advice is to give them what they require, but also prepare a clear summary page that highlights the information your doctor actually needs and bring this summary with you to the appointment. I created a resource called "Template – Monitoring Report" that you can use to organize this; it's available in the online resources.

Here is what you should gather and summarize for each egg retrieval:

- **Bloodwork:** AMH, FSH, LH, estrogen, and progesterone (all taken between cycle days 2 and 4, except AMH, which can be taken anytime)
- **Follicle count:** done on cycle days 2–4
- **Medication calendars:** the medications you took, at what doses, and for how long
- **Monitoring reports:** follicle sizes and hormone levels from each monitoring appointment, starting at baseline and continuing through stimulation until the trigger shot
- **Embryology reports:** how each egg developed into an embryo
- **Summary overview:** a short page that the doctor can read quickly (Place this on top or in a separate document.)

Pro Tip: Always send the records to yourself first before passing them on to the clinic. That way, you keep your own copy, and if another clinic ever needs them, you will not have to wait for your old clinic to process the request again.

THE QUESTIONS TO ASK DURING A CONSULTATION

The last client I got from a country other than my own (the USA) was from Kenya. I don't know any IVF doctors or clinics in Kenya, but I did know that I could help her select the best one for her because I knew the *questions* to ask and the answers I wanted to hear.

> DEPENDING ON HOW THEY RESPOND AND THE REASONING BEHIND THEIR CHOICES, YOU'LL HAVE A MUCH CLEARER SENSE OF WHETHER THIS DOCTOR IS TRULY CREATING A PLAN AROUND YOUR BIOLOGY OR OFFERING A ONE-SIZE-FITS-ALL APPROACH TO IVF.

These questions are how you find out if you are going to get "okay" IVF or "optimized" IVF. And not every question belongs to the doctor. If you want to know about the lab, ask the embryologist. If you want to know about costs, ask the financial advisor. Keep your face time with the doctor for what only they should handle: your protocol and its execution.

Here is a chart of key questions to ask the clinic you are considering, along with what you might want to hear as an answer. I also include a digital version of this in the online resources so you can print it out and use it at the meeting.

CONSULTATION QUESTIONS TO ASK

QUESTION	WHO SHOULD ANSWER	WHAT YOU WANT TO HEAR
What do you think of my previous cycle? Would you do anything differently?	Doctor	A new approach if the last cycle was not successful. Not "same protocol, new lab."
Here is a protocol I got from a second opinion. What do you think of it?	Doctor	Thoughtful feedback, not defensiveness.
Here were my issues (uneven growth, fast growth, immature eggs, poor fertilization, poor embryo growth, abnormal blasts). What would you do to solve them?	Doctor	A true change in strategy, not repeating the same thing.
Tell me about your lab. What is your mature egg to blast ratio?	Doctor or Embryologist	Around 40-50%.
How many days do you like to see patients on stimulation drugs before the trigger shot?	Doctor	Around 11 days (plus or minus 1). If they say it depends on the growth you can agree but then ask again what they like to see in an ideal situation plus or minus one day.
What follicle size do you like to see before trigger?	Doctor	Around 16-19 mm (plus or minus 1mm). If they give a bigger range like 15-22mm, ask what would be their *ideal* size within 2 mm for your trigger.
Do you freeze embryos on Day 3 or only blasts?	Doctor or Embryologist	You will likely want both options if you have a hard time making it to blast or have a lower egg reserve.
What percentage of your patients do genetic testing?	Doctor or Embryologist	Less than 80% is best. If 80%+, and you do not want to test, make that clear up front and ask if it will be an issue if you don't test.
How many cases do you do per year in my age group?	Doctor, Embryologist, or CDC.gov	100+ per year.

What are your donor egg success rates and how many cases per year?	Doctor, Embryologist, or CDC.gov	50%+ transfer success, ideally 50+ cases. This will tell you how good they are at transfer protocols since the eggs should be very young and healthy.
What is your embryo thaw survival rate?	Doctor or Embryologist	95% or higher.
When doing genetic testing, do you hatch embryos on Day 1, 3, or 5?	Doctor or Embryologist	Day 3 or Day 5.
Does your clinic batch cycles? Are you open every day for monitoring and procedures?	Doctor, Nurse, or Coordinator	No batching is best and you need a clinic that is open every day of the week for monitoring and/or procedures because your follicular growth doesn't pause just because it a weekend.
Tell me about your embryologists. How many are junior vs. senior? How long has your senior embryologist been in practice? Where have they worked?	Doctor, Nurse, Coordinator, or Embryologist	A senior embryologist should always be on staff. Their extra years of training can make or break your cycle.
Are you board certified in reproductive endocrinology and infertility (REI)?*	Doctor, Nurse, or Coordinator	Yes. REI certification means advanced training beyond OB/GYN and ongoing education. But I am not sure if this is applicable in all countries
(If you need to travel far to use this clinic) Do you allow outside monitoring? If yes, will I be paying for monitoring twice – once in the IVF package with your clinic and again at the outside monitoring clinic? And how far in advance do you want me at your clinic?	Nurse, or Coordinator	Ideally yes, outside monitoring is allowed. Not having to pay twice is rare unless the IVF clinic offers à la carte pricing instead of bundles, which is uncommon.
Do you offer financing or multi-round discounts? If yes, what are the terms?	Coordinator	Clear terms, including refund options if you stop early.

If I have a question for the doctor specifically, and it needs a timely answer such as during stimulation medications, how do I get it answered? What about after hours?	Doctor, Nurse, or Coordinator	Easy access to the doctor when needed, especially during stimulation.
Will a nurse ever make protocol or medication decisions?	Doctor	The only acceptable answer is no.
Can I switch doctors or nurses within the clinic?	Doctor, Nurse, or Coordinator	Yes.

***A Note on Certification**
REI board certification is specific to the United States. In the UK, the equivalent is subspecialty training in reproductive medicine through RCOG. In Canada, it is a certification through the Royal College of Physicians and Surgeons. Most countries have their own version of advanced reproductive medicine training, so look for the highest level available where you live.

TURNING YOUR CONSULTATION INTO A REAL STRATEGY SESSION

The first question on the chart asks about the protocol your doctor would consider for you. After reading the previous section on IVF medications and strategies for success, you might already have a general idea of what your protocol should look like.

Now that you have these resources, you can evaluate your doctor's answers about protocols and execution with more confidence. Depending on how they respond and the reasoning behind their choices, you'll have a much clearer sense of whether this doctor is truly creating a plan around *your* biology or offering a one-size-fits-all approach to IVF.

AFTER THE CONSULTATION

> IF YOU DID NOT FEEL GOOD WITH THAT DOCTOR OR IN THAT CLINIC, MOVING FORWARD COULD LEAD TO REGRET FOR NOT LISTENING TO YOUR GUT

The very first thing I ask my private clients after a consultation is, "How did you feel?" Not "What did they say?" or "What's their protocol?" But "How did you feel being in that room or on that Zoom call with that doctor?"

Your intuition is your superpower.

Even if the doctor has a reputation as "the best" (and you already know how I feel about so-called "best" doctors), or even if it is someone I personally recommended, there are always other talented doctors to consider.

If you did not feel good with that doctor or in that clinic, moving forward could lead to regret for not listening to your gut.

And if you doubt your inner voice because you feel like you have made too many mistakes in the past when it comes to your fertility or IVF journey, first, remember what I wrote in Spirit Protocol: they were not mistakes if you learned from them, and they are helping you move forward smarter today. Keep practicing the exercises in that section.

Second, if you need more support to quiet that inner critic and strengthen your inner voice, you can learn more in the video series I created, *Conscious Creation: Elevating Your Mindset,* which is available in the online resources.

And lastly, I know that this version of you might feel off or broken, but I do not agree. **I think you are smart, persistent, and extraordinary in the best ways possible, and I know you are going to be an amazing mom.**

I THINK YOU ARE SMART, PERSISTENT, AND EXTRAORDINARY IN THE BEST WAYS POSSIBLE, AND I KNOW YOU ARE GOING TO BE AN AMAZING MOM

Now that we've established that fact, let's shift gears and start making precise decisions that get you there.

EXERCISE: MAKING DECISIONS WITH PRECISION

Below are the steps from a document I created for my clients years ago titled "Making a Decision with Precision." I even did a podcast episode on it ("IVF Uncovered," Episode 75). I am going to walk you through this process that uses your conscious mind, your subconscious mind, your analytic skills, and even your physical body to help you make the best decisions possible.

Promise me one thing: you will not skip steps.

Okay, let's say you are deciding between Clinic A and Clinic B.

STEP 1: START WITH THANKS AND LOVE

I know it sounds cheesy, but this is why I made you promise not to skip steps. And I promise this one is not fluff. Pinky promise.

This step should help shift your energy up the Levels of Energy Alignment. When done correctly, it moves you out of fear and second-guessing and into courage, reason, and acceptance by intentionally covering all of your bases.

Here is what I mean.

Step 1: Give thanks for having options

Start by offering gratitude, love, or prayer for the choices you have. Even in a hard season, options are a privilege not everyone has, and recognizing it is grounding. It reminds your body and brain that you are not trapped.

Step 2: Send love to those without the same opportunities

Next, send love or prayers to the women who do not have the same health, resources, or opportunities to build their families. This perspective is humbling and softens the nervous system, pulling you out of panic and into compassion.

Step 3: Send love to those who achieved what you want

Finally, send love or prayers to the women who were successful in the very thing you want to achieve. This step is essential to keeping your energy out of scarcity. It reminds you that what you want exists in abundance. If it can happen for them, it can happen for you.

AND THE HIGHER YOU MOVE ON THE LEVELS OF ENERGY ALIGNMENT, THE MORE CLEARLY YOU ARE ABLE TO SEE YOUR PATH TO PARENTHOOD

This practice naturally shifts your energy up the Levels of Energy Alignment. It moves you out of fear and into courage, reason, and acceptance. **And the higher you move on the Levels of Energy Alignment, the more clearly you are able to see your path to parenthood.**

STEP 2: GATHER ALL *THE INFORMATION*

Using the online resources that go along with this book, create strategic questions to discuss with your doctor and clinic. Resist the urge to fill in blanks or assume answers, and pause your brain from mapping out a path until all of your questions have been answered.

Most of the overwhelm I see in clients, and in myself, comes from trying to make a decision before having all the information. When you gather the full picture first, many options naturally fall away. From there, decisions feel simpler, more confident, and rooted in facts.

Example: If you are choosing between clinics, that means you have gone through all the filters for choosing a clinic, fully understand the costs to you, have had conversations with all the doctors you are considering, gathered their complete answers to your questions, and know how you feel about each one.

STEP 3: PROS VS. CONS (PART 1)

Now it is time to get everything out of your head and onto paper. Do a total brain dump of every pro and con you can think of. Don't edit, organize, or overthink it, and definitely don't judge yourself for what you write down.

When your thoughts stay in your head, they spin and overlap, which makes everything feel ten times more confusing. Writing them down helps you see your situation more clearly and separates emotion from logic. Sometimes, putting it on paper reveals what truly matters to you and what does not.

Example: Pros for Clinic A might include liking and trusting the doctor, knowing the staff, easy communication, quick responses, an exceptional lab, and a convenient location. Cons might be that they are not making changes to the protocol, and your results have not improved.

STEP 4: PROS VS. CONS (PART 2)

Now, cross off anything that does not directly affect your chance of success. Be honest and as objective as possible. This part is about clarity, not comfort.

Your brain's natural instinct is to keep you safe, and sometimes that means clinging to what feels comfortable rather than what moves you forward. By taking as much emotion out of it as possible, you focus only on what gets you closer to your goal. Ask yourself, *if my only objective was to get and stay pregnant, what would I keep on this list?*

Example: From the list above in Step 3 (Part 1), I would keep "communication is easy," "I trust the doctor," and "they have a great lab."

STEP 5: WORST-CASE SCENARIO

Talk through the absolute worst outcome for each choice, then ask yourself how you would feel and notice what your body does when you imagine it. Your body often knows the truth before your mind does.

We are often told to think positively and avoid focusing on negative outcomes so we do not "invite" them in. While it is true that what you focus on grows, avoiding difficult possibilities does not make them disappear. It simply pushes the emotional response deeper into your body, where it sits unresolved and adds to internal noise and tension.

Facing possible outcomes directly clears that backlog. It creates space for logic and calm to step in. Fear loses its grip when it is acknowledged instead of avoided.

And when you let yourself imagine the worst-case scenario and explore how you would actually feel and respond, you might be surprised.

Example: "If I stay with Clinic A and they agree to change the protocols, but we get the same results (no embryos), at least I'll know I gave it my best before moving to Clinic B. I can afford to do a couple more retrievals, and getting these results will finalize things for me." Or, "If I stay with Clinic A and, even if we change the protocol and I get the same results, I'll be furious with myself for not switching sooner."

By this point, you might already have your answer, but if not, that's okay. Keep going.

STEP 6: MUSCLE TESTING

This is where your body and subconscious help you decide. Take a few deep breaths or do a quick brain break from the Survive to Thrive Protocol to clear your mind. Assign Clinic A to leaning forward and Clinic B to leaning backward. Stand up, ask the question, and notice what your body does. Did you lean forward or back? That's your subconscious giving you the answer.

Your subconscious already knows what feels right, but your conscious mind often gets in the way with logic, fear, and "what ifs." This step helps your inner wisdom speak up.

And if your body doesn't move forward or backward, I give you my full compassion for that. This kind of resistance usually means something deeper is protecting you. It's often tied to past experiences where you were taught that if you don't stay guarded, you will get hurt again. It might also mean that your heart doesn't know how to open up and be vulnerable, and that makes perfect sense.

But this doesn't make you strong; it keeps you suffering. **You can't give or receive true, unconditional love with a closed, protected heart.**

YOU CAN'T GIVE OR RECEIVE TRUE, UNCONDITIONAL LOVE WITH A CLOSED, PROTECTED HEART

If you are ready to finally feel free, it will take some uncomfortable action, but you can do it. And it will be worth it, especially before your baby arrives earthside.

I urge you to focus your energy on Spirit Protocol. In the online resource guide for this book, I have included additional tools and a few of the books that helped break my own heart wide open.

STEP 7: STOP THINKING AND START RECEIVING

"WE CANNOT SOLVE OUR PROBLEMS WITH THE SAME THINKING WE USED WHEN WE CREATED THEM" -ALBERT EINSTEIN

Remember the section on getting superpowers from your higher power? This is where you put that into practice. Ask the question, then pause and wait for the answer. It may arrive as a quiet thought, a sense of knowing, or a not-so-subtle sign pointing you in the right direction.

The answers you are looking for rarely come from overthinking or forcing clarity. They tend to show up when you slow down enough to listen or when you allow guidance from someone or something you trust for perspective and wisdom.

Einstein said it best: ***"We cannot solve our problems with the***

same thinking we used when we created them." New answers come from new sources, or sometimes from *The* Source.

Practice expanding where you look for guidance. Open yourself to support from a higher power that loves you and wants the best for you. The answers are already available. You simply need to quiet the conscious mind enough to let them come through.

CHANGING CLINICS: THE HARDEST (AND SMARTEST) MOVE IN IVF

New Client: "I'll do anything you tell me. Whatever you say, I'll do it."

Me: "Okay, you've had four failed retrievals. The doctor isn't willing to make key changes that could lead to better results, and if we keep doing the same thing, we'll get the same outcome. I highly recommend switching clinics."

New Client: "Well... I just changed to this clinic... my clinic knows me so well... I love the nurses... changing will be so much work... this is the best clinic... the idea of starting over feels so overwhelming..."

Changing clinics, even when the results and doctor feedback make it clear that what they are doing is not working, is one of the hardest things for my clients to accept.

The other, as shared before, is doing Spirit Protocol, because it can feel "silly," "fluffy," or "woo woo." It is worth saying again that mindset work is scientifically proven to be effective, so that "woo woo" deserves a "woop woop!"

I completely understand why it's hard. It's not easy to walk away when you feel depleted, exhausted, and emotionally attached to your doctor and staff. When you've already given so much, putting even an ounce more energy into something like changing clinics or "doctor dating" again can feel soul-sucking.

But if your goal is to do as little IVF as possible, as soon as possible, and you are not seeing success with your current clinic, then switching might be the smartest move you can make.

My *general* rule is this:

- If your second treatment is not *more* successful than your first, or if

you've done three total treatments at a clinic with no success, it's probably time to move on.
- If you change clinics and immediately get worse results, cut your losses and don't go back.

Of course, your exact results and situation are the main drivers in making this decision, but those are usually clear signs that it's time for a change.

I'll say it again. **Nothing is more inconvenient or costly than IVF that is not working.** Yes, there's always a chance that switching clinics will give you similar results, but the odds are much higher that staying where you are will continue to produce the same results.

NOTHING IS MORE INCONVENIENT OR COSTLY THAN IVF THAT IS NOT WORKING

And if you do decide to switch clinics, try to see it as both smart and strategic (and yes, a total pain in the butt too).

Using the Levels of Energy Alignment from Spirit Protocol, you can be ***willing*** to see that changing clinics could lead to greater success. You can ***accept*** that the clinic you thought would work well for you did not, and while that's frustrating, it's also okay. You can recognize that it was ***reasonable*** for you to choose that clinic in the first place. You made the best decision you could with the information you had at the time. And now, with new information, you can be ***courageous*** enough to go back to a previous clinic or move on to a new one, even if every part of you wants to resist it.

When you make decisions from those higher energies, you give yourself the best chance at creating your family while keeping more peace in the process.

WHEN YOU MAKE DECISIONS FROM THOSE HIGHER ENERGIES, YOU GIVE YOURSELF THE BEST CHANCE AT CREATING YOUR FAMILY WHILE KEEPING MORE PEACE IN THE PROCESS

Or, you can wait until you hit rock bottom to finally make a change. I hate seeing that happen, but I understand it because I've been there. I ignore the little nudges (a tap on the shoulder), then the louder ones (a slap on the face), until eventually it becomes a full punch in the mouth. It hurts, there's blood everywhere, and it takes a long time to clean up and recover. But I finally learn the lesson and do what I should have done months, or even years, ago.

Please don't be like me. Dodge the beatdown and make the move without the bloody drama.

BREAKING UP IS NOT *HARD TO DO*

From People-Pleaser to Parent

(Record screech.) Wait, what crossed your mind when you read the last section? Did you instantly think about how you might hurt your doctor's or nurse's feelings if you leave? If so, keep reading. If not, feel free to skip ahead.

PROTECTING FEELINGS SHOULD NEVER OUTRANK PROTECTING YOUR CHANCE AT A CHILD

If the thought of telling your clinic you are moving on makes you feel uncomfortable, you probably have the same disease I am still recovering from: people-pleaseritis.

Now, I could remind you that your doctor is part of a business and that they will "break up" with you in a heartbeat if your case becomes "bad for business," like after too many failed rounds. But since you and I are similar, I know that probably will not help. You will still say, "That is fine if they break up with me. I can handle that. But me breaking up with them? No way. I would feel terrible if I hurt their feelings."

So, I am going to bring out the big guns for this one. I didn't want to, but if you are unshakable in putting their feelings ahead of your own, you need to hear this.

Here it goes.

If you do not change clinics when you need to because you do not want to hurt your doctor's or nurse's feelings, you are choosing the feelings of an adult professional over your child's chance to come to life and be loved by you.

Protecting feelings should never outrank protecting your chance at a child.

BE THE PARENT WHO UNAPOLOGETICALLY PUTS HER FAMILY AND HER NEEDS ABOVE ANY OTHER HUMAN ON THE PLANET

And let me tell you, as a recovering people pleaser myself, that was uncomfortable to write because it probably made you uncomfortable to read. But I refuse to sit back and watch you delay your dream of motherhood because you have decided it is your job to make sure everyone else is okay… including your doctor.

So instead, **be the parent who unapologetically puts her family and her needs above any other human on the planet.** The kind of parent your future child will one day thank you for being.

When it is time to move on from a clinic, there is an easy process that, in my experience, has never led to the awkwardness or confrontation so many of my clients fear.

Here's an email I put together for a client who was transitioning from her current clinic. You can send this as a short note to your doctor, nurse, or both:

> **Subject:** Next Steps
> Dear [Doctor or Nurse's Name],
> Thank you so much for all of your efforts in helping me build my family.
> For this next round, I've decided to go in a different direction and won't be moving forward with your clinic for IVF.
> With gratitude,
>
> [Your Name]

That's it. You don't need to say anything else.

If they ask for more details (which they rarely do), you can simply reply, *"It's a new direction. Thank you for everything."* Period.

If they keep pressing, which would surprise me, you could respond again with: *"The most comfortable I am with sharing is that we are going in a new direction. Thank you again."*

And from there, you can write, *"See previous response,"* even if it doesn't make sense.

But in all of my years consulting, I have never had a client go back and forth like this. The clinic's response is almost always short, very kind, and supportive.

And if they respond rudely or with judgment, I know it would be tempting, but do not reply. Take it as clear confirmation that you made the right move.

TURNING QUESTIONS INTO CONVERSATIONS WITH YOUR DOCTOR

My clients often ask me how I get doctors to follow the protocols I want them to follow. I tell them the truth: I don't.

Most of us would not appreciate someone walking into our workplace and giving instructions on something we've trained for our entire careers. Doctors are no different.

But what I've found is that **when you ask talented and professional IVF doctors specific and strategic questions, and you ask them in a kind and curious tone, you will get specific and strategic answers back.**

WHEN YOU ASK TALENTED AND PROFESSIONAL IVF DOCTORS SPECIFIC AND STRATEGIC QUESTIONS, YOU WILL GET SPECIFIC AND STRATEGIC ANSWERS BACK

Think of your conversations with your doctor like a business meeting where you are hiring a professional for an important service. The key is to respect that they are the trained professionals while remembering that you are the client.

Let's say you had a low embryo development rate and you ask, "What could we do next time to get more embryos?" It's a fair question, but it's not specific. Vague questions usually get vague answers. You might nod along, unsure what else to ask, and leave without much clarity.

Now imagine you've learned how to read your monitoring reports (which you will in this book). Instead, you say, "I noticed that my follicles grew unevenly from the start. What do you recommend we do differently to help keep them growing more evenly?" Then you listen.

If your doctor does not mention something you know could help with that issue, you can follow up with, "Since the follicles were uneven from the beginning, do you think we should look at different priming strategies? If so, which ones?"

It is much harder for a doctor to give a vague answer to those kinds of questions. And at no point are you telling them what to do. You are genuinely asking what they think about strategies you have learned.

Here is what that formula could look like:

Start by stating the issue professionally: "I would like to address my low fertilization rate."

Next, respect that they are the professionals and get curious about their solutions: "What would you recommend we try to improve this?"

Listen and write down all of their answers. If you have a suggestion that was not mentioned, you can ask: "I've heard about calcium activation to improve fertilization rates. What do you think of that?"

If they do not give a clear preference, you can gently follow up with something like, "Would you feel comfortable trying it this time?" or "If this option cannot hurt but may or may not help, could we try it?"

Keep in mind that, with any strategy like calcium activation, you also want to make sure the clinic does it regularly and that they have personally seen success with it.

Use a Kind and Curious Tone. One IVF doctor once told me, "Can you please teach your followers how to better communicate with their doctors?" Apparently, some patients were coming in hot, demanding specific protocols or treatments without leaving room for discussion. The problem was not what they were asking; it was how they were asking.

When you lead with curiosity instead of confrontation, your doctor is far more likely to listen, think carefully, and collaborate with you.

Here is a sample email you can send before your next appointment that follows this approach:

> **Subject:** Questions for Our Upcoming Appointment
> Dear Dr. [Name],
> Thank you for your continued support in helping me build my family.
> As I prepare for our next appointment, I wanted to share a few specific questions so you have time to review them beforehand. I would appreciate it if these could be passed directly to you, as I would like to hear your perspective.
> I am concerned about my [insert issue]. What would you recommend we try to improve this for the next [insert treatment plan]?
> I have heard about [insert solution] to improve [insert issue]. Does your clinic do that, and if so, is that something you would recommend for me?
> I appreciate your perspective and look forward to your thoughts.
>
> With gratitude,
> [Your Name]

When you approach the conversation with curiosity instead of control, you keep the relationship respectful, strengthen trust, and build a real partnership with your doctor that leads to better decisions and better outcomes.

KNOW THE "NO"

It is completely okay for your doctor to say no to a strategy you ask about. You are not there to steamroll anyone into doing something they are uncomfortable with, that they are not allowed to do, or that they believe is not right for you. There are many reasons a doctor may or may not be able to use a certain strategy. Your goal is to understand how they think, what they have tried before, how often, with what success, what they are willing to do now, and what they know enough to advise you on.

But what you do deserve is to understand *why* they may give a "no."

Let's start with what they actually know enough to advise you on. If your question is about supplements, nutrition, or the latest trend in holistic health, you will probably get a no right away. This is not something most doctors are formally trained in, and for good reason. Because of liability concerns, they cannot officially recommend anything outside their expertise. Save those questions for the experts who specialize in those areas. It will save both of you time and frustration.

Now, for questions that *are* within their specialty, a solid no should come with a solid reason. And to me, a solid reason is one based on the doctor's own clinical experience or the experience of their peers. The best doctors give clear, confident, experience-backed answers.

But if a no comes without much explanation, like "that's not how we do it," or if it's based only on research, that's the time to follow up in a kind and curious way so you can truly understand the no.

If your doctor gives you a vague no, here are some ways to follow up without sounding pushy:

- "I definitely don't want to do anything you are not comfortable with. I'm curious, have you tried this approach with other patients like me, and it wasn't successful, or is this something your clinic doesn't offer?"
- "I completely understand that your approach is research-based, and I really respect that your recommendations come from published studies. I'm curious, does your clinic only allow strategies that already have research behind them, or are there times when you consider options that seem promising but haven't been formally studied yet?"

Or

- "I totally understand if you prefer to stick to evidence-based methods. I'm curious, does this particular strategy have research showing it doesn't work, or is it more that there just isn't enough research showing it does work?"
- Would you consider this more of a "probably won't help but can't hurt" option, or could it actually hurt my results?"

Once you have asked and listened, and if the doctor is clear that it is a strategy they are not willing to try, you move on. You do not want a doctor doing something they are uncomfortable with.

IT IS OKAY FOR A DOCTOR TO SAY NO. IT IS ALSO OKAY FOR YOU TO KNOW WHY, AND IT IS ABSOLUTELY OKAY FOR YOU TO SAY "NO THANK YOU"

However, if the doctor is unwilling to try anything different from what has already proven ineffective for you, that might be a sign that it is time for a second opinion.

In short, **it's okay for a doctor to say no. It's also okay for you to ask why, and it's absolutely okay for you to say, "No, thank you."**

WHAT IF THE DOCTOR DOESN'T LIKE QUESTIONS?

My first suggestion when someone asks me this? "Well, tell them you don't like bills, but they're required for you to work together, right? Well, so are your questions."

(Okay, okay, that's not exactly "kind and curious" like I taught you, but come on.)

Thankfully, this isn't a common issue. But let's talk about those rare and very revealing moments when a doctor refuses to answer your questions.

One of my clients once asked a new doctor how she could contact him during treatment if she had questions. His response? "I don't do questions." He was a very popular doctor in an affluent area, but I never liked his protocol, and this response confirmed that I didn't like him either.

Another client at another clinic had a great stimulation response with beautiful follicles but ended up with no embryos. When she asked the doctor what changes he would recommend for the next protocol, he answered, "None." So she brought up some of the strategies I had suggested. His response? A full-on toddler tantrum. "I've been doing this for thirty years!" he yelled over and over. Wow. Just wow.

Turns out, this doctor wasn't board-certified in reproductive endocrinology and infertility, so yes, he probably had been doing IVF the same way for thirty years, without additional training since, and that was the problem.

TRULY SKILLED IVF DOCTORS DON'T MIND HAVING REAL CONVERSATIONS OR ANSWERING YOUR QUESTIONS. THE ONES I KNOW RESPOND WITH CALM, CONFIDENT ANSWERS, NOT EMOTIONAL REACTIONS

These kinds of reactions are what many clients fear, but they are *not at all* common and should never be considered normal. They are rare and outrageous exceptions. But if a doctor ever gets defensive, dismissive, or shuts the conversation down completely, be grateful for the clarity. That's not a red flag; that's a neon sign to leave that clinic.

Truly skilled IVF doctors don't mind having real conversations or answering your questions. The ones I know respond with calm, confident answers, not emotional reactions.

If you're feeling nervous about asking thoughtful, curious questions in a calm and kind tone, I want you to remember a few things.

- You have every right to ask questions. IVF is costly, and not just financially. One miscommunication can ruin an entire cycle. Asking questions prevents mistakes and helps you feel confident in what's happening.
- If asking questions makes you worry about offending your doctor, remember this: you're not insulting their intelligence; you're sharing yours by asking for clarity and inviting them to fill in the gaps with their expertise.
- Doctors are human, and everyone has bad days or tough seasons. Maybe your doctor is dealing with exhaustion, loss, or burnout. While that doesn't excuse unprofessional behavior, it can help you approach the situation with compassion and perspective.

And remember your role and your worth. You are the client paying a lot of money for an important service that means everything to your family, and it's your job to protect that investment.

And even if it doesn't always feel like it, remember this: they need you more than you need them.

WHAT IF I DON'T LIKE TO ASK THE DOCTOR QUESTIONS?

(If you saw the last section heading and thought, *Too bad for them. I'll ask whatever I please before I put my body and dollars down for IVF,* first, I applaud you and hope to be like you when I grow up. Also, you can skip this section.)

Maybe you feel like asking questions makes it seem like you're telling your doctor what to do, or maybe you feel deeply uncomfortable speaking up in front of certain professionals. If either one sounds like you, let's talk through both.

Remember, you're not telling your doctor what to do. They have the final say in the treatment plan. You're simply asking questions to better understand what's being recommended and to make sure the plan truly aligns with what you want and feel good about. If you don't ask questions before, during, and after treatments, you'll never know if it's the right doctor or clinic to trust with something as important as your family.

I know it can feel uncomfortable to ask questions, but I'm challenging you to be incredibly brave and do it anyway.

Here's your fertility fuel to give you the courage to speak up even when it feels awkward.

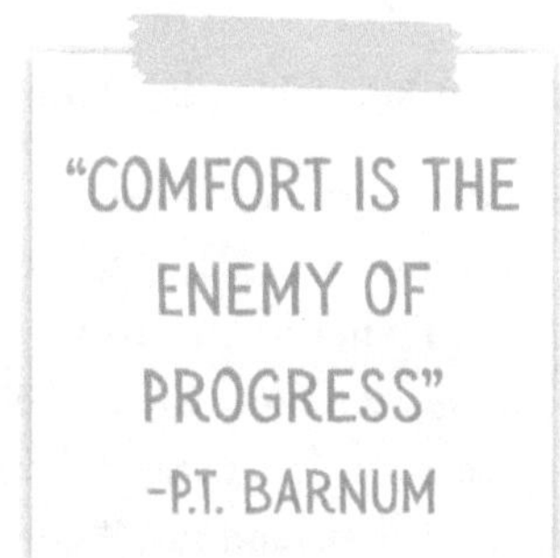

Comfort is the Enemy of Progress

One of my favorite quotes, often attributed to P. T. Barnum, says, ***"Comfort is the enemy of progress."***

This might be one of those moments when you choose the simple but uncomfortable step now by asking the hard question, changing clinics, or having the honest conversation so you don't end up in a far more complicated and painful situation later, realizing it wasn't your biology that stopped you. Instead, it was something that should have changed sooner.

If someone is offended by you doing what's best for your finances, body, time, energy, and family, that's not your problem... and they would likely do the same thing.

YOU NEED TO PRACTICE USING YOUR VOICE TO GET YOUR NEEDS MET. EVEN IF IT UPSETS SOMEONE TODAY, IT COULD PROTECT YOUR FAMILY TOMORROW

Parenting Practice

You need to practice using your voice to get your needs met. Even if it upsets someone today, it could protect your family tomorrow.

How you approach your fertility journey is often how you'll approach other difficult moments in life... including parenthood. If you struggle to advocate for yourself, you'll struggle to advocate for your children, too. Take it from someone who learned the hard way: you do not want to be "too nice" to get uncomfortable for their sake.

You might think it'll be different once your kids are involved, but in most cases, it isn't. So start practicing polite, firm boundaries and advocacy now, starting with IVF.

Protect Yourself Like You Would Your Child

If neither of those reasons lit a fire under you, let me try this.

Imagine your daughter is going through IVF, and you are in the room with her during her follow-up after a failed round. She's in tears because nothing is working after many cycles. You find a third party who offers solutions that have worked countless times for other women in her situation, but her IVF doctor dismisses them and says, "I don't do questions."

What would you do or say next to that doctor?

(Okay, wow, that was more than I expected... and illegal.)

But that fire? That protectiveness? Use it for yourself, too.

Ask yourself: *Would I ever allow someone to perform a medical procedure on my child without being able to ask questions?*

Would I spend tens of thousands of dollars on a procedure for my child without fully understanding the plan?

Would I continue spending tens of thousands of dollars on a procedure for

my child if it wasn't working and the doctor wasn't willing to make changes?

If your answer is no, then why would you accept that for yourself?

When you ask thoughtful, curious questions to advocate for your family, you are being the kind of parent your future child will one day thank you for.

You're doing some hard work, Mama. I have to say it again: your baby is already so lucky to have you. **The love, effort, and heart you're putting into your own growth will be the foundation for theirs too.**

THE LOVE, EFFORT, AND HEART YOU'RE PUTTING INTO YOUR OWN GROWTH WILL BE THE FOUNDATION FOR THEIRS TOO

CHAPTER 10 SUMMARY

- **Reputation Is Not the Same as Results:** Popular clinics and celebrity doctors can still deliver "eh" IVF. What matters is whether they can execute optimized IVF for cases like yours.
- **The Power Team Behind Success:** Your doctor sets the plan, the embryologist handles the eggs and embryos, and the lab determines whether they thrive. You want strength in all three, not only one.
- **Beware and Avoid Profit-First IVF:** Batching, delayed stims, minimal monitoring, weekend closures, quotas, MIA doctors, and charging for questions are all clues that the clinic is built for profit and convenience, not patient success.
- **Filters That Actually Help:** Insurance, stats, and smart travel plans can be useful. Referrals matter only if the person is truly similar to you, and online reviews are mostly noise unless clear patterns emerge everywhere.
- **Make the Consultation a Strategy Session:** Come prepared with your data, your monitoring reports, and your questions. Know upfront how long you have, what the consultation includes, and whether the doctor has reviewed your records, so your time and expectations are protected.
- **How You Feel Matters:** After the consultation, your first question is not "What did they recommend?" It is "How did I feel?" Your intuition is data, and it deserves a vote.
- **Curious Questions in a Kind Tone:** You are not there to tell the doctor what to do. You are there to ask specific, respectful questions that reveal how they think, what they do often, and what they are willing to change.
- **Know the No and Know Why:** A good "no" comes with a clear reason rooted in experience or policy. A vague no, defensiveness, or "I don't do questions" is a huge red flag.
- **Changing Clinics Could Be the Smartest Move:** If results do not improve by cycle two, or you have done three cycles with no success, it is likely time to switch. Do not choose comfort and familiarity over your family.

- **IVF Advocacy Is Parenting Practice:** Using your voice trains you how to protect your future family.

Before heading to the next section...

If you'd like the list of questions to discuss with your doctor and the answers I hope you hear, a customizable worksheet for "Making a Decision with Precision," a link to the letter you can copy and paste for your doctor, and more, just scan the QR code.

11. Exact Execution for Egg Retrievals

It's showtime! The next step is all about execution. You'll learn what to expect at each monitoring appointment, what key results to look for, and how to interpret what they mean for your cycle. We'll also go over how to decode embryo grading and review strategies to discuss with your doctor if certain challenges arise, like cysts, uneven follicle growth, or lower-than-expected fertilization rates.

But wait, is this your first time doing IVF?

If so, I am officially excited for you! You're getting informed, protecting your investment, and taking charge before you even start. I can't tell you how many times I've heard, "I wish I knew all this before my first IVF." Me too, by the way. I went in blind and way too confident. You're already miles ahead of where I started.

Also, if this is your first IVF cycle, read this section first.

If you've already done IVF before, skip to the next section called "Exact Execution for Your Egg Retrieval."

THE EGG RETRIEVAL PROCESS FOR ROOKIES

When I first heard I had to do IVF, I was terrified. The medications, the procedures, the needles. It all felt so foreign. It was the classic fear of the unknown. While you really do have to experience it once to understand how it feels (and every clinic does it a little differently), I want to share the most common questions and concerns I've heard from clients over the years... and the ones I once had myself.

So think of this section as your what-to-expect guide for IVF, filled with the things your clinic probably won't tell you.

GETTING YOUR MEDICATIONS

I remember stressing about whether my medications would arrive on time, but most fertility pharmacies ship overnight. Still, don't rely on that as your backup. To avoid last-minute panic, call the pharmacy to confirm shipping times and order about a week in advance. You can also ask your doctor or nurse if they keep extra medication on hand in case something doesn't show up when it should.

HOW THE MEDICATIONS FEEL

I was convinced the medications would turn me into an emotional wreck since I felt like a raging monster on birth control. But they didn't. I also had major anxiety about the injections, certain they'd be unbearably painful, and they weren't, especially once I figured out a few tricks I'll share with you later.

Most people don't feel much from the meds. Side effects like headaches, mood swings, or trouble sleeping can happen, but they're unusual. The two medications I hear the most about are Clomid and Depot Lupron.

Clomid (clomiphene citrate) is one of those meds people either breeze through or absolutely hate. It blocks estrogen receptors, tricking your brain into thinking estrogen levels are low. That makes your brain pump out more FSH and LH to get your ovaries working. The downside is that blocking estrogen can make your body react like it's in estrogen withdrawal, which is why some women get hot flashes, mood swings, or headaches, while others feel almost nothing at all.

Depot Lupron, often used before an embryo transfer, works differently from Clomid but still causes that estrogen drop. It temporarily shuts down your ovaries, which can lead to hot flashes, night sweats, or mood changes. Some women really feel it; others hardly notice.

As for stimulation meds, the main thing you might feel leading up to retrieval is bloating. I remember waddling around New York City during my first round because I felt so puffy. But I didn't bloat at all during my next eight retrievals. And of course, because I didn't have bloating, I worried something was wrong. But the results were the same either way. For me, bloating or no bloating didn't make a difference.

THE MORNING OF RETRIEVAL

After you check in, you'll change into a hospital gown. Double-check that you've removed all jewelry and contact lenses.

A nurse will check your vitals and ask standard questions, like whether you followed the no-food-after-midnight rule. She'll also place your IV. Here's something important: nurses usually don't numb the area before inserting an IV, but anesthesiologists do. So you can ask the nurse to numb you or request to wait for the anesthesiologist. You'll meet the anesthesiologist before going under anyway.

If that's not an option, let your nurse try twice. If they miss both times, don't let them keep poking you. Two tries are enough. There should be someone else on staff to try again.

Where you go next depends on the clinic. You might be in a private room for everything, or you might be in a shared space with other couples (yes, in your gown and IV). Have a few things ready to lift your mood: music, a funny video, or your favorite person. At one of our clinics, Brian always made me laugh by putting on a surgical glove and sticking his finger straight up like he was about to give someone an exam. Totally immature, but when nerves are high, a little humor helps a lot.

Anesthesia

When it's time, you'll walk into the operating room, lie on the table, and wait for anesthesia. If you've never been under before, it can feel a little scary. I was nervous my first time, too, but it turned out to be one of the best surprises of IVF. Most clinics use propofol, which, for me, was hands down the best nap of my life. Waking up from it felt like bliss.

This next tip is for embryo transfer, not retrieval: ask for Valium. It's prescribed for anxiety and helps calm your nervous system. A friend told me to ask for it, but I brushed it off until my eighth transfer, when the clinic gave it routinely. Wow. For that hour, I didn't have a single care in the world, and it was glorious.

And if you're still anxious before going under, distract yourself with people-watching. I used to scan the room, guessing which staff members were secretly dating, as if it were a medical soap opera. I probably looked ridiculous, but it worked.

Recovery Room

Recovery is quick. You'll wake up and rest for about twenty minutes while the nurses check your vitals and bring you juice and a snack. Once you're stable and dressed, they'll give you your post-care instructions and tell you how many eggs were retrieved. Whoever came with you to the appointment can usually join you once you're awake.

If you had a rough time with anesthesia, ask which one was used and write it down for future reference. Everyone reacts differently, and now you'll know which one doesn't agree with your biology.

AFTER THE EGG RETRIEVAL

Drink plenty of water with electrolytes to help with recovery.

That night, follow your doctor's instructions and do what feels comfortable. Most people feel fine by the next day and can return to work, maybe a little sore. If you have a high follicle count, you may need extra rest. Gentle walking, nutritious meals, and daily electrolytes can all help your body bounce back.

But if walking feels wrong or your discomfort increases, you could be experiencing OHSS (ovarian hyperstimulation syndrome). According to the Mayo Clinic, symptoms to watch for include:

- Mild to moderate OHSS may cause bloating, nausea, vomiting, diarrhea, or tenderness near the ovaries.
- Severe OHSS can include rapid weight gain (more than two pounds in 24 hours), intense abdominal pain, persistent nausea or vomiting, shortness of breath, or a swollen, tight abdomen.

If you experience any of these symptoms, call your doctor right away.

THE FERTILIZATION REPORT

The next morning, the lab will call with your fertilization report and let you know how many eggs were fertilized successfully. After that, expect updates every few days as your embryos grow.

THE EMOTIONAL SIDE OF WAITING

IVF is an emotional roller coaster, and retrieval results are one of the biggest drops. There are so many mini results to process: how many eggs were retrieved, how many were mature, how many were fertilized, and how many made it to the blastocyst stage. The numbers may shift at every stage, and it's easy to panic before you even reach the more important outcome: the embryo count.

One of my clients is a perfect example. On her first cycle, back before I was her consultant, she had ten eggs retrieved. Eight were mature, five were fertilized, and two reached the blastocyst stage. One was normal, but the transfer failed. On her next cycle, with me as her consultant, she had ten eggs again. She called me up in tears when she found out only six were mature this time. I reminded her that we don't have the results yet and the changes the doctor agreed to make were great ones.

Five of the six mature eggs were fertilized, and all five reached the blastocyst stage. She transferred one untested embryo, and it worked on the very first try.

CELEBRATE THIS STEP

Most importantly, celebrate ASAP after the egg retrieval, even before learning the results. Assuming you feel well enough, plan something similar to what you would do on your birthday (assuming you don't have ragers anymore). Have a nice celebratory dinner or treat yourself to something special. Your hardest job, making the eggs, is done, and that is worth toasting.

EXACT EXECUTIONS FOR YOUR EGG RETRIEVAL

When One More Day Was Two Too Many

I got a text with a monitoring report that made my stomach drop.

The person texting was my client, but the results she sent me were her friend's. I'm stopping short on details to protect privacy, but just know it was the first monitoring report I had seen from her because the friend was not my client.

Here were the follicle sizes:

25, 22, 21, 21, 20, 20, 20, 20, 20, 19, 19, 18, 18, 16, 16, 15, 14, 12, 10.

My first thought? Based on her age, these were overgrown by at least a day, and she should have triggered *yesterday*.

I asked how many days she had been on stimulation medication and what her doctor's next step was. In my head, I already knew the answer would be to trigger that day.

Her reply: She had been on stimulation for 12 days. And the plan was to trigger the *next* day.

The next day? The *next* day? No way. My stomach went from sinking to fully nauseous.

If they had triggered the day before, she likely would have had 11 follicles in the ideal range. Triggering that day would still give her about 6 in range. Waiting one more day would likely drop it to 4.

I told my client to have her friend contact her doctor immediately and ask, even beg, to trigger that day. If she did, she still had a chance at some viable embryos.

The doctor disagreed and wanted one more day of stimulation.

I knew at that moment the retrieval was compromised.

Here's what happened:

- 14 follicles retrieved
- 12 mature
- 11 fertilized

On paper, those numbers looked exciting. But I had seen this too many times before. I was certain that only 4 follicles were in the right size range to have a real shot at becoming blastocysts.

The final result:

- 3 blastocysts
- 1 genetically normal

The doctor called this "great results" for a 40-year-old. By her texts, my client agreed.

But I didn't.

I fully believed her embryo development could have been much stronger if they had triggered 2 days earlier. My heart broke again that day. Another round of IVF that could have been better. Another doctor believing this is just what happens at that age. And another woman believing her body was the problem when it wasn't.

And I could do nothing about it.

That moment became one more story fueling my fire to keep writing and creating the resources you need. I have seen that the longer women stay connected to my work, whether through the podcast or what I share here, the less they believe their body or age is to blame, because they finally have clarity and strategies to bring to their doctor.

Promise me something. If you have the capacity, please share this book with anyone you know who is trying to get pregnant. More women need to know the truth about what their incredibly capable bodies can do when given the right protocols and precise timing.

A great protocol sets the plan, but execution is where IVF is won or lost. Without that precision, issues like uneven follicle growth, follicles maturing too quickly, or mistimed medication adjustments can arise. Those small execution errors can lead to poor egg maturation, low fertilization rates, or weak embryo development. And for those doing genetic testing, they can mean fewer healthy embryos.

I have seen it firsthand. Same doctor, same clinic, and the same medications. But when the dosing and how the medication was used were adjusted, my clients ended up with more healthy embryos at their oldest age than they ever thought possible.

The next section walks you through how I analyze monitoring reports and the strategies that I suggest my clients discuss with their doctor based on real-time results.

Your *exact* execution will always depend on your *data*, but I want to show you, in general, what I look for, the details I expect to see, and how I use that information to help clients make decisions mid-cycle.

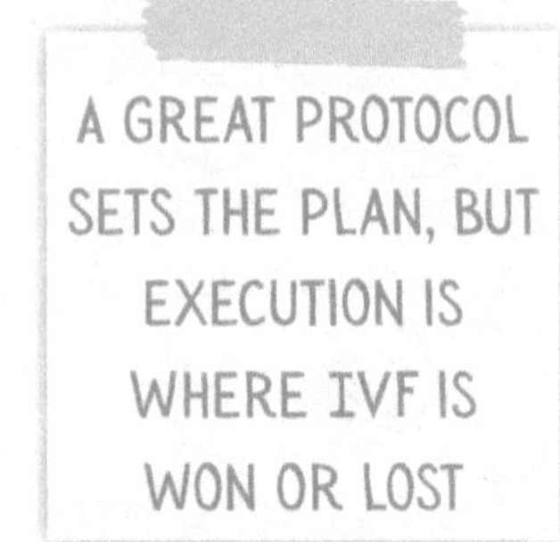

MONITORING APPOINTMENTS: EXPECTATIONS AND TARGETS

Monitoring appointments are the play-by-play of IVF. They show how your follicles and hormones are responding to medications, and without this data, it is impossible to know what is really happening in your cycle, whether adjustments are needed to optimize results now, or how to improve outcomes next time.

Hopefully, this is your last egg retrieval; if not, missing data makes it almost impossible to improve your next one.

At each appointment, you will want to chart every level that is monitored. And yes, it is your responsibility to write down your results at every visit. If your clinic does not post follicle sizes and hormone levels in a portal, ask during the ultrasound for the measurements of each follicle and record them in your phone, or if they are displayed on a screen, take a photo. When the nurse calls with your next steps, ask for the hormone levels from that day as well.

All of this data can be easily organized using the monitoring report template found in the online resources for this book.

Your IVF Data Belongs to You

Wait, what was that? Your clinic doesn't share results? (buzzer sound!)

In the United States, patients have the legal right to access their own medical records under HIPAA (Health Insurance Portability and Accountability Act). This includes lab results, imaging, ultrasounds, hormone levels, procedure reports, and anything else that is part of your medical chart.

The only exceptions are if your doctor believes releasing the information would cause you direct harm (for example, in certain psychiatric cases), but that does not apply to IVF monitoring or embryology reports.

Without this information, you are handing over responsibility for your family-building journey and relying on blind trust. I know, because that's exactly what I did for nine egg retrievals to have two children. You have the chance to do it better. Protecting your IVF investment starts with having your data in hand.

So if their "policy" is to withhold your medical information, that is a big red flag, and I would seriously wonder what they are trying to hide.

Follicle Measurement Variability

Follicle measurements are not an exact science. Size can vary depending on which technician performs the ultrasound and how the follicles are measured. Even small differences in angle or placement can change the numbers.

Because of that, some variation from scan to scan is normal, but the measurements still need to make sense overall. If you notice results that do not line up, like a lead follicle measuring 19 mm one day and then 17 mm the next, it is reasonable to ask for another set of eyes on the scan.

Follicle measurements play a big role in deciding stimulation dosing adjustments and the best timing for your trigger shot. While some variability is unavoidable, the goal is to minimize it as much as possible so decisions are based on the most accurate information available.

Bottom line: **data leads to decisions with precision**. Without it, you are stuck assuming, and, like I said before, assumptions in IVF can be an *ass-tronomically* expensive mistake.

Monitoring Report #1: Baseline

This first monitoring report is usually done on cycle days 1–3 and should not be later if you are starting in the follicular phase. At this point, you have not started stimulation medication (stims) yet, but you will likely begin that day.

Because this is the very first check, the goal is simple: we want the ovaries to be quiet. Shhhh. Quiet ovaries mean no follicles have taken the lead yet, and growth has not already been decided.

Low hormone levels, especially LH and progesterone, are a sign that ovulation is still far away. At this stage, everything should be calm and undeveloped —low hormones, small follicles, and a thin lining. This quiet baseline gives you the best chance for the medications to step in and guide follicle growth evenly, instead of starting with one or two "alpha" follicles already ahead of the pack.

MONITORING REPORT 1: BASELINE		
TIMING	BLOODWORK	ULTRASOUND
Cycle day 1-3	FSH, estradiol, LH, progesterone	Antral follicle count (AFC), follicle sizes, lining thickness

TARGETS (for a follicular phase start of medication only)	
ESTRADIOL	< 80 pg/mL (or < 200 pg/mL if on estrogen priming)
PROGESTERONE	< 1.5 ng/mL
FSH	< 10 mIU/mL
LH	< 5 mIU/mL
FOLLICLES ALL	< 10 mm (ideally < 7 mm)
LINING	< 5 mm

Strategies for Egg Retrieval Execution Based on Data

If your hormone levels or follicle sizes are not nice and low at baseline, that is often a sign to pause and discuss a pivot with your doctor. This could mean starting priming about 4–6 days after ovulation to bring levels and follicle sizes down by the next cycle start, or if you already primed, switching to a different priming medication.

Cysts can also be a reason to pause and reassess. If one shows up at baseline, do not panic, but do not ignore it either. We go into much more detail about specific strategies to discuss with your doctor in the upcoming section, "Hurdles to Hatchlings: Egg Retrievals," including how to determine the type of cyst and when it may be smarter to clear it before moving forward.

In general, if a cyst appears, it is worth a thoughtful conversation about whether you are truly starting stimulation under optimal conditions or whether giving your ovaries a little time could set you up for a stronger cycle.

Log It!

Always record your results. Write down each follicle size. I recommend logging by size group instead of by ovary so you see the total number by size. Also, record the hormone levels tested and any medications you are on. Keeping a clear record makes it much easier to spot unusual patterns and make decisions about whether to move forward or pause.

Side Note on Mid-Luteal Starts

If you are doing a mid-luteal start, your hormone levels will likely be much higher than the follicular phase targets. As the stimulation medication begins, most of the levels start high and then drop before rising again. Only use the targets for hormone levels listed above with a follicular phase start.

Monitoring Report #2: Day 3–5 (max) on Stims

The second monitoring report is ideally done three days after starting stimulation medication if this is your first time on this protocol. If there are no changes from a prior cycle, or if the only change is a lower dose of the same medication and you previously had no medication changes for the first five days, it is usually fine to wait until day five from baseline.

If you are on a different protocol or your medication dose has been increased, I recommend asking your doctor to check you after three days on the new plan. The goal is for most follicles to move forward as a group, not for a few to race ahead while the rest lag behind.

When it comes to monitoring hormones this early in stimulation, estrogen is usually the main lab being followed. The exact level will depend on how many follicles are growing and the type of medications you are using. In general, the more follicles growing, the higher the estrogen. As a rough guide, I like to see estrogen rising steadily and close to doubling about every two days. If it climbs much faster than that, it may be time to consider lowering the dose. If you are taking letrozole, which suppresses estrogen, your levels may stay lower until you have been off it for a couple of days.

Strategies for Egg Retrieval Execution Based on Data

The usual growth rate of follicles is about 2 mm per day, so this is when you start doing the math. The goal is for the follicles most likely to become embryos, not always the lead ones, since doctors sometimes let the biggest one or two go and focus on the group behind them, to reach about 19 mm ± 1 mm by stimulation day 11. The target may be a little smaller if you are 43 or older and a little bigger if you are under 35. See the section on trigger shot timing for details.

For example, if a follicle is already 10 mm on day 5, it could be about 22 mm by day 11. Unless you are under 35 and know that your body does best with larger follicles, I suggest talking to your doctor about reducing the medication slightly to slow growth. The exact timing and dose depend on your individual results, but in general, if estrogen is rising steadily and follicles are growing at about 2 mm per day, lowering medication a bit often helps more eggs mature together.

As for estrogen levels, as a rough guide, I like to see them rising steadily and close to doubling about every two days. If they climb much faster than that, it may be time to consider lowering the dose. If you are taking letrozole, which suppresses estrogen, your levels may stay lower until you have been off letrozole for a couple of days. You do not necessarily need to increase medication if your estrogen is lower. You may just need to let the letrozole clear your system.

These approaches are what I see the most successful IVF doctors do to get the best results. Remember, low and slow is the way to go. Lower medication, but not too much, and steady follicle growth, but not too slow, usually create healthier embryos. If estrogen is rising and follicles are growing, even slowly, that is a positive sign. You must always consider your full results and history, but I have seen this strategy consistently support stronger embryo development.

Log It!

Write down every medication change, follicle size, and hormone level. The details matter for this cycle and for future planning.

Monitoring Report #3: Day 5–7 on Stims

By day 5–7 of stimulation, you should be seen again to confirm follicle growth and hormone levels are on track. Around stimulation day 5 or 6, or when the lead follicle in the group that is most likely to become embryos reaches about 14 mm, an ovulation suppressor is often added if you are not already on one. The goal is to prevent ovulation from happening too early while supporting steady follicle development.

We are checking to make sure estradiol is rising in proportion to both follicle size and number. Progesterone should remain under 1.5 ng/mL to confirm ovulation is not approaching too soon. LH should also stay under 15 IU/L, ideally closer to 5, to show that ovulation is suppressed. We are also watching to ensure that most follicles are growing together rather than a few racing ahead of the group.

Strategies for Egg Retrieval Execution Based on Data

Same as before, the ideal growth rate of follicles is about 2 mm per day, so start doing the math again. Are your follicles on target to have the lead follicles reach about 19 mm ± 1 mm by stimulation day 11? The target may be a little smaller if you are 43 or older and a little bigger if you are under 35. See the section on trigger shot timing for details.

If you have diminished ovarian reserve (DOR) and estrogen is not rising as expected, or if follicles are not growing at all, there is a strategy to consider. Ask your doctor to check your FSH. If it is high, over 30 mIU/mL, one approach to discuss is pausing stimulation for about five days or adding estrogen support for five days without any other medication to allow levels to normalize before restarting. If a monitoring appointment after five days shows that follicles are getting bigger and estrogen is rising, you may be able to restart stimulation, assuming you are taking the correct dose for your biology, and reset the clock on your stimulation day count.

I have seen many successful egg retrievals that produced strong embryos using this approach.

Log It!

Write down every medication change, follicle size, hormone level, and lining measurement. These details matter for optimizing this cycle and for planning future ones.

Monitoring Report #4+: Daily Monitoring Reports Until Trigger Shot Day

Once your lead follicles, which are likely to provide eggs for fertilization, reach about 14 to 16 mm, you should ideally move to daily monitoring until the trigger shot. This is essential for tracking rapid changes in growth and hormone levels, as well as for timing the trigger shot on the most ideal day possible.

At this stage, we are making sure ovulation is still being held off and that follicles are growing steadily. Ideally, follicles should grow about 1 to 2 mm per day, with estradiol rising in proportion to that development. We are also watching that growth stays steady rather than accelerating too quickly, since follicles can occasionally jump more than 4 mm in a single day as you approach the trigger shot. That is why daily monitoring becomes especially important in the final days leading up to the trigger and on trigger day itself.

If you are planning a fresh transfer, progesterone should remain under 1.5 ng/mL before the trigger, and the lining should be progressing well, ideally between 8 and 12 mm.

Strategies for Egg Retrieval Execution Based on Data

Daily monitoring at this stage is the only way to catch the exact timing for your trigger shot and to protect against risks such as early ovulation or OHSS (Ovarian Hyperstimulation Syndrome).

If progesterone or LH starts rising early, that signals a higher risk of ovulation before retrieval, and you may need to discuss adjustments with your doctor right away.

If estradiol climbs above 3,000 pg/mL with 20 or more follicles, this increases your risk of OHSS. Ask your doctor about strategies to reduce that risk, such as using a Lupron-only trigger or adding Cabergoline around the time of retrieval.

One approach I do not recommend is increasing medications in the back half of stimulation. At this stage, follicles are already primed to grow quickly. Adding more medication can push them too far, too fast, which may reduce embryo quality. This condition becomes even riskier if paired with fewer monitoring visits, which can leave important days untracked. That combination is a recipe for "Oh No" IVF results.

If estradiol suddenly drops, the decrease may mean follicles have collapsed.

That does not always mean the cycle is canceled, but you do need to confirm that follicles will still be available for retrieval. Ask your doctor if this decline was expected and whether the plan now involves targeting a different group of follicles for fertilization.

Do you have a history of empty follicles or early ovulation, or do your hormone levels, such as progesterone or LH, suggest ovulation may happen before the trigger shot? Ask for an ultrasound the day after your trigger shot and another on retrieval day. Make sure your team schedules these ahead of time, since the ultrasound on retrieval day may be done at a different location. This helps ensure you do not risk missing your ideal retrieval window.

Log It!

Write down every medication change, follicle size, hormone level, and lining measurement. These details are key to optimizing this cycle and planning future ones.

Monitoring Report: The Day After the Trigger Shot

Not everyone is monitored the day after the trigger shot, but here are the reasons your doctor might recommend it:

- You have a history of, or concern for, early ovulation.
- You are doing a fresh transfer.
- You are using a Lupron-only trigger, and they want to check progesterone and LH levels.

If any of these apply, it is worth discussing with your doctor whether the day after monitoring makes sense for you.

MONITORING REPORT: THE DAY AFTER THE TRIGGER SHOT	
BLOODWORK	**ULTRASOUND**
Progesterone, LH, hCG (sometimes)	An ultrasound typically is not done unless your doctor is checking for early ovulation of the follicles.

TARGETS	
PROGESTERONE	> 3 ng/mL
LH	< 15 IU/L
HCG	> 25 mIU/mL

Strategies for Egg Retrieval Execution Based on Data

After your trigger shot, many clinics will check bloodwork the next morning to confirm that your body responded appropriately. Depending on the trigger used, they may measure progesterone, LH, or hCG.

If hCG was part of your trigger, most doctors want to see the level above 25 mIU per mL to confirm it was absorbed. Think of 25 as the minimum threshold, not necessarily the ideal number. With a full 10,000 IU hCG trigger shot, levels are often much higher the next day. If the number is barely above that cutoff after a full dose, it may raise questions about absorption or timing. Lower doses will naturally produce lower levels. If you used a Lupron-only trigger, hCG will not rise the same way, and your doctor may check LH and progesterone instead to confirm an adequate response.

If progesterone, LH, or hCG do not meet the target levels, your doctor may recommend an additional trigger shot to fully release the eggs from the follicular walls and improve maturation rates.

If you are doing a fresh transfer and your progesterone, LH, or lining measurement is not ideal, ask your doctor whether pivoting to a frozen transfer would be the better option.

If you have a history of early ovulation or empty follicles, the most reliable way to know whether eggs are still present is with an ultrasound the day after the trigger and again on retrieval day. Too many clients have told me the heartbreaking story of going under anesthesia expecting a good number of eggs, only to wake up and hear that many or all were missing. A simple ultrasound could have prevented the cost, anesthesia, and disappointment of an unnecessary retrieval.

If your doctor schedules an ultrasound the day of retrieval to confirm eggs are still in the follicles, confirm the time and location in advance. Sometimes it is done at a different facility than the retrieval itself, and you cannot risk being late.

Log It!

Write down hormone levels, follicle sizes, and lining measurements from this check if it is performed. These details matter for understanding how your body responds to the trigger and for planning future cycles.

MONITORING REPORTS: EGG RETRIEVAL AND AFTER

On the day of your egg retrieval, there is usually no monitoring at the clinic unless you are in a special situation where an ultrasound is needed to confirm the eggs are still in place and you have not ovulated already.

After the egg retrieval, clinical monitoring shifts to how you feel. Pay attention to bloating, pain, or nausea, and follow the list of red flags your doctor gives you. Drink electrolytes daily until you are fully recovered.

The last step is to gather and organize your records. Keep your medication calendar with names, doses, and start and stop dates, all monitoring reports from the clinic, and your own notes so you can compare them, along with the full embryology report detailing everything from eggs retrieved to embryos created.

The details in your monitoring reports are *gold* for understanding what worked, what did not, and how to make the next step even stronger if another cycle is needed.

EMBRYO REPORTS: EMBRYO GRADING

Healing the "Not Good Enough" Voice IVF Can Trigger

I once had a client (now a mama) who spiraled into an anxiety attack after hearing the grades of her embryos because they weren't "A's." I've had clients feel upset about grades before, but usually, I can reassure them by explaining how I've seen "A" embryos fail to implant and "B" or "C" embryos create the most beautiful, healthy babies. But this time was different. So, I helped her explore what those grades really meant to her.

It turned out that hearing about her embryos' grades brought her straight back to childhood memories of the pressure and shame she felt whenever she didn't get an "A" in school. Fascinating, right?

PROTECTING FEELINGS SHOULD NEVER OUTRANK PROTECTING YOUR CHANCE AT A CHILD

I believe that any difficult journey, especially a fertility journey, doesn't create new fears or anxieties; it simply puts a spotlight on what's already there. What surfaces during hard times is often the emotional clutter we've tried to forget. So when you notice the same patterns popping up, that's your cue not to ignore them but to stay present and face them.

Use the exercises you learned in the Survive to Thrive Protocol from the "Brain Breaks" section to quiet your mind and get into the present moment. Then ask what this trigger is trying to teach you. See what comes up.

Next, ask yourself if what you're feeling is something you still want to believe and carry, or if it's old news that needs to be released. Chances are, you're holding on to an outdated version of yourself, the one that still believes she needs to earn her worth. It's time to declutter those old thoughts, release the heaviness of the past that no longer fits you, and finally feel free.

Before we get started, if you're not totally clear on the difference between an embryo and a blastocyst, or how they're named and graded, here's a quick, simple overview (because there are much fancier words we could use).

Once the egg and sperm are fertilized, they're considered an embryo. The number of days after fertilization determines the name. For example, three days after fertilization, it's called a *day-3 embryo*.

When you hear the term "blastocyst," that simply means the embryo has reached a more advanced developmental stage or shape. This usually happens around day five, six, or seven after fertilization.

Now, let's talk about grading.

Here's what I think (but don't always say out loud) when someone tells me their embryo grade: *I don't care.*

Grading is subjective. An "A" at one clinic could easily be a "B" at another. To me, an embryo is a chance at your baby, and that alone is something to celebrate.

Plus, I've seen "average" graded embryos create the most beautiful, healthy babies.

But it is important to understand the grading you are given.

BLASTOCYST GRADING EXPLAINED

Blastocyst grading uses letters (A, B, and C, with A being "best") to describe two things:

1. The *trophectoderm*: the outer cells that will form the placenta
2. The *inner cell mass*: the cluster of cells that will become the baby

The more even and organized the cells look, the higher the grade. Blastocysts also get a number from 2 to 6 that describes how expanded or "grown" they are, with "6" being the most advanced.

DAY-3 GRADING EXPLAINED

Day-3 grading looks at two things: how fast the embryo is growing (the number of cells) and how even those cells are (called fragmentation). Some clinics rate fragmentation from 1 to 5, but each lab's system is slightly different, so don't get hung up on the scale.

There are things I look for in embryos that tend to tell me whether there is a better chance that the embryo will become a baby.

For day-3 embryos, you want at least 6 cells, ideally 8 or more, and fewer fragments.

For blastocysts, I pay more attention to when they reach that stage than to the grade itself. Embryos that become blastocysts on day 5 or 6 tend to have a higher chance of success. But let me also tell you this: two of my clients in a row became pregnant and stayed pregnant with day-7 blastocysts. So, just when I thought I had the "rules" figured out, life proved me wrong in the best way.

So here's my advice, especially for those concerned that your embryos didn't make the grade: love all of your embryos that decide to show up with you, because the "average" ducklings often become the most beautiful swans.

HURDLES TO HATCHLINGS: EGG RETRIEVALS

Here's your at-a-glance guide to the factors that can shape your medication plan and treatment options. Some come from your current unique biology, while others are based on what may have happened in previous egg retrievals that didn't go as planned.

For each situation, you'll see the strategies I've found most helpful to discuss with your doctor, followed by example questions you can ask.

You'll notice the strategies are detailed, often including specific protocols or adjustments that I've seen make a measurable difference in improving outcomes during egg retrievals. The questions for your doctor, though, are phrased more broadly, and that's intentional. As you learned in the section "Turning Questions Into Conversations With Your Doctor," we don't tell doctors what to do. Instead, we stay kind, curious, and collaborative. Ask what they would recommend, then, based on their response, see if they would consider specific strategies you've learned in this book.

REACTIONS TO MEDICATIONS

Some women already live with health conditions like frequent migraines, high blood pressure, or a history of blood clots. Adding synthetic estrogen in these cases is not only uncomfortable; it can be unsafe. Estrogen can trigger severe migraines, raise blood pressure further, or increase the risk of dangerous clots.

Success Strategies to Discuss with Your Doctor

If you already have these conditions, your protocol should be designed with safety as the priority from the very beginning. Safer options include skipping estrogen priming altogether, using Norethisterone (Aygestin) instead of combination birth control that contains estrogen, or, in some cases, adding letrozole to support follicle development while keeping estrogen levels lower. If you start treatment and develop new symptoms like migraines, that is not the time to push through. It is time to ask for adjustments.

Questions to Discuss with Your Doctor:

- Given my history of [migraines, high blood pressure, or blood clots], what other medications would you recommend for me other than estrogen?
- What do you think about trying Aygestin or a no-priming approach instead of synthetic estrogen?
- I have heard that letrozole can help keep estrogen levels lower while still supporting follicle development. What do you think?

OVARIAN HYPERSTIMULATION / OHSS

If your antral follicle count is over 20, especially over 30, or your estradiol climbs above 3,000 pg/mL during stimulation, you are at higher risk for OHSS. Remember, OHSS is not only uncomfortable; it can even land you in the hospital. And from what I have seen, OHSS = "Oh No" embryo development.

Other risk factors can include being under 35, having a low BMI (under 18 kg/m^2), or starting off with high estrogen before the trigger.

Success Strategies to Discuss with Your Doctor:

Lower dosing (but not too low) and steady growth usually lead to more even follicles, stronger embryos, and a lower risk of OHSS. Strategies can include beginning with a lower dose right away, slightly lowering the dose as estrogen increases, using Letrozole to lower estrogen levels, avoiding high hCG at the trigger, using only Lupron for the trigger, and adding a medication like Cabergoline before retrieval to help prevent fluid buildup and protect against OHSS.

Questions to Discuss with Your Doctor:

- Based on my AFC and rising estrogen, should we be doing anything differently to help avoid OHSS?

- Since I am prone to OHSS, will I be given a Lupron-only trigger shot? If so, is it possible to check my progesterone the next day to make sure it worked?
- I have heard that adding cabergoline around retrieval could help reduce my risk of OHSS. What do you think?

CYSTS ON OVARIES

If a cyst appears at baseline, the first step is determining its type. A cyst that produces estrogen is called a functioning cyst. If your estrogen is high at baseline without priming, for example, above 80 pg/mL, that cyst is likely functioning and moving forward could set you up for uneven results.

Nonfunctioning cysts, meaning those that do not produce estrogen, are sometimes considered harmless, but I do not agree. I say cysts sort of suck. Science may say nonfunctioning cysts do not matter, but my clinical experience says otherwise. I rarely see my clients get their best results when a cyst is present, functioning or not. That makes sense. If there is a cyst, something is already a little off. When you are investing in IVF, the goal should be optimal conditions whenever possible, not pushing ahead, getting poor results, and regretting not waiting.

Success Strategies to Discuss with Your Doctor:

If a cyst appears and it was not there before, ask about clearing it before moving forward. Many cysts resolve after ovulation, which usually takes about two weeks, or ovulation can be induced with a trigger shot to help release it. Once the cyst has resolved, you could consider starting stimulation in a mid-luteal cycle. This approach is often best for women with a natural FSH (follicle-stimulating hormone) under 10, a follicular phase of at least 11 days, and typically, though not always, an antral follicle count between 6 and 30.

If cysts are something you see frequently, that still deserves a plan. Your doctor may be able to shrink or clear some before stimulation using certain priming medications, such as luteal phase norethisterone or Aygestin, which is less suppressive, or combination birth control pills. If you are a candidate for no priming, you can also ask about shifting to a mid-luteal start, which can sometimes bypass cyst interference and allow you to begin stimulation sooner under better conditions.

The Survive to Thrive Protocols can also support your body by reducing inflammation and balancing hormones, giving you a better chance of having cyst-free cycles or fewer cysts showing up at baseline.

Questions to Discuss with Your Doctor:

- Since this cyst is not usually there and I want to begin stimulation in the best possible conditions, could we clear it first? If so, what would you recommend? I have heard that ovulating or taking a trigger shot could help to remove the cysts. Do you agree?

OR

- Since these cysts are always present for me, could we try to shrink or clear them before starting stimulation? If so, what would you recommend that would help without overly suppressing my ovaries? I hear that Aygestin could help with this. Do you agree?

ENDOMETRIOSIS

When I work with clients who have endometriosis or fibroids, I often say they are fiery in the best way. That spark is part of their strength. But for IVF, we want to gently turn down the flames. Adding estrogen on top of endometriosis is like pouring lighter fluid on a fire. It makes the flames grow, and in this case, that growth can work against you.

Most people talk about endometriosis in terms of transfers and implantation, and it definitely plays a role there. But for egg retrieval, if your endometriosis is around the ovaries, it can almost suffocate them, lowering egg reserve or speeding up a decline in Anti-Müllerian Hormone (AMH) levels if it is not addressed.

Yes, you can get and stay pregnant with endometriosis. But like cysts, it is not an ideal environment. Since IVF is such an investment, and since we want to hold our babies sooner, it makes sense to calm anything that is not optimal before treatment, and endometriosis is one of those things. That is why I often recommend looking into the Survive to Thrive Protocol as a way to reduce inflammation and calm endometriosis before you even begin IVF.

Success Strategies to Discuss with Your Doctor:

Many women with endometriosis do better with approaches that reduce estrogen exposure. That could mean no priming, using norethisterone/Aygestin instead of combination birth control or estradiol priming, or adding letrozole to the stimulation medications. If your AMH is declining faster than expected, that may be a sign your ovaries are being affected, and adjusting your stimulation plan could help protect egg quality.

Questions to Discuss with Your Doctor:

- Since I have endometriosis, what protocols would you recommend for me? Would you suggest avoiding estrogen-based approaches to the priming protocols?
- If my AMH is lower than expected for my age, do you believe endometriosis could be playing a role? If so, should I focus on reducing or removing it before my next egg retrieval?

PCOS

PCOS changes how a stimulation cycle should be run. Your response depends on whether you ovulate on your own, your AMH, and your exact follicle count before starting stims. These details shape the best priming plan, medication dose, and monitoring schedule.

Success Strategies to Discuss with Your Doctor

One size does not fit all. With PCOS, lower daily dosing (but not too low), closer monitoring, and a slower, steadier pace usually work best to help follicles grow more evenly. If you have 20 or more follicles, you may need lower total daily units, frequent every-other-day scans, and sometimes Letrozole-supported stims to keep growth steady and estrogen from climbing too quickly. To get a clearer picture of the priming and dosing strategies most likely to work best for you, see the *"Your Perfect Protocol–IVF"* software in the resource section, which can show you the options to discuss with your doctor.

Outside of medication, the Survive to Thrive Protocols are another powerful way to support your body before IVF. They could help lower inflammation, improve metabolic balance, and set the stage for a steadier and more synchronized response to stimulation.

Questions to Discuss with Your Doctor:

- Are we concerned with my starting AMH or AFC (antral follicle count), and do we need to think about OHSS with this egg retrieval?
- Do I need medications to help lower my estrogen throughout the stimulation medication? If so, what do you recommend? I have heard that letrozole could help with this. What do you think?
- If follicles start to separate into uneven groups or if estrogen rises too quickly in the middle of the stimulation medication, what will your strategy be?

EARLY OVULATION OR MISSING EGGS AT RETRIEVAL

It is heartbreaking to expect a strong number of eggs at retrieval and wake up to find most were not there. This usually happens when ovulation occurs early or when follicles collapse before retrieval. Women with shorter cycles, a history of early ovulation, or progesterone and LH rising too soon are most at risk.

Success Strategies to Discuss with Your Doctor:

Early ovulation can often be prevented with the right monitoring and safeguards. Red flags include follicles growing too large, too quickly (for example, many over 20 mm before day 9), or progesterone rising above 1.5 ng/mL and LH rising above 15 IU/L before trigger. Strategies can include starting the antagonist earlier when follicles are 11–14 mm (closer to 11 mm in women with lower ovarian reserve), taking the antagonist twice a day instead of once, or using a progestin such as Provera from the start of stimulation rather than a GnRH antagonist. Another option is an extended Clomid protocol, where Clomid is continued throughout stimulation to block estrogen receptors and help prevent an LH surge. For those with a history of early ovulation, it can also help to confirm follicles are still present with an ultrasound on trigger day, the day after trigger, and again on retrieval day before anesthesia. Retrieval-day scans must be scheduled in advance since they take extra time.

Questions to Discuss with Your Doctor:

- Given my [early ovulation or missing eggs at retrieval], what would you recommend we do differently next time to lower that risk? Would you consider a different priming medication, a different dosing of the stimulation medication, or a different ovulation suppressor?
- Why do you think we had this issue?
- My progesterone and LH seem to be rising quickly. Do you agree? If so, what are the options you would consider to help prevent it? Should I be taking more of the antagonist? Could I continue to get my LH and progesterone monitored daily?
- For the next egg retrieval, can we plan ultrasounds after the trigger shot day and on the day of retrieval to confirm that the follicles are still intact?

UNEVEN OR RAPID FOLLICULAR GROWTH

Uneven follicle sizes and rapid growth often show up together, and when they do, the results are usually weaker eggs and poor embryo development. If your lead follicles are racing ahead while the rest lag behind, or if the main group is already over 20 mm by day 9, growth is moving too quickly. This often happens when the starting dose of medication is too high, when the estrogen is rising quickly and the dosing of the stimulation medication is not adjusted to slow it down, when there is no priming protocol with a higher FSH or estrogen level at the baseline ultrasound (for a follicular start of the stimulation meds), or when more medication is added mid-cycle to push things along.

Slowing down the growth of the follicles and using strategies to keep the follicles growing evenly throughout the stimulation medication will give you the best chance at the most embryos, and they should be healthy and strong, too.

Success Strategies to Discuss with Your Doctor:

Uneven or rapid growth usually points to a mismatch between your biology and the plan. Adjusting the medication type, dose, or timing could significantly improve how your follicles grow together. That might mean starting at a lower dose, planning an earlier step-down based on your prior cycle pattern, or monitoring estrogen more closely and adjusting sooner instead of reacting late.

A thoughtful priming approach could help follicles grow more synchronously before stimulation even begins. Use the priming chart previously outlined to guide the conversation with your doctor. Start with the least suppressive option first, then choose based on your specific biology and past response patterns. The goal is to create a more level starting line so one follicle does not take off ahead of the group. You can learn exactly which priming protocols I would recommend based on your data inside the software I created, *"Your Perfect Protocol IVF."*

In certain cases, a "standard then mini-stim" approach could help maintain more even growth by reducing intensity once follicles are recruited. Others may benefit from avoiding mid-cycle dose increases unless absolutely necessary, since pushing harder often accelerates the lead follicle instead of helping the smaller ones catch up.

If you have three or fewer follicles growing and they are uneven, another option could be converting to timed intercourse or IUI, assuming sperm parameters are adequate and fallopian tubes are open. This could allow you to use the cycle instead of canceling it. However, this option should not be considered if more than three mature follicles develop, since the risk of multiples would be too high.

Trigger timing is another key lever. In some cases, triggering slightly earlier could prevent over-maturation of the lead follicles and protect overall egg quality.

Questions to Discuss with Your Doctor:

- Why do you think my follicles grew unevenly or too quickly in my last cycle?
- Based on my prior monitoring, we can see the day that growth accelerated (or the follicles started to grow unevenly). Is there something we can do to prevent that from happening again?
- Since I only have three follicles growing and they are uneven, would this be the time to discuss converting to timed intercourse or IUI (intrauterine insemination) instead of canceling?

POOR OVARIAN RESPONSE

If you start with a healthy number of follicles at baseline but only a few grow once stimulation begins, you may be what doctors call a "poor responder." This is not the same as having a low ovarian reserve. It means the follicles are there, but they are not being recruited effectively.

This kind of situation often happens when the starting dose of medication is too high and essentially overwhelms the follicles instead of encouraging steady growth, or when priming is overly suppressive and prevents them from waking up and responding. It can feel especially frustrating when your baseline scan looked pretty and promising.

Success Strategies to Discuss with Your Doctor:

Getting a strong response at the start of your cycle really comes down to three simple things: the right kind of priming, the right medication for *your* body, and a starting dose that encourages growth without overwhelming your ovaries.

Very high starting doses, like 450 units or more, can sometimes backfire. Instead of helping, they can cause a few follicles to grow while the rest just sit there, especially if your ovarian reserve is lower. For some women, starting at a lower dose actually helps more follicles grow together because the ovaries are not being shocked by too much medication at once.

Priming can also play a big role. If it is too suppressive, like being on combination birth control for a long time, your ovaries may stay too "quiet" and not respond well when stimulation begins. Using the priming chart we discussed and starting with the least suppressive option that fits your biology may help your ovaries wake up and respond better.

Choosing the right medication is another key piece. If your testosterone is low, it could affect how well follicles are recruited, so it is worth checking before your next cycle. Some women respond better when pills are used at the beginning to help recruit follicles. Others do better going straight to injectable medications like FSH and LH. If one approach did not work well before, trying a different strategy could lead to a better response.

In some cases, doctors talk about adding human growth hormone to possibly support follicle growth and egg development. When it is used, it is usually started early in the stimulation phase so it is already in your system before follicles are fully recruited. It is not right for everyone, and not every doctor will try it, but I tend to recommend it and believe it is a conversation worth having.

Questions to Discuss with Your Doctor:

- Since I had a good number of follicles at the start, but only some of them grew, what do you think stopped the others from responding?
- Do you think my starting dose was too high for my body? Would starting lower help more follicles grow together?
- Was my priming too suppressive? Based on my hormone levels and how I responded before, would you try a less suppressive option next time?
- I hear that testosterone priming has been used to help recruit more follicles when there is a poor response. What do you think? Should we test my testosterone to see if it is low?
- Do you like the flare protocols with Clomid or Letrozole?
- What do you think of adding in human growth hormone to the start of the stimulation medications? Could this possibly help and not hurt?

SLOW OR NO GROWTH WITH STIMULATION DRUGS

If you are 4 to 6 days into stimulation and your estradiol is still around 100 pg/mL or lower, and your follicles are under 6 mm, it can feel like the cycle is going nowhere. Some clinics cancel quickly in this situation. But many times, the cycle could still be turned around with the right adjustments. I have seen women go on to create healthy embryos from cycles that started with almost no response once the plan was corrected.

Success Strategies to Discuss with Your Doctor:

If this happens mid-cycle, one of the first things to check is your FSH level. If FSH is very high, for example, over 30 mIU/mL, your ovaries may be under stress. In that case, taking a short break from medication could give your body time to reset.

Instead of canceling right away, you could pause stimulation for about five days and then recheck FSH, estradiol, and follicle sizes. During that pause, some doctors will stop all medications completely, while others may continue estrogen only to help stabilize hormone levels.

If estradiol starts to rise, follicles begin to grow, and FSH drops, restarting stimulation at a dose that better matches your follicle count could still lead to a usable cycle.

It is also important to look at the bigger picture. Was your priming too suppressive? Was your starting dose too high or too low for your biology? Do you tend to respond better to certain stimulation medications than others? These patterns should guide changes in the current cycle, if possible, and definitely in the next one.

Questions to Discuss with Your Doctor:

- Why do you think my follicles have stalled in this cycle?
- What would you recommend we do right now since growth seems very slow?
    - Would checking my FSH help us understand whether my ovaries are under stress or just moving slowly?
    - If my FSH is very high, could we pause the cycle instead of canceling? During that pause, would you stop all medications or continue estrogen only?
    - After a pause, what numbers would we be looking for to decide if it makes sense to restart stimulation?
    - If we restart, how would you adjust the dose or medication choice to better match how my ovaries are responding?
- Have you had patients whose cycles looked as if they stalled early on but improved after a pause? What changes did you make that helped them move forward?

FEWER THAN 80 PERCENT OF THE EGGS RETRIEVED WERE MATURE

When fewer than 80 percent of your eggs are mature, it is often a sign that the follicles were not given enough time or the right support to fully develop before retrieval. This is one of the most common hurdles I see. Egg maturity depends on two key factors: how evenly the follicles grew during stimulation and whether the trigger shot was timed and dosed correctly. If eggs are retrieved too early, too late, or after uneven growth, maturity rates can drop.

Success Strategies to Discuss with Your Doctor:

Start by reviewing follicle sizes on the day of the trigger shot. Were most follicles in the 16 to 20 mm range after at least 10 days of stimulation, or was growth uneven? If growth was uneven, the next cycle may require adjustments to priming, starting dose, or pacing during stimulation.

Next, look closely at the trigger shot. Some women may need a higher hCG dose, sometimes up to 20,000 units. Others respond better to a dual trigger that combines hCG and Lupron. For women at risk of OHSS, a Lupron-only trigger shot with careful follow-up labs may be the safer choice.

If low maturity happens despite evenly growing follicles and adequate stimulation time, it may also be reasonable to review lab timing and handling practices.

Questions to Discuss with Your Doctor:

- Why do you think we had lower maturity rates in this cycle?
- Do you think uneven follicle growth contributed? If so, what changes would you make to help improve synchronization next time?
- Would adjusting the trigger shot, either by increasing hCG or using a dual trigger, potentially improve maturity in my case? Why do you think we had this issue?

FEWER THAN 80 PERCENT OF THE MATURE EGGS WERE FERTILIZED

If fertilization rates are under 80 percent, I start by reviewing follicle growth, overall protocol execution, sperm quality, and what happened in the lab. Eggs that are too small, too large, or uneven in growth may not fertilize well. If stimulation was too aggressive or poorly paced, the eggs may also be more fragile at retrieval.

Fertilization outcomes can also depend on the method used, whether conventional insemination or ICSI (Intracytoplasmic Sperm Injection). And sometimes sperm issues, such as DNA fragmentation, are the hidden factor, even when a basic semen analysis appears normal.

Success Strategies to Discuss with Your Doctor:

First, review follicle growth to determine whether uneven development may have contributed. Next, discuss the fertilization method used and whether a different approach could improve outcomes. Some cases benefit from ICSI, and in select situations, calcium ionophore activation may be considered.

If low fertilization rates occur despite evenly growing follicles and appropriate stimulation length, it is reasonable to also ask about lab conditions and consistency.

Questions to Discuss with Your Doctor:

- What do you believe contributed to our lower fertilization rate?
- Do you think follicle growth or stimulation pacing played a role? If so, what changes would you recommend for the next cycle?
- Would ICSI potentially improve fertilization compared to conventional insemination in my case?
- Is calcium ionophore activation something your lab uses, and in what situations do you recommend it?
- Would sperm DNA fragmentation testing provide useful information for us? Why do you think we had this issue?

FEWER THAN 80 PERCENT OF THE FERTILIZED EGGS MADE IT TO DAY-3 EMBRYOS

If fewer than 80 percent of fertilized eggs made it to day-3 embryos, I look closely at follicle growth, overall stimulation pacing, sperm quality, and lab conditions. Eggs that did not grow evenly or were exposed to overly aggressive medication may lack the energy reserves needed to keep dividing.

Even subtle lab variables, such as differences in culture media, equipment, or staffing, can influence early embryo development. And sometimes sperm DNA fragmentation is the hidden factor, especially when fertilization initially appears normal but embryos arrest soon after.

Success Strategies to Discuss with Your Doctor:

Start by reviewing your stimulation cycle. Were most follicles in the 16 to 20 mm range after at least 10 days of medication, or was growth uneven or rushed? Uneven growth can leave eggs less prepared to support early embryo division.

Next, ask about lab consistency. Were there any changes in culture media, equipment, or embryology staff during your cycle?

Finally, consider sperm quality more deeply. DNA fragmentation testing may uncover issues that a standard semen analysis would miss.

Questions to Discuss with Your Doctor:

- What do you believe contributed to fewer embryos reaching day 3?
- Do you think follicle growth or stimulation pacing played a role? If so, what would you adjust next cycle?
- Were there any lab changes or variables that could have influenced embryo development?
- Would sperm DNA fragmentation testing help clarify why embryos are arresting at this stage?

FEWER THAN 80 PERCENT OF DAY-3 EMBRYOS MADE IT TO THE BLASTOCYST STAGE, OR THE BLASTOCYSTS WERE NOT NORMAL

When fewer than 80 percent of your day-3 embryos make it to the blastocyst stage, or when most blastocysts come back abnormal after genetic testing, several variables could be involved. Blastocyst development builds on everything that affects day-3 embryos, including protocol design, medication dosing, and trigger timing. It is also influenced by age, sperm quality, lab conditions, and how embryos are handled during biopsy and testing.

Egg health during stimulation and sperm integrity both play major roles in whether embryos continue developing. The lab environment and biopsy technique can also influence outcomes. If PGT (preimplantation genetic testing) was performed, the number of normal embryos could be affected by how and when the biopsy was done and which lab processed the samples. While uncommon, variability between genetic testing labs has been reported, which is why transparency and data are important.

Success Strategies to Discuss with Your Doctor:

Start by reviewing stimulation and follicle growth. Were most follicles in the 16 to 20 mm range at trigger after at least 10 days of stimulation, or was growth uneven or rushed?

Next, discuss the lab environment. Ask about consistency in culture media, equipment, and embryo handling.

If genetic testing was performed, confirm who performed the biopsy and which laboratory analyzed the samples. In some cases, adjusting biopsy timing or technique, or even using a different testing lab, may be worth discussing for a future cycle.

Questions to Discuss with Your Doctor:

- What do you believe contributed to fewer embryos reaching blastocyst or testing normal?
- Could my stimulation protocol or follicle growth pattern have influenced blastocyst development?
- Were there any lab variables that could have affected development beyond day 3?
- Who performed the biopsy, and could timing or technique have influenced the results?
- What are your lab's typical blastocyst and euploid rates for patients my age?
- Would there be any benefit to using a different genetic testing lab in a future cycle?

CARDIAC DISEASE, CARDIOMYOPATHY, OR BLOOD CLOTS DESPITE MEDICATION

If you have a history of serious heart disease, cardiomyopathy, or blood clots, IVF planning requires an added layer of caution. Pregnancy increases blood volume and clotting factors, which can strain the heart and raise clot risk. For some women, a gestational carrier is the safest path. For others who are fully cleared by their cardiologist and hematologist to carry, the focus shifts to keeping hormone levels as steady and as low as safely possible.

Success Strategies to Discuss with Your Doctor:

In these cases, synthetic estrogen is usually avoided or used only with extreme caution because it can increase clotting risk. That includes oral estrogen and sometimes even patches, depending on your specific history. These decisions should always be made in coordination with your cardiologist and fertility team.

Doctors may consider gentler stimulation approaches, such as lower-dose gonadotropins or letrozole-supported cycles, to help keep estradiol levels from climbing too high. The goal is to support follicle growth without overwhelming your cardiovascular system.

Questions to Discuss with Your Doctor:

- Am I medically cleared to carry a pregnancy, or should we consider a gestational carrier?
- Should synthetic estrogen be avoided in my case?
- What stimulation approach would help keep estradiol levels lower and safer for me?
- How will my heart function and clotting risk be monitored during stimulation and early pregnancy?

TRANSGENDER PATIENTS

If you are in transition and currently taking testosterone, egg retrieval will usually require a pause. This pause can be challenging, both physically and emotionally. Some people experience mood shifts, increased anxiety, or low energy when stopping testosterone. Knowing this ahead of time and planning for support can make a big difference.

Working with your fertility doctor, prescribing physician, and therapist as a coordinated team can help you feel safer and more supported during this phase. Clear communication and a plan for both your physical and emotional health are essential.

Success Strategies to Discuss with Your Doctor:

The focus here is timing, safety, and emotional support. You will want clarity on how long testosterone should be paused before stimulation and retrieval and what support systems can be in place during that time.

Questions to Discuss with Your Doctor:

- How long should I be off testosterone before starting stimulation?
- What lab values will you monitor to determine when it is safe to proceed?
- Have you worked with transgender patients before, and how do you support them during this process?
- If I experience emotional changes while off testosterone, what support options are available through your clinic? How long should I be off testosterone before starting treatments?

MOSAIC TURNER SYNDROME (MISSING AN X CHROMOSOME)

If you have mosaic Turner syndrome and are still cycling, you may still produce eggs, though ovarian reserve is often lower. IVF may be possible, but there are two major considerations.

First, embryos should typically undergo PGT to assess chromosomal health, since Turner syndrome increases the risk of chromosomal abnormalities in embryos.

Second, carrying a pregnancy with Turner syndrome can involve significant medical risks, particularly related to the heart and blood vessels. A thorough cardiac evaluation is essential before attempting pregnancy. In some cases, a gestational carrier may be the safest option depending on your individual health profile. The priority is protecting your long-term health while also giving you the best chance at a healthy baby.

Success Strategies to Discuss with Your Doctor:

Start with embryo testing. PGT, or preimplantation genetic testing, can help identify which embryos are chromosomally normal.

Next, review your overall health, especially cardiac screening and pregnancy safety. Make sure a clear plan is in place before moving forward.

Finally, discuss whether any protocol adjustments could support ovarian response or uterine preparation based on your specific hormone levels and reserve.

Questions to Discuss with Your Doctor:

- Should we plan to test all embryos with PGT given my diagnosis?
- What specific pregnancy risks apply to me, particularly regarding cardiac health?
- Do I need updated cardiac imaging or clearance before attempting pregnancy?
- Based on my medical profile, would you recommend that I consider a gestational carrier?
- Are there protocol adjustments you would suggest to optimize ovarian response or uterine safety in my case?

CHAPTER 11 SUMMARY

- **Execution Makes or Breaks a Great Protocol:** A perfect plan on paper does not matter if the timing, monitoring, and adjustments are off. Precision during stims is where strong embryos are won or lost.
- **Monitoring Visits Are Your Play-by-Play:** Ultrasounds and hormone levels tell you if the dosing of the medication needs to shift to help create healthy embryos.
- **Baseline Sets the Tone:** Quiet ovaries, low hormones, and no cyst drama give you the best chance at even growth. If baseline levels are off, a short pause or pivot could save the whole cycle.
- **Low and Slow Is the Way to Go:** Slow (but not too slow) and steady follicle growth tends to create hardier eggs with a better chance of becoming embryos. One of the most effective ways to support that is to use lower (but not too low) stimulation dosing, especially in the second half of stims, when follicles can start growing too fast and outpace quality.
- **The Trigger Shot Is the Final Exam:** Timing and dosing decide egg maturity. One extra day can be the difference between a strong cohort and a compromised retrieval.
- **OHSS Is Not Only Uncomfortable:** High estrogen, high follicle count, and aggressive dosing can trigger OHSS (preimplantation genetic testing), and OHSS often goes hand in hand with weaker embryo development.
- **What Numbers Matter:** The number that matters most in determining the success of an egg retrieval is *embryo development* and not the number of eggs retrieved, matured, or fertilized.
- **Grades Don't Decide Your Baby:** Embryo grading is subjective and varies by clinic. A "perfect" grade can fail, and an "average" grade can become your healthy baby.
- **Every Problem Has a Strategy:** Cysts, uneven growth, early ovulation, low maturity, low fertilization, and stalled development all have possible pivots. The win is knowing what to ask and catching issues early enough to fix them.

Before heading to the next section...

If you'd like checklists for preparing for an egg retrieval, monitoring report templates to properly track and analyze results, and more, just scan the QR code.

12. Retrieval's Done! What's Next?

You Know You've Done Too Much IVF When...

Last year, I went in for a routine mammogram, took off all my clothes, and put on the robe, and as I started walking out of the dressing room, it hit me: this robe is *really* short.

And then it really hit me... I wasn't supposed to take off my pants. I giggled and thought, *You know you've done too much IVF when...*

And then more came to me. I made a post about it, and here is what I wrote:

"You know you have done too much IVF when...

... you used to care if your OB/GYN was male or female, and now you don't even expect them to be a doctor.

... not only do needles not scare you anymore, but you're pretty sure you could get stabbed with a knife and not flinch.

... you hear that someone got pregnant naturally, and you think, Wow, that's unusual.

... you giggle when someone says their $150 medication is outrageously expensive and they can't believe it isn't covered by insurance."

My tribe on Instagram added even more gems to the list, along with tons of laughing emojis. It reminded me that while IVF is heartbreaking and heavy, it can also be funny. Not in a "*that was hilarious*" way, but in a "*can you believe what we're doing (or did) to have a baby?!*" kind of way.

After an egg retrieval, some of my clients know exactly what they want to do next, while others have decisions to make. If you are in the decision-making camp, your next step depends on what happened in your retrieval, your family goals, and your available resources: financial, emotional, and physical.

I'm going to walk you through the most common decisions my clients face after retrieval. I'll share the same objective information I give them, along with the questions I encourage them to ask, so you can figure out your next best step to get closer to kissing your baby sooner.

BANK OR TRANSFER YOUR EMBRYOS

One of the most common questions I hear is, "Should I go straight into a transfer or do another retrieval and bank more embryos first?"

While I usually know a client's history well enough to guide them quickly, if I were walking someone through this without any context, these are the questions I would ask to help them find their right next step.

Like with most decisions when you're trying to figure out a plan of action, I tend to start tactically to see if any data could immediately rule out some options.

Can you afford another retrieval right now? Sometimes finances make the decision for you. Maybe you can't afford another retrieval now but could in a few months. If that's the case, another retrieval is simply off the table for now. If finances allow for either option, we keep asking more questions.

Do you have insurance coverage right now? If your insurance currently covers retrievals, it may be worth taking advantage of that while you have it. Jobs and coverage can change, and I've seen clients regret not using insurance when it was available. The first step is to understand your coverage completely. Confirm whether your plan allows another retrieval even if you already have embryos frozen. If it does, depending on your answers to the next question, I would likely recommend another egg retrieval.

How many embryos do you have on ice, and how many chil-

dren do you want? How many embryos do you have on ice, and how many children do you hope to have? There is no guaranteed number that equals a baby. Even strong embryos do not always lead to a live birth. That said, I like to see at least four day-3 embryos or two to three blastocysts per desired child frozen.

For example, if you have two blastocysts frozen and hope for two children, I would usually recommend considering another retrieval before moving to transfer. It is much easier to create embryos now than to wish you had later.

How do you feel about having extra embryos? Some people feel fine having more embryos than they may use, while others find that idea stressful. It's important to explore this early because your comfort level shapes whether you'll want to bank more embryos or move to transfer once you have what feels like enough for at least one baby.

How old are you, and how easily can you make more embryos? Your age and biology play a huge role in this decision. If you are thirty-six, have a strong AMH, and plan for one child, you may feel comfortable transferring now, knowing you could return for another retrieval in two years. That timeline usually accounts for a nine-month pregnancy and about a year after your baby is born. If you are forty or have a low AMH or high FSH, and hope to have two children but only have one or two embryos, I would usually suggest doing another retrieval before transferring.

How does your body feel about another retrieval? This is often the ultimate decision-maker. Even when the logic points one way, your body's reaction usually gives the clearest answer. When I do this exercise with clients, I have them close their eyes and imagine two scenarios. First, I say, "The choice is made. You're going to do another retrieval." I pause and ask what they feel in their body. Then I say, "The choice is made. You're going to do a transfer next." Again, I pause and ask them to notice their reaction.

Sometimes clients feel calm about retrieval. Other times their body says a loud "no." And when that happens, forcing another cycle rarely brings great results. IVF works best when your mind and body are aligned.

You can also revisit the "Making a Decision with Precision" exercise from earlier in the book to help you choose what's right for you. With the combination of these questions and your final gut check, I've always seen clients land on the path that's right for them.

BACK-TO-BACK RETRIEVAL: PAUSE OR PLAY?

Many clients feel like they have to jump straight into another egg retrieval before they are even fully awake from anesthesia because they are told, "You're too old to wait." As if taking one month to rest would cause their eggs to shrivel up, disappear, and send them straight into menopause, never to make another egg again.

Nope. That is not how biology works.

When clinics push urgency, they are often pulling you toward the lowest place on the Levels of Energy Alignment scale: fear and shame. Fear sounds like, "Your eggs already look bad. You cannot afford to wait." Shame sounds like, "You should have started sooner. You focused on your career or waited too long for the right partner." Both create pressure. Both create blame.

That is not how you operate anymore. You make decisions from clarity. And clarity creates confidence. You look at your data, your age, your ovarian reserve, your actual response. You know that dramatic, sweeping statements are not the same thing as evidence. And you trust yourself enough to pause if something does not feel right.

So let's decide whether to hit pause or play on another retrieval using your numbers, not someone else's pressure.

GET THE RESULTS

If you do not know the results of your last egg retrieval, I would pause. Too often, I see women told to start priming for the next retrieval without knowing the results of the last.

This scenario usually happens when you do genetic testing on embryos and end up with about a three-week wait for results. That waiting period is not just downtime; it's data collection.

Those results should drive your very next move. If the report comes back poor, like no healthy embryos, repeating the exact same protocol or execution is rarely the right call. That is essentially asking your body to respond differently without giving it a different plan.

If your results were successful, excellent! You can move to the next step.

COMPARE CYCLE TO CYCLE

Even when your next protocol looks identical to the previous one on paper, your current biology and the execution of that protocol are what actually determine the outcome.

I had a client repeat her exact protocol back-to-back, and the second time her results were far worse. Why? Two small but important differences. First, her baseline labs were different. Estradiol and FSH were higher than they had been in the previous cycle. Second, her doctor delayed the start of her stimulation medications past cycle day 4. Same protocol, slightly different execution, completely different results.

This is why you never want to assume that the same protocol will give the same results. Always compare cycle to cycle. **The same protocol can only give you similar outcomes if the conditions and the execution are the same.**

THE SAME PROTOCOL CAN ONLY GIVE YOU SIMILAR OUTCOMES IF THE CONDITIONS AND THE EXECUTION ARE THE SAME

CHECK IN WITH YOURSELF

Fertility is a byproduct of overall health and wellness. When you do not feel well, your results usually reflect that. Before committing to another round, answer these questions honestly:

- How is your energy?
- How are you sleeping?
- Physically, mentally, and emotionally, do you feel ready to do this again?

Taking a month or two off will not destroy your egg reserve. In some cases, it may give your body the energy it needs.

I have watched too many women push forward on empty, hoping grit alone will carry them through. More often than expected, the next cycle performs worse. Not because they were one month older, but because they never gave their body a chance to recover.

There is one more question I want you to ask. How do you *feel* when you hear that you should do another retrieval right away?

I recently spoke with a woman preparing for back-to-back retrievals without even knowing the results of her last one. She was 43 and had been told she could not wait another second. When we walked through this exact check-in and reviewed her data, it became clear that waiting made more sense. She said it felt like a weight had been lifted.

Your body gives signals when a decision is right. The hard part is quieting the fear-driven voice long enough to hear them. But you know how to do that now.

DO YOU NEED AN EGG DONOR?

What if My Child Wants a Different Mom?

Many of my clients worry that if they use a donor egg, their child will eventually find out and reject them or push them out of their life.

When I hear that, I tell them they're absolutely right… But the same conversation can happen when a parent raises a child who is genetically their own.

I remember thinking I wanted a different mom in fourth grade because mine wouldn't let me have two sleepovers in a row. Right then, I determined that she was the *strictest mom ever*!

And when Hudson was four or five, he had his own version of that moment. One night, I said, for what must have been the hundredth time, "Thank you for picking me to be your mom." But that night, he looked right at me and said, "I would like to choose a new mom."

When I asked who he had in mind, he didn't hesitate before saying, "Auntie Rosa."

That's my sister, who's the funniest, most brilliant, beautiful, fun, generous, and talented person I know. She had the best house with way too many animals and is the mom of his cousin Kaia, whom he thinks of like a sister.

Oh, and she is also a superhero.

Yup. My sister is an actress, and, at the time Hudson uttered those words to me, she was playing the mom of a family of superheroes on the very popular Nickelodeon show *The Thundermans*. Hudson got all the perks of being on set, going to the Nickelodeon award shows and events with her, and meeting other TV stars and athletes he loved. Of course he wanted to join her family. What kid wouldn't?

I thought that what Hudson told me was adorable and couldn't wait to tell Rosa. But when I walked into my room to tell Brian, I didn't even get a full sentence out before I started sobbing, "Hudson doesn't want me to be his mooooom…"

Now, if I had been living higher on the Levels of Energy Alignment, I would have understood why he wanted my sister to be his mom. I could have seen it for what it was: my son wanted to be a super cool superhero, too.

But I was living on a much lower level. That one comment landed right on my deepest fear that I was failing as a mom. That if I just did more, did better, and was more and better, my son would be happy with me.

Do you know what vibration that is? Shame: the lowest emotion on the Alignment scale.

How I interpreted what Hudson said revealed everything about me. Remember the statement from Spirit Protocol: your external world reflects your internal beliefs. If I hadn't been living in shame, I would never have filtered what he said through that lens and turned it into a spiral about what I was doing wrong.

When you practice the Spirit Protocol, you reset your natural vibration so that when things are said or done around you, you filter them through a higher frequency level. While I still have those moments when I feel like I should be doing more or doing better (just ask me how long it took me to edit this book!), I don't live there anymore.

And for the record, Mila wants a new mom right now, too, because she's not getting a smartphone anytime soon. That apparently makes me the *strictest mom ever*!

(To be fair, I told her she could get a phone, just not a smartphone. I also told her that if she could find research proving it's healthy and safe for an eleven-year-old to have one, I would gladly reconsider.)

(And I reminded her that giving her a phone would be the easy thing to do because she'd "STOP ASKING MEEEEE," and I usually end with, "This is hard for both of us… and we can do hard things.")

(… And yes, I know I'm "so annoying." But why would I stop giving life lessons when I get to see her eyes roll all the way back into her head so impressively when I do?)

Overall, you get to choose what exchanges like this mean to you. If your reaction is shame, that's your signal to spend more time on the Spirit Protocol.

And if your child wants to find a new mom, that means you are probably being a great mom, helping your children grow up healthy and safe, and setting them up for success in life.

Or it simply means your sister's also a superhero, and you really can't win that one.

Note: While I've had clients use sperm donors, embryo donors, and surrogates, most of the women I work with are trying to decide whether or not to use an egg donor. The same decision-making process and mindset I'm about to share can absolutely apply to any third-party assistance, but to keep this already-too-long-because-I-talk-too-much book a bit shorter, we're going to stick with egg donors here.

I am probably the worst person to ask if there is "hope" that you can get pregnant with your own eggs or if you should keep trying to build your family, and here's why.

1. **I have personally seen too many miracles happen.** When you have seen as many healthy babies created from situations that looked impossible as I have, statistics start to lose their power.
2. **When I decide I want something, I don't stop until I get it.** Hence, the eight additional rounds of IVF for baby number two. But that doesn't mean I am unrealistic about what my clients are capable of. It means that when a woman decides she is going to have a baby, I believe her, so it's happening. From there, my job is to help her find the best path forward.
3. **Around 70 percent of my clients come to me saying they were told they need an egg donor, and less than 5 percent end up using one before creating a healthy baby.** So when I hear my clients say that they were told they need an egg donor, that doesn't hold much weight.

But whenever someone does want to discuss using an egg donor, the reason to move forward with one is not always about hormone levels or egg reserve. It is also about your resources: emotional, physical, and financial.

Here are the same questions I walk my clients through to help them figure out whether their next right step is to keep going with their own eggs or consider a donor.

1. **Have you done "optimized" IVF (the right protocol, executed correctly, and with an excellent lab)?** If yes, move to the next question. If not, it might be worth trying one round of optimized IVF first and then basing your next decision on those results. The goal is to give your own eggs their best possible shot without doing endless, exhausting cycles that are less likely to work.
2. **Are you currently making embryos that reach the day-3 or blastocyst stage with optimized IVF?** If not, and if

you have already done multiple rounds of optimized IVF, it may be time to explore other incredible paths to parenthood.

If you are making day-3 embryos or blastocysts, the next step is to look closely at your transfer strategies. Assuming those are solid, then I will ask:

3. **Can you afford to continue IVF with your own eggs for one or two more retrievals and still have the resources to move to donor eggs, if needed?** Avoid draining your resources and leaving no options for next steps. If you know that after these final retrievals, you will not have the means to pursue a donor, and your heart is set on building your family in any way possible, then finances alone might make the right choice for you.
4. **How do you feel?** There's that question again. Even if you passed questions one, two, and three, this is usually when I recommend pausing with your own eggs because, say it with me, "When it does not feel right, it usually is not."

You can always revisit this decision later, but for now, the answer might be to pause. Which brings me to the most important truth of all:

You have done enough.

If you are reading this part with hesitation or even anxiety, chances are you have already poured in more than enough effort, time, money, and heart. Oh, so much heart. You have shown up again and again, even when it was hard. You are not ready to give up, but you are tired... *really* tired.

I have seen this before, and I want to tell you again something I have told others in the past: You have done enough. This is something I know with 100 percent certainty about people doing IVF, even when they could not see it for themselves. And failing to see that they've done enough is what kept them stuck.

Let that sink in. **You really have done enough.**

No, deciding to pause is not you giving up. This is not you failing in any way. This is not the second-best choice or a consolation prize. This is the right choice based on results. This is a great strategy. As the CEO of your family, you are making the most of your resources and moving toward your goal using a different strategy. That is not losing anything; that is leadership.

Think of it like this. You are driving when the road suddenly closes for an unknown period. You could sit there waiting, frustrated and stuck, wasting time, money, and energy, not knowing when or if it will reopen. So you start researching it online, calling friends for advice, even though they're not on the road with you and can't understand, and doing more and more, trying to force that road to work.

Or you could simply turn and take a different road. The destination is the same. Yes, it truly is. The same child is waiting for you, and I will explain more about that in a moment.

All you are doing is choosing a new route because the one ahead has shown you it is not available right now. Anyone with an important destination would do the same.

YOU HAVE DONE ENOUGH. AND IT IS OKAY TO ALLOW YOURSELF TO CONSIDER A DIFFERENT ROAD THAT COULD LEAD YOU TO YOUR BABY

You have too big a life to sit stuck in endless unknowns. You are ready for the next chapter, the one where your child is finally here. So let me say my next words clearly and with absolute certainty: **you have done enough. And it is okay to allow yourself to consider a different road that could lead you to *your* baby.**

REFRAMING EGG DONATION

"What will people say?" "What will I say to my children?"

These are common questions I hear from my clients. Here is what I share with them about egg donation, and really, about anything people have opinions on:

What you believe about something feels real, but it is not always the truth.

If you believe egg or sperm donation is strange, then it will feel strange. But that is a belief, not a truth. You can choose to see it differently.

For example, I do not think egg donation is strange at all, because in my experience, I have only seen joy, peace, love, and beautiful, healthy babies come from it.

The perfect child arrives at the perfect time. Always. End of story.

Egg donation is simply one of the ways that the perfect child for your family finds their way to you.

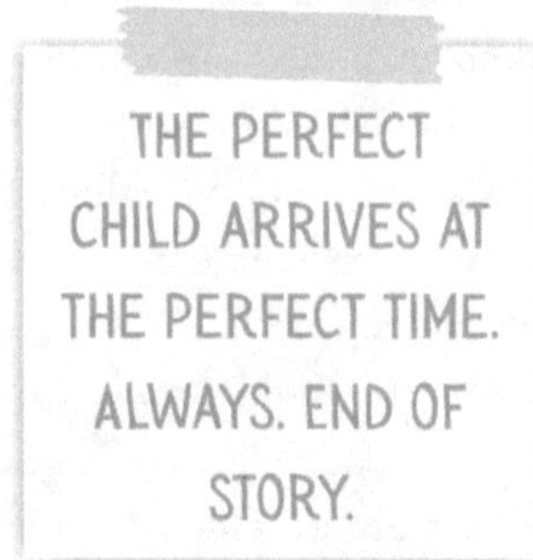

But egg donation probably isn't something you talk about with many friends or family, and when something feels unfamiliar, the brain labels it as uncomfortable or strange in some way. That is where the shame begins. It can start to feel like a secret that you are embarrassed about.

If I am working with someone who feels weighed down by the shame of possibly needing an egg donor, here are a few things I walk through with her:

1. **Choose to see it from a higher place on the Levels of Energy Alignment.**

If that feels hard, go back to the Spirit Protocol and keep practicing. Remember, what you see outside, like shame for needing an egg donor or fear of what people will think, is a mirror of what is happening inside.

And you can choose to see it differently. You can decide that using an egg donor is not something shameful; it is simply one of the many beautiful ways families are created.

2. **Replace Fear With Facts**

Beliefs are often formed from what you have seen, heard, or experienced. So if your experience with egg donation is limited, it may be time to level up.

Find people who have used egg donors and talk to them. Ask them what the process was like, what surprised them, and how they feel about it now. I will also include online resources and podcast interviews I have done with clients who used egg donors, some for their first child and some for their second after having a baby with their own eggs.

You can also speak with your fertility clinic about their experience supporting donor-egg cycles. Hearing real stories and understanding the process helps replace fear with facts.

IF IT'S NOT MY DNA, IT WON'T FEEL LIKE MY CHILD

This is a belief you can choose to hold, but I challenge you not to. I say that because of what I've seen over and over again with the families who welcome donor-conceived children. Not only does the perfect child show up at the perfect time, but (this might sound wild) so many of these babies look or act exactly like their moms.

I tell clients about this phenomenon ahead of time, and they usually giggle politely, thinking I'm just trying to be their supportive BFF (best fertility friend). But I'm not. I mean it. And later, when they send me pictures of themselves with their babies, I get to text back, *"Sooo... do people tell you your baby looks just like you?"* And when they reply, *"All the time,"* I can't help but obnoxiously add, *"I told you so!!!"* At this point, after seeing it happen so many times, I've come to expect it.

Some women have one child with their own eggs and another with donor eggs, and you would never know the difference. They simply look like a family, and it is beautiful.

Now, when you think about what you want for your child, how they'll look, act, or who they'll take after, I challenge you to rethink what parenthood really is. You're not choosing to create a mini version of anyone already in your family. **By choosing parenthood, you're choosing to invite a whole new human being into your world, someone with their own quirks, talents, and life lessons to share with you.** From what I've seen, pushing your children into a box of expectations often pushes them away from you. You might have even felt that yourself.

BY CHOOSING PARENTHOOD, YOU'RE CHOOSING TO INVITE A WHOLE NEW HUMAN BEING INTO YOUR WORLD, SOMEONE WITH THEIR OWN QUIRKS, TALENTS, AND LIFE LESSONS TO SHARE

My two children could not be more different, and both of them have incredible gifts that teach me exactly what I need to learn, though not always what I want to learn. Take my daughter Mila, for example, the child who took three years and eight additional rounds before she decided to show up. The difficulty getting her here was a preview of the strong, brave, take-it-or-leave-it little powerhouse she is. She was born with sensibilities that it took me decades to figure out, and I'm still working on them. No part of her DNA seemed to match mine. Instead, she has every feature I wished for as a kid and as an adult.

And her spirit is so different from mine, my son's, and my husband's that I hired someone to teach me how to parent her best without squashing her incredible spirit. Is it hard raising someone so different from me? Absolutely. Do I wish she'd just listen to me and do what I say because I am always right?

YES! Will she? NO! Am I learning that my triggers are my story, not her issue? (Ugh, stop asking such annoying questions.) Okay, yes.

When I think about why Mila and I were paired, two words come to mind: life lessons.

Mila isn't the perfect daughter *for me* because she looks or acts like me, but because our differences teach *me* every single day and make *me* a better human.

So whether it's your DNA or not, the soul that joins yours will be the perfect match for you. And that child will be 100 percent *your child.*

And yes, if you use a donor and your child is having a tantrum and being totally unreasonable, that's when you should absolutely blame the egg donor.

BUT WHAT WILL MY FAMILY THINK?

This question often carries a lot of layers, including generational ones. When it comes up, there are usually three different things that need to be unpacked.

Shame vs Stigma

Shame is an internal judgment that makes you feel less than. Stigma is an external judgment that comes from other people. They often work together because your internal and external worlds tend to mirror each other. You can work on the shame that lives inside you. You cannot fix the shame that lives inside someone else. Part of peace is accepting your family as they are today, not who you hope they will become.

Understanding Where Opinions Come From

When it comes to family opinions, remember this: beliefs are shaped by experience. If someone offers advice or judgment without education or real exposure to egg donation, that limitation is theirs, not yours. Staying uninformed is a choice, and in my experience, the most uninformed are often the loudest. What they say may sting, but you cannot and should not try to control what others think or do. Just as you want your choices respected, you can choose to extend that same respect. This is where the Spirit Protocol helps. It supports you in staying grounded in the higher Levels of Energy Alignment, where other people's opinions lose their grip on you.

You Are the CEO of Your Family

As I have mentioned before, you are the CEO of your family. Right now, the most important decision is how you bring that family together. No one outside of you, not even your parents, gets to decide what is right for your family. This is where I challenge you again to take full responsibility for your family-building journey, because it is yours.

Love the family you came from. Lead the family you are creating.

LOVE THE FAMILY
YOU CAME FROM.
LEAD THE FAMILY
YOU ARE CREATING

SUCCESS STRATEGIES FOR EGG DONORS

Before you make any big decisions, start small. The goal is to gather data without investing too much time or emotional energy. The more you learn about the process from different sources, the more familiar and less foreign it will feel. I will include resources in the online resource guide for this book.

Next, talk to your fertility clinic about the options they offer, their process for someone using an egg donor, the agencies they work with, and the costs from start to finish.

You will likely be given the option to use fresh eggs or frozen eggs. A fresh donor is a woman who goes through an egg retrieval cycle specifically for you, or sometimes for you and one other family. The eggs are fertilized right away with your partner's or donor sperm.

Using frozen eggs means the retrieval has already happened and the eggs were frozen for later use. Those eggs are then thawed, fertilized, and grown into embryos.

My preference is usually a fresh donor who has already successfully created embryos before. I like this option because it gives you a repeatable formula to follow, and it often results in a higher number of embryos. The downside is cost. This option is typically the most expensive. And if you are looking for a very specific donor profile, it may be harder to find with a fresh donor compared to frozen eggs.

While having many embryos can feel reassuring to some women, it can feel overwhelming to others. If you know that abundance might add pressure instead of comfort, frozen eggs may be the better option for you.

And here is something very important that often gets overlooked. Do not forget about the transfer. A donor egg embryo is not a guaranteed pregnancy. The transfer still needs the right strategy and timing to give you the best possible chance of success.

And lucky for you, that is exactly what we will cover next.

CHAPTER 12 SUMMARY

- **Do the Math:** Aim for 2–3 blastocysts per desired child before stopping retrievals. If you don't have that "cushion," consider banking more now.
- **Check Your Resources:** Let your finances, insurance coverage, and age dictate the logistics. If the money or coverage is there now, use it.
- **Ignore the Panic:** A one- to two-month pause will not undo your fertility. Avoid making big decisions in a rush, fueled by clinic pressure instead of data.
- **Audit Your Results:** Before starting a new round, make sure you have all the information from the last one. If a protocol failed, whether an egg retrieval or embryo transfer, the next step is to figure out why beyond age and egg quality and build a strategy that could prevent another failure whenever possible.
- **"You've Done Enough":** Choosing a donor is not failure or giving up. It is a strategic pivot that takes a different route to the same goal.
- **The Donor Is Only Part of the Strategy:** An egg donor does not guarantee pregnancy. Your body still needs the right signals to feel safe to implant, and the transfer protocol must be built around your biology.

Before heading to the next section...

If you'd like some of the resources I give my clients who are curious about egg donation, just scan the QR code.

13. Precise Protocols for Embryo Transfers

Let me start by saying how exciting it is to reach the embryo transfer stage. Your embryos have been created with so much love, and they are lucky to have you as their mama. This is a stage to celebrate!

Of course, I know you may feel nervous about the procedure and the outcome, but remember what I said earlier about choosing to love your embryos. Your job now is to love them and make sure that, with what you can control, you're doing things right.

So let's talk strategy.

My personal experience, and my experience with my clients, has been that most IVF doctors assume the best when it comes to your body accepting an embryo. Never been pregnant? They assume you'll implant easily. Been pregnant before? They assume it will happen again. Had one or two losses? They often chalk it up to bad luck or statistics.

My approach to embryo transfers is opposite. I assume the worst, so my clients have the best chance at success.

Put another way, I assume there's an issue with everything that could get in the way of a successful pregnancy until it's fixed or managed.

I know I've said how much I don't like assumptions in IVF, but in this case, my assumptions are the start of more discovery instead of the final answer.

For example, if a client has a pregnancy loss with an abnormal embryo, I assume she is at risk for more losses. Yes, even though we know the embryo was abnormal, there could still be something in the body that makes it harder to hold a pregnancy long-term. If we only focus on the embryo being abnormal, we might miss something that could be prevented next time.

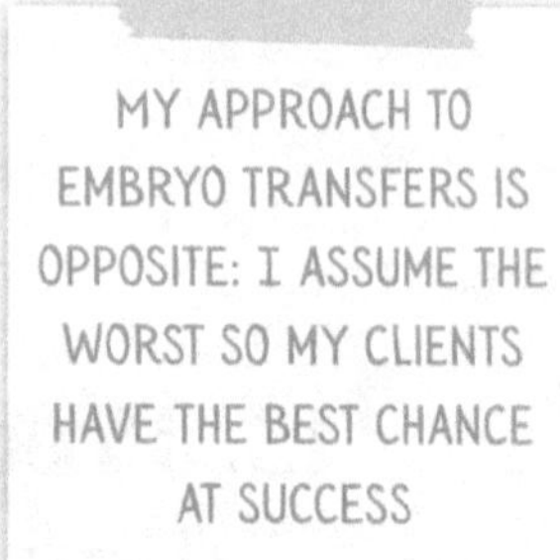

After investing so much to create these precious embryos, you deserve to put as much energy into making sure nothing stands in their way of implanting and growing.

There are two main ways to do that:

- Run the tests to confirm there's probably no issue that could block implantation or make it harder to stay pregnant.
- When you don't know or can't find out for sure if something could block implantation, proactively use medications that could help and won't hurt.

My goal is to help you understand what can block an embryo from implanting and, with what you can control, clear the path for success.

"OKAY" VS. "OPTIMIZED" IVF STRATEGIES FOR EMBRYO TRANSFERS

The embryo transfer is another time not to settle for "okay" IVF. Too often, I hear my clients say that they discussed the situation with their doctor when they had a virus and felt run down, their lining wasn't ideal but was "good enough," or their hormone levels were off without a clear reason, and yet the doctor assured them it was okay to move forward with the transfer.

If you can't tell, I dislike "good enough" approaches to IVF.

I like to assume that any of those *temporary* issues could interfere with implantation and fix the issues before moving forward. If your lining isn't where you want it to be, your body is still recovering, you feel exhausted, or other hormone levels are out of range, I usually recommend waiting instead of pushing forward. For our precious embryos, we want energy and optimized conditions.

I know how frustrating it is to prepare your entire life around a transfer only to have it canceled, sometimes several months in a row (see callout box below). But I am so glad I waited. **I beg you to choose the inconvenience of delaying a treatment over the heartbreak of needing to start another costly egg retrieval because a transfer failed.**

I BEG YOU TO CHOOSE THE INCONVENIENCE OF DELAYING A TRANSFER OVER THE HEARTBREAK OF NEEDING TO START ANOTHER COSTLY EGG RETRIEVAL BECAUSE A TRANSFER FAILED

And while I don't love saying this, it is important to remember that the person telling you to move forward when conditions are okay, rather than optimized, isn't the one losing if the transfer fails.

So what do I mean by "okay" IVF? It usually looks something like this:

- Diagnostic tests: a saline ultrasound (and sometimes not even that)
- Protocol: Hormone Replacement Therapy (HRT), whether needed or not (birth control, or not, followed by estrogen and progesterone)
- Minimal monitoring throughout the estrogen phase
- Minimal monitoring of progesterone after transfer

Here's why this approach falls short, especially after failed transfers:

The diagnostic testing isn't always thorough enough. Saline ultrasounds are subjective and only as good as both the technician and the equipment. I know some doctors who can pick up almost anything with their version of a saline ultrasound, but far more often, things like scar tissue, fluid, or inflammation from infection are missed. These issues can absolutely block implantation.

Another miss in my book is when your doctor doesn't check for chronic endometritis. Among infertile women, chronic endometritis has been found in about 30-57 percent, especially in those with repeated implantation failures. A simple biopsy can check for infection. It's quick, though not always comfortable, but worth it because an infection makes implantation almost impossible.

If you are estrogen-dominant, more estrogen can throw everything off. Estrogen doesn't always help build the lining. If your estrogen is already high in the luteal phase (around cycle day 19), adding more can disrupt everything. Estrogen prepares the uterus, but it only works when progesterone rises at the right time to balance it out. If progesterone support isn't strong enough or estrogen climbs too high, that balance tips, and implantation can fail. Sometimes the lining even retracts instead of staying stable. This is why checking estradiol and progesterone during transfer prep is important.

Overall, if your cycle is healthy, your hormones are balanced, and your lining grows beautifully on its own, why add unnecessary medication?

It also ignores the possibility of mild or silent endometriosis. If you have symptoms like painful or heavy periods, digestive issues around your cycle, unexplained fatigue, or pelvic pain, endometriosis could be playing a role. In those cases, adding more estrogen is like pouring lighter fluid on a fire. Sometimes the right step is medication to suppress estrogen or keep it low before transfer, giving the embryo a much better chance.

The bottom line is that this cookie-cutter approach doesn't uncover and address the issues that could cause healthy embryos to fail before they even have a chance to implant. And when the transfer fails, similar to when egg retrievals don't go as planned, the reason is often blamed on the embryo or egg quality.

WHEN YOUR TRANSFER PROTOCOL IS BUILT AROUND YOUR REAL DATA, THAT IS OPTIMIZED IVF AND THAT IS WHEN YOUR SUCCESS RATES CAN TRULY SOAR

When your transfer protocol is built around your real data, that is optimized IVF, and that is when your success rates can truly soar.

OPTIMIZED IVF TRANSFER STRATEGY

So what could get in the way of a successful embryo transfer? Usually three things:

1. The embryos
2. The uterus
3. The body

The Embryos

Let's start with the one thing we cannot control at the time of transfer: the embryos. Whether you opted for testing or not, the embryos are perfect just the way they are.

I'm not naive enough to think embryos can't be abnormal or fail to implant. But there is no strategy to correct them, so no energy should go toward trying to. These embryos are the ones that showed up, and our only job is to love them, no matter what they choose to do next.

So when I'm preparing someone for transfer, I like to put a quick check mark next to the embryos. Done. On to the things we can influence.

The Uterus

Now let's move to something you can control when it comes to embryo transfer: the uterus. This part is usually straightforward. A few well-chosen tests can rule out most of the common barriers to implantation. If you flip back to Chapter 5, "Tests for the Uterine Lining," you will see the specific testing that could uncover issues interfering with implantation. Here is a quick overview:

Endometrial Biopsy: Checks for hidden infection or inflammation in the uterine lining that could make implantation harder.
Saline Ultrasound: Checks the shape of the uterus and looks for fibroids, polyps, scar tissue, or fluid inside the uterus that could interfere with implantation.
Hysteroscopy: Uses a small camera to directly look inside the uterus for scar tissue, polyps, shape issues, or persistent fluid. It only evaluates the uterine cavity.
Hysterosalpingogram (HSG): Identifies damaged fallopian tubes, including hydrosalpinx. Fluid from a damaged tube can leak into the uterus and lower implantation rates.
MRI: Used when adenomyosis or deeper endometriosis is suspected and more detail is needed than ultrasound can provide.
Laparoscopy: A surgical procedure used to treat problems outside the uterus, such as removing a damaged fallopian tube or treating endometriosis or scar tissue that could interfere with implantation.

The Body

This is the tricky one. Unlike the uterus, where a couple of tests give us a pretty clear picture, there isn't one test or one medication I can recommend for everyone.

But there are patterns. The body can typically get in the way of implantation in two main ways:

- The body is stuck in survival mode instead of conception mode.
- The body doesn't like the medication it's given for the transfer and pushes back.

You already know the Survival to Thrive Protocol and the Spirit Protocol from earlier, which walk you through how to shift your body from survival mode to conception mode. If this is what's stopping you from getting or staying pregnant, remember that nothing needs to be perfect. It just needs to be a little bit better.

So in this section, I'm going to focus on the second piece: protocols for embryo transfers that your body either accepts or rejects. This way, you can have more strategic conversations with your doctor and know what to push back on if something does not feel right.

PROTOCOLS FOR EMBRYO TRANSFERS

Three Transfers, Three Cancellations

When I see a check mark for "thin lining" on one of my new client intake forms, the first thing I ask on our call is, "What medications were you on when it was measured?" If estrogen was part of the mix, I usually say, "You might not actually have a thin lining. Your body might reject synthetic estrogen."

That was exactly the case for me. I had to cancel my tenth transfer three times. The doctor kept repeating the same protocol that wasn't working. I don't remember if I was on birth control at the start or not, but I do remember the estrogen… lots of estrogen. And while estrogen is supposed to grow the lining, it did the opposite for me.

Finally, I asked my doctor, "Do I even need to be on estrogen? I've never had an issue building my lining before, and my cycle is normal." The doctor said no, stopped the estrogen, and sure enough, my lining grew beautifully. That was the transfer when the embryo that became Mila implanted.

It wasn't until after I had Mila that I learned why that probably happened. My friend, who was a traditional OB/GYN and had started practicing integrative medicine, discovered I was estrogen-dominant. Suddenly, everything clicked. That's why I went full-on crazy on the birth control pill, too.

Now, it could have been the watermelon and molasses I tossed into the ocean that led to my successful transfer with Mila… (Wait, have you listened to that podcast yet? If not, it's Episode 51.) And please remember, I was very, very, very desperate at that point. But in reality, I believe it was getting my body out of survival mode and finally using a protocol that actually matched my biology.

When it comes to preparing your uterine lining, there isn't just one way to do it. The right protocol depends on what your body needs, how it responds to medication, and what has already been tried. Some approaches work beautifully for certain women and fall flat for others. If one isn't working for you, repeating it rarely fixes the problem. Instead, this is where you bring other options to your doctor using the question-asking framework you learned earlier.

Now, let's get you informed about the different transfer protocols, which ones you might want to consider, and why they're worth discussing with your doctor.

NATURAL PROTOCOL

This protocol relies on your body to implant an embryo and build up your uterine lining without medication.

Protocol: Track your ovulation at home (I prefer ovulation tests with 2 lines instead of "digital" with words or symbols so you can see the second line get darker) and confirm ovulation with a blood test. For more precise ovulation, your doctor might provide a trigger shot. Progesterone may or may not be part of the protocol, depending on your natural levels.

Consider it if:

- Your hormone levels are naturally balanced
- You naturally have good lining and a normal menstrual cycle
- You want to take as little medication as possible
- You are doing a fresh transfer after an egg retrieval
- You should avoid synthetic estrogen

LETROZOLE-MODIFIED NATURAL TRANSFER CYCLE

The goal of this protocol is to use a stimulant, such as letrozole (Femara), to create more follicles. Your uterus gets the signal that eggs are developing, so it starts building the uterine lining to prepare for implantation. When you are close to ovulation, you take a trigger shot to release the follicles, which also signals your body to produce progesterone more naturally.

For fresh transfers, letrozole is sometimes used instead of Clomid to build up follicles because it has less negative impact on the uterine lining. It may also be chosen for women with endometriosis (a condition where tissue similar to the lining inside the uterus grows outside it), suspected endometriosis, migraines, PCOS (polycystic ovary syndrome), high AMH (anti-Müllerian hormone, a marker of ovarian reserve), or a history of blood clots because it suppresses estrogen.

For Frozen Embryo Transfers (FETs), letrozole helps build follicles that support ovulation and natural progesterone production after the trigger shot. Research also suggests it may increase beta-3 integrin expression, which is important for implantation.

Protocol: Take letrozole on cycle days 2–6, and then track your lining and LH to make sure the lining is building properly and to detect when you are approaching ovulation. Once the lining is 8–13 mm, the trigger shot is given. Progesterone may or may not be added depending on your natural levels.

Consider it if:

- You have trouble building your lining, or you feel you need more support than a natural cycle provides
- Your body does not respond well to estrogen, you should avoid it (such as with high blood pressure, migraines, or heart disease), you are estrogen dominant, or you suspect silent endometriosis
- You are doing a fresh transfer after an egg retrieval

STIMULATED

In this protocol, you use the same injectables (e.g., FSH, LH) given for an egg retrieval, but typically at much lower doses, to stimulate the follicles to grow. Similar to the above protocol, your uterus gets the message that eggs are being created and starts to build up the uterine lining and prepare for implantation.

Protocol: You'll take injectables like FSH and LH to build up the follicles and signal your body to build the lining. Your uterine lining, follicles, and hormones will be tracked to know when to give the trigger shot. After the trigger shot, progesterone may or may not be part of the protocol depending on your levels.

Consider it if:

- You're having a hard time building your lining, or you naturally have a thin lining, but it grew well during the stimulation medications for your egg retrieval.
- Your body doesn't respond well to estrogen, you should avoid it (you have high blood pressure, are prone to migraines, or have heart disease), you're estrogen dominant, or you suspect or have endometriosis.
- You're doing a fresh transfer after an egg retrieval.

MEDICATED TRANSFER CYCLE OR HORMONE REPLACEMENT THERAPY (HRT)

This is the protocol that's typically done first and the one I see most often. The goal is to help your body do what it naturally does when it can't do it on its own.

Protocol: Start with or without birth control, based on whether the goal is to calm hormones or simply line up timing for the transfer.

Add in estrogen (patches, oral, or vaginal) until the lining is 8–13 mm, then start progesterone.

Consider it if:

- You don't ovulate on your own
- You have naturally low estrogen, and your lining doesn't build up
- You need to control the timing of the transfer
- You have imbalanced hormones or are in menopause
- You know you don't have endometriosis or estrogen dominance

SUPPRESSION

This protocol takes your own hormones out of the equation in case they are quietly interfering with implantation or making it harder to stay pregnant. Suppression puts your body into a temporary menopause-like state, where the ovaries go into a deep sleep. The longer suppression is used, the deeper that sleep becomes.

This approach is often used when there are concerns about inflammation, hormone imbalance, endometriosis, adenomyosis, fibroids, or repeated failed transfers with healthy embryos. By removing your hormones from the picture, suppression helps answer an important question. Is your body getting in the way of implantation?

The goal is to calm the uterine environment before transfer. That means reducing inflammation, quieting hormone-driven conditions, and in some cases, shrinking fibroids. Please always start with the Survive to Thrive Protocol to support these areas naturally before moving to medication. Give your body the best chance to get and stay pregnant first. Then, if needed, you could consider suppression medications as the next step.

After suppression, you move into a transfer protocol to rebuild the uterine lining, most commonly HRT or a letrozole-modified natural cycle. A fully natural transfer is also an option, but cycles may take a month or two to normalize, which can delay timing.

Here are the main suppression options:

Combination Birth Control and Letrozole/Femara (daily pills for two months)

Pros:

- Strong suppression that's effective for conditions like endometriosis, adenomyosis, and fibroids
- Typically fewer side effects than Depot Lupron
- Since it's taken as daily pills, you can stop if side effects become too intense for you

Cons:

- Limited research on this exact combination, so many doctors are unfamiliar with it or hesitant to prescribe it

Depot Lupron (one shot each month for two months)

Pros:

- Strong suppression that's effective for conditions like endometriosis, adenomyosis, and fibroids
- Well-researched and widely used, so most doctors are comfortable with it

Cons:

- Once the injection is given, it stays in your system. If you react badly, you can't stop it
- Side effects are usually stronger and more intense compared to other options

- Can cause significant bone loss if used long-term (6 months or more)

Elagolix (brand name Orilissa, daily pill for two months)

Pros:

- Moderate hormone suppression that could help with endometriosis, adenomyosis, and fibroids
- Researched and available, so most doctors are comfortable using it
- A daily pill makes it flexible: you can stop if side effects become too intense for you
- It may be paired with small amounts of estrogen and progesterone to help limit side effects from low estrogen.

Cons:

- Side effects can be similar to Depot Lupron
- Without small amounts of estrogen and progesterone, it can be hard to tolerate for more than a few months

Daily Lupron Injections (three weeks)

Pros:

- Shorter duration, so side effects are usually milder and go away faster
- Flexible dosing: you can adjust or stop if needed
- Works as a lighter "reset" before transfer without shutting your hormones down for months
- Less risk of bone loss compared to longer suppression

Cons:

- Suppression isn't as strong, so it may not fully calm endometriosis, adenomyosis, or fibroids
- Requires daily injections, which can feel inconvenient

- Not enough time to shrink fibroids effectively

My personal suppression favorites for my clients to discuss with their doctor are combination birth control with letrozole or daily Lupron injections for about three weeks. I like these options because, for many of my clients, they tend to have fewer side effects while still being very effective at calming the uterine environment before transfer.

PROGESTERONE PLEASE!

The other medication that will likely be a part of the protocol is *the* pregnancy hormone: progesterone! Once your lining is ready and thick enough, progesterone is what adds the texture that makes it cozy.

This next section will walk you through the types and timing of progesterone, what I like to see with monitoring and administration, how to make sure your levels stay right where they need to be for implantation and early pregnancy, and how to safely wean off once you're pregnant.

Let this guide you in asking better questions and making sure your progesterone plan matches your specific needs.

TIMING OF PROGESTERONE

Once your lining has built up to the thickness your doctor is looking for, the next step is adding progesterone. The timing depends on both the type of transfer protocol you are using and the age of the embryo being transferred.

The chart below shows two things:

1. The signal that it is time to start progesterone, based on the type of transfer
2. How many days of progesterone your uterus needs before transfer, which should match the number of days the embryo has already developed

When you are reading this chart, remember that the first day you take progesterone is labeled as "P+0."

For example, If P+0 is Monday, then a day-5 embryo transfer would be on Saturday (P+5), after your uterus has had 5 full days of progesterone exposure.

TIMING OF PROGESTERONE AND TRANSFER	
TRANSFER TYPE	**THE SIGNAL THAT STARTS PROGESTERONE (Day 0 = P+0)**
HRT (MEDICATED)	Lining is ready (typically 8–13 mm) and progesterone is started → P+0
TRUE NATURAL (NC)	Body's own LH surge → counted as P+0
MODIFIED NATURAL (MOD-NC)	hCG trigger shot given → counted as P+0
FRESH TRANSFER	Day of egg retrieval (trigger already started progesterone rise) → OR = P+0

Once P+0 is set, transfer timing is universal:

- Day 3 embryo → P+3
- Day 5 blastocyst → P+5
- Day 6 blastocyst → P+6
- Day 7 blastocyst → P+7

What about 5.5 days on progesterone?

That timing can work too! Most of the time, your doctor will want to line up the number of progesterone days with the age of the embryo, like I shared in the chart above. But if you've had several failed transfers with good-quality embryos, it may be worth asking your doctor whether shifting the timing slightly could help. Some studies suggest that about 5.5 days of progesterone exposure before transferring a Day 5 embryo may be the sweet spot for certain women. It is not something everyone needs, but if you keep hitting roadblocks, this is one more detail to explore in the timing conversation with your doctor.

TYPE OF PROGESTERONE

When it comes to progesterone support, there are two main options: suppositories or intramuscular shots (progesterone in oil). Some women use one; others use both.

I got pregnant using each. With Hudson, a fresh transfer and a day-3 embryo, I used progesterone in oil shots. With Mila, a frozen transfer of a blastocyst, I used suppositories.

Here's what I personally prefer for my clients: progesterone in oil every day only, or progesterone in oil every 2 to 3 days combined with daily suppositories.

Here's why:

- Suppositories are harder to measure. They absorb directly through vaginal tissue into the uterus (the "first uterine pass effect"), which makes blood levels appear lower than they really are. With shots, progesterone enters your bloodstream, giving a more accurate reading. If low progesterone could affect a client's ability to stay pregnant, and it's hard to know if the low level is accurate or not with suppositories, I don't want to assume the levels are fine. I want to *know* for sure. Which is why I prefer the shots.
- Suppositories are also messy. I know you probably don't care and will do anything to get and stay pregnant, but progesterone support can last for months, and those messy suppositories get irritating (physically and mentally) fast.
- Low progesterone usually means you'll end up on shots anyway. If your doctor monitors levels, drops in progesterone almost always lead to injections. So, following my "assume the worst, plan for the best" mindset, I suggest starting with shots or adding them every three days, especially if weekly testing isn't available. It helps, doesn't hurt, and lets you catch both low and rarely high levels early.

While those are the reasons I prefer progesterone in oil, if you're doing a natural, letrozole, or modified natural transfer cycle, your body *should* be making enough progesterone on its own, so you may not need extra support at all. Just make sure you *know* your progesterone levels.

Yikes, I Don't Want to Do the Progesterone Shots!

And yes, I know progesterone shots are intramuscular, the needle is long, and for some people, the idea of sticking it into a muscle is pretty gross (It was for me, too!). But I created a proven technique that makes them painless.

I teach the technique in a video available in the online resources for this book. (Yes, you'll see me grabbing my own "chunk of butt"... in clothes, of course!).

Once you learn this technique, you'll have such an easy time doing the progesterone shots, with or without someone helping you, and you shouldn't feel a thing.

So I guess what I am saying is: progesterone shots don't need to be a pain in the ass!

(I'll be here all week.)

PROGESTERONE STRATEGY: TESTING, ADJUSTING, AND PROTECTING YOUR EMBRYOS

The Power of Staying on Progesterone

I have a client who has now been pregnant longer than ever before. She lives in another country and has a doctor who basically says yes to everything she asks, which makes my job fun. When we prepared her for her next transfer, we discovered that she naturally had lower progesterone levels. Could that have been the reason she struggled for so long to get or stay pregnant? I assumed yes and put strategies in place. She got her progesterone into what I consider the ideal range before transfer and kept it there in the critical weeks afterward.

When it came time to stop progesterone, we weaned. The first reduction didn't change much, but after the second, her levels started to drop. They were still technically in a good range, but I had her discuss with her doctor returning to the previous dose for another couple of weeks before trying again. She kept testing, and the progesterone kept dropping when she reduced the dose again, even through her 11-week ultrasound. So her doctor agreed to keep her on progesterone support.

My simple strategy of assuming the worst at the beginning—that she's one of the few women who truly need progesterone support longer into pregnancy than most—is why I believe she is finally staying pregnant. Whoo hoo!

This is one of those areas where even the doctors I love, and who tolerate me right back, do not always agree with me. And that is okay. When it comes to progesterone, my goal is simple. If there is something we can measure, adjust, or support earlier rather than later, I want to take that shot. Progesterone is not the place where I like to cross my fingers and hope for the best.

I do this consulting in three ways:

1. Progesterone Levels I Like to See

For my clients, I like to see progesterone around 20 ng/mL the day before transfer, about 30 ng/mL one week later, close to 40 ng/mL at the pregnancy test, and then continuing to rise steadily through early pregnancy. It does not have to be that high for success, but I believe those ranges tend to support a smoother transfer and a stronger, more stable pregnancy.

If progesterone comes in much lower than this, I usually have my clients ask about increasing support sooner rather than waiting to see what happens.

On the flip side, I also do not want progesterone too high. Research published in *Reproductive Biology and Endocrinology* shows that super-physiologic progesterone levels or an unusually high progesterone-to-estrogen ratio can push the uterine lining out of sync with the embryo, narrowing or mistiming the implantation window. In simple terms, it is not just about having progesterone. Its level and balance with estrogen influence whether the lining and embryo stay in sync.

Clinically, this also matches what I see. Progesterone levels over 100 ng/mL before transfer or in the first two weeks after are rare, but when I have seen them, I have not seen positive pregnancy tests. Because of that, increasing progesterone levels has become part of the protection strategy I use with clients. Progesterone is essential, but fertility is about balance. Enough to support implantation, but not so much that timing gets thrown off.

2. Progesterone Testing Timing

The only way to know if progesterone is too low or too high is to test it. Some clinics skip this, and I will never fully understand why.

I have seen pregnancies supported because a drop was caught early. I have also seen losses where no one knew progesterone was falling because no one checked. Did the low progesterone cause the loss, or was there already going to be a loss, and the progesterone dipped as a result? We may not always know for sure. But measuring progesterone between transfer and the pregnancy test could give us critical information and a chance to intervene if needed.

I believe progesterone should be checked the day before transfer and then weekly afterward. This confirms your level is high enough going into transfer and that it continues to rise appropriately if pregnancy begins.

3. **Progesterone Weaning to Protect Pregnancy**

I do not love stopping progesterone cold turkey and assuming the placenta has taken over. Even though that is usually true, I prefer proof over "probably."

One protective strategy I use is weaning progesterone while testing it. This allows you to confirm that your body is doing what it needs to do to support the pregnancy, rather than guessing. This is the only way I know for sure that the placenta is truly running the show, instead of assuming it is.

What this can look like is this: when it is time to stop progesterone, get a progesterone blood level and talk to your doctor about reducing the dose by half instead of stopping completely. Then repeat blood work in 4 to 5 days. If the level remains stable, discuss reducing it by half again and rechecking in another 4 to 5 days. If levels stay stable, you will likely be fine stopping progesterone completely. If it dips, talk to your doctor about staying on progesterone for another week or two before attempting to wean again.

These strategies are not always standard in IVF care. They do involve more testing and closer tracking. But **when it comes to protecting embryos and early pregnancies, I'll always choose precise over probably right.**

WHEN IT COMES TO PROTECTING EMBRYOS AND EARLY PREGNANCIES, I'LL ALWAYS CHOOSE PRECISE OVER PROBABLY RIGHT

SHOULD I SEE AN AUTOIMMUNE SPECIALIST?

Short answer: *probably not.*

Boy, am I going to get crap from some people for that one... even a few of my former clients. But hear me out. While I've worked with many clients who were already seeing an autoimmune specialist when they came to me, I've never recommended one myself, and here's why:

1. **My clients are usually successful without them.**

Most of my clients never see an autoimmune specialist, and yet their success rates are much higher than the national average. As a reminder, my success rates from transfers over the last decade have fluctuated between 1.2 and 1.5 transfers before having a healthy baby, regardless of age.

2. **The protocols don't always change outcomes.**

If autoimmune protocols consistently made a difference, I'd be the first to recommend them. But that's not what I usually see. I've had clients spend months, tons of money, and energy on these approaches only to feel they were a waste.

3. **You find what you're looking for.**

Specialists almost always find something. Take natural killer (NK) cells, for example. Many women are told they have "high NK cells" based on blood work, but those are peripheral NK cells that circulate in the blood. They don't necessarily reflect what's happening inside the uterine lining. There are things worth checking, like clotting issues that could interfere with staying pregnant, but you don't need an autoimmune specialist for that, and the treatment is usually simple.

4. **Root causes before really expensive medications.**

The first step to calming the immune system should not be aggressive, high-cost medications. It should be the Survive to Thrive Protocol you've already learned, along with uncovering root causes. I've seen clients completely turn around autoimmune issues and even improve hormones (including ones they were told would never change, like AMH) by focusing on eating whole food, sleep, "brain breaks," and movement. I understand the urge to reach for anything that might work fast because you have already been waiting long enough to kiss your baby. But as I've said before, you cannot force a pregnancy. Many of these autoimmune medications end up being nothing more than an expensive band-aid. And in some cases, the so-called quick fix creates more harm than good.

5. **The costs can be outrageous.**

Like so many things in IVF, the price tag here is staggering. The consultations and some of the medications cost thousands, sometimes tens of thousands, of dollars. Take IVIG (intravenous immunoglobulin) infusions, for example. My clients who've done them spent about $3,000 USD per session and were told to do *nine* sessions. Would I have said yes to that after seven failed transfers if someone had told me it was the missing piece? Absolutely. I would have done *anything* at that point to finally get pregnant and would have taken out a loan to cover whatever was needed to make that happen. But I do not believe these expensive infusions are the key for most women to get or stay pregnant. From what I have seen, there are often simpler, more effective, and far less costly steps that are effective. I'll walk you through some of the more common medications below so you can see what may be worth discussing with your doctor.

6. **Some protocols are simply reckless.**

I've seen women put on combinations of medications that are too heavy, too long, and in doses that don't make sense. You can't strong-arm your body into pregnancy. For transfers, yes, we assume the worst and use medications when they might help and won't hurt. But drowning the body in overly aggressive protocols doesn't create babies. It creates women who are drained of money, energy, and time.

Now, to be fair, I can think of three clients who are absolutely convinced it was the autoimmune protocol that finally helped them get and stay pregnant. And I believe them. But that is not enough for me to recommend it to most women, and the doctors I respect and learn from typically agree.

What I see far more often are women taking on extra costs, both financial and emotional, in an already exhausting process. That depletion adds up fast and can actually push them further from the family they are working so hard to build.

AUTOIMMUNE MEDICATIONS TO DISCUSS WITH YOUR DOCTOR

It's worth mentioning for the millionth time that before loading up on medications, you should pause and ask the better question: *why is this happening in the first place?* The goal is to address the root cause of inflammation and immune activation in a natural, sustainable way. Once that foundation is in place using the Survive to Thrive Protocol, then you can talk to your doctor about adding medications strategically.

These medications can often be prescribed by IVF doctors or hematologists who are open to it, which saves you the extra time, energy, and money of seeing an official autoimmune specialist. From what I've seen, these medications can be surprisingly effective in helping women finally get or stay pregnant.

So if you know or suspect you might have an autoimmune or blood-clotting issue affecting your ability to get or stay pregnant, or if you have test results that suggest you might benefit from extra support, here are some medication options to discuss with your doctor.

Corticosteroids

Prednisone and Medrol both belong to the corticosteroid family, which means they are steroids that calm inflammation and suppress the immune system. The main difference is in strength and timing. Medrol is slightly stronger on a milligram-to-milligram basis and works a little differently in the body. Because of that, some doctors prefer Medrol in short bursts around transfer, while others use Prednisone for longer courses. Neither one is always better; it usually depends on your doctor's strategy and what they believe will give you the best chance.

Medrol (methylprednisolone)

- Usually taken for 5 days, starting before transfer
- An anti-inflammatory steroid that may help support implantation
- Generally mild with fewer side effects
- This is the one I tend to favor because it's a shorter course and, from what I've seen, very effective

Prednisone

- Often taken for 1 to 4 weeks (talk with your doctor before going longer than that)
- An anti-inflammatory steroid that may also support implantation
- Typically prescribed at 5–10 mg per day, with a taper once implantation occurs
- Can cause more side effects than Medrol, such as mood changes, stomach upset, or sleep issues

Other Autoimmune Suppressors

There are a few other medications sometimes used as immunosuppressants that are added to transfer protocols. Two examples I commonly see in the U.S. are Neupogen (filgrastim) and Plaquenil (hydroxychloroquine). I don't have enough personal data on their effectiveness to fully recommend them, but if your doctor has experience using these safely and successfully, I would place them in the "could help and can't hurt" category.

Blood Thinners

If you tend to implant but lose the pregnancy before 8 to 10 weeks, blood clotting could be part of the problem. Even if your doctor has ruled out common clotting disorders but you are still experiencing pregnancy losses, here is what I usually recommend my clients discuss with their doctors:

Low-Dose Aspirin (75–81 mg of acetylsalicylic acid)

- Take daily.
- Timing depends on the reason you are taking it:
  - If it is for building your lining, you will likely start about a month before the transfer.
  - If it is for early losses or suspected micro-clotting, you will likely start about a week before the transfer or the day of.
- It is easy to buy on your own and often a good first step as a blood thinner.
- If pregnancy losses continue on baby aspirin, or you suspect a blood-clotting disorder, talk to your doctor about the next option.

Blood Thinners: Heparin and Enoxaparin (Lovenox, Clexane)

Enoxaparin sodium (Lovenox, Clexane) is the most common prescription blood thinner I see in transfer protocols. Heparin is a shorter-acting alternative that requires more frequent dosing and may be used in certain situations.

If your clinic will not consider prescribing a blood thinner, a hematologist could be the right specialist for additional blood work and input.

If you have had more than one pregnancy loss before 12 weeks and there is no clear medical reason to avoid anticoagulation, this is still a reasonable conversation to have, even if prior clotting tests were negative. We cannot test for every possible clotting factor. The goal is not to add medication by default, but to consider whether a clotting contribution not identified on routine testing could be playing a role.

Understanding A Doctor's "Nope" On Blood Thinners

Some doctors are cautious about adding blood thinners, while others include them in their standard protocol.

The hesitation from some doctors is that blood thinners increase the risk of bleeding. If you were in an accident, needed surgery, or hit your head hard, the bleeding could be more serious. Though it is unlikely such an event would happen, doctors are trained to prescribe medications only when there is a clear medical reason. If a blood thinner is given without a diagnosed clotting disorder or history of pregnancy loss, and a rare complication occurs, it could create legal risk for them.

This is why some doctors say no unless the evidence is very clear or another specialist, such as a hematologist or an autoimmune specialist, is willing to monitor you.

Another reason some doctors wait to start blood thinners until after the transfer is to reduce the chance of bleeding inside the uterus. During an embryo transfer, small tools are used to guide the catheter through the cervix and into the uterus. Occasionally, those tools can irritate or lightly touch the uterine lining. If someone is already on a blood thinner, that irritation could increase the chance of bleeding. Blood in the uterus during a transfer is not ideal, so some doctors prefer to start blood thinners right after the embryo is placed instead of before.

Ultimately, your doctor's opinion matters most, and you want insight into the repeated successes that shaped the strategies they trust.

ULTIMATELY, YOUR DOCTOR'S OPINION MATTERS MOST, AND YOU WANT INSIGHT INTO THE REPEATED SUCCESSES THAT SHAPED THE STRATEGIES THEY TRUST

As long as your doctor confirms that a blood thinner, such as low-dose aspirin or Lovenox, is safe for you, I usually recommend including it in your transfer plan, especially after a loss. And if your doctor decides it is not the right fit for your protocol, you can feel confident knowing the decision is based on their experience and what they believe will best support your success.

NUMBER OF EMBRYOS AND STRATEGY

The number of embryos you transfer should always start with a conversation with your doctor, since every clinic has its own policy. Don't spend time stressing over how many embryos you'd feel comfortable transferring until you know what your options actually are and hear what your doctor recommends and why, based on the outcomes they've seen.

If multiple embryos are an option, here's how I typically look at it:

For Day-3 Embryos: If you are over forty, consider transferring as many day-3 embryos as you feel comfortable with and your doctor is willing to do, since the drop-off rate between day-3 and blastocyst can be higher. I would not usually recommend transferring only one or two at a time if you have several available. While each day-3 embryo has the potential to become a healthy baby (and I've seen it happen often), they generally have a lower success rate than blastocysts. Transferring them one by one can become expensive and emotionally draining.

If you are under forty, I usually suggest transferring two to three day-3 embryos at once. I've only had one client who ended up with twins after transferring three day-3 embryos, but it shows the possibility is there.

For Blastocysts: One to two embryos is usually the sweet spot. If you're comfortable with twins, two may be an option. If not, stick with one.

CHAPTER 13 SUMMARY

- **"Okay" IVF vs. Optimized Transfers:** Minimal testing, routine HRT, and settling for "good enough" conditions put embryos at risk. Optimized IVF pauses, tests, pivots, and moves forward based on true readiness.
- **Assume Nothing, Verify Everything:** Optimized transfers start by assuming something could interfere, then ruling it out or managing it before risking an embryo.
- **Three Things Decide Transfer Success:** The embryo, the uterus, and the body. You can't change the embryo at transfer, but you can clear the uterus and support the body to remove silent barriers.
- **The Uterus Must Be Clear:** Strategic testing, like a biopsy, saline ultrasound, hysteroscopy, and imaging when needed, helps confirm nothing is physically blocking implantation.
- **Your Body Has a Vote:** Survival mode, inflammation, and hormone intolerance can quietly block success, even with a strong embryo.
- **Protocols Should Match Your Data:** Natural, letrozole-modified, stimulated, medicated, and suppression-based transfer protocols should be chosen based on your data and not a clinic's default.
- **Progesterone Is a Process:** Timing, type, dose, and testing all play a role. When progesterone is monitored and adjusted, it could help protect implantation and early pregnancy.
- **More Medication Isn't Always Better:** Steroids, blood thinners, and immune support could help in the right cases, but aggressive add-ons without clear reasons often drain energy, money, and momentum.
- **Strategy Over Speed:** Canceling or delaying a transfer when conditions are not optimized is annoying, but it could be the move that gets you to your baby faster.

14. Exact Execution For Embryo Transfers

Monitoring for a transfer is much simpler than for an egg retrieval. The main goal is to make sure your lining is ready, your progesterone stays in the right range, and your other hormones, like TSH, stay steady without any wild spikes.

Here is a summary of the monitoring appointments that should be happening and what to look for so that you know, with what you can control, you are maximizing the success rates of your embryo transfer.

MONITORING FOR EMBRYO TRANSFERS

MONITORING BEFORE PROGESTERONE STARTS: UTERINE LINING THICKNESS

This phase is all about your uterine lining. Most women get checked every 4–6 days to see how it's growing. If you're doing a true natural or modified natural cycle, you may need more frequent checks since your doctor will also be watching for your LH surge.

I don't recommend staying on medication to build your lining for more than 6 days before getting checked. If your lining isn't developing the way it should, the sooner you know, the sooner you can adjust medications and still move forward with the transfer.

And if it's the day before the transfer and your lining still isn't where it needs to be, please don't settle for "good enough." **It's far better to pause, reset, and try a different protocol than to risk an embryo on conditions that aren't optimal.** I know how frustrating it is to wait another month, but it's worth the frustration if the alternative is losing an embryo because you moved forward too soon.

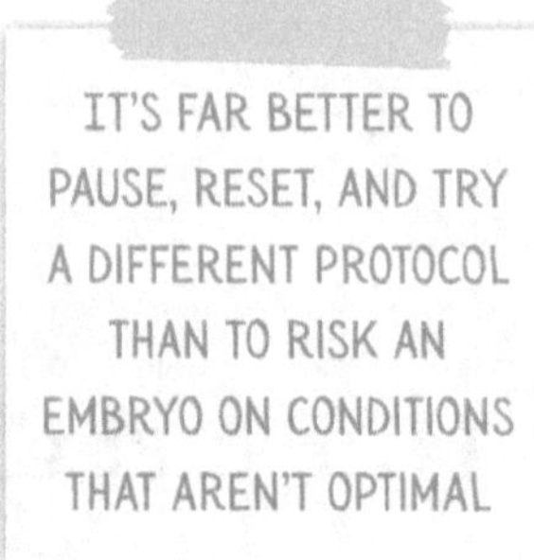

Target Levels

- Lining thickness: 8–13 mm
- Lining appearance: trilaminar (triple stripe)

Some women do get pregnant with a thinner or non-trilaminar lining, but that's rare. Unless you already know this is your personal "normal," aim for optimal before transferring.

One way to figure out what's normal for you is by looking at your own history. Discuss the following with your doctor or nurse:

- What's the thickest lining I've ever achieved in past cycles without medication?
- When I was doing stimulation medication for the egg retrieval, what was my lining at the trigger shot?
- What was my lining measurement in the cycle when I had implantation, whether it led to an ongoing pregnancy or a biochemical pregnancy?

This helps you and your doctor see how your lining grows with and without specific medications. You get a clearer picture of what your body is capable of. That way, if you are on medication and your lining is not growing, you can better tell whether it is the medication affecting it or simply your personal baseline.

What to Discuss with Your Doctor if Your Lining Is Not Growing

See "Strategies for Thin Uterine Lining" below.

MONITORING ESTROGEN LEVELS

Estrogen plays a key role in preparing your uterine lining for implantation, but how closely it's monitored depends on the type of transfer cycle you're doing.

True Natural, Modified Natural, or Fresh Transfer:

In these cycles, your body produces its own estrogen, so it's not always measured before or after progesterone starts. The main focus is on how your lining looks, the timing of ovulation, and whether your progesterone levels are rising appropriately.

Questions to Discuss with Your Doctor About Estrogen Monitoring in Natural, Modified Natural, or Fresh Transfers:

- How often should my estrogen levels be checked based on my type of transfer?
- What is the ideal estrogen range for building a healthy lining?
- If my lining isn't growing, should we test estrogen before adjusting my protocol?
- Could too much estrogen be affecting my lining or implantation potential?
- When should estrogen support stop once I'm pregnant?

HRT (Medicated FET):

In this type of cycle, estrogen is usually tracked through bloodwork while your lining is monitored by ultrasound. Estrogen support typically continues through the transfer and into early pregnancy to help maintain a stable environment for implantation.

Questions to Discuss with Your Doctor About Estrogen Monitoring in HRT (Medicated FET) Cycles:

- How often will my estrogen be checked while we are building my lining?
- What estrogen range are you aiming for before starting progesterone?
- If my lining is not responding, will we adjust the estrogen dose before moving forward?
- Will my estrogen be rechecked after transfer to ensure levels remain stable in early pregnancy?

Suppression Protocols:

When any of the suppression protocols we discussed are used before a transfer cycle, estrogen levels are intentionally lowered to calm the uterine environment. During this phase, estrogen is not expected to be in a fertile range. The goal is to reduce hormone stimulation and inflammation, particularly in cases of endometriosis, adenomyosis, or repeated implantation failure.

Once suppression is complete and you begin building your lining, estrogen is added back in, and monitoring typically follows the same approach as a hormone replacement therapy (HRT) cycle, since you are now actively using estrogen to prepare for transfer.

Questions to Discuss with Your Doctor About Estrogen Monitoring in Suppression Cycles:

- Should my estrogen be checked during suppression to confirm adequate suppression?
- What estrogen level indicates that suppression has been effective?
- Once we begin adding estrogen back in, how often should levels be monitored before transfer?

MONITORING AFTER PROGESTERONE STARTS

Once you begin progesterone, you usually will not have another appointment until a day or two before your transfer. That visit is the ideal time to check your progesterone levels and confirm your body is ready for implantation.

Use the recommendations from Chapter 13, "Progesterone Strategy: Testing, Adjusting, and Protecting Your Embryos," to guide progesterone monitoring after progesterone starts.

Estrogen typically is not rechecked at this point because the focus shifts to making sure progesterone is strong enough to support the embryo. If you tend to run lower in estrogen, rechecking it could still be worthwhile.

If you have had thyroid issues in the past, this is also a smart time to check levels and make sure they are in range before transfer. If levels are off, thyroid medications usually work quickly to rebalance things, so delaying a transfer is not typically necessary, but medication support is important.

MONITORING AFTER TRANSFER

Continue using the recommendations from Chapter 13, "Progesterone Strategy: Testing, Adjusting, and Protecting Your Embryos," to guide progesterone monitoring after transfer.

Thyroid levels should also be monitored, especially if you have had issues in the past. TSH (thyroid-stimulating hormone) can spike early in pregnancy, and the goal is to keep it in a healthy range.

THE PREGNANCY TEST

On the day of your pregnancy test, your clinic will likely check hCG (human chorionic gonadotropin), progesterone, and TSH. Some doctors may also check estrogen.

If your pregnancy test is positive, you'll usually go back the next day to confirm that your hCG is doubling. After that, you'll likely have another blood test and ultrasound about a week later.

As for *target ranges*, they can vary depending on how many days you are past transfer. I personally like to see a beta (hCG) level over 70 mIU/mL 9 days after transfer, though plenty of healthy pregnancies have started at lower levels.

So instead of focusing too much on that first number, focus on whether it keeps doubling; steady increases are what count most.

Log It!

Track everything. Keep a simple log of your results so you can spot patterns and know exactly what worked for you in your embryo transfer prep. That information is gold for future cycles and for maintaining early pregnancy.

STRATEGIES FOR THIN UTERINE LINING

When my clients struggle to build their uterine lining, I always look at two things: the protocol being used and whether their bodies are stuck in survival mode instead of conception mode.

What still amazes me is how few different approaches most doctors try when a lining will not grow, especially if they have only attempted to build it with one form of estrogen. To me, your body not responding well to synthetic estrogen is not a signal that your uterus has a problem. It is a clue that a different strategy, possibly one without estrogen, needs to be tried.

Below are strategies that could help you build your lining so you can walk into your appointments prepared for a more strategic and informed conversation with your doctor. I start with medication options to consider and then move into holistic health strategies you can layer on top. But none of this replaces the Survive to Thrive Protocol. That always comes first. Please, please, please! Yes, I am officially begging you.

MEDICATIONS TO DISCUSS WITH YOUR DOCTOR

These are not the actual transfer protocols, such as HRT (medicated), True Natural (NC), Modified Natural (mod-NC) with Letrozole, or Fresh Transfer. Choosing the right protocol and strategy always comes first. Once you know that piece is in place and you still need extra support to build your lining, here are some additions you can bring up with your doctor.

Vaginal Viagra: This is not the same as the Viagra you may have heard of. It is a compounded version made specifically for fertility treatment. This is often the first thing I encourage my clients to ask about if estrogen alone insufficiently thickens the lining or if they know they naturally have a thin lining. The earlier you start it, the sooner it can help, which is why monitoring every 4 to 6 days is key when you begin medications for transfer.

Other Forms of Estrogen: If you are already on estrogen and your doctor suggests increasing it because it is not working as well as it should, ask about adding more in a *different* form. Estrogen can be taken orally, vaginally, or through patches, and everyone absorbs it differently. If one form is not effective for you, it is worth asking about switching or combining different types.

Baby Aspirin: Baby aspirin may help improve blood flow to the uterus, which can support lining growth. Many doctors recommend starting it on cycle day 1 of the transfer cycle, though you should always confirm with your doctor since it also thins the blood.

Human Growth Hormone (Omnitrope, Zomacton): This can be added with letrozole or around cycle day 7 and continued until the lining reaches the thickness your doctor is aiming for.

HOLISTIC HEALTH TOOLS TO HELP BUILD YOUR LINING

When I work with a client who has a naturally thin uterine lining, you and I already know what that usually means. There is an imbalance or depletion somewhere that needs attention. The reproductive system does not scale back without a reason. When the body lacks key resources, it shifts away from conception and toward survival.

The strategies below are natural ways to restore balance and increase blood flow to the uterus while your medical protocol manages the hormonal timing. Think of it as strengthening the soil while your doctor manages the planting schedule.

Plan to use most of these for at least 30 days, and aim for 60 days if you can. As you add them in, ask your doctor to monitor your natural lining each cycle, usually one to two days before ovulation or on ovulation day, to see how your body responds.

Survive to Thrive Protocol

Did you almost skip this since you are probably sick of hearing me talk about this protocol? Okay, okay, I get it, and I deserve it. But it is so important if the goal is to reclaim your health, wellness, and fertility.

Here is the key thing to remember: a thin lining is often your brain's very precise way of telling your body that now is not the time to reproduce.

So please do not skip it. It is basically nature's fertility fountain of youth. Or the closest thing we have to one.

And another reminder (ok, wow, I actually heard you sigh). Nothing needs to be perfect. It just needs to be a little better.

Ok, now for the rest of the holistic health practices that give targeted support to the uterus. They should always be *paired with* the Survive to Thrive Protocol because that supports the whole body. That combination gives your body the best chance to get baby-body ready as quickly as possible.

Supplements: L-Arginine, Vitamin E

These supplements may help improve circulation and blood flow to the uterus, which can encourage lining development. Vitamin E is also an antioxidant, which supports cellular health. Be sure to talk with your doctor if you are also taking baby aspirin, since baby aspirin and vitamin E both thin the blood, and together they could be too much.

Red Light Therapy

Look for a device with both red light at 660 nm and near-infrared light around 850 nm. Red light helps improve blood flow right at the surface level, which could boost circulation and stimulate the endometrial cells directly. Near-infrared light penetrates deeper into the pelvic tissue. This helps increase overall circulation, oxygen delivery, and energy production in cells, which may encourage the uterine lining to grow from the inside out.

Acupuncture or Laser Acupuncture

Acupuncture may help improve blood flow to the uterus and balance hormone signaling, which can support a thicker, healthier lining. Laser acupuncture is another option that uses light rather than needles to achieve a similar effect. (Listen to my podcast episode on acupuncture for what to look for in an appointment specifically meant to improve fertility and IVF outcomes.)

Therapeutic Massage

Therapies such as Mercier or myofascial release may help by improving blood flow, releasing tension, and restoring mobility in the pelvic region. This can increase circulation to the uterus and ovaries, supporting the growth of the uterine lining. Ideally, you would see a physical therapist specializing in pelvic floor care, and in many cases, such treatments can be covered by insurance.

Herbs: Red Raspberry Leaf Tea

Drinking 2–3 cups daily for about two months is a classic remedy for uterine health. It is thought to support better blood flow to the uterus and help the uterine muscles work smoothly, creating an environment that may encourage a stronger, healthier lining.

Foods: Phytoestrogen-Rich Options

Beans, ground flax seeds, red clover, nettles, alfalfa, royal jelly, and maca all contain plant-based compounds that can gently mimic estrogen in the body. These foods and herbs may support your natural hormones and give your lining an extra boost.

Hyperbaric Oxygen Chambers

This one is a commitment that can be harder to find, time-consuming, and expensive, but some doctors trust it because research has shown that flooding the body with concentrated oxygen may improve tissue healing and circulation. For women with a thin lining that does not respond well to other approaches, this therapy may provide another option to discuss with your doctor.

Hurdles to Hatchlings: Embryo Transfers

Before we get into the most common hurdles that can block implantation, I want to clarify how this section fits with what you already learned in "Part 1: The Book on Fertility."

In Part 1, we focused on understanding these conditions and supporting the body over time. This section is not about re-explaining any of that or revisiting general healing. This section is about giving your transfer the best possible chance.

The focus now shifts to execution. These strategies are about protecting embryos, optimizing implantation conditions, and reducing the risk of failed transfers.

FIBROIDS

With embryo transfer, fibroids become less about whether they exist and more about where they are and what they are doing to the uterine environment. Fibroids inside the uterine cavity or pressing into it can block implantation or interfere with the blood flow an embryo needs to grow. Even fibroids outside the cavity can become a concern if they distort the uterus or affect the lining or ovaries.

Success Strategies to Discuss with Your Doctor

The first step is confirming size, location, and whether anything has changed. A hysteroscopy is often the best way to get clear answers when transfer success is the goal. Once fibroids are confirmed, you and your doctor can decide whether medication, suppression, or surgery makes the most sense before another transfer.

Suppression protocols may be used to reduce fibroid size or quiet their impact before transfer. Fibroids that sit inside the cavity or clearly press into it are often recommended for removal before another attempt, but timing is important. Recovery can take eight weeks or longer, so in many cases it makes sense to freeze enough embryos to cover your family goals before surgery.

Your doctor will know whether your fibroids are likely to interfere with implantation. But if you keep hearing, "Your embryos look perfect. We don't know why it didn't work," and you also have fibroids, it may be time to seriously consider that they could be contributing before transferring another embryo or moving to third-party options like surrogacy.

Questions to Discuss with Your Doctor

- Should we evaluate my fibroids with a hysteroscopy before my next retrieval or transfer?

- Even if my fibroids are considered small or unlikely to interfere, could they be playing a role, given my transfer history?
- If surgery is recommended, how should we time it so I do not lose momentum with my family-building goals?

ENDOMETRIOSIS

Preparing for an embryo transfer with endometriosis starts with calming the uterine environment. Inflammation, scar tissue, and fluid associated with endometriosis can quietly interfere with implantation, even when embryos look perfect on paper.

Success Strategies to Discuss with Your Doctor

One of the most useful first steps before transfer is imaging, often an MRI, to get a clearer picture of whether endometriosis may be active. This can help guide decisions without jumping straight to surgery.

Suppression protocols are commonly used before transfer to quiet inflammation and reduce the impact of endometriosis. This is often the best short-term strategy when surgery is not needed, not possible right now, or not something you want to pursue.

This is another situation where assuming endometriosis is not affecting implantation could delay success. If you have healthy embryos and repeated failed transfers, it is reasonable to consider that inflammation may be interfering and to create a plan that addresses it before another transfer.

Questions to Discuss with Your Doctor

- Given my failed transfers, should we consider suppression even if endometriosis has not been definitively diagnosed?
- Would imaging, such as an MRI, help us understand whether inflammation is still active before my next transfer?
- If surgery is recommended, how should we time it so it does not unnecessarily slow down my chances of getting pregnant?

CHAPTER 14 SUMMARY

- **Monitoring Creates Clarity:** Regular ultrasounds and bloodwork before and after progesterone starts help ensure your body is responding optimally, not just clearing the minimum bar.
- **Protecting Embryos with Smart Timing:** Choosing to pause when lining or hormones are not ideal preserves embryos and sets you up for stronger outcomes.
- **Thin Lining Is Actionable Information:** When lining will not grow, it points to a protocol adjustment or deeper support through survival mode shifts, both of which can be improved.
- **Protocols Are Meant to Evolve:** If one transfer approach is not working, refining the strategy opens the door to better results.
- **Clear the Path for Implantation:** Addressing fibroids, inflammation, and endometriosis before transfer increases the chance that a healthy embryo can implant and grow.
- **Data Builds Forward Momentum:** Tracking hormone levels before and after transfer turns each cycle into insight that guides smarter decisions.

Before heading to the next section...

If you'd like a downloadable guide to the monitoring reports, the link to the video on how to do progesterone shots that don't hurt, and more about transfer success, just scan the QR code.

15. You're PREGNANT! Wait... Now What?

Why Communication Is a Medical Intervention

When I was pregnant with Hudson, I did the NT scan. His Down syndrome risk shifted from 1 in 600 to about 1 in 300. That is still only a 0.3 percent chance, but my OB/GYN still recommended CVS (chorionic villus sampling).

It was not a small biopsy like I was told. The person performing the procedure moved the instrument back and forth aggressively to collect tissue. I was not warned at all about how physical or painful it would be. I was caught completely off guard and went into a trauma response, freezing from pain and the fear that if I moved, something could go wrong. Afterward, I stayed frozen for a bit, and then my whole body started shaking. No one knew because the person doing the procedure was gone. Once I could, I put my pants back on and left.

Common sense tells me that it was probably not healthy for a newly pregnant woman to go into a trauma response. Nor was it necessary. A simple conversation about what to expect and how to prepare would have prevented it.

And for context, I am not someone who avoids discomfort. I am very much a no pain, no gain person. You should see the lasers I willingly let burn the top layer of my face off while zapping deep enough that my skin thinks it has been ripped away and needs to rebuild itself. As it's happening, I'm thinking, *Bring it on,* clenching my hands together so hard they might break, tears streaming down my face.

So this is not about being too sensitive, needing hand-holding, or being unable to tolerate discomfort. This is about communication.

When things happen *without warning*, your brain believes it needs to stay on guard *at all times*. This is how so many of us end up stuck in chronic stress, hormone imbalance, infertility, and disease.

With Mila, there was also a lack of communication that left my nervous system unnecessarily on high alert for the last three months of her pregnancy. At 26 weeks, her stomach measured two weeks behind. I was told it could mean nothing at all, or it could indicate a genetic condition incompatible with life. No additional explanation.

So I did what we all do and went online, which sent me into a full spiral of unanswered questions.

I was monitored weekly until her birth, when we would finally find out if she was healthy… or not.

Mila was born healthy (thank God!). And yes, she has a very small waist.

I believe this points to a much bigger conversation about healthcare, especially for women.

(Excuse me while I step onto this soapbox…)

From the various conversations I have with women about their healthcare all over the world, it seems like many aspects of women's healthcare involve trauma responses that leave our nervous systems on high alert and push us into chronic survival mode without us even realizing it.

Relationship experts often say women need to feel *seen, heard, and safe*. In healthcare, I feel like those could all be possible with our medical professionals.

Seen. Too many women receive life-altering news like "there is no heartbeat" or "your baby could have a life-threatening condition" delivered without compassion or context. In those moments, patients are left stunned, trying to process what happened and how to cope. It feels impossible that words that heavy could be delivered so coldly from one human to another, yet I hear such messages from my clients far too often.

Heard. There are countless stories of patients experiencing real pain from procedures or menstrual cycles who speak up and are then dismissed or given medications to cover it up instead of understanding the root cause. When discomfort is minimized or brushed off, to me, it seems like the healthcare professional is saying, "So what?" This typically leaves a lasting impression that patients shouldn't speak up.

Safe. When something happens without warning and your body reacts with, "Stop. This is not right," that loss of safety is profound and, for some, permanent. Far too many women know that feeling. And so much of it could be prevented with a simple conversation.

The question I keep coming back to is this: how do we make communication and preparation standard in healthcare?

I do not have the answer. But I do know this: simple, calm, and, dare I say, caring conversation can make an enormous difference in keeping patients healthy. For example, looking someone in the eyes so they feel *seen*. Listening to their questions so they feel *heard*. Being transparent about what is about to happen, what most people experience, and the risks and benefits so they can feel *safe* making an informed choice.

If the real goal of healthcare is healthcare, I believe conversations like this should be foundational.

(... okay, stepping down from the soap box before I fall.)

When one of my clients texts me that they're pregnant, my first step is to celebrate! A big woo hoo, lots of yesss with extra s's and too many exclamation marks!!!!!!!!

And then, we both switch gears. I go into my consultant mode, double-checking their labs and medications and coming up with questions to discuss with the doctor, and they tend to shift into what I lovingly call "mission pregnant" mode, where joy collides with panic and every thought is about making this pregnancy stick.

Let's start with what I look into with my clients and then what I tell them to help shift "mission pregnant" mode into something positive, not panicked.

SUPPLEMENTS

First, I review their supplements if they are on any. The supplements you take once you're pregnant could shift from the ones you took to get pregnant. Your body has different needs now, and it's important to update accordingly. If you would like a list of general supplements we might recommend once you are confirmed pregnant, you can find it in our online resources by scanning the QR code, which you'll find at the end of most chapters.

MEDICATIONS AND LABS

Next, I check their lab results, as they likely received them along with their pregnancy test. You already know the strategy I like for timing and testing progesterone, which you can discuss with your doctor.

Other tests to discuss right away are thyroid panels, especially if you've had thyroid issues in the past. Also, an RH factor test if they haven't discussed that with you already (this checks whether your blood type is positive or negative and whether there's a potential incompatibility with the baby's blood type).

If you're on a blood thinner, like baby aspirin or Lovenox, I would discuss when to stop with your OB/GYN, as well as with a high-risk OB/GYN if you've had recurrent pregnancy losses in the past, for a second opinion.

Most stay on it until around the end of the first trimester. But if you've had multiple miscarriages and this is the first pregnancy holding steady while on Lovenox, your OB/GYN may want you on it the entire pregnancy. Yes, it's annoying to do daily shots, but the women who've had to do it often feel that taking Lovenox daily through pregnancy was the reason they finally carried to term.

MINDSET

It's really hard to stay present and calm early in pregnancy, after you have invested so much into getting pregnant (and I am not just talking financially). You want this pregnancy to stick more than anything, and you are willing to do whatever it takes. On top of that, you are used to being very active in making things happen, so suddenly sitting back and waiting feels wrong. There has to be something to do, right?

Yes and no. There is very little you can do to make this pregnancy continue or end, assuming you are not doing anything dangerous. Whether this pregnancy goes to term is not up to you. It is up to the baby and God.

That said, because you are like me and strategic action always feels better than doing nothing, I put together a checklist. Think of it as a way to stay in "mission pregnant" mode without letting it turn into panic mode.

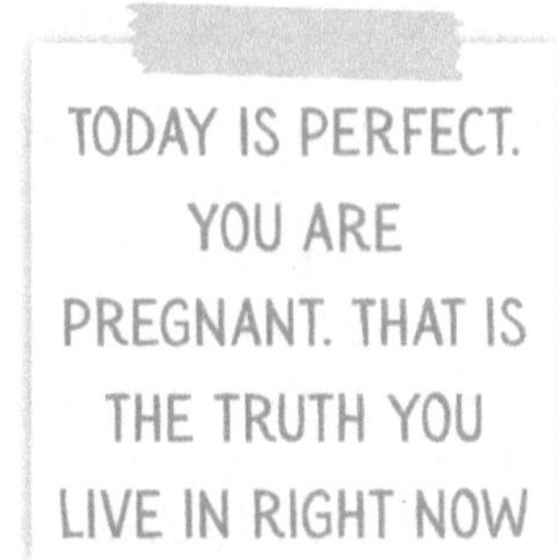

- Protect your baby by safeguarding what you are seeing, hearing, feeling, and believing. Fuel your body and mind with what supports growth, safety, and calm.
    - If you need help, revisit the Spirit Protocol in "Part 1: The Book on Fertility." Focus on choices, quieting the mean girl in your head like you learned in Chapter 4, and working through the Levels of Energy Alignment from Chapter 4 as well. Use the exercises found in this book as your daily mental hygiene.
    - If you want deeper support, use the *Conscious Creation: Elevating Your Mindset* video series and worksheets in the online resources (Scan the QR code at the end of any chapter). These tools are not just for fertility or pregnancy. They are especially powerful for postpartum and parenthood, too.
- Anchor yourself to *today's* reality.
    - **Today is perfect. You are pregnant. That is the truth you live in right now.**
    - Remind yourself that fears about what could happen are not facts. They are imagined futures, not your current reality.
    - When worry shows up, bring yourself back to this thought: today, your baby chose to stay.
- Trust that if things ever change, it will be painful and heartbreaking, and you will still be okay. You always have been. For now, stay here. Stay present.

Simple, but not easy, right? I know. And I also know how much this journey will help you become the woman and mother this precious baby needs.

Your job right now is not to control the outcome. It is to become the present mother this baby already chose.

Congratulations!

BABY NO. 2 (OR MORE!) READINESS CHECKLIST

Deciding when to try for another baby is a big question, and it's one my clients often bring up to me. But the correct answer is very specific to the person asking it. So when my clients ask whether they're ready for baby No. 2 (or No. 3, or more), we start with the data to get a clear, objective picture. Then I look at the emotional and spiritual data, too. That often tells me more than the numbers ever could.

Here's how I walk my clients through it.

BIRTH RECOVERY

Did you have a vaginal birth or a C-section? Most OB/GYNs will recommend waiting a year before trying again, and I agree. That's especially important if you had a C-section. Your uterus needs time to heal properly so it can support another pregnancy safely.

BREASTFEEDING

Breastfeeding can take a lot out of you, and we know that we don't want to be in a state of depletion when trying to have a baby. Most OB/GYNs will suggest waiting at least 3–6 months after you stop nursing, but I recommend waiting until your menstrual cycle has returned and is normal for about 2–3 months before moving forward. Your cycle is one of the clearest signs of your overall health and wellness.

DATA TO DECISIONS: BLOOD WORK

Once your cycle has been steady for 2–3 months, then it's time to check your blood work. Start with hormone levels around cycle day 3, such as FSH, AMH, and estrogen, and also run the comprehensive blood panel I outlined in the "Blood Tests That Get You Wise To Your Whys" section. This will check for vitamin and mineral deficiencies and show you if your body is fully replenished or still running on empty.

DATA TO DECISIONS – DIAGNOSTIC TESTS

Then go back to the testing section in the Science Protocol, starting with a semen analysis and a DNA fragmentation test. Please don't skip that step, even if there has never been a sperm issue in the past. Things change.

Once you have the sperm results, move on to the other tests I covered in the Science Protocol to make sure conception is truly possible. Can the egg and sperm meet? Is fertilization likely? Is anything blocking implantation? These tests will let us know for sure.

And if you've had a C-section, I urge you to get a hysteroscopy so your scar can be properly analyzed as well. Any scar tissue can block implantation, and I believe the hysteroscopy is the easiest way to find it.

HOW DO YOU FEEL?

And now for the most important question: how do you feel? I save this question for last because the women I work with are some of the toughest people I've ever met. They can push through exhaustion and pain without blinking, and many of them could literally run the world if given the chance. But just because you can push doesn't mean you should.

If you are still exhausted, if you experienced postpartum depression, or if you're recently coming out of "the fog" that so many of my clients describe, it is not the time to ask your body to create another body. The answer will be either "No," "Nope," or my personal answer for many years: "Are you out of your f-ing mind, woman?!"

It is time to pause and replenish your reserves. Trying again before your body and brain are ready will result in significant losses. Your body is wise. It will put up roadblocks to protect you if you are not ready yet, and I urge you to take out the stubborn earplugs and limiting blinders that I wore for years and stop, look, and listen.

> READINESS FOR BABY #2+ IS ABOUT MORE THAN BIOLOGY. IT'S ABOUT HEALING, REPLENISHMENT, AND HONESTY WITH YOURSELF

At the end of the day, **readiness for baby No. 2+ is about more than biology. It's about healing, replenishment, and honesty with yourself.** The labs and numbers can guide us, but the emotional and spiritual data are just as important. Trust your body and your spirit, and give yourself the space to be truly ready before you begin again.

PREPARING FOR BABY #2+

About half of my clients already have a baby and are now facing secondary infertility. Some are former clients, and others are new and completely confused about why it was so easy the first time but so hard the second.

Here is the mistake I see over and over.

They assume that because a protocol worked once, it will work again.

But you are not the same woman you were the first time.

You are likely more depleted. You are sleeping less. You are managing more stress. You may still be recovering hormonally, emotionally, or physically. Add a toddler running the house, and your energy bank account looks very different from what it did before baby number one.

A SECOND CHILD MEANS A DIFFERENT LITTLE SOUL AND A DIFFERENT VERSION OF YOU, WHICH OFTEN CALLS FOR A DIFFERENT APPROACH

If you are preparing for another egg retrieval or embryo transfer, do not assume the old plan still fits. Base your strategy on your biology today, not on who you were two or three years ago.

A second child means a different little soul and a different version of you, which often calls for a different approach.

Secondary infertility is often about skipped preparation and assumed resilience.

Go back to the fundamentals... yup, yes, and heck yeah, I mean the Survive to Thrive Protocol! (Gosh, it felt good to get that in one more time before this book ended.)

That is how you give yourself the best shot at welcoming that next beautiful baby to your family.

CHAPTER 15 SUMMARY

- **Celebrate First, Then Stabilize:** A positive pregnancy deserves full celebration, followed by a thoughtful review of labs, medications, and next steps. Early pregnancy is protected by steady support, not panic-driven control.
- **Stay in Today's Reality:** What could go wrong is not the same as what is happening. Today, you are pregnant. Let that be the truth you live in until the data says otherwise.
- **Support the Body You're In Now:** Supplements, medications, and labs often change once pregnancy begins. Updating care based on current needs helps the body stay steady through early pregnancy.
- **Before Baby Two, Rebuild You:** A green light from your doctor is not the same as full recovery. Real readiness means replenished nutrients, stable hormones, healthy testing, and emotional strength to go again.
- **Each Baby Deserves a Fresh Plan:** A second or third pregnancy is not a repeat of the first. New demands, a new season of life, and a different version of you often require a new approach.

Conclusion

Congratulations, Mama!

You've walked through ten years of research, five years of writing, and three years of refining strategies and formulas, guided by one former IVF warrior-turned-consultant who giggles at her own jokes.

With this knowledge, you're now a key player in the mission to reduce infertility, miscarriage rates, and the number of IVF cycles needed, while boosting IVF success rates *worldwide*.

Along the way, you've discovered truths about the infertility disease, starting with how it's a byproduct of overall health and wellness, but also learning that you can manage and even reverse it.

You've gotten wise by finally understanding the *whys* behind your infertility and ailments.

And that mean girl in your head? She's now like that neighbor with way too many opinions. She starts talking, you smile politely, and then you change the subject and go live your truth.

And oh, oh, OH, do you know IVF.

With what you now know, you can stop accepting dead-end answers about why IVF treatments aren't working. You understand the real factors that go into success and the strategies to overcome them.

You get to have more strategic conversations with your doctor and know if they are the right partner to build your family with because you can measure them by their strategy, their execution, and, most importantly, the results you see for yourself.

You get to move forward with confidence because you now have clarity. And with what you can control, you are doing it with precision.

That is how you take 100 percent responsibility for your family-building journey without taking 100 percent of the blame.

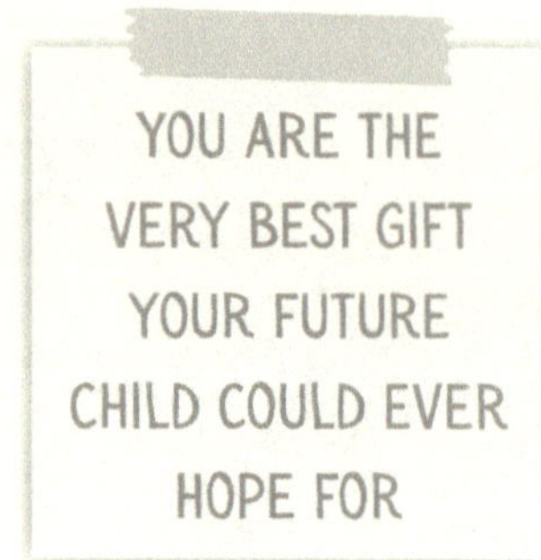

That is being the CEO of your family-building journey.

That is how you will kiss your baby sooner.

I can't thank you enough for investing the time and energy to learn how to be the best version of yourself and the mama you were always meant to be.

Your child is so lucky to have you.

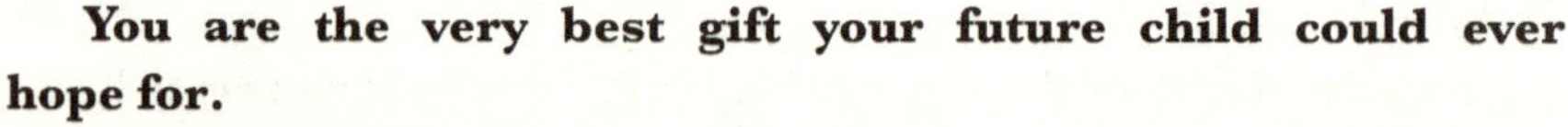

You are the very best gift your future child could ever hope for.

You are extraordinary.

I love you.

Acknowledgments

This book would not be possible without divine intervention, and I mean that literally. Thank you, God, for Your guidance and patience with me. For the lessons I did not ask for but clearly needed, and for loving me through every stubborn, worrying season. Thank you for qualifying me for this mission and for walking beside me as I step into it. Honestly, it feels too big for me, but I trust You.

Thank you to the brilliant IVF doctors, functional medicine experts, and mindset leaders I have studied and learned from over the last decade. If you ever felt like you were being watched, it is because you were.

A special thank you to the incomparable Dr. Debra Minjarez. Your work and teachings have raised the standard for what IVF care should be. The way you show up for your patients and push for better medicine is rare. You lead with integrity, high standards, and a true mission to do what is right for the families who trust you with their dreams.

To my amazing team throughout the years, and especially to Steph, who has been with me from the very beginning and believes in our mission wholeheartedly. Your loyalty and fierce devotion to our clients are truly out of this world.

To every woman who has allowed me to stand beside you on your path to parenthood, I am humbled to be part of your journey. We are forever family.

To my first ever editor, Laura Baginski, who started by correcting the notes I passed her in fourth grade and has been my favorite writer, editor, and friend ever since. Now, please stop using big words with me.

To the brilliant editors who stepped in throughout this book's evolution because Laura was too busy: Kate Rouze and Game Changer Publishing, especially Jessica, Cris, and Jeff. Thank you for letting me obsessively overedit every detail. It really is a disease.

To the business minds who helped me turn my genius into a real business, even when I tried my hardest to fight it, thank you. Taylor Welch and his incredible wife, Lindsey, you helped me take an idea and turn it into a mission. You pulled a leader out of me when I did not want to be one. And yes, you were right... about everything.

Sarah Walton, you told me to be an IVF consultant before that was even a thing and pushed me to make it happen when I said, "nope," because it was not a thing.

Dan Martell and his amazingly talented wife, Renée. Learning from you through coaching has been an incredible gift, but becoming real friends along the way has meant even more. I'm grateful for your belief in me and for the example you set. Looking forward to our next trip and to Brian being mistaken for your bodyguard again.

And then there is my family.

To my mom, Joyce, also known as Goppy, your resilience, strength, generosity, and love redefine extraordinary. I admire you more than you will ever know. To my dad in heaven, we love you and miss you. You were the dreamer who believed we could do anything and the first book writer in the family.

To my sister, Rosa, you are a trailblazer who taught me how to be bold. You are the funniest person I know, other than Rocky, and my favorite person to dance, laugh, and sing with.

To my baby brother, Rocky, you should not be as successful and grounded as you are, given the sisters you grew up with, so congratulations on that miracle. I am endlessly proud of the man you are.

To my half-sister, Marina, you are loyal, wildly talented, and so fun. Thank you for always loving and supporting me fully.

To my in-laws, whom I am truly in love with: Lisa, my insanely talented and loving sister-in-law who helps me raise my babies like they are her own; the very fertile, funny, and fabulous Alicia; Paul, we love you; and Todd, we would be so bored without you.

To my nieces and nephews, Kaia, Ryan, Liv, Lucia, Erik, and Kevin, I love you more than your parents do, but do not tell them I said that.

To my incredible friends who let me rope you into the making of this book, especially Gina, Lesley, and Missy. Thank you for helping me shape not only this book but also a beautiful life.

To my babies, Hudson and Mila, thank you for choosing me to be your mom and for letting me be a bit much with the hugs and kisses. I am so lucky to have you and even luckier to learn from you, though it would be great if you could let me learn a little less often (you know who I am talking to). Because of you two, I count my billions of blessings every day.

And to my love, my husband, my Brian. You are my rock and my person. You are my favorite date and partner. I love that we are a team in everything, and I am sorry you have to be on my team for anything athletic. I am so grateful we chose to stay married even when it felt impossible, and I am so proud of how we keep working to build an extraordinary life and marriage together. Now take your shirt off!

Before You Go...

Could I ask you for a huge favor?

Mama,

I am so grateful you spent your time with me inside these pages. That truly means more to me than you know, and I have one big favor to ask.

If this book helped you in any way, would you take two minutes to leave a review on Amazon? Your words could be the reason another woman finds this book at exactly the right moment instead of losing more time, money, or strength to create her family.

When we share resources that could reduce infertility, unnecessary IVF cycles, and pregnancy loss, we help more women kiss their babies sooner.

Thank you for being part of this family and for helping move this mission forward.

With thanks and love,
Tasha

P.S. To leave a review on Amazon, go to "Your Orders," find the book, and click "Write a Product Review" on the right side near the bottom. Thank you for being amazing!

References

Instead of filling these pages with long citations, I organized every study by chapter in our online resources. Use the QR code to access and explore the data behind some of the recommendations shared in this book.

www.ingramcontent.com/pod-product-compliance
Lightning Source LLC
LaVergne TN
LVHW100502110826
845146LV00002B/485

* 9 7 9 8 9 0 1 5 8 1 0 8 7 *